高等学校专业英语系列教材

给水排水工程专业

高　湘　等编
刘文君　主审

中国建筑工业出版社

图书在版编目(CIP)数据

给水排水工程专业/高湘等编. ——北京：中国建筑工业出版社，2006 (2022.8重印)
(高等学校专业英语系列教材)
ISBN 978-7-112-06654-4

Ⅰ. 给… Ⅱ. 高… Ⅲ. ①给水工程-英语-高等学校-教材 ②排水工程-英语-高等学校-教材 Ⅳ. H31

中国版本图书馆 CIP 数据核字(2006)第 134884 号

高等学校专业英语系列教材
给水排水工程专业
高 湘 等编
刘文君 主审

*

中国建筑工业出版社出版、发行（北京西郊百万庄）
各地新华书店、建筑书店经销
北京天成排版公司制版
北京圣夫亚美印刷有限公司印刷

*

开本：787×1092 毫米 1/16 印张：18¾ 字数：452 千字
2007 年 1 月第一版 2022 年 8 月第九次印刷
定价：**32.00** 元
ISBN 978-7-112-06654-4
(20757)

版权所有 翻印必究
如有印装质量问题，可寄本社退换
(邮政编码 100037)

本社网址：http://www.cabp.com.cn
网上书店：http://www.china-building.com.cn

考虑到给水排水工程专业近年的发展、专业外语课时的限制，为扩大读者获知面，提高读者阅读理解的能力，本教材主要设计了三大部分内容，即水的输送和水处理部分、建筑给水排水部分以及水泵站部分的有关内容，共24课。在编排上，设有课文、阅读材料、单词以及课后简答。课文语言规范，容易理解，阅读材料（Reading Material）主要是课文的拓展部分，收入了一些与课文相关的文章，以加深读者对这些专业理论知识的全面理解。

在内容安排设置上，第1~2课介绍了取水、废水收集、水的输送以及水循环等基础知识，第3~19课主要介绍了水质及其基本检测方法、废水处理基础、废水回用以及生物污泥处理基础、筛滤、混凝、沉淀、过滤、吸附、化学氧化和消毒、离子交换、膜处理、高级氧化、水的生物处理、污泥处理与处置等方面的基本理论及应用，第20~22课介绍了室内的冷热水供应系统的基本知识，第23、24课介绍了泵的基本理论及水泵站设计的相关知识。

本书知识面覆盖较宽，既有基础理论，也有一定的设计和管理知识，适用于给水排水工程专业本科生、硕士研究生的专业英语阅读之用，同时也可作为给水排水工程技术人员、环境工程专业的学生及工程技术人员的参考书。

责任编辑：齐庆梅
责任设计：郑秋菊
责任校对：张景秋　兰曼利

前言

随着世界科学技术交流的日趋广泛，增强给水排水工程专业学生的专业外语阅读能力的任务就日趋紧迫与重要。为适应现代教育的发展，同时考虑到当代水处理技术的发展现状，为给水排水工程专业师生以及相关科学技术人员提供一本题材新颖、语言规范、覆盖专业课程主要内容、语言难度适宜的专业英语教材，已成为一种广泛而迫切地需要。

考虑到专业技术的发展、课堂教学的时间以及学生知识结构等多方面因素，本教材主要介绍了三大部分内容，即水的输送和水处理部分、建筑给水排水部分以及水泵站部分的有关内容，共计24课。采用一篇课文带一篇阅读材料的形式，其中阅读材料大多数是课文内容的拓宽或延续，但也有部分阅读材料的内容与课文内容相近或相关。第1、2课主要介绍取水、废水收集、水的输送以及水文循环等基础知识；第3～19课主要介绍水质及其基本检测方法、废水处理基础、废水回用以及生物污泥处理基础、筛滤、混凝、沉淀、过滤、吸附、化学氧化和消毒、离子交换、膜处理、高级氧化、水的生物处理、污泥处理与处置等方面的基本理论及应用；第20～22课介绍室内的冷热水供应系统的基本知识；第23、24课介绍泵的基本理论及水泵站设计的相关知识。在选材上，本教材以世界名校所用教材为主线，结合一定量的设计内容，使得本教材的知识面覆盖较宽，既有基础理论简介，也有一定的设计及管理知识。

本教材共24课，其中1～14课由高湘编写，15～19课由王瑞编写，20～21课由张建锋编写，22课由王涛编写，23、24课由杨玉思编写。

本教材适用于给水排水工程专业本科生、硕士研究生的专业英语阅读，同时也可作为给水排水工程技术人员、环境工程专业的学生及科技人员的参考书。

在本书的编写过程中，得到了齐庆梅编辑的大力支持，正是由于她的努力及勤奋工作才使得本书得以撰写及出版，在此作者表示由衷的谢意。感谢清华大学刘文君先生在百忙之中对本书进行的认真细致的审校，其中肯、科学的建议使得本书更加完善。同时对其他给予作者支持的人士表示深深的谢意。可以说，本书的完成是那些关心和支持作者的朋友共同努力的结果，真心希望本书能够给广大读者以帮助。

鉴于作者视野和学术能力的局限，在文章选材和编排等方面还存在着不足之处，恳请读者给予批评指正，作者在此表示衷心的感谢。

CONTENTS

LESSON 1　Water Supply ··· 1
　Reading Material　Water Circulation ························· 7
LESSON 2　Collection Of Wastewater ························ 9
　Reading Material　Water Transmission ····················· 13
LESSON 3　Measurement Of Water Quality: Ⅰ ············ 16
　Reading Material　Measurement Of Water Quality: Ⅱ ········· 23
LESSON 4　Fundamentals Of Wastewater Treatment ············ 33
　Reading Material　Fundamentals Of Wastewater Reuse And
　　　　　　　　　　Biosolids Management ················· 42
LESSON 5　Classification Of Screening And Coarse Screens ········ 48
　Reading Material　Fine Screens, Microscreens And
　　　　　　　　　　Screenings ································· 54
LESSON 6　Coagulation and Flocculation: Ⅰ ················ 60
　Reading Material　Coagulation and Flocculation: Ⅱ ············· 66
LESSON 7　Gravity Separation Theory: Ⅰ ···················· 75
　Reading Material　Gravity Separation Theory: Ⅱ ············· 81
LESSON 8　Filtration ·· 90
　Reading Material　Rapid Filters ································· 96
LESSON 9　Adsorption: Ⅰ ·· 102
　Reading Material　Adsorption: Ⅱ ······························ 108
LESSON 10　Chemical Oxidation ································ 118
　Reading Material　Disinfection ·································· 122
LESSON 11　Ion Exchange ·· 129
　Reading Material　Application of Ion Exchange ············· 135
LESSON 12　Membrane Filtration Processes ··············· 138
　Reading Material　Membrane Fouling ························ 146
LESSON 13　Application of Membranes ···················· 150
　Reading Material　Electrodialysis ······························ 157
LESSON 14　Advanced Oxidation Processes ··············· 162
　Reading Material　Distillation ···································· 167
LESSON 15　Introduction to the Activated-sludge Process ········ 170

Reading Material　Operational Problems Of the Activated-
　　　　　　　　　　　sludge Process ………………………………… 175
LESSON 16　Trickling Filters ……………………………………… 182
　　　Reading Material　Physical Facilities Design of
　　　　　　　　　　　Trickling Filters ………………………………… 186
LESSON 17　Anaerobic Treatment ………………………………… 193
　　　Reading Material　Anaerobic Treatment Processes …………… 200
LESSON 18　Rotating Biological Contactors …………………… 206
　　　Reading Material　Physical Facilities and Process
　　　　　　　　　　　Design for RBC ………………………………… 210
LESSON 19　Sludge Treatment, Utilization, and Disposal ……… 214
　　　Reading Material　Sludge Characteristics ……………………… 220
LESSON 20　Cold Water Supply：Ⅰ ……………………………… 223
　　　Reading Material　Cold Water Supply：Ⅱ ……………………… 231
LESSON 21　Hot Water Supply：Ⅰ ……………………………… 240
　　　Reading Material　Hot Water Supply：Ⅱ ……………………… 247
LESSON 22　Preservation Of Water Quality：Ⅰ ………………… 252
　　　Reading Material　Preservation Of Water Quality：Ⅱ ………… 257
LESSON 23　Pump Stations for Municipal Wastewater：Ⅰ …… 263
　　　Reading Material　Pump Stations for Municipal
　　　　　　　　　　　Wastewater：Ⅱ ………………………………… 269
LESSON 24　Pump Stations for Industrial Wastewater,
　　　　　　　Stormwater, Sediments and Sludges ……………… 274
　　　Reading Material　Other Lifting Devices ……………………… 281
REFERENCES ……………………………………………………………… 290

LESSON 1

Water Supply

A supply of water is critical to the survival of life, as we know it. People need water to drink, animals need water to drink, and plants need water to drink. The basic functions of society require water: cleaning for public health, consumption for industrial processes, and cooling for electrical generation. In this lesson, we discuss water supply in terms of:
1. Groundwater supplies
2. Surface water supplies

Groundwater Supplies

Groundwater is an important direct source of supply that is tapped by wells, as well as a significant indirect source since surface streams are often supplied by subterranean water.

Near the surface of the earth, in the *zone of aeration*, soil pore spaces contain both air and water. This zone, which may have zero thickness in swamplands and be several hundred feet thick in mountainous regions, contains three types of moisture. After a storm, *gravity water* is in transit through the larger soil pore spaces. *Capillary* water is drawn through small pore spaces by capillary action and is available for plant uptake. *Hygroscopic moisture* is held in place by molecular forces during all except the driest climatic conditions. Moisture, from the zone of aeration cannot be tapped as a water supply source.

In the *zone of saturation*, located below the zone of aeration, the soil pores are filled with water, and this is what we call *groundwater*. A stratum that contains a substantial amount of groundwater is called an *aquifer*. At the surface between the two zones, called the *water table* or *phreatic surface*, the hydrostatic pressure in the groundwater is equal to the atmospheric pressure. An aquifer may extend to great depths, but because the weight of overburden material generally closes pore spaces, little water is found at depths greater than 600m(2000ft). The amount of water that will drain freely from an aquifer is known as *specific yield*.

The flow of water out of a soil can be illustrated using Figure 1. The flow rate must be proportional to the area through which flow occurs times the velocity, or

$$Q = Av \qquad (1)$$

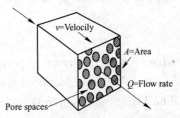

Figure 1 Flow through soil

where Q = flow rate, in m³/sec

A = area of porous material through which flow occurs, in m²

v = superficial velocity, in m/sec

The superficial velocity is of course not the actual velocity of the water in the soil, since the volume occupied by the soil solid particles greatly reduces the available area for flow. If a is the area available for flow, then

$$Q = Av = av' \tag{2}$$

where v' = actual velocity of water flowing through the soil

a = area available for flow

Solving for v',

$$v' = \frac{Av}{a} \tag{3}$$

If a sample of soil is of some length L, then

$$v' = \frac{Av}{a} = \frac{AvL}{aL} = \frac{v}{porosity} \tag{4}$$

since the total volume of the soil sample is AL and the volume occupied by the water is aL.

Water flowing through the soil at a velocity v' loses energy, just as water flowing through a pipeline or an open channel does. This energy loss per distance traveled is defined as

$$\text{energy lose} = \frac{\Delta h}{\Delta L} \tag{5}$$

where h = energy, measured as elevation of the water table in an unconfined aquifer or as pressure in a confined aquifer, in m

L = horizontal distance in direction of flow, in m

The symbol (delta) simply means "a change in," as in "a change in length, L." Thus this equation means that there is a change (loss) of energy, h, as water flows through the soil some distance, L.

In an unconfined aquifer, the drop in the elevation of the water table with distance is the slope of the water table in the direction of flow. The elevation of the water surface is the potential energy of the water, and water flows from a higher elevation to a lower elevation, losing energy along the way. Flow through a porous medium such as soil is related to the energy loss using the Darcy equation,

$$Q = KA \frac{\Delta h}{\Delta L} \tag{6}$$

where K = coefficient of permeability, in m/day

A = cross-sectional area, in m²

The Darcy equation makes intuitive sense, in that the flow rate (Q) increases with increasing area (A) through which the flow occurs and with the drop in pressure, $\Delta h / \Delta L$. The greater the driving force (the difference in upstream and downstream pressures), the greater the flow. The factor, K, is the *coefficient of permeability*, an indirect measure of the ability of a soil sample to transmit water, can be measured by a permeameter shown in Figure 2; it varies dramatically for different soils, ranging from about 0.0005m/day for clay to over 5000m/day for gravel. The coefficient of permeability is measured commonly in the laboratory using *permeameters*, which consist of a soil sample through which a fluid such as water is forced. The flow rate is measured for a given driving force (difference in pressures) through a known area of soil sample, and the permeability calculated.

If a well is sunk into an unconfined aquifer, shown in Figure 3, and water is pumped out, the water in the aquifer will begin to flow toward the well. As the water approaches the well, the area through which it flows gets progressively smaller, and therefore a higher superficial (and actual) velocity is required. The higher velocity of course results in an increasing loss of energy, and energy gradient must increase, forming a *cone of depression*. The reduction in the water table is known in groundwater terms as a *drawdown*. If the rate of water flowing toward the well is equal to the rate of water being pumped out of the well, the condition is at equilibrium, and the drawdowm remains constant. If, however, the rate of water pumping is increased, the radial flow toward the well has to compensate, and this results in a deeper cone or drawdown.

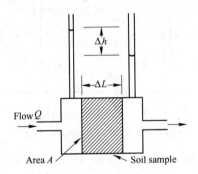

Figure 2 Permeameter used for measuring coefficient of permeability using the Darcy equation

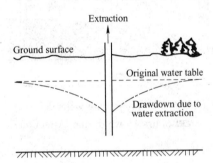

Figure 3 Drawdown in water table due to pumping from a well

Consider a cylinder, shown in Figure 4, through which water flows toward the center. Using Darcy's equation,

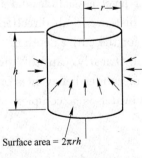

$$Q = KA \frac{\Delta h}{\Delta L} = K(2\pi rh) \frac{\Delta h}{\Delta r} \quad (7)$$

where r is the radius of the cylinder, and $2\pi rh$ is the cross-sectional surface area of the cylinder. If water is pumped out of the center of the cylinder at the same rate, as water is moving in through the cylinder surface area, the above equation can be integrated to yield

$$Q = \frac{\pi K(h_1^2 - h_2^2)}{\ln \frac{r_1}{r_2}} \quad (8)$$

Figure 4 Cylinder with flow though the surface

where h_1 and h_2 are the height of the water table at radial distances r_1 and r_2 from the well.

This equation can be used to estimate the pumping rate for a given drawdown any distance away from a well, using the water level measurements in two observation wells in an unconfined aquifer, as shown in Figure 5. Also, knowing the diameter of a well, it is possible to estimate the drawdown at the well, the critical point in the cone of depression. If the drawdown is depressed all the way to the bottom of the aquifer, the well "goes dry"——it cannot pump water at the desired rate. Although the derivations of the above equations are for an unconfined aquifer, the same situation would occur for a confined aquifer, where the pressure would be measured by observation wells.

Multiple wells in an aquifer can interfere with each other and cause excessive drawdown. Consider the situation in Figure 6, where a single well creates a cone of depression. If a second production well is installed, the cones will overlap, causing greater drawdown at each well. If many wells are sunk into an aquifers, the combined effect of the wells can deplete the groundwater resources and all wells will "go dry".

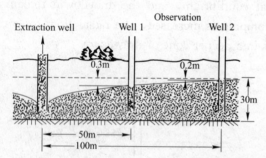

Figure 5 Two monitoring wells define the extent of drawdown during extraction

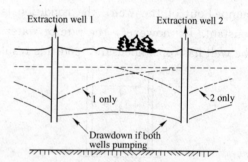

Figure 6 Multiple wells and the effect of extraction on the groundwater table

The reverse is also true, of course. Suppose one of the wells is used as an injection well, then the injected water flows from this well into the others, building up the groundwater table and reducing the drawdown. The judicious use of extraction and injection wells is one way that the flow of contaminants from hazardous waste or refuse dumps can be controlled.

Finally, many assumptions are made in the above discussion. First, we assume that the aquifer is homogeneous and infinite—that is, it sits on a level aquaclude and the permeability of the soil is the same at all places for an infinite distance in all directions. The well is assumed to penetrate the entire aquifer and is open for the entire depth of the aquifer. Finally, the pumping rate is assumed to be constant. Clearly, any of these conditions may cause the analysis to be faulty, and this model of aquifer behavior is only the beginning of the story. Modeling the behavior of groundwater is a complex and sophisticated science.

Surface Water Supplies

Surface water supplies are not as reliable as groundwater sources since quantities often fluctuate widely during the course of a year even a week, and water quality is affected by pollution sources. If a river has an average flow of 10 cubic feet per second (cfs), this does not mean that a community using the water supply can depend on having 10 cfs available at all times.

The variation in flow may be so great that even a small demand cannot be met during dry periods and so storage facilities must be built to save water during wetter periods. Reservoirs should be large enough to provide dependable supplies. However, reservoirs are expensive and, if they are unnecessarily large, represent a waste of community resources.

One method of estimating the proper reservoir size is to use a *mass curve* to calculate historical storage requirements and then to calculate risk and cost using statistics. Historical storage requirements are determined by summing the total flow in a stream at the location of the proposed reservoir and plotting the change of total flow with time. The change of water demand with time is then plotted on the same curve. The difference between the total water flowing in and the water demanded is the quantity that the reservoir must hold if the demand is to be met.

A mass curve like Figure 7 is not very useful if only limited stream flow data are available. Data for one year yield very little information about long-term variations.

Long-term variations may be estimated statistically when actual data are not available. Water supplies are often designed to meet demands of 20-year cycles, and about once in 20 years the reservoir capacity will not be adequate to offset the drought. The community may choose to build a larger reservoir that will prove inadequate only every 50 years, for example. A calculation comparing the additional capital investment to the added benefit of increased water supply will assist in making such a decision. One calculation method requires first assembling required reservoir capacity data for a number of years, ranking these data according to the drought severity, and calculating the drought probability for each year. If the data are assembled for n year and the rank is designated by m, with $m=1$ for the largest reservoir requirement during the most severe drought, the probability that the supply will be adequate for any year is given by $m/(n+1)$. For example, if storage capacity will be inadequate, on the average, one year out of every 20 years,

$$m/(n+1) \approx 1/20 = 0.05 \tag{9}$$

If storage capacity will be inadequate, on the average, one year out of every 100 years,

$$m/(n+1) \approx 1/100 = 0.01 \tag{10}$$

This procedure is a *frequency analysis* of a recurring natural event. The frequencies

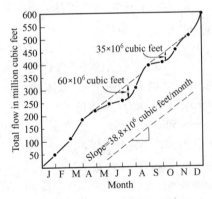

Figure 7 Mass curve for determining required reservoir capacity

chosen for investigation were once in 10 years and once in 5 years, or a "10-year drought" and a "5-year drought", but droughts occurring 3 years in a row and then not again for 30 years still constitute "10-year droughts". Planning for a 30-year drought will result in the construction of a large expensive reservoir; planning for a 10-year drought will result in the construction of a smaller less-expensive reservoir.

New Words and Phrases

specific yield　单位产水量
mass curve　累积曲线
capital investment　投资
recurring natural event　重现历史事件
subterranean　*adj.* 地下的
groundwater　*n.* 地下水
surface water　*n.* 地表水
tap　*n.* 开关、龙头
　　v. 在…上开空(导出液体)
swampland　*n.* 沼泽地
capillary　*n.* 毛细管
　　adj. 毛状的，毛细作用的
hygro-　［词头］湿(气)，液体
hygroscopic　*adj.* 吸湿的
hygroscopic moisture　吸湿水
stratum　*n.* ［地］地层，［生］(组织的)层
aquifer　*n.* 含水层，蓄水层
saturation　*n.* 饱和(状态)，浸润，浸透，饱和度
hydrostatic　*adj.* 静水力学的，流体静力学的
hydrostatic pressure　静水压力
water table　*n.* 地下水位，［建］承雨线脚
phreatic surface　*n.* 地下水(静止)水位，浅层地下水面
superficial　*adj.* 表面的，表观的，浅薄的
porosity　*n.* 多孔性，有孔性，孔隙率
unconfined　*adj.* 无限制的，无约束的

permeability　*n.* 渗透性
permeameter　*n.* 渗透仪
clay　*n.* 黏土，泥土
gravel　*n.* 砂砾，砾石
cone of depression　*n.* 下降锥体，下降漏斗
drawdown　*n.* (抽水后)水位降低(量)
integrate　*v.* 求积分
observation well　*n.* 观测井
extraction　*n.* 抽取，取出，提取(法)，萃取(法)
derivation　*n.* 引出，来历，出处，(语言)词源，衍生
deplete　*vt.* 耗尽，使衰竭
refuse　*vt.* 拒绝，谢绝
　　n. 废物，垃圾
dump　*vt.* 倾倒(垃圾)，倾卸
　　n. 堆存处，垃圾堆
unconfined aquifer　*n.* 潜水含水层
confined aquifer　*n.* 承压含水层
homogeneous　*adj.* 同类的，相似的，均匀的，均相的
aquaclude　*n.* 不透水层，难渗透水的地层
offset　*n.* 偏移量，抵消，弥补，分支，平版印刷，胶印，支管，乙字管
　　vt. 弥补，抵消，用平版印刷
　　vi. 偏移，形成分支
sophisticated　*adj.* 复杂的，需要专门技术的

Questions

1. Please give the meaning of *drawdown*.
2. Try to explain the method of estimating the proper reservoir size.

3. Please give the definition of *aquifer*.
4. What is the use of *permeameter*?
5. What is the definition of *porosity* of a soil sample?

Reading Material

Water Circulation

The hydrologic cycle is a useful starting point for the study of water supply. This cycle, illustrated in Figure 8, includes precipitation of water from clouds, infiltration into the ground or runoff into surface water, followed by evaporation and transpiration of the water back into the atmosphere.

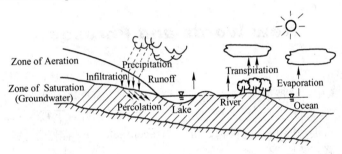

Figure 8 The hydrologic cycle

The rates of precipitation and evaporation/transpiration help define the baseline quantity of water available for human consumption. *Precipitation* is the term applied to all forms of moisture falling to the ground, and a range of instruments and techniques have been developed for measuring the amount and intensity of rain, snow, sleet, and hail. The average depth of precipitation over a given region, on a storm, seasonal, or annual basis, is required in many water availability studies. Any open receptacle with vertical sides is a common rain gauge, but varying wind and splash effects must be considered if amounts collected by different gauges are to be compared.

Evaporation and *transpiration* are the movement of water back to the atmosphere from open water surfaces and from plant respiration. The same meteorological factors that influence evaporation are at work in the transpiration process: solar radiation, ambient air temperature, humidity, and wind speed. The amount of soil moisture available to plants also affects the transpiration rate. Evaporation is measured by measuring water loss from a pan. Transpiration can be measured with a *phytometer*, a large vessel filled with soil and potted with selected plants. The soil surface is hermetically sealed to prevent evaporation; thus moisture can escape only through transpiration. The rate of moisture escape is determined by weighing the entire system at intervals up to the life of the plant. Phytometers cannot simulate natural conditions, so results have limited value. However, they can be used as an index of water demand by a crop under field conditions and thus relate to calculations that help an engineer determine water supply requirements for that crop. Because it is often not necessary to distinguish between evaporation and transpiration, the two processes are often linked as *evapotranspiration*, or the total water loss to the atmosphere.

The direction of our discussion is that sufficient water supplies exist, but many areas are water poor while others are water rich. Adequate water supply requires engineering the supply and its transmission from one area to another, keeping in mind the environmental effects of water transmission systems. In many cases, moving the population to the water may be less environmentally damaging than moving the water. This section concentrates on measurement of water supply, and the following section discusses treatment methods available to clean up the water once it reaches areas of demand.

New Words and Phrases

keep in mind　紧记
concentrate on　集中，全神贯注于
hydrologic　*adj.* 水文的
precipitation　*n.* 沉淀(作用)，沉积物，沉降；降水(量)
infiltration　*n.* 渗透
runoff　*n.* 径流(量)，流量；流出；流出口；决赛
evaporation　*n.* 蒸发(作用)
transpiration　*n.* 蒸发(物)，散发，[生]蒸腾作用，[物]流逸
baseline　*n.* 基线
sleet　*n.* 冰雨，雨夹雪
　　vi. 下雨雪，下冰雹
hail　*n.* 冰雹，致敬，招呼

　　vt. 向…欢呼，致敬，招呼，使像下雹样落下
　　vi. 招呼，下雹
receptacle　*n.* 容器，[植]花托，[电工]插座
meteorological　*adj.* 气象(学)的
ambient　*adj.* 周围的
　　n. 周围环境
humidity　*n.* 湿气，潮湿，湿度
phyto-　[词头]植物
phytometer　*n.* 植物剂、植物蒸腾表
hermetically　*adj.* 密封地，不透气地
simulate　*vt.* 模拟，模仿
evapotranspiration　*n.* 土壤水分蒸发蒸腾损失总量

LESSON 2

Collection Of Wastewater

The "Shambles" is a street or area in many medieval English cities, like London and York. During the eighteenth and nineteenth centuries, Shambles were commercialized areas, with meat packing as a major industry. The butchers of the Shambles would throw all of their waste into the street, where it was washed away by rainwater into drainage ditches. The condition of the street was so bad that it contributed its name to the English language originally as a synonym for butchery or a bloody battlefield.

In old cities, drainage ditches like those at the Shambles were constructed for the sole purpose of moving storm water out of the cities. In fact, discarding human excrement into these ditches was illegal in London. Eventually, the ditches were covered over and became what we now know as *storm sewers*. As water supplies developed and the use of the indoor water closet increased, the need for transporting domestic wastewater, called *sanitary waste*, became obvious. In the United States, sanitary wastes were first discharged into the storm sewers, which then carried both sanitary waste and stormwater and were known as *combined sewers*. Eventually a new system of underground pipes, known as sanitary sewers, was a constructed for removing the sanitary wastes. Cities and parts of cities built in the twentieth century almost all built separate sewers for sanitary waste and stormwater.

Estimation Wastewater Quantities

Domestic wastewater (sewage) comes from various sources within the home, including the washing machine, dishwasher, shower, sinks, and of course the toilet. The toilet, or water closet (WC), as it is still known in Europe, has become a standard fixture of modern urban society. As important as this invention is, however, there is some dispute as to its inventor. Some authors credit John Bramah with its invention in 1778; others recognize it as the brainchild of Sir John Harrington in 1596. The latter argument is strengthened by Sir John's original description of the device, although there is no record of his donating his name to the invention. The first recorded use of that euphemism is found in a 1735 regulation at Harvard University that decreed, "No Freshman shall go to the Fellows' John."

The term *sewage* is used here to mean only domestic wastewater. Domestic wastewater flows vary with the season, the day of the week, and the hour of the day. Note the wide variation in flow and strength. Typically, average sewage flows are in the range of 100 gallons per day per person, but especially in smaller communities that average can range widely.

Sewers also commonly carry industrial wastewater. The quantity of industrial wastes may usually be established by water use records, or the flows may be measured in manholes that serve only a specific industry, using a small flow meter. Industrial flows also often vary considerably throughout the day, the day of the week, and the season.

In addition to sewage and industrial wastewater, sewers carry groundwater and surface water that seeps into the pipes. Since sewer pipes can and often do have holes in them (due to faulty construction, cracking by roots, or other causes), groundwater can seep into the sewer pipe if the pipe is lower than the top of the groundwater table. This flow into sewers is called *infiltration*. Infiltration is least for new, well-constructed sewers, but can be as high as 500 $m^3/(km \cdot day)$ (200000 gal/(mi · day)). For older systems, 700 $m^3/(km \cdot day)$ (300000 gal/(mi · day)) is the commonly estimated infiltration. Infiltration flow is detrimental since the extra volume of water must go through the sewers and the wastewater treatment plant. It should be reduced as much as possible by maintaining and repairing sewers and keeping sewerage easements clear of large trees whose roots can severely damage the sewers.

Inflow is storm-water collected unintentionally by the sanitary sewers. A common source of inflow is a perforated manhole cover placed in a depression, so that stormwater flows into the manhole. Sewers laid next to creeks and drainage ways that rise up higher than the manhole elevation, or where the manhole is broken, are also a major source. Illegal connections to sanitary sewers, such as roof drains, can substantially increase the wet weather flow over the dry weather flow. The ratio of dry weather flow to wet weather flow is usually between 1 : 1.2 and 1 : 4.

For these reasons, the sizing of sewers is often difficult, since not all of the expected flows can be estimated and their variability is unknown. The more important the sewer and the more difficult is to replace it, the more important it is to make sure that it is sufficiently large to be able to handle all the expected flows for the foreseeable future.

System Layout

Sewers collect wastewater from residences and industrial establishments. A system of sewers installed for the purpose of collecting wastewater is known as a *sewerage system* (*not* a sewage system). Sewers almost always operate as open channels or gravity flow conduits. Pressure sewers are used in a few places, but these are expensive to maintain and are useful only when there are severe restrictions on water use or when the terrain is such that gravity flow conduits cannot be efficiently maintained.

A typical system for a residential area is shown in Figure 1. Building connections are usually made with clay or plastic pipe, 6 inches in diameter, to the collecting sewers that run under the street. *Collecting sewers* are sized to carry the maximum anticipated peak flows without surcharging (filling up) and are ordinarily made of plastic, clay, cement, concrete, or cast iron pipe. They discharge into *intercepting sewers*, or *interceptors*, that collect from large areas and discharge finally into the wastewater treatment plant.

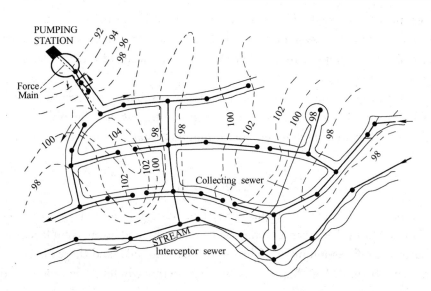

Figure 1 Typical wastewater collection system layout

Collecting and intercepting sewers must be constructed with adequate slope for adequate flow velocity during periods of low flow, but not so steep a slope as to promote excessively high velocities when flows are at their maximum. In addition, sewers must have manholes, usually every 120 to 180 m (400 to 600 ft) to facilitate cleaning and repair. Manholes are necessary whenever the sewer changes slope, size, or direction. Typical manholes are shown in Figure 2.

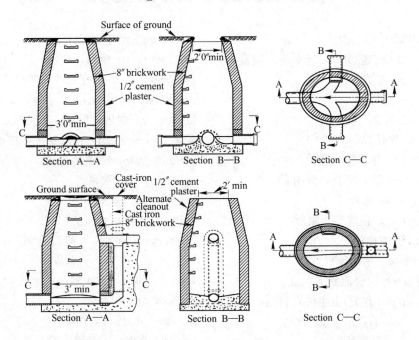

Figure 2 Typical manholes used in sewerage systems

Gravity flow may be impossible, or uneconomical, in some locations so that the wastewater must be pumped. This requires the installation of pumping stations at various locations throughout the system. The pumping station collects wastewater from a collecting sewer and pumps it to a higher elevation by means of a force main. The end of a force main is always into a manhole.

A power outage would render the pumps inoperable, and eventually the sewage would back up into homes. As you can imagine, this would be highly undesirable; therefore, a good system layout minimizes pumping stations and/or provides auxiliary power.

Conclusion

Sewers have been a part of civilized settlements for thousands of year, and in the modem United States we have become accustomed to and even complacent about the sewers that serve our communities. They never seem to fail, and there never seems to be a problem with them. Most important, we can dump whatever we want to down the drain, and it just disappears.

Of course, it doesn't just disappear. It flows through the sewer and ends up in a wastewater treatment plant. The stuff we often thoughtlessly dump down the drain can in fact cause serious problems in wastewater treatment and may even cause health problems in future drinking water supplies. Therefore, we must be cognizant of what we flush down the drain and recognize that it does not just disappear.

New Words and Phrases

drainage ditch　排水沟
shambles　*n.* 肉店(市)，屠宰场，混乱的地方
synonym　*n.* 同义词
discard　*vt.* 丢弃，抛弃
　　　　v. 放弃
excrement　*n.* 排泄物，大便
sewer　*n.* 污水管，缝具，缝纫者
storm sewer　雨水管
water closet　*n.* 盥洗室，厕所
indoor　*adj.* 室内的
sanitary waste　生活废水
combined sewer　合流制下水道
sanitary　*adj.* (有关)卫生的，(保持)清洁的，清洁卫生的
　　　　n. 公共厕所
sanitary sewer　生活污水管道
separate sewer　分流制下水道

sewerage　*n.* 排水工程
easement　*n.* 缓和，减轻，地役权
perforated　*adj.* 穿孔的，凿孔的
creek　*n.* 小溪，小河，小港，小湾
layout　*n.* 规划，设计，布局图，版面设计
sewerage system　排水系统，排水工程
conduit　*n.* 管道，导管，沟渠，泉水，喷泉
terrain　*n.* 地形
collecting sewer　污水支管
interceptor sewer　截流管道，污水［管］截砂阱
force main　压力干管
cement　*n.* 水泥
outage　*n.* 停机，停电
mi　*n.* 英里，大音阶的第三音
auxiliary　*adj.* 辅助的，补助的
brickwork　*n.* 砌砖

domestic wastewater（sewage） 生活废水，家庭污水
brainchild   n. 指计划、想法、创作等脑力劳动的创造物
euphemism   n. 委婉的说法
sink   n. 洗涤盆，污水池，接收器
decree   n. 法令，政令
         v. 颁布
manhole   n. 检查井，检修孔
seep   v. 渗出，渗漏
cracking   n. 破裂，裂化
detrimental   adj. 有害的

Questions

1. What is the meaning of *Shambles*?
2. Try to describe the development history of sewer.
3. Please explain the meaning of *infiltration* in wastewater collection system.
4. For what reasons, the sizing of sewers is often difficult?
5. What is *sewerage system*?

Reading Material

Water Transmission

Water can be transported from a ground or surface supply either directly to the water users in a community or initially to a water treatment facility. Water is transported by different types of conduits, including:

1. Pressure conduits, tunnels and pipelines
2. Gravity-flow conduits, channels and canals

The location of the river or well field as well as the location of the water treatment facility defines the length of these conduits. Long, gentle slopes allow canal and aqueducts to be used, but in most instances, pressurized systems are constructed for water transmission from the water supply watershed. The water then enters a water treatment facility where it is cleaned into potable water and subsequently distributed to the community of residential, commercial, and industrial users through a system of pressurized pipes. Because the demand for water is variable, we use more water during the daylight hours and for random fire control; for example, this distribution system must include storage facilities to even out the fluctuations.

Flow In Pipes Under Pressure

When water flows in a pipeline, there is friction acting between the flowing water and the pipe wall, and between the layers of water moving at different velocities in the pipe. This is because of the *viscosity* of the water. The flow velocity is actually zero at the pipe wall and maximum along the centerline of the pipe. When the term *velocity of flow* is used in this text, it means the average velocity over the cross section of flow.

The frictional resistance to flow causes a loss of energy in the system. This loss of energy is manifested as a continuous pressure drop along the path of flow. It is often necessary to be able to compute the expected pressure drop in a given system or to design a new system with a specified maximum pressure loss.

In Figure 3a, a straight section of pipe filled with water under pressure is shown attached to a tank. There is no flow in the system and therefore no pressure loss when the valve in the pipe is closed. It can be seen that the pressure head at section 1 equals the pressure head at section 2.

When the valve is opened, flow begins to occur with corresponding energy loss due to friction. This loss can be seen by measuring the pressures along the pipeline. In Figure 3b, the difference in pressure heads between sections 1 and 2 can be seen in the piezometer tubes attached to the pipe. A line connecting the water surface in the tank with the water levels at sections 1 and 2 shows the pattern of continuous pressure loss along the pipeline. This is called the *hydraulic grade line* (*HGL*) of the system. It is a very useful graphical aid when analyzing pipe flow problems.

The HGL is actually a graph of the pressure head along the pipe, plotted above the pipe centerline. It is not necessary to draw the piezometer tubes, as in Figure 3. *The HGL always slopes downward in the direction of flow* unless additional energy is added to the system by a pump. The vertical drop in the HGL between two sections separated by a distance L is called the *head loss* (h_L). The ratio of h_L to L is the slope (S) of the HGL or *hydraulic gradient*. In equation form, $S = h_L/L$.

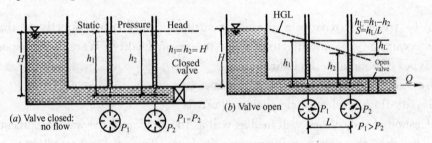

Figure 3 The hydraulic grade line, or HGL, is a graph of the pressure
head above the pipe centerline. Its downward slope in the direction
of flow shows pressure loss due to friction

The HGL always passes through the free water surface of any storage tank in the system, since that elevation is equivalent to the system's pressure head at that point. The greater is the flow rate in a given pipeline, the greater is the rate of pressure loss, and the steeper is the slope of the HGL.

Gravity Flow In Pipes

When water flows in a pipe or channel with a *free surface* exposed to the atmosphere, it is called *open channel* or *gravity flow*. Gravity provides the moving force, while friction resists the motion and causes energy loss. Stream or river flow is open channel flow. Flow in storm and sanitary sewers is also open channel flow, except when the water is pumped through a pipe under pressure (a *force main*).

In most routine problems in the design or analysis of storm or sanitary sewer systems, a condition called *steady uniform flow* is assumed. Steady flow means that the discharge is constant with time. Uniform flow means that the slope of the water surface and the cross-sectional flow area are also constant. A length of a stream, channel, or pipeline that has a relatively constant slope and cross section is called a *reach*.

Under steady uniform flow conditions, the slope of the water surface is the same as the slope of the channel bottom. The HGL lies along the water surface and, as in pressure flow in pipes, it slopes downward in the direction of flow. Energy loss is manifested as a drop in elevation of the water surface. A typical profile view of uniform steady flow is shown in Figure 4. The slope of the water surface represents the rate of energy loss. It may be expressed as the ratio of the drop in elevation of the surface in the reach to the length of the reach.

Typical cross sections of open channel flow are shown in Figure 5. In Figure 5a, the pipe is only partially filled with water and there is a free surface at atmospheric pressure. It is still open channel flow, even though the pipe is a closed conduit underground. The important factor is that gravity, not a pump, is moving the water.

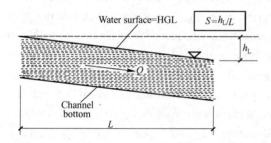

Figure 4　In steady uniform open channel flow, the slope of the water surface, or HGL, is equal to the slope of the channel bottom

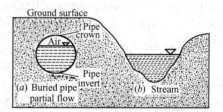

Figure 5　Any flow that occurs with a free surface exposed to atmospheric pressure is open channel flow, whether it occurs in a surface stream or in an underground pipe
(Note: ▽ indicates a free surface.)

New Words and Phrases

tunnel　　*n.* 隧道，隧洞
pipeline　　*n.* 管道(线)
canal　　*n.* 运河，小道，导管，槽，沟渠
channel　　*n.* 流道，渠道，沟渠，河槽，河床
aqueduct　　*n.* 输水管，渡槽
watershed　　*n.* 流域
even out　　*v.* 使平坦
fluctuation　　*n.* 波动，起伏

friction　　*n.* 摩擦，摩擦力
viscosity　　*n.* 黏度，黏性
cross section　　*n.* 横截面
specified　　*adj.* (技术规范中)规定的
valve　　*n.* 阀，[英] 电子管，真空管
piezometer　　*n.* 压力计，压强计
reach　　*n.* 河段

LESSON 3

Measurement Of Water Quality: I

Quantitative measurements of pollutants are obviously necessary before water pollution can be controlled. However, measurement of these pollutants is fraught with difficulties. Sometimes specific materials responsible for the pollution are not known. Moreover, these pollutants are generally present at low concentrations, and very accurate methods of detection are required.

Only a representative sample of the analytical tests available to measure water pollution is discussed in this section. A complete volume of analytical techniques used in water and wastewater engineering is compiled as *Standard Methods for the Examination of Water and Wastewater*. This volume is the result of a need for standardizing test techniques. It is considered definitive in its field and has the weight of legal authority.

Many water pollutants are measured in terms of milligrams of the substance per liter (mg/L). In older publications pollutant concentrations are expressed as parts per million (ppm), a weight/weight parameter. If the liquid involved is water, ppm is identical with mg/L, since one liter (L) of water weights 1000 grams (g). For pollutants present in very low concentrations (<10 mg/L), ppm is approximately equal to mg/L. However, because of the possibility that some wastes have specific gravity different from water, mg/L is preferred to ppm. A third commonly used parameter is percent, a weight/weight relationship. Note that 10000 ppm=1% and is equal to 10000 mg/L only when 1 mL=1 g.

Sampling

Some tests require the measurement to be conducted in the stream since the process of obtaining a sample may change the measurement. For example, if it is necessary to measure the dissolved oxygen (DO) in a stream, the measurement should be conducted right in the stream, or the sample must be extracted with great care to ensure that no transfer of oxygen from the air and water (in or out) occurs.

Most tests may be performed on a water sample taken from the stream. The process by which the sample is obtained, however, may greatly influence the result. The three basic types of samples are grab, composite, and flow-weighted composite.

The *grab sample*, as the name implies, measures water quality at only one sampling point. Its value is that it accurately represents the water quality at the moment of sampling, but it says nothing about the quality before or after the sampling. The *composite sample* is obtained by taking a series of grab samples and mixing them together. The *flow-weighted composite* is obtained by taking each sample so that the volume of the sample is proportional to the flow at that time. The last method is especially useful when daily loadings to wastewater treatment plants are calculated. Whatever the technique or method, however, the analysis can only be as accurate as the sample, and often the sampling methods are far more sloppy than the analytical determination.

Solids

Wastewater treatment is complicated by the dissolved and suspended inorganic material the wastewater contains. In discussion of water treatment, both dissolved and suspended materials are called solids. The separation of these solids from the water is one of the primary objectives of treatment.

Strictly speaking, in wastewater anything other than water is classified as solids. The usual definition of solids, however, is the residue after evaporation at 103℃ (slightly higher than the boiling point of water). The solids thus measured are known as total solids. Total solids may be divided into two fractions: the total dissolved solids (TDS) and the total suspended solids (TSS). A filtration step is used to separate the total suspended solids (TSS) from the total dissolved solids (TDS).

Total Suspended Solids. Because a filter is used to separate the TSS from the TDS, the TSS test is somewhat arbitrary, depending on the pore size of the filter paper used for the test. Filters with nominal pore sizes varying from 0.45 μm to about 2.0 μm have been used for the TSS test. More TSS will be measured as the pore size of the filter used is reduced.

Total Dissolved Solids. By definition, the solids contained in the filtrate that passes through a filter with a nominal pore size of 2.0 μm or less are classified as dissolved (Standard Methods. 1998). Yet it is known that wastewater contains a high fraction of colloidal solids. The size of colloidal particles in wastewater is typically in the range from 0.01 to 1.0 μm. It should be noted that some researchers have classified the size range for colloidal particles as varying from 0.001 to 1.0 μm, others from 0.003 to 1.0 μm. The size range for colloidal particles considered in this text is from 0.01 to 1.0 μm. The number of colloidal particles in untreated wastewater and after primary sedimentation is typically in the range from 10^8 to 10^{12}/mL. The fact that the distinction between colloidal particles and truly dissolved material has not been made routinely has led to confusion in the analysis of treatment plant performance and in the design of treatment processes.

pH

The pH of a solution is a measure of hydrogen ion concentration, which in turn is a measure of its acidity. The hydrogen-ion concentration in water is connected closely with the extent to which water molecules dissociate. Pure water dissociates slightly into equal concentrations of hydrogen and hydroxyl (OH^-) ions.

$$H_2O \rightleftharpoons H^+ + OH^- \tag{1}$$

An excess of hydrogen ions makes a solution acidic, whereas a dearth of H^+ ions, or an excess of hydroxyl ions, makes it basic. The equilibrium constant for this reaction, K_w, is the product of H^+ and OH^- concentrations and is equal to 10^{-14}. This relationship may be expressed as

$$[H^+][OH^-] = K_w = 10^{-14} \tag{2}$$

where $[H^+]$ and $[OH^-]$ are the concentration of hydrogen and hydroxyl ions, respectively, in moles per liter. Considering Equation 1 and solving Equation 2, in pure water,

$$[H^+] = [OH^-] = 10^{-7} \text{ moles/L} \tag{3}$$

The hydrogen-ion concentration is an important quality parameter of both natural waters and wastewaters. The usual means of expressing the hydrogen-ion concentration is as pH, which is defined as the negative logarithm of the hydrogen-ion concentration.

$$pH = -\log_{10}[H^+] = \log_{10}\left[\frac{1}{H^+}\right] \tag{4}$$

or

$$[H^+] = 10^{-pH} \tag{5}$$

For a neutral solution, $[H^+]$ is 10^{-7}, or pH = 7. For larger hydrogen ion concentrations, then, the pH of the solution is <7. For example, if the hydrogen ion concentration is 10^{-4}, the pH=4 and the solution is acidic. In this solution, we see that the hydroxyl ion concentration is $10^{-14}/10^{-4} = 10^{-10}$. Since $10^{-4} \gg 10^{-10}$, the solution contains a large excess of H^+ ions, confirming that it is indeed acidic. A solution containing a dearth of H^+ ions would have $[H^+] < 10^{-7}$, or pH>7, and would be basic. The pH range of dilute solutions is from 0 (very acidic; 1 mole of H^+ ions per liter) to 14 (very alkaline). Solutions containing more than 1 mole of H^+ ions per liter have negative pH.

The measurement of pH is now almost universally by electronic means. Electrodes that are sensitive to hydrogen ion concentration (strictly speaking, the hydrogen ion activity) convert the signal to electric current. Various pH papers and indicator solutions that change color at definite pH values are also used. The pH is determined by comparing the color of the paper or solution to a series of color standards. pH is important in almost all phases of water and wastewater treatment. Aquatic organisms are sensitive to pH changes, and biological treatment requires either pH control or monitoring. In water treatment as well as in disinfection and corrosion control, pH is important in ensuring proper chemical treatment. Mine drainage often involves the formation of sulfuric acid (high H^+ concentration), which is extremely detrimental to aquatic life. Continuous acid deposition from the atmosphere may substantially lower the pH of a lake.

Alkalinity

A parameter related to pH is alkalinity, or the buffering capacity of the water against acids. Water that has a high alkalinity can accept large doses of acid without lowering the pH significantly. Waters with low alkalinity, such as rainwater, can experience a drop in the pH with only a minor addition of hydrogen ion.

LESSON 3

In natural waters much of the alkalinity is provided by carbonate/bicarbonate buffering system. Carbon dioxide (CO_2) dissolves in water and is in equilibrium with the bicarbonate and carbonate ions.

$$CO_2 \text{(gas)} \rightleftharpoons CO_2 \text{(dissolved)}$$
$$CO_2 \text{(disolved)} + H_2O \rightleftharpoons H_2CO_3 \qquad (6)$$
$$H_2CO_3 \rightleftharpoons H^+ + HCO_3^-$$
$$HCO_3^- \rightleftharpoons H^+ + CO_3^{2-}$$

Any change that occurs in the components of this equation influences the solubility of CO_2. If acid is added to the water, the hydrogen ion concentration is increased, and this combines with both the carbonate and bicarbonate ions, driving the carbonate and bicarbonate equilibria to the left, releasing carbon dioxide into the atmosphere. The added hydrogen ion is absorbed by readjustment of all the equilibria, and the pH does not change markedly. Only when all of the carbonate and bicarbonate ions are depleted will the additional acid added to the water cause a drop in pH.

Alkalinity is determined by titrating against a standard acid; the results are expressed in terms of calcium carbonate, mg/L as $CaCO_3$. For most practical purposes alkalinity can be defined in terms of molar quantities, as

$$\text{Alk, eq/m}^3 = \text{meq/L} = [HCO_3^-] + 2[CO_3^{2-}] + [OH^-] - [H^+] \qquad (7)$$

The corresponding expression in terms of equivalents is

$$\text{Alk, eq/m}^3 = (HCO_3^-) + (CO_3^{2-}) + (OH^-) - (H^+) \qquad (8)$$

In practice, alkalinity is expressed in terms of calcium carbonate. To convert from meq/L to mg/L as $CaCO_3$, it is helpful to remember that:

$$\text{Milliequivalent mass of } CaCO_3 = \frac{100 \text{mg/mmole}}{2 \text{meq/mmole}}$$
$$= 50 \text{mg/meq} \qquad (9)$$

Thus 3 meq/L of alkalinity would be expressed as 150 mg/L as $CaCO_3$.

$$\text{Alkalinity, Alk as } CaCO_3 = \frac{3.0 \text{meq}}{L} \times \frac{50 \text{mgCaCO}_3}{\text{meqCaCO}_3}$$
$$= 150 \text{mg/L as } CaCO_3$$

Dissolved Oxygen

Probably the most important measure of water quality is the dissolved oxygen (DO). Oxygen, although poorly soluble in water, is fundamental to aquatic life. Without free DO, streams and lakes become uninhabitable to gill-breathing aquatic organisms. The actual quantity of oxygen (other gases too) that can be present in solution is governed by (1) the solubility of the gas, (2) the partial pressure of the gas in the atmosphere, (3) the temperature, and (4) the concentration of the impurities in the water (e.g., salinity, suspended solids, etc.).

Because the rate of biochemical reactions that use oxygen increases with increasing temperature, dissolved oxygen levels tend to be more critical in the summer months. The problem is compounded in summer months because stream flows are usually lower, and thus the total quantity of oxygen available is also lower. The presence of dissolved oxygen in wastewater is desirable because it prevents the formation of noxious odors.

The amount of oxygen dissolved in water is usually measured either with an oxygen probe or by iodometric titration. The latter method is the Winkler tests for DO, developed about 100 years ago and the standard against which all other measurements are compared.

Biochemical Oxygen Demand

The *rate* at which oxygen is used is perhaps even more important than the determination of DO. A very low rate of use would indicate either clean water, that the available microorganisms are uninterested in consuming the available organic compounds, or that the microorganisms are dead or dying. The rate of oxygen use is commonly referred to as biochemical oxygen demand (BOD). BOD is not a specific pollutant but rather a measure of the amount of oxygen required by bacteria and other microorganisms engaged in stabilizing decomposable organic matter.

The most widely used parameter of organic pollution applied to both wastewater and surface water is the 5-day BOD (BOD_5). This determination involves the measurement of the dissolved oxygen used by microorganisms in the biochemical oxidation of organic matter. Despite the widespread use of the BOD test, it has a number of limitations. It is hoped that, through the continued efforts of workers in the field, one of the other measures of organic content, or perhaps a new measure, will ultimately be used in its place. Why, then, if the test suffers from serious limitations, is further space devoted to it in this text? The reason is that BOD test results are now used (1) to determine the approximate quantity of oxygen that will be required to biologically stabilize the organic matter present, (2) to determine the size of waste-treatment facilities, (3) to measure the efficiency of some treatment processes, and (4) to determine compliance with wastewater discharge permits.

Chemical Oxygen Demand

Among many drawbacks of the BOD test, the most important is that it takes five days to run. If the organic compounds are oxidized chemically instead of biologically, the test can be shortened considerably. Such oxidation is accomplished with the chemical oxygen demand (COD) test. Because nearly all organic compounds are oxidized in the COD test and only some are decomposed during the BOD test, COD values are always higher than BOD values. One example of this is wood pulping waste, in which compounds such as cellulose are easily oxidized chemically (high COD) but are very slow to decompose biologically (low BOD).

The COD test is used to measure the oxygen equivalent of the organic material in wastewater that can be oxidized chemically using dichromate in an acid solution, as illustrated in the following equation, when the organic nitrogen is in the reduced state (oxidation number = −3).

$$C_nH_aO_bN_c + dCr_2O_7^{2-} + (8d+c)H^+ \longrightarrow nCO_2 + \frac{a+8d-3c}{2}H_2O + cNH_4^+ + 2dCr^{3+} \quad (10)$$

where $d = \dfrac{2n}{3} + \dfrac{a}{6} - \dfrac{b}{3} - \dfrac{c}{2}$

Although it would be expected that the value of the ultimate carbonaceous BOD would be as high as the COD, this is seldom the case. Some of the reasons for the observed differences are as follows: (1) many organic substances which are difficult to oxidize biologically, such as lignin, can be oxidized chemically, (2) inorganic substances that are oxidized by the dichromate increase the apparent organic content of the sample, (3) certain organic substances may be toxic to the microorganisms used in the BOD test, and (4) high COD values may occur because of the presence of inorganic substances with which the dichromate can react. From an operational standpoint, one of the main advantages of the COD test is that it can be completed in about 2.5h, compared to 5 or more days for the BOD test. To reduce the time further, a rapid COD test that takes only about 15 min has been developed.

As new methods of biological treatment have been developed, especially with respect to biological nutrient removal, it has become more important to fractionate the COD. The principal fractions are particulate and soluble COD. In biological treatment studies, the particulate and soluble fractions are fractionated further to assess wastewater treatability. Fractions that have been used include: (1) readily biodegradable soluble COD, (2) slowly biodegradable colloidal and particulate (enmeshed) COD, (3) nonbiodegradable soluble COD, and (4) nonbiodegradable colloidal and particulate COD. The readily biodegradable soluble COD is often fractionated further into complex COD that can be fermented to volatile fatty acids (VFAs) and short chain VFAs. Unfortunately, as noted previously, there is little standardization on the definition of soluble versus particulate COD. Where filtration is the technique used to fractionate the sample, the relative distribution between soluble and particulate COD will vary greatly depending on the pore size of the filter. An alternative method used to determine the soluble COD involves precipitation of the suspended solids and a portion of the colloidal material. The COD of the clarified liquid corresponds to the soluble COD.

New Words and Phrases

concentration　　 n. 集中，浓缩，浓度
definitive　　 adj. 最后的，确定的，权威性的
milli-　　 [词头] 千分之一，毫
extract　　 vt. 提炼，萃取
sloppy　　 adj. 湿透的，水多的，液体的；草率的，粗心大意的
residue　　 n. 残留物，剩余物
TDS (the total dissolved solids)　　 总溶解性固体
TSS (the total suspended solids)　　 总悬浮性固体
filtration　　 n. 过滤
filtrate　　 v. 过滤，筛选
　　 n. 滤出液
nominal　　 adj. 名义上的，名字的，[语] 名词性的，公称的，额定的
hydrogen　　 n. 氢
ion　　 n. 离子
dissociate　　 v. 分离，游离，分裂

hydroxyl *n.* 羟(基)，氢氧基
acidic *adj.* 酸的，酸性的
dearth *n.* 缺乏
basic *n.* 基本，要素，基础
        adj. 基本的，碱性的
product *n.* 产品，产物，乘积
logarithm *n.* 对数
electrode *n.* 电极，焊条
hydrogen ion activity 氢离子活性(度)
indicator *n.* 指示剂，指示菌，指示基因
aquatic *adj.* 水的，水上的，水生的，水栖的
organism *n.* 生物体，有机体
disinfection *n.* 消毒
mine drainage 矿山排水
sulfuric acid 硫酸
alkalinity *n.* 碱度
buffering capacity 缓冲能力
carbonate *n.* 碳酸盐
bicarbonate *n.* 重碳酸盐
CO_2 (Carbon dioxide) 二氧化碳
titrate *v.* 用滴定法测量
          n. 滴定法被测溶液
calcium carbonate 碳酸钙
DO (dissolved oxygen) 溶解氧
gill *n.* 腮，腮下肉，峡谷，峡流，锶
       v. 用刺网捕鱼
salinity *n.* 含盐量，咸度，盐浓度
odor *n.* 气味，名声
iodo- (构词成分)碘

titration *n.* 滴定
BOD (biochemical oxygen demand) 生化需氧量
microorganism *n.* 微生物
bacteria *n.* 细菌
decomposable *adj.* 可分解的
decomposition *n.* 分解，腐烂
oxidation *n.* 氧化
stabilize *v.* 稳定
COD (chemical oxygen demand) 化学需氧量
drawback *n.* 缺点，障碍
decompose *v.* 分解，(使)腐烂
cellulose *n.* 纤维素
dichromate *n.* 重铬酸盐
nitrogen *n.* 氮
reduced state 还原态
carbonaceous *adj.* [化]碳的，碳质的，含碳的
lignin *n.* 木质素
nutrient *adj.* 有营养的
fractionate *vt.* 使分馏，分级，把…分为几部分
particulate *n.* 微粒，颗粒
              adj. 微粒的
biodegradable *adj.* 生物可降解的
ferment *n.* 酵素，发酵
          v. (使)发酵
VFAs (volatile fatty acids) 挥发性脂肪酸

Questions

1. What can pollutant concentration be expressed?
2. What are basic types of samples?
3. What are the meanings of TDS and TSS?
4. What are the definitions of pH and alkalinity?
5. In natural water, why do the alkalinity have the buffering capacity against acids?
6. By what methods is the amount of oxygen dissolved in water usually measured?
7. Please explain the meanings of BOD and COD.
8. Why are COD values always higher than BOD values?

Reading Material

Measurement Of Water Quality: II

Turbidity

Water that is not clear but "dirty", in the sense that light transmission is inhibited, is considered *turbid*. In the treatment of water for drinking purposes, turbidity is of great importance, first because of aesthetic considerations and second because pathogenic organisms can hide on (or in) the tiny colloidal particles.

Turbidity is another test used to indicate the quality of waste discharges and natural waters with respect to colloidal and residual suspended matter. The measurement of turbidity is based on comparison of the intensity of light scattered by a sample to the light scattered by a reference suspension under the same conditions (Standard Methods, 1998). *Formazin* suspensions are used as the primary reference standard. The results of turbidity measurements are reported as nephelometric turbidity units (NTU). Colloidal matter will scatter or absorb light and thus prevent its transmission. It should be noted that the presence of air bubbles in the fluid would cause erroneous turbidity readings. In general, there is no relationship between turbidity and the concentration of total suspended solids in untreated wastewater. There is, however, a reasonable relationship between turbidity and total suspended solids for the settled and filtered secondary effluent from the activated sludge process. The general form of the relationship is as follows:

$$TSS, \text{ mg/L} \approx (TSS_f)(T) \tag{11}$$

where TSS = total suspended solids, mg/L

TSS_f = factor used to convert turbidity readings to total suspended solid, (mg/L TSS)/NTU

T = turbidity, NTU

The specific value of the conversion factor will vary for each treatment plant, depending primarily on the operation of the biological treatment process. The conversions factors for settled secondary effluent and for secondary effluent filtered with a granular-medium depth filter will typically very from 2.3 to 2.4 and 1.3 to 1.6, respectively.

One of the problems with the measurement of turbidity (especially low values in filtered effluent) is the high degree of variability observed, depending on the light source (incandescent light versus light-emitting diodes) and the method of measurement (reflected versus transmitted light). Another problem often encountered is the light-absorbing properties of the suspended material. For example, the turbidity of a solution of lampblack will essentially be equal to zero. As a result, it is almost impossible to compare turbidity values reported in the literature. However, turbidity readings at a given facility can be used for process control. Some on-line turbidity meters used to monitor the performance of microfiltration units are affected by the air used to clean the membranes.

Turbidimeters are photometers that measure the intensity of scattered light. Opaque particles scatter light, so the scattered light measured at right angles to a beam of incident light is proportional to the turbidity.

The standard for calibrating turbidimeters is defined as

$$1\text{mg/L of } SiO_2 = 1 \text{ normalized turbidity unit}$$

Nitrogen

The elements nitrogen and phosphorus, essential to the growth of microorganisms, plants, and animals, are known as nutrients or biostimulants. Trace quantities of other elements, such as iron, are also needed for biological growth, but nitrogen and phosphorus are, in most cases, the major nutrients of importance. Because nitrogen is an essential building block in the synthesis of protein, nitrogen data will be required to evaluate the treatability of wastewater by biological processes. Insufficient nitrogen can necessitate the addition of nitrogen to make the waste treatable. Where control of algal growths in the receiving water is necessary, removal or reduction of nitrogen in wastewater prior to discharge may be desirable.

Sources of Nitrogen. The principal sources of nitrogen compounds are (1) the nitrogenous compounds of plant and animal origin, (2) sodium nitrate, and (3) atmospheric nitrogen. Ammonia derived from the distillation of bituminous coal is an example of nitrogen obtained from decayed plant material. Sodium nitrate ($NaNO_3$) is found principally in mineral deposits in Chile and in the manure found in seabird rookeries. The production of nitrogen from the atmosphere is termed *fixation*. Because fixation is a biologically mediated process and because $NaNO_3$ deposits are relatively scarce, most sources of nitrogen in soil/groundwater are of biological origin.

Forms of Nitrogen. The chemistry of nitrogen is complex, because of the several oxidation states that nitrogen can assume and the fact that changes in the oxidation state can be brought about by living organisms. To complicate matters further, the oxidation state changes brought about by bacteria can be either positive or negative depending upon whether aerobic or anaerobic conditions prevail. The oxidation states of nitrogen are summarized below.

$$-\text{III} \quad 0 \quad \text{I} \quad \text{II} \quad \text{III} \quad \text{IV} \quad \text{V}$$
$$NH_3 - N_2 - N_2O - NO - N_2O_3 - NO_2 - N_2O_5 \qquad (12)$$

The most common and important forms of nitrogen in wastewater and their corresponding oxidation state in the water/soil environment are ammonia (NH_3, $-\text{III}$), ammonium (NH_4^+, $-\text{III}$), nitrogen gas (N_2, 0), nitrite ion (NO_2^-, $+\text{III}$), and nitrate ion (NO_3^-, $+\text{V}$). The oxidation state of nitrogen in most organic compounds is $-\text{III}$.

Total nitrogen, is comprised of organic nitrogen, ammonia, nitrite, and nitrate. The organic fraction consists of a complex mixture of compounds including amino acids, amino sugars, and proteins (polymers of amino acids). The compounds that comprise the organic fraction can be soluble or particulate. The nitrogen in these compounds is readily converted to ammonium through the action of microorganisms in the aquatic or soil environment. Urea, readily converted to ammonium carbonate, is seldom found in untreated municipal wastewaters.

Definition of the various terms used to define various nitrogen species Table 1

Form of nitrogen	Abbrev.	Definition
Ammonia gas	NH_3	NH_3
Ammonium ion	NH_4^+	NH_4^+
Total ammonia nitrogen	TAN	$NH_3 + NH_4^+$
Nitrite	NO_2^-	NO_2^-
Nitrate	NO_3^-	NO_3^-
Total inorganic nitrogen	TIN	$NH_3 + NH_4^+ + NO_2^- + NO_3^-$
Total Kjeldahl nitrogen	TKN	Organic N $+ NH_3 + NH_4^+$
Organic nitrogen	Organic N	$TKN - (NH_3 + NH_4^+)$
Total nitrogen	TN	Organic N $+ NH_3 + NH_4^+ + NO_2^- + NO_3^-$

Organic nitrogen is determined analytically using the Kjeldahl method. The aqueous sample is first boiled to drive off the ammonia, and then it is digested. During digestion the organic nitrogen is converted to ammonium through the action of heat and acid. Total Kjeldahl nitrogen (TKN) is determined in the same manner as organic nitrogen, except that the ammonia is not driven off before the digestion step. *Total Kjeldahl nitrogen is therefore the total of the organic and ammonia nitrogen.*

As biological nutrient removal has become more common, information on the various organic nitrogen fractions has become important. The principal fractions are particulate and soluble. In biological treatment studies, the particulate and soluble fractions of organic nitrogen are fractionated further to assess wastewater treatability. Fractions that have been used include (1) free ammonia, (2) biodegradable soluble organic nitrogen, (3) biodegradable particulate organic carbon, (4) nonbiodegredable soluble organic nitrogen, and (5) nonbiodegradable particulate organic nitrogen. Unfortunately, there is little standardization on the definition of soluble versus particulate organic nitrogen. Where filtration is the technique used to fractionate the sample, the relative distribution between soluble and particulate organic nitrogen will vary depending on the pore size of the filter used. In many cases, colloidal organic nitrogen has been classified as soluble or dissolved. The lack of standardized definition will also affect other aggregate constituents (i.e., chemical oxygen demand and total organic carbon).

Phosphates

Phosphorus is also essential to the growth of algae and other biological organisms. Because of noxious algal blooms that occur in surface waters, there is presently much interest in controlling the amount of phosphorus compounds that enter surface waters in domestic and industrial waste discharges and natural runoff. Municipal wastewaters, for example, may contain from 4 to 16mg/L of phosphorus as P.

The usual forms of phosphorus that are found in aqueous solutions include the orthophosphate, polyphosphate, and organic phosphate. The orthophosphates, for example, PO_4^{3-}, HPO_4^{2-}, $H_2PO_4^-$, H_3PO_4, are available for biological metabolism without further breakdown. The polyphosphates include those molecules with two or more phosphorus atoms, oxygen atoms, and, in some cases, hydrogen atoms combined in a complex molecule. Polyphosphates undergo hydrolysis in aqueous solutions and revert to the orthophosphate forms; however, this hydrolysis is usually quite slow. The organically bound phosphorus is usually of minor importance in most domestic wastes, but it can be an important constituent of industrial wastes and wastewater sludges.

Orthophosphate can be determined by directly adding a substance such as ammonium molybdate, which will form a colored complex with the phosphate. The polyphosphates and organic phosphates must be converted to orthophosphates using an acid digestion step before they can be determined in a similar manner.

Color

Color and odor are both important measurements in water treatment. Along with turbidity they are called physical parameters of drinking water quality. Color and odor are important from the standpoint of aesthetics. If water looks colored or smells bad, people instinctively avoid using it, even though it might be perfectly safe from the public health aspect. Both color and odor may be and often are caused by organic substances such as algae or humic compounds.

Color is measured by comparison with standards. Colored water made with potassium chloroplatinate when tinted with cobalt chloride closely resembles the color of many natural waters. When multicolored industrial wastes are involved, such color measurement is meaningless.

Odor

Effects of Odors. The importance of odors at low concentrations in human terms is related primarily to the psychological stress they produce rather than to the harm they do to the body. Offensive odors can cause poor appetite for food, lowered water consumption, impaired respiration, nausea and vomiting, and mental perturbation. In extreme situations, offensive odors can lead to the deterioration of personal and community pride, interfere with human relations, discourage capital investment, lower socioeconomic status, and deter growth. Also, some odorous compounds (e.g., H_2S) are toxic at elevated concentrations.

Detection of Odors. The malodorous compounds responsible for producing psychological stress in humans are detected by the olfactory system, but the precise mechanism involved is at present not well understood. Since 1870, more than 30 theories have been proposed to explain olfaction. One of the difficulties in developing a universal theory has been the inadequate explanation of why compounds with similar structures may have different odors and why compounds with very different structures may have similar odors.

At present, there appears to be some general agreement that the odor of a molecule must be related to the molecule as a whole.

Odor Characterization and Measurement. It has been suggested that four independent factors are required for the complete characterization of an odor: intensity, character, hedonics, and detectability. To date, detectability is the only factor that has been used in the development of statutory regulations for nuisance odors. As shown on Figure 1, odor can be measured by sensory methods, and specific odorant concentrations can be measured by instrumental methods. It has been shown that, under carefully controlled conditions, the sensory (organoleptic) measurement of odors by the human olfactory system can provide meaningful and reliable information. Therefore, the sensory method is often used to measure the odors emanating from wastewater-treatment facilities. The availability of a direct reading meter for hydrogen sulfide, which can be used to detect concentrations as low as 1 ppb, is a significant development.

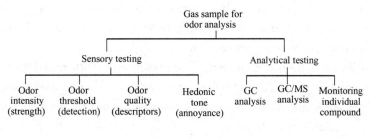

Figure 1 Classification of methods used to detect odors

The threshold odor of a water or wastewater sample is determined by diluting the sample with odor-free water. The "threshold odor number" (TON) corresponds to the greatest dilution of the sample with odor-free water at which an odor is just perceptible. The recommended sample size is 200mL. The numerical value of the TON is determined as follows:

$$\text{TON} = \frac{A+B}{A} \tag{13}$$

where   TON=threshold odor number
         A=mL of sample
         B=mL of odor-free water

Bacteriological Measurements

From the public health standpoint, the bacteriological quality of water is as important as the chemical quality. A large number of infectious diseases may be transmitted by water, among them typhoid and cholera. However, it is one thing to declare that water must not be contaminated by *pathogens* (disease-causing organisms) and another to determine the existence of these organisms. First, there are many pathogens. Each has a specific detection procedure and must be screened individually. Second, the concentration of these organisms, although large enough to spread disease, may be so small as to make their detection impossible, like the proverbial needle in a haystack.

How then can we measure for bacteriological quality? The answer lies in the concept of *indicator organisms* that, while not particularly harmful, indicate the possible presence of bacteria that are pathogenic. The indicator most often used is a group of microbes of the family *Escherichia coli* (*E. coli*), often called coliform bacteria, which are organisms normal to the digestive tracts of warm-blooded animals. In addition, *E coli are*:

1. Plentiful and hence not difficult to find
2. Easily detected with a simple test
3. Generally harmless expect in unusual circumstances
4. Hardy, surviving longer than most known pathogens

Coliforms have thus become universal indicator organisms. The presence of coliforms does not prove the presence of pathogens. If a large number of coliforms are present, there is a good chance of recent pollution by wastes from warm blooded animals, and therefore the water may contain pathogenic organisms.

This last point should be emphasized. The presence of coliforms does not prove that there are pathogenic organisms in the water, but indicates that such organisms might be present. A high coliform count is thus suspicious, and the water should not be consumed, even though it may be safe.

Coliforms are measured by first filtering the sample through a sterile micropore filter by suction, thereby capturing any coliforms on the filter. The filter is then placed in a petri dish containing a sterile agar that soaks into the filter and promotes the growth of the coliforms while inhibiting other organisms. After 24 or 48 hours of incubation the number of shiny black dots, indicating coliform colonies, is counted. If we know how many milliliters of sample poured through the filter, the concentration of coliforms may be expressed as coliforms/mL.

Viruses

More than 100 different types of enteric viruses capable of producing infection or disease are excreted by humans. Enteric viruses multiply in the intestinal tract and are released in the fecal matter of infected persons. From the standpoint of health the most important human enteric viruses are the enteroviruses (polio, echo, and coxsackie), Norwalk viruses, rotaviruses, reoviruses, caliciviruses, adenoviruses, and hepatitis A virus. Of the viruses that cause diarrhea disease, only the Norwalk virus and rotavirus have been shown to the major waterborne pathogens. The reoviruses and adenoviruses, known to cause respiratory illness, gastroenteritis, and eye infections, have been isolated from wastewater. There is no evidence that the human immunodeficiency virus (HIV), the pathogen that causes the acquired immunodeficiency syndrome (AIDS), can be transmitted via the waterborne route.

Because of their minute size and extremely low concentration and the need to culture

LESSON 3

them on living tissues, pathogenic (or animal) viruses are fiendishly difficult to measure. Moreover, there are as yet no standards for viral quality of water supplies, as there are for pathogenic bacteria.

One possible method of overcoming this difficulty is to use an indicator organism, much like the coliform group is used as an indicator for bacterial contamination. This can be done by using a *bacteriophage*—a virus that attacks only a certain type of bacterium. For example, coliphages attack coliform organisms and, because of their association with wastes from warm-blooded animal seem to be an ideal indicator. The test for coliphages is performed by inoculating a petri dish containing an ample supply of a specific coliform with the wastewater sample. Coliphages will attack the coliforms, leaving visible spots, or plaques, that can be counted, and an estimation can be made of the number of coliphages per unit volume.

Heavy Metals

Heavy metals such as arsenic and mercury can harm fish even at low concentrations. Consequently, the method of measuring these ions in water must be very sensitive. The method of choice is *atomic absorption spectrophotometry*, in which a solution of lanthanum chloride is added to the sample, and the treated sample is sprayed into a flame using an atomizer. Each metallic element in the sample imparts a characteristic color to the flame, whose intensity is then measured spectrophotometrically.

Trace quantities of many metals, such as cadmium (Cd), chromium (Cr), copper (Cu), iron (Fe), lead (Pb), manganese (Mn), mercury (Hg), nickel (Ni), and zinc (Zn) are important constituents of most waters. Many of these metals are also classified as priority pollutants. However, most of these metals are necessary for growth of biological life, and absence of sufficient quantities of them could limit growth of algae, for example. The presence of any of these metals in excessive quantities will interfere with many beneficial uses of the water because of their toxicity; therefore, it is frequently desirable to measure and control the concentrations of these substances.

Note: polio means poliomyelitis

Importance of Metals All living organisms require varying amounts (macro and micro) of metallic elements, such as iron, chromium, copper, zinc, and cobalt, for proper growth. Although macro and micro amounts of metals are required for proper growth, the same metals can be toxic when present in elevated concentrations. As more use is made of treated wastewater effluent for irrigation and landscape watering, a variety of metals must be determined to assess any adverse effects that may occur. Calcium, magnesium, and sodium are of importance in determining the sodium adsorption ratio (SAR), which is used to assess the suitability of treated effluent for agricultural use. Where composted sludge is applied in agricultural applications, arsenic, cadmium, copper, lead, mercury, molybdenum, nickel, selenium, and zinc must be determined.

Sources of Metals The sources of trace metals in wastewater include the discharges from residential dwellings, groundwater infiltration, and commercial and industrial discharges. For example, cadmium, chromates, lead, and mercury are often present in industrial wastes. These are found particularly in metal-plating wastes and should be removed by pretreatment at the site of the industry rather than be mixed with the municipal wastewater. Fluoride, a toxic anion, is found commonly in wastewater from electronics manufacturing facilities.

Sampling and Methods of Analysis Methods for determining the concentrations of these substances vary in complexity according to the interfering substances that may be present (Standard Methods, 1998). Metals are determined typically by flame atomic absorption, electrothermal atomic absorption, inductively coupled plasma, or IPC/mass spectrometry. Various classes of metals are defined as: (1) *dissolved metals* are those metals present in unacidified samples that pass through a 0.45-μm membrane filter, (2) *suspended metals* are those metals present in unacidified samples that are retained on a 0.45-μm membrane filter, (3) *total metals* is the total of the dissolved and suspended metals or the concentration of metals determined on an unfiltered sample after digestion, and (4) *acid extractable metals* are those metals in solution after an unfiltered sample is treated with a hot dilute mineral acid.

Trace Toxic Organic Compounds

Very low concentrations of chlorinated hydrocarbons and other agrichemical residues in water can be assayed by gas *chromatography*. Oil residues in water are generally measured by extracting the water sample with Freon and then evaporating the Freon and weighing the residue from this evaporation.

New Words and Phrases

turbidity n. 浑浊，浊度
pathogenic adj. 致病的，病原的，发病的
intensity n. 强烈，剧烈，强度
scatter v. 分散，散开
formazin n. 福尔马肼
nephelometric adj. （散射）浊度计的
sludge n. 沉泥，淤泥
activated sludge process 活性污泥工艺
incandescent adj. 遇热发光的，白炽的
light-emitting diodes 发光二极管
transmit v. 透射，传输，转送，传达，传导，发射，遗传，传播
lampblack n. 灯烟，灯黑
on-line adj. 在线的，即时的
microfiltration n. 微滤
membrane n. 膜，隔膜

turbidimeter n. 浊度计，浊度表
photometer n. 光度计，曝光计
scattered light 散射光
incident light 入射光
opaque n. 不透明物
　　　　adj. 不透明的，不传热的
phosphorus n. 磷
biostimulant n. 生物刺激物质
trace n. 痕量，微量，示踪
building block 构件，结构单元，砌块
synthesis n. 综合，合成
protein n. 蛋白质
　　　　adj. 蛋白质的
nitrogenous adj. 氮的，含氮的
sodium nitrate 硝酸钠
ammonia n. 氨，氨水

LESSON 3

distillation   *n.* 蒸馏，蒸馏法，蒸馏物
bituminous coal   生煤，烟煤
manure   *n.* 肥料
           v. 施肥于
rookery   *n.* 白嘴鸦的群居地，海豹等之穴，破旧而拥挤的住房群，贫民窟
fixation   *n.* 固定［作用］，结合
aerobic   *adj.* 好氧的，需氧的
ammonium   *n.* 铵
nitrite   *n.* 亚硝酸盐
nitrate   *n.* 硝酸盐
total Kjeldahl nitrogen   总基耶达氮
amino acid   氨基酸
amino sugar   氨基糖
urea   *n.* 尿素
digestion   *n.* 消化［作用］，老化，蒸煮
phosphate   *n.* 磷酸盐
orthophosphate   *n.* 正磷酸盐
polyphosphate   *n.* 聚磷酸盐
alga   *n.* 藻类，海藻
noxious   *adj.* 有毒的
metabolism   *n.* 新陈代谢，变形
hydrolysis   *n.* 水解
molybdate   *n.* 钼酸盐
humic compound   腐殖化合物，腐殖质
potassium   *n.* 钾
chloroplatinate   *n.* 氯铂酸盐
tint with   给…染色
cobalt   *n.* 钴（符号为 Co），钴类颜料，由钴制的深蓝色
chloride   *n.* 氯化物
resemble   *vt.* 像，类似
offensive   *adj.* 讨厌的，攻击性的
           n. 进攻，攻势
psychological   *adj.* 心理（上）的
appetite   *n.* 食欲，胃口，欲望，爱好
impair   *v.* 削弱
nausea   *n.* 反胃，晕船，恶心
vomit   *n.* 呕吐，呕吐物，催吐剂
         v. 呕吐，吐出

mental   *adj.* 精神的，智力的
perturbation   *n.* 混乱，小扰动
deterioration   *n.* 变坏，退化
discourage   *vt.* 阻碍
socioeconomic   *adj.* 社会经济学的
deter   *v.* 阻止
malodorous   *adj.* 有恶臭的
olfactory   *adj.* 嗅觉的
olfaction   *n.* 嗅觉
mechanism   *n.* 机理，机械装置，机构
character   *n.* 特性，性质，字符，性格，特征，人物
hedonics   *n.* 享乐，享乐论
detectability   *n.* 探测能力
statutory   *adj.* 法令的，法定的
sensory   *adj.* 感觉的，感官的
organoleptic   *adj.* 器官（尤指味觉、嗅觉或视觉器官）的
hydrogen sulfide   硫化氢
mass spectrometry   质谱测量，质谱分析
threshold   *n.* 阈值
perceptible   *adj.* 可察觉的，显而易见的，感觉得到的
bacteriological   *adj.* 细菌学的，细菌学上的
infectious   *adj.* 有传染性的，易传染的
typhoid   *n.* 伤寒症
         adj. 伤寒的，斑疹伤寒症的
cholera   *n.* 霍乱
pathogen   *n.* 病原体(物)
Escherichia coli   大肠埃希氏菌
coliform bacteria   大肠型细菌
digestive tract   消化道
sterile   *adj.* 无菌的
micropore   *n.* 微孔
suction   *n.* 吸入，抽气
petri dish   培养皿
agar   *n.* 琼脂（一种植物胶，用海产石花菜类制成，可作冷食或微生物的培养基等），石花菜
colony   *n.* 集落；菌落

virus　n. 病毒，滤过性微生物
enteric　adj. 肠的
infection　n. 传染，传染病，影响，感染
multiply　v. 繁殖，乘，增加
intestinal tract　肠道
fecal　adj. 排泄物的
enterovirus　n. 肠道病毒
poliovirus　n. 脊髓灰质炎病毒
poliomyelitis　n. 小儿麻痹症，急性骨髓灰白质炎
ECHO virus　n. ECHO 病毒，埃柯病毒
Coxsackie　n. 柯萨奇病毒（一种引起呼吸道疾病等的病毒）［首先发现于美国纽约州的 Coxsackie 镇］
norwalk virus　n. 诺沃克病毒［可引起腹泻，属杯状病毒科］
rotavirus　n. 轮状病毒
reovirus　n. 呼肠(孤)病毒
calicivirus　n. 杯状病毒
adenovirus　n. 腺病毒
hepatitis　n. 肝炎
diarrhea　n. 痢疾，腹泻
waterborne　adj. 水传染的
respiratory illness　n. 呼吸疾病
gastroenteritis　n. 肠胃炎
immunodeficiency　n. 免疫缺陷
AIDS　abbr. 艾滋病，获得性免疫功能丧失综合症
tissue　n. (生物)组织
fiendishly　adv. 恶魔似地，极坏地
viral　adj. 病毒的
bacteriophage　n. 噬菌体
bacterium　n. 细菌(pl.) bacteria
coliphage　n. 大肠杆菌噬菌体
inoculate　vt. 接种，嫁接

plaque　n. 斑点
arsenic　n. 砷，砒霜
mercury　n. 水银，汞
atomic absorption spectrophotometry　原子吸收分光谱测量
lanthanum　n. 镧
atomizer　n. 喷雾器
cadmium　n. 镉
chromium　n. 铬
copper　n. 铜，警察
lead　n. 铅
manganese　n. 锰
nickel　n. 镍，镍币
zinc　n. 锌
irrigation　n. 灌溉，冲洗
molybdenum　n. 钼
selenium　n. 硒
chromate　n. 铬酸盐
landscape watering　景观水
composted sludge　堆肥
plating　n. 电镀，被覆金属
fluoride　n. 氟化物
anion　n. 阴离子
electrothermal　adj. 电热的
inductively　adv. 诱导地
plasma　n. 等离子体，等离子区，原生质，血浆
acidify　vt. 使酸化，使成酸
　　　　　vi. 变酸
hydrocarbon　n. 烃，碳氢化合物
chlorinated hydrocarbon　氯化烃
assay　n. & v. 化验
gas chromatography　气相色谱
Freon　n. 氟利昂

LESSON 4

Fundamentals Of Wastewater Treatment

Every community produces both liquid and solid wastes and air emissions. The liquid waste—wastewater—is essentially the water supply of the community after it has been used in a variety of applications (see Figure 1). From the standpoint of sources of generation, wastewater may be defined as a combination of the liquid or water-carried wastes removed from residences, institutions, and commercial and industrial establishments, together with such groundwater, surface water, and stormwater as may be present.

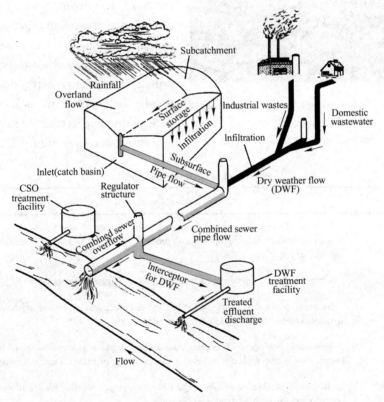

Figure 1 Schematic diagram of a wastewater management infrastructure

When untreated wastewater accumulates and is allowed to go septic, the decomposition of the organic matter it contains will lead to nuisance conditions including the production of malodorous gases. In addition, untreated wastewater contains numerous pathogenic microorganisms that dwell in the human intestinal tract.

Wastewater also contains nutrients, which can stimulate the growth of aquatic plants, and may contain toxic compounds or compounds that potentially may be mutagenic or carcinogenic. For these reasons, the immediate and nuisance-free removal of wastewater from its sources of generation, followed by treatment, reuse, or dispersal into the environment is necessary to protect public health and the environment.

Treatment Methods

Methods of treatment in which the application of physical forces predominate are known as *unit operations*. Methods of treatment in which the removal of contaminants is brought about by chemical or biological reactions are known as *unit processes*. At the present time, unit operations and processes are grouped together to provide various levels of treatment known as preliminary, primary, advanced primary, secondary (without or with nutrient removal), and advanced (or tertiary) treatment (see Table 1). In preliminary treatment, gross solids such as large objects, rags, and grit are removed that may damage equipment. In primary treatment, a physical operation, usually sedimentation, is used to remove the floating and settleable materials found in wastewater (see Figure 2).

Figure 2 Typical primary sedimentation tanks used to remove floating and settleable material from wastewater

Levels of wastewater treatment　　Table 1

Treatment Level	Description
Preliminary	Removal of wastewater constituents such as rags, sticks, floatables, grit, and grease that may cause maintenance or operational problems with the treatment operations, processes, and ancillary systems
Primary	Removal of a portion of the suspended solids and organic matter from the wastewater
Advanced primary	Enhanced removal of suspended solids and organic matter from the wastewater. Typically accomplished by chemical addition or filtration
Secondary	Removal of biodegradable organic matter (in solution or suspension) and suspended solids. Disinfection is also typically included in the definition of conventional secondary treatment
Secondary with nutrient removal	Removal of biodegradable organics, suspended solids, and nutrients (nitrogen, phosphorus, or both nitrogen and phosphorus)
Tertiary	Removal of residual suspended solids (after secondary treatment), usually by granular medium filtration or microscreens. Disinfection is also typically a part of tertiary treatment. Nutrient removal is often included in this definition
Advanced	Removal of dissolved and suspended materials remaining after normal biological treatment when required for various water reuse applications

For advanced primary treatment, chemicals are added to enhance the removal of suspended solids and, to a lesser extent, dissolved solids. In secondary treatment, biological and chemical processes are used to remove most of the organic matter. In advanced treatment additional combinations of unit operations and processes are used to remove residual suspended solids and other constituents that are not reduced significantly by conventional secondary treatment. A listing of unit operations and processes used for the removal of major constituents found in wastewater is presented in Table 2.

Unit operations and processes used to remove constituents found in wastewater   Table 2

Constituent	Unit operation or process
Suspended solids	Screening Grit removal Sedimentation High-rate clarification Flotation Chemical precipitation Depth filtration Surface filtration
Biodegradable organics	Aerobic suspended growth variations Aerobic attached growth variations Anaerobic suspended growth variations Anaerobic attached growth variations Lagoon variations Physical-chemical systems Chemical oxidation Advanced oxidation Membrane filtration
Nutrients	
Nitrogen	Chemical oxidation (breakpoint chlorination) Suspended-growth nitrification and denitrification variations Fixed-film nitrification and denitrification variations Air stripping Ion exchange
Phosphorus	Chemical treatment Biological phosphorus removal
Nitrogen and Phosphorus	Biological nutrient removal variations
Pathogens	Chlorine compounds Chlorine dioxide Ozone Ultraviolet (UV) radiation
Colloidal and dissolved solids	Membranes Chemical treatment Carbon adsorption Ion exchange
Volatile organic compounds	Air stripping Carbon adsorption Advanced oxidation
Odors	Chemical scrubbers Carbon adsorption Biofilters Compost filters

About 20 years ago, biological nutrient removal (BNR)—for the removal of nitrogen and phosphorus—was viewed as an innovative process for advanced wastewater treatment. Because of the extensive research into the mechanisms of BNR, the advantages of its use, and the number of BNR systems that have been placed into operation, nutrient removal, for all practical purposes, has become a part of conventional wastewater treatment. When compared to chemical treatment methods, BNR uses fewer chemicals, reduces the production of waste solids, and has lower energy consumption. Because of the importance of BNR in wastewater treatment, BNR is integrated into the discussion of theory, application, and design of biological treatment systems.

Land treatment processes, commonly termed "natural systems", combine physical, chemical, and biological treatment mechanisms and produce water with quality similar to or better than that from advanced wastewater treatment. Natural systems are not covered in this text as they are used mainly with small treatment systems.

Current Status

Up until the late 1980s, conventional secondary treatment was the most common method of treatment for the removal of BOD and TSS. In the United States, nutrient removal was used in special circumstances, such as in the Great Lakes area, Florida, and the Chesapeake Bay, where sensitive nutrient - related water quality conditions were identified. Because of nutrient enrichment that has led to eutrophication and water quality degradation (due in part to point source discharges), nutrient removal processes have evolved and now are used extensively in other areas as well.

As a result of implementation of the Federal Water Pollution Control Act Amendments, significant data have been obtained on the numbers and types of wastewater facilities used and needed in accomplishing the goals of the program. Surveys are conducted by U.S. EPA to track these data. The number and types of facilities needed in the future (~20yr) are shown in Table 3. These data are useful in forming an overall view of the current status of wastewater treatment in the United States.

Number of U.S. wastewater treatment facilities by design capacity in 1996 and in the future when needs are met[a] Table 3

Level of treatment	Existing facilities		Future facilities(when needs are met)	
	Number of facilities	m³/s	Number of facilities	m³/s
Less than secondary	176	133.80	61	26.33
Secondary	9388	776.98	9738	779.65
Greater than secondary	4428	876.96	6135	1252.53
No discharge[b]	2032	62.26	2369	78.99
Total	16024	1850.00	18303	2137.50

[a] Adapted from U.S. EPA (1997a).

[b] Plants that do not discharge to a water body and use some form of land application.

LESSON 4

In the last 10 years, many plants have been designed using BNR. Effluent filtration has also been installed where the removal of residual suspended solids is required. Filtration is especially effective in improving the effectiveness of disinfection, especially for ultraviolet (UV) disinfection systems, because (1) the removal of larger particles of suspended solids that harbor bacteria enhances the reduction in coliform bacteria and (2) the reduction of turbidity improves the transmittance of UV light. Effluent reuse systems, except for many that are used for agricultural irrigation, almost always employ filtration.

New Directions and Concerns

New directions and concerns in wastewater treatment are evident in various specific areas of wastewater treatment. The changing nature of the wastewater to be treated, emerging health and environmental concerns, the problem of industrial wastes, and the impact of new regulations, all of which have been discussed previously, are among the most important. Further, other important concerns include: (1) aging infrastructure, (2) new methods of process analysis and control, (3) treatment plant performance and reliability, (4) wastewater disinfection, (5) combined sewer overflows, (6) impacts of stormwater and sanitary overflows and nonpoint sources of pollution, (7) separate treatment of return flows, and (8) odor control and the control of VOC emissions.

Aging Infrastructure. Some of the problems that have to be addressed in the United States deal with renewal of the aging wastewater collection infrastructure and upgrading of treatment plants. Issues include repair and replacement of leaking and undersized sewers, control and treatment of overflows from sanitary and combined collection systems, control of nonpoint discharges, and upgrading treatment systems to achieve higher removal levels of specific constituents.

Portions of the collection systems, particularly those in the older cities in the eastern and midwestern United States, are older than the treatment plants. Sewers constructed of brick and vitrified clay with mortar joints, for example, are still used to carry sanitary wastewater and stormwater. Because of the age of the pipes and ancillary structures, the types of materials and methods of construction, and lack of repair, leakage is common. Leakage is in the form of both infiltration and inflow where water enters the collection system, and exfiltration where water leaves the pipe. In the former case, extraneous water has to be collected and treated, and oftentimes may overflow before treatment, especially during wet weather. In the latter case, exfiltration causes untreated wastewater to enter the groundwater and/or migrate to nearby surface water bodies. It is interesting to note that while the standards for treatment have increased significantly, comparatively little or no attention has been focused on the discharge of untreated wastewater from sewers through exfiltration. In the future, however, leaking sewers are expected to become a major concern and will require correction.

Treatment Process Performance and Reliability. Important factors in process selection and design are treatment plant performance and reliability in meeting permit requirements. In most discharge permits, effluent constituent requirements, based on 7-day and 30-day average concentrations, are specified. Because wastewater treatment effluent quality is variable because of varying organic loads, changing environmental conditions, and new industrial discharges, it is necessary to design the treatment system to produce effluent concentrations equal to or less than the limits prescribed by the discharge permit. Reliability is especially important where critical water quality parameters have to be maintained such as in reuse applications. On-line monitoring of critical parameters such as total organic carbon (TOC), transmissivity, turbidity, and dissolved oxygen is necessary for building a database and for improving process control. Chlorine residual monitoring is useful for dosage control, and pH monitoring assists in controlling nitrification systems.

Treatment plant reliability can be defined as the probability that a system can meet established performance criteria consistently over extended periods of time. As improved microbiological techniques are developed, it will be possible to optimize the disinfection process.

Wastewater Disinfection. Changes in regulations and the development of new technologies have affected the design of disinfection systems. Gene probes are now being used to identify where specific groups of organisms are found in treated secondary effluent (i.e., in suspension or particle-associated). Historically, chlorine has been the disinfectant of choice for wastewater. With the increasing number of permits requiring low or nondetectable amounts of chlorine residual in treated effluents, dechlorination facilities have had to be added, or chlorination systems have been replaced by alternative disinfection systems such as ultraviolet (UV) radiation (see Figure 3). Concerns about chemical safety have also affected design considerations of chlorination and dechlorination systems. Improvements that have been made in UV lamp and ballast design within the past 10 years have improved significantly the performance and reliability of UV disinfection systems. Effective guidelines have also been developed for the application and design of UV systems. Capital and operating costs have also been lowered. It is anticipated that the application of UV for treated drinking water and for stormwater will continue to increase in the future. Because UV produces essentially no troublesome byproducts and is also effective in the reduction of other related compounds, its use for disinfection is further enhanced as compared to chlorine compounds.

Figure 3 UV lamps used for the disinfection of wastewater

Combined Sewer Overflows (CSOs), Sanitary Sewer Overflows (SSOs), and Nonpoint Sources. Overflows from combined sewer and sanitary sewer collection systems have been recognized as difficult problems requiring solution, especially for many of the older cities in the United States. The problem has become more critical as greater development changes the amount and characteristics of stormwater runoff and increases the channelization of runoff into storm, combined, and sanitary collection systems. Combined systems carry a mixture of wastewater and stormwater runoff and, when the capacity of the interceptors is reached, overflows occur to the receiving waters. Large overflows can impact receiving water quality and can prevent attainment of mandated standards.

A combination of factors has resulted in the release of untreated wastewater from parts of sanitary collection systems. These releases are termed sanitary system overflows (SSOs). The SSOs may be caused by (1) the entrance of excessive amounts of stormwater, (2) blockages, or (3) structural, mechanical, or electrical failures. Many overflows result from aging collection systems that have not received adequate upgrades, maintenance, and repair. The U. S. EPA has estimated that at least 40000 overflows per year occur from sanitary collection systems. The untreated wastewater from these overflows represents threats to public health and the environment.

The effects of pollution from nonpoint sources are growing concerns as evidenced by the outbreak of gastrointestinal illness in Milwaukee traced to the oocysts of *Cryptosporidium parvum*, and the occurrence of *Pfiesteria piscicida* in the waters of Mary-land and North Carolina. *Pfiesteria* is a form of algae that is very toxic to fish life. Runoff from pastures and feedlots has been attributed as a potential factor that triggers the effects of these microorganisms.

Treatment of Return Flows. Perhaps one of the significant future developments in wastewater treatment will be the provision of separate facilities for treating return flows from biosolids and other processing facilities. Treatment of return flows will be especially important where low levels of nitrogen are to be achieved in the treated effluent. Separate treatment facilities may include(1) steam stripping for removal of ammonia from biosolids return flows; (2) high-rate sedimentation for removing fine and difficult-to-settle colloidal material that also shields bacteria from disinfection; (3) flotation and high-rate sedimentation for treating filter backwash water to reduce solids loading on the liquid treatment process; and (4) soluble heavy metals removal by chemical precipitation to meet more stringent discharge requirements. The specific treatment system used will depend on the constituents that will impact the wastewater treatment process.

Control of Odors and VOC Emissions. The control of odors and in particular the control of hydrogen sulfide generation is of concern in collection systems and at treatment facilities. The release of hydrogen sulfide to the atmosphere above sewers and at treatment plant headworks has occurred in a number of locations. The release of excess hydrogen sulfide has led to the accelerated corrosion of concrete sewers, head-works structures, and equipment, and to the release of odors. The control of odors is of increasing environmental concern as residential and commercial development continues to approach existing treatment plant locations. Odor control facilities including covers for process units, special ventilation equipment, and treatment of odorous gases need to be integrated with treatment plant design. Control of hydrogen sulfide is also fundamental to maintaining system reliability.

The presence of VOCs and VTOCs in wastewater has also necessitated the covering of treatment plant headworks and primary treatment facilities and the installation of special facilities to treat the compounds before they are released. In some cases, improved industrial pretreatment has been employed to eliminate these compounds.

Future Trends in Wastewater Treatment

In the U.S. EPA Needs Assessment Survey, the total treatment plant design capacity is projected to increase by about 15 percent over the next 20 to 30 years (see Table 3). During this period, the U.S. EPA estimates that approximately 2300 new plants may have to be built, most of which will be providing a level of treatment greater than secondary. The design capacity of plants providing greater than secondary treatment is expected to increase by 40 percent in the future (U.S. EPA, 1997). Thus, it is clear that the future trends in wastewater treatment plant design will be for facilities providing higher levels of treatment.

Some of the innovative treatment methods being utilized in new and upgraded treatment facilities include vortex separators, high rate clarification, membrane bioreactors, pressure-driven membrane filtration (ultrafiltration and reverse osmosis), and ultraviolet radiation (low-pressure, low-and high-intensity UV lamps, and medium-pressure, high-intensity UV lamps). Some of the new technologies, especially those developed in Europe, are more compact and are particularly well suited for plants where available space for expansion is limited.

In recent years, numerous proprietary wastewater treatment processes have been developed that offer potential savings in construction and operation. This trend will likely continue, particularly where alternative treatment systems are evaluated or facilities are privatized. Privatization is generally defined as a public-private partnership in which the private partner arranges the financing, design, building, and operation of the treatment facilities. In some cases, the private partner may own the facilities.

New Words and Phrases

wastewater   n. 废水
generation   n. 产生，[世]代
residence   n. 居住，住处
mutagenic   adj. 诱变的，致诱变的
septic   adj. 腐败的，败血病的，脓毒性的
       n. 腐烂物
malodorous   adj. 有恶臭的
dwell   vi. 居住

carcinogenic   adj. 致癌物(质)的
dry weather flow   枯季流量
catch basin   集水池，截流井，雨水口
overland flow   地表径流，地面水流
subcatchment   n. 子流域
rainfall   n. 雨量；降雨
subsurface   adj. 表面下的，地下的
effluent   adj. 流出的

LESSON 4

     n. 流出物，废水，污水，排水渠
discharge *n.* 流量，排放物，排出，排放
overflow *n.* 溢流
term *n.* 学期，期间，条款，条件，术语
contaminant *n.* 致污物，污染物
preliminary treatment 预处理
rag *n.* 抹布，碎屑，石板瓦，破旧衣服
grit *n.* 粗砂
primary treatment 初级处理
constituent *n.* 构分，成分，组分
stick *n.* 棍，棒
floatable *adj.* 可漂浮的，可浮起的
grease *n.* 油脂
ancillary *adj.* 辅助的，附属的
secondary treatment 二级处理
tertiary treatment 三级处理
chemical precipitation 化学沉淀
anaerobic *adj.* 厌氧的
lagoon *n.* 污水塘，环礁，泻湖
advanced oxidation 高级氧化
membrane filtration 膜滤
breakpoint chlorination 折点加氯
denitrification *n.* 反硝化作用，脱氮作用
air stripping 空气吹脱，气提
ion exchange 离子交换
chlorine dioxide 二氧化氯
ozone *n.* 臭氧
colloidal *adj.* 胶体的，胶质的
volatile organic compounds（VOCs） 挥发性有机化合物
chemical scrubber 化学洗涤塔
biofilter *n.* 生物滤池
compost *n.* 混合肥料，堆肥
advanced treatment 高级处理
innovative *adj.* 创新的，革新(主义)的
eutrophication *n.* 富营养化作用
amendment *n.* 改善，改正

harbor *n.* 海港，*v.* 隐藏
aging *n.* 衰老，老化，陈化
infrastructure *n.* 下部构造，基础(结构)
nonpoint source 非点源
point source 点源
retrofit *n.* & *v.* 改型，改进
renewal *n.* 更新，复兴，续借
undersized *adj.* 较一般为小的，不够大的
vitrified *adj.* 陶瓷的，玻璃化的，上釉的，陶化的
mortar *n.* 灰浆，砂浆，胶泥
    vt. 用灰泥涂抹，用灰泥结合
exfiltration *n.* (逐渐)漏出，渗出
transmissivity *n.* 透射比，透射率，透射系数
gene *n.* 基因
ballast *n.* 整流器，压舱物，道碴
byproduct *n.* 副产品
channelization *n.* 管［渠］道化
interceptor *n.* 截砂阱
upgrade *n.* 升级，上升，上坡
    vt. 提高(等级)，提升，浓缩
gastrointestinal tract 胃肠道
oocyst *n.* 卵囊
cryptosporidium *n.* 隐孢子虫属
cryptosporidium parvum 小隐孢子虫
pfiesteria piscicida 幽灵藻
pasture *n.* 牧地，草原，牧场
feedlot *n.* 饲育场
trigger *vt.* 引发，引起，触发
vortex separator 旋流分离器
membrane bioreactor 膜生物反应器
ultrafiltration 超滤
reverse osmosis 反渗透
ultraviolet radiation 紫外线辐射
headworks *n.* 渠首工程，脑力劳动

Questions

1. What is the difference between unit *operation* and *unit processes*?

2. Please describe the characteristic of preliminary, primary, advanced primary, secondary, secondary with nutrient removal, tertiary and advanced wastewater treatment.
3. In what unit of the operation and process can colloidal and dissolved solids be removed from wastewater?
4. What is the definition of treatment plant reliability?
5. What kinds of wastewater disinfection methods are there?
6. What are the advantages of ultraviolet (UV) radiation disinfection systems?
7. For what reason may the SSOs happen?
8. What are the future trends in wastewater treatment?

Reading Material

Fundamentals Of Wastewater Reuse And Biosolids Management

Terminology

In the literature, and in governmental regulations, a variety of terms have been used for individual constituents of concern in wastewater. The terminology used commonly for key concepts and terms in the field of wastewater management is summarized in Table 4. In some cases, confusion and undue negative perceptions arise with the use of the terms *contaminants*, *impurities*, and *pollutants*, which are often used interchangeably. To avoid confusion, the term *constituent* is used in this text in place of these terms to refer to an individual compound or element, such as ammonia nitrogen. The term *characteristic* is used to refer to a group of constituents, such as physical or biological characteristics.

Terminology commonly used in the field of wastewater engineering   Table 4

Term	Definition
Biosolids	Primarily an organic, semisolid wastewater product that remains after solids are stabilized biologically or chemically and are suitable for beneficial use
Class A biosolids[a]	Biosolids in which the pathogens (including enteric viruses, pathogenic bacteria, and viable helminth ova) are reduced below current detectable levels
Class B biosolids[a]	Biosolids in which the pathogens are reduced to levels that are unlikely to pose a threat to public health and the environment under specific use conditions. Class B biosolids cannot be sold or given away in bags or other containers or applied on lawns or home gardens
Characteristics (wastewater)	General classes of wastewater constituents such as physical, chemical, biological, and biochemical
Composition	The makeup of wastewater, including the physical, chemical, and biological constituents

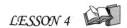

Table 4(Continued)

Term	Definition
Constituents[b]	Individual components, elements, or biological entities such as suspended solids or ammonia nitrogen
Contaminants	Constituents added to the water supply through use
Disinfection	Reduction of disease-causing microorganisms by physical or chemical means
Effluent	The liquid discharged from a processing step
Impurities	Constituents added to the water supply through use
Nonpoint sources	Sources of pollution that originate from multiple sources over a relatively large area
Nutrient	An element that is essential for the growth of plants and animals. Nutrients in wastewater, usually nitrogen and phosphorus, may cause unwanted algal and plant growths in lakes and streams
Parameter	A measurable factor such as temperature
Point sources	Pollutional loads discharged at a specific location from pipes, outfalls, and conveyance methods from either municipal wastewater treatment plants or industrial waste treatment facilities
Pollutants	Constituents added to the water supply through use
Reclamation	Treatment of wastewater for subsequent reuse application or the act of reusing treated wastewater
Recycling	The reuse of treated wastewater and biosolids for beneficial purposes
Repurification	Treatment of wastewater to a level suitable for a variety of applications including indirect or direct potable reuse
Reuse	Beneficial use of reclaimed or repurified wastewater or stabilized biosolids
Sludge	Solids removed from wastewater during treatment. Solids that are treated further are termed biosolids
Solids	Material removed from wastewater by gravity separation (by clarifiers, thickeners, and lagoons) and is the solid residue from dewatering operations

[a] U. S. EPA (1997b).

[b] To avoid confusion, the term "constituents" is used in this text in place of contaminants, impurities, and pollutants.

The term "sludge" has been used for many years to signify the residuals produced in wastewater treatment. In 1994, the Water Environment Federation adopted a policy defining "biosolids" as a primarily organic, solid wastewater treatment product that can be recycled beneficially. In this policy, "solids" are defined as the residuals that are derived from the treatment of wastewater. Solids that have been treated to the point at which they are suitable for beneficial use are termed "biosolids." In this text, the terms of solids and biosolids are used extensively, but "sludge" continues to be used, especially in cases where untreated solid material and chemical residuals are referenced.

Wastewater Reuse

In many locations where the available supply of fresh water has become inadequate to meet water needs, it is clear that the once-used water collected from communities and municipalities must be viewed not as a waste to be disposed of but as a resource that must be reused. The concept of reuse is becoming accepted more widely as other parts of the country experience water shortages. The use of dual water systems, such as now used in St. Petersburg in Florida and Rancho Viejo in California, is expected to increase in the future. In both locations, treated effluent is used for landscape watering and other nonpotable uses.

Current Status. Most of the reuse of wastewater occurs in the arid and semiarid western and southwestern states of the United States; however, the number of reuse projects is increasing in the south especially in Florida and South Carolina. Because of health and safety concerns, water reuse applications are mostly restricted to nonpotable uses such as landscape and agricultural irrigation. In a report by the National Research Council (1998), it was concluded that indirect potable reuse of reclaimed water (introducing reclaimed water to augment a potable water source before treatment) is viable. The report also stated that direct potable reuse (introducing reclaimed water directly into a water distribution system) was not practicable. Because of the concerns about potential health effects associated with the reclaimed water reuse, plans are proceeding slowly about expanding reuse beyond agricultural and landscape irrigation, groundwater recharge for repelling saltwater intrusion, and nonpotable industrial uses (e.g., boiler water and cooling water).

New Directions and Concerns. Many of the concerns mentioned in the National Research Council (NRC, 1998) report regarding potential microbial and chemical contamination of water supplies also apply to water sources that receive incidental or unplanned wastewater discharges. A number of communities use water sources that contain a significant wastewater component. Even though these sources, after treatment, meet current drinking water standards, the growing knowledge of the potential impacts of new trace contaminants raises concern. Conventional technologies for both water and wastewater treatment may be incapable of reducing the levels of trace contaminants below where they are not considered as a potential threat to public health. Therefore, new technologies that offer significantly improved levels of treatment or constituent reduction need to be tested and evaluated. Where indirect potable reuse is considered, risk assessment also becomes an important component of a water reuse investigation.

Future Trends in Technology. Technologies that are suitable for water reuse applications include membranes (pressure-driven, electrically driven, and membrane bioreactors), carbon adsorption, advanced oxidation, ion exchange, and air stripping. Membranes are most significant developments as new products are now available for a number of treatment applications. Membranes had been limited previously to desalination, but they are being tested increasingly for wastewater applications to produce high-quality treated effluent suitable for reclamation. Increased levels of contaminant removal not only enhance the product for reuse but also lessen health risks. As indirect potable reuse intensifies to augment existing water supplies, membranes are expected to be one of the predominant treatment technologies.

Biosolids Management

The management of the solids and concentrated contaminants removed by treatment has been and continues to be one of the most difficult and expensive problems in the field of wastewater engineering. Wastewater solids are organic products that can be used beneficially after stabilization by processes such as anaerobic digestion and composting. With the advent of regulations that encourage biosolids use, significant efforts have been directed to producing a "clean sludge" that meets heavy metals and pathogen requirements and is suitable for land application.

Other treatment plant residuals such as grit and screenings have to be rendered suitable for disposal, customarily in landfills. Landfills usually require some form of dewatering to limit moisture content. With the increased use of membranes, especially in wastewater reuse applications, a new type of residual, brine concentrate, requires further processing and disposal. Solar evaporation ponds and discharge to a saltwater environment are only viable in communities where suitable and environmental geographic conditions prevail; brine concentration and residuals solidification are generally too complex and costly to implement.

Current Status. Treatment technologies for solids processing have focused on traditional methods such as thickening, stabilization, dewatering, and drying. Evolution in the technologies has not occurred as rapidly as in liquid treatment processes, but some significant improvements have occurred. Centrifuges that produce a sludge cake with higher solids content, egg-shaped digesters that improve operation, and dryers that minimize water content are just a few examples of products that have come into use in recent years. These developments are largely driven by the need to produce biosolids that are clean, have less volume, and can be used beneficially.

Landfills still continue to be used extensively for the disposal of treatment plant solids. The number and capacity of landfills, however, have been reduced, and new landfill locations that meet public and regulatory acceptance and economic requirements are increasingly difficult to find. Incineration of solids by large municipalities continues to be practiced, but incineration operation and emission control are subject to greater regulatory restrictions and adverse public scrutiny. Alternatives to landfills and incineration include land application of liquid or dried biosolids and composting for distribution and marketing. Land application of biosolids is used extensively to reclaim marginal land for productive uses and to utilize nutrient content in the biosolids. Composting, although a more expensive alternative, is a means of stabilizing and distributing biosolids for use as a soil amendment. Alkaline stabilization of biosolids for land application is also used but to a lesser extent.

New Directions and Concerns. Over the last 30 years, the principal focus in wastewater engineering has been on improving the quality of treated effluent through the construction of secondary and advanced wastewater treatment plants. With improved treatment methods, higher levels of treatment must be provided not only for conventional wastewater constituents but also for the removal of specific compounds such as nutrients and heavy metals. A byproduct of these efforts has been the increased generation of solids and biosolids per person served by a municipal wastewater system. In many cases, the increase in solids production clearly taxes the capacity of existing solids processing and disposal methods.

In addition to the shear volume of solids that has to be handled and processed, management options continue to be reduced through stricter regulations. Limitations that affect options are: (1) landfill sites are becoming more difficult to find and have permitted, (2) air emissions from incinerators are more closely regulated, and (3) new requirements for the land application of biosolids have been instituted. In large urban areas, haul distances to landfill or land application sites have significantly affected the cost of solids processing and disposal. Few new incinerators are being planned because of difficulties in finding suitable sites and obtaining permits. Emission control regulations of the Clean Air Act also require the installation of complex and expensive pollution control equipment.

Future Trends in Biosolids Processing. New solids processing systems have not been developed as rapidly as liquid unit operations and processes. Anaerobic digestion remains the principal process for the stabilization of solids. Egg-shaped digesters, developed in Europe for anaerobic digestion, are being used more extensively in the United States because of advantages of easier operation, lower operation and maintenance costs, and, in some cases, increased volatile solids destruction (which also increases the production of reusable methane gas) (see Figure 4). Other developments in anaerobic and aerobic digestion include temperature-phased anaerobic digestion and autothermal aerobic digestion (ATAD), another process developed in Europe. These processes offer advantages of improved volatile solids destruction and the production of stabilized biosolids that meet Class A requirements.

Figure 4 Egg-shaped digesters used for the anaerobic treatment of biosolids

High solids centrifuges and heat dryers are expected to be used more extensively. High solids centrifuges extract a greater percentage of the water in liquid sludge, thus providing a dryer cake. Improved dewatering not only reduces the volume of solids requiring further processing and disposal, but allows composting or subsequent drying to be performed more efficiently. Heat drying provides further volume reduction and improves the quality of the product for potential commercial marketing.

New Words and Phrases

terminology   n. 专门名词,术语,词汇   perception   n. 理解,感知,感觉

undue   *adj.* 不适当的
impurity   *n.* 杂质，混杂物
pollutant   *n.* 污染物质
helminth   *n.* 寄生虫，蠕虫
ova   *n.* ovum 的复数
ovum   *n.* [生] 卵，卵子
dual water systems   双水道系统
nonpotable use   非饮用的利用
arid   *adj.* 干旱的，贫瘠的（土地等）
semiarid   *adj.* 半干旱的
viable   *adj.* 能养活的，能生育的，可行的
desalination   *n.* 除盐作用
reclamation   *n.* 回收、开垦、改良、驯化
intrusion   *n.* 闯入，侵入
boiler   *n.* 煮器（锅，壶的统称），汽锅，锅炉
disposal   *n.* 处理，处置
anaerobic digestion   厌氧消化
composting   *n.* 堆制肥料

methane gas   沼气
regulate   *vt.* 管制，控制，调节
screenings   *n.* 筛渣，筛余物
landfill   *n.* 垃圾填埋
brine   *n.* 盐水
concentrate   *v.* 集中，浓缩
centrifuge   *n.* 离心分离机
incineration   *n.* 焚烧
scrutiny   *n.* 详细审查
alkaline   *adj.* 碱的，碱性的
tax   *n.* 税，税款，税金
    vt. 使负重担，对…征税
incinerator   *n.* 焚化装置，焚化炉
haul distance   拖运距离，动距
outfall   *n.* 河口，排水口
volatile   *adj.* 挥发性的，不稳定的，爆炸性的
thermal   *adj.* 热的，热量的

LESSON 5

Classification Of Screening And Coarse Screens

The first unit operation generally encountered in wastewater-treatment plants is screening. A screen is a device with openings, generally of uniform size, that is used to retain solids found in the influent wastewater to the treatment plant or in combined wastewater-collection systems subject to overflows, especially from storm-water. The principal role of screening is to remove coarse materials from the flow stream that could (1) damage subsequent process equipment, (2) reduce overall treatment process reliability and effectiveness, or (3) contaminate waterways. Fine screens are sometimes used in place of or following coarse screens where greater removals of solids are required to (1) protect process equipment or (2) eliminate materials that may inhibit the beneficial reuse of biosolids.

All aspects of screenings removal, transport, and disposal must be considered in the application of screening devices, including (1) the degree of screenings removal required because of potential effects on downstream processes, (2) health and safety of the operators as screenings contain pathogenic organisms and attract insects, (3) odor potential, and (4) requirements for handling, transport, and disposal, i.e., removal of organics (by washing) and reduced water content (by pressing), and (5) disposal options. Thus, an integrated approach is required to achieve effective screenings management.

Classification of Screens

The types of screening devices commonly used in wastewater treatment are shown on Figure 1. Two general types of screens, coarse screens and fine screens, are used in preliminary treatment of wastewater. Coarse screens have clear openings ranging from 6 to 150 mm (0.25 to 6 in); fine screens have clear openings less than 6 mm (0.25 in). Microscreens, which generally have screen openings less than 50 μm, are used principally in removing fine solids from treated effluents.

The screening element may consist of parallel bars, rods or wires, grating, wire mesh, or perforated plate, and the openings may be of any shape but generally are circular or rectangular slots. A screen composed of parallel bars or rods is often called a *"bar rack"* or a coarse screen and is used for the removal of coarse solids. Fine screens are devices consisting of perforated plates, wire cloth that have smaller openings. The materials removed by these devices are known as *screenings*.

Coarse Screens (Bar Racks)

In wastewater treatment, coarse screens are used to protect pumps, valves, pipelines, and other appurtenances from damage or clogging by rags and large objects. Industrial waste-treatment plants may or may not need them, depending on the character of the wastes. According to the method used to clean them, coarse screens are designated as either hand-cleaned or mechanically cleaned.

Hand-Cleaned Coarse Screens. Hand-cleaned coarse screens are used frequently ahead of pumps in small wastewater pumping stations and sometimes used at the headworks of small-to medium-sized wastewater-treatment plants. Often they are used for standby screening in bypass channels for service during high-flow periods, when mechanically cleaned screens are being repaired, or in the event of a power failure. Normally, mechanically cleaned screens are provided in lieu of hand-cleaned screens to minimize manual labor required to clean the screens and to reduce flooding due to clogging.

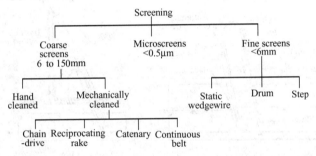

Figure 1 Definition sketch for types of screens used in wastewater treatment

The screen channel should be designed to prevent the accumulation of grit and other heavy materials in the channel ahead of the screen and following it. The channel floor should be level or should slope downward through the screen without pockets to trap solids. Fillets may be desirable at the base of the sidewalls. The channel preferably should have a straight approach, perpendicular to the bar screen, to promote uniform distribution of screenable solids throughout the flow and on the screen.

Mechanically Cleaned Bar Screens. The design of mechanically cleaned bar screens has evolved over the years to reduce the operating and maintenance problems and to improve the screenings removal capabilities. Many of the newer designs include extensive use of corrosion-resistant materials including stainless steel and plastics. Mechanically cleaned bar screens are divided into four principal types: (1)chain-driven, (2)reciprocating rake, (3)catenary, and(4)continuous belt. Cable-driven bar screens were used extensively in the past but largely have been replaced in wastewater applications by the other types of screens. Typical design information for mechanically cleaned is also included in Table 1. Examples of the different types of mechanically cleaned bar screens are shown on Figure 2.

Parameter	U.S. customary units			SI units		
		Cleaning method			Cleaning method	
	Unit	Manual	Mechanical	Unit	Manual	Mechanical
Bar size						
Width	in	0.2~0.6	0.2~0.6	mm	5~15	5~15
Depth	in	1.0~1.5	1.0~1.5	mm	25~38	25~38
Clear spacing between bars	in	1.0~2.0	0.6~3.0	mm	25~50	15~75
Slope from vertical	°	30~45	0~30	°	30~45	0~30
Approach velocity						
Maximum	ft/s	1.0~2.0	2.0~3.25	m/s	0.3~0.6	0.6~1.0
Minimum	ft/s		1.0~1.6	m/s		0.3~0.5
Allowable headloss	in	6	6~24	mm	150	150~600

Typical design information for manually and mechanically cleaned bar racks   Table 1

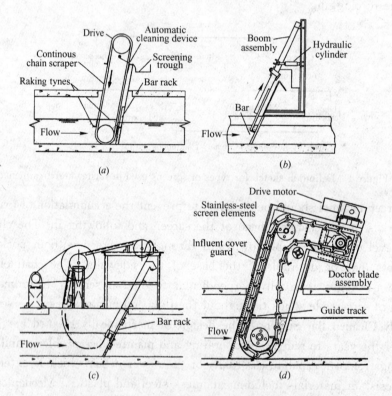

Figure 2   Typical mechanically cleaned coarse screens:
(a) front-cleaned, front-return chain-driven, (b) reciprocating rake,
(c) catenary, (d) continuous belt

Chain-Driven Screens Chain-driven mechanically cleaned bar screens can be divided into categories based on whether the screen is raked to clean from the front (upstream) side or the back (downstream) side and whether the rakes return to the bottom of the bar screen from the front or back. Each type has its advantages and disadvantages, although the general mode of operation is similar. In general, front cleaned, front return screens (see Figure 2a) are more efficient in terms of retaining captured solids, but they are less ragged and are susceptible to jamming by solids that collect at the base of the rake. Front cleaned, front return screens are seldom used for plants serving combined sewers where large objects can jam the rakes. In front cleaned, back return screens, the cleaning rakes return to the bottom of the bar screen on the downstream side of the screen, pass under the bottom of the screen, and clean the bar screen as the rake rises. The potential for jamming is minimized, but a hinged plate, which is also subject to jamming, is required to seal the pocket under the screen.

Reciprocating Rake (Climber) Screen The reciprocating-rake-type bar screen (see Figure 2b) imitates the movements of a person raking the screen. The rake moves to the base of the screen, engages the bars, and pulls the screenings to the top of the screen where they are removed. Most screen designs utilize a cogwheel drive mechanism for the rake. The drive motors are either submersible electric or hydraulic type. A major advantage is that all parts requiring maintenance are above the waterline and can be easily inspected and maintained without dewatering the channel. The front cleaned, front return feature minimizes solids carryover. The screen uses only one rake instead of multiple rakes that are used with other types of screens. As a result, the reciprocating rake screen may have limited capacity in handling heavy screenings loads, particularly in deep channels where along "*reach*" is necessary. The high overhead clearance required to accommodate the rake mechanism can limit its use in retrofit applications.

Catenary Screen A catenary screen is a type of front cleaned, front retuned chain-driven screen, but it has no submerged sprockets. In the catenary screen (see Figure 2c), the rake is held against the rack by the weight of the chain. If heavy objects become jammed in the bars, the rakes pass over them instead of jamming. The screen, however, has a relatively large "footprint" and thus requires greater space for installation.

Continuous Belt Screen The continuous belt screen is a relatively new development for use in screening applications in the United States. It is a continuous, self-cleaning screening belt that removes fine and coarse solids (see Figure 2d). A large number of screening elements (rakes) are attached to the drive chains; the number of screening elements depends on the depth of the screen channel. Because the screen openings can range from 0.5 to 30 mm (0.02 to 1.18 in), it can be used as either a coarse or a fine screen. Hooks protruding from the belt elements are provided to capture large solids such as cans, sticks, and rags. The screen has no submerged sprocket.

Design of Coarse Screen Installations. Considerations in the design of screening installations include(1)location; (2)approach velocity; (3)clear openings between bars or mesh size; (4)headloss through the screens; (5)screenings handling, processing, and disposal; and(6)controls.

Because the purpose of coarse screens is to remove large objects that may damage or clog downstream equipment, in nearly all cases, they should be installed ahead of the grit chambers. If grit chambers are placed before screens, rags and other stringy material could foul the grit chamber collector mechanisms, wrap around air piping, and settle with the grit. If grit is pumped, further fouling or clogging of the pumps will likely occur.

In hand-cleaned installations, it is essential that the velocity of approach be limited to approximately 0.45 m/s (1.5 ft/s) at average flow to provide adequate screen area for accumulation of screenings between raking operations. Additional area to limit the velocity may be obtained by widening the channel at the screen and by placing the screen at a flatter angle to increase the submerged area. As screenings accumulate, partially plugging the screen, the upstream head will increase, submerging new areas for the flow to pass through. The structural design of the screen should be adequate to prevent collapse if it becomes plugged completely.

For most mechanically cleaned coarse screen installations, two or more units should be installed so that one unit may be taken out of service for maintenance. Slide gates or recesses in the channel walls for the insertion of stop logs should be provided ahead of, and behind, each screen so that the unit can be dewatered for screen maintenance and repair. If only one unit is installed, it is absolutely essential that a bypass channel with a manually cleaned bar screen be provided for emergency use. Sometimes the manually cleaned bar screen is arranged as an overflow device if the mechanical screen should become inoperative, especially during unattended hours. Flow through the bypass channel normally would be prevented by a closed slide or sluice gate. The screen channel should be designed to prevent the settling and accumulation of grit and other heavy materials. An approach velocity of at least 0.4 m/s (1.25 ft/s) is recommended to minimize solids deposition in the channel. To prevent the pass-through of debris at peak flowrates, the velocity through the bar screen should not exceed 0.9 m/s (3 ft/s).

The velocity through the bar screen can be controlled by installation of a downstream head control device such as a Parshall flume, or, for screens located upstream of a pumping station, by controlling the wetwell operating levels. If the channel velocities are controlled by wetwell levels, lower velocities can be tolerated provided flushing velocities occur during normal operating conditions.

Headloss through mechanically cleaned coarse screens is typically limited to about 150 mm (6 in) by operational controls. The raking mechanisms are operated normally based on differential headloss through the screen or by a time clock.

Hydraulic losses through bar screens are a function of approach velocity and the velocity through the bars. The headloss through coarse screens can be estimated using the following equation:

$$h_L = \frac{1}{C}\left(\frac{V^2 - v^2}{2g}\right) \tag{1}$$

where h_L = headloss, m
  C = an empirical discharge coefficient to account for turbulence and eddy losses, typically 0.7 for a clean screen and 0.6 for a dogged screen
  V = velocity of flow through the openings of the bar screen, m/s

v = approach velocity in upstream channel, m/s
g = acceleration due to gravity, 9.81 m/s^2

The headloss calculated using Eq. (1) applies only when the bars are clean. Headloss increases with the degree of clogging. The buildup of heedloss can be estimated by assuming that a part of the open space in the upper portion of the bars in the flow path is clogged.

Although most screens use rectangular bars, optional shapes, i.e., "teardrop" and "trapezoidal", are available. For the optional shapes, the wider width dimension is located on the upstream side of the bar rack to make it easier to dislodge materials trapped between the bars. The alternative shapes also reduce headloss through the rack.

Screenings from the rake mechanism are usually discharged directly into a hopper or container or into a screenings press. For installations with multiple units, the screenings may be discharged onto a conveyor or into a pneumatic ejector system and transported to a common screenings storage hopper. As an alternative, screenings grinders may be used to grind and shred the screenings. Ground screenings are then returned to the wastewater; however, ground screenings may adversely affect operation and maintenance of downstream equipment such as clogging weir openings on sedimentation tanks or wrapping around air diffusers.

New Words and Phrases

fine screen 细格栅,细筛
coarse screen 粗格栅,粗筛
microscreen 微筛
parallel bar 平行棒
grating *n.* 栅栏,栅
wire mesh 金属丝网,铁丝网,钢丝网
perforated plate 穿孔板,多孔板
standby *n.* 备用
bypass *n.* 旁路,旁通管
in lieu of 代替
fillet *n.* 圆角,凸起,缘边,嵌条
chain *n.* 链(条)
reciprocating *adj.* 往复的,来回的
rake *n.* 耙子,齿耙
catenary *adj. & n.* 悬链线;悬链线的
trough *n.* 槽,水槽
ragged *adj.* 粗糙的
jam *n. & vi.* 堵塞,拥挤
hinge *n. & v.* (门、盖等的)铰链
SI units 国际标准单位

approach velocity 行近流速
headloss *n.* 水头损失
cogwheel *n.* 齿轮
carryover *n.* 携带,带出,遗留,遗留物
overhead *adj.* 在头上的,高架的
sprocket *n.* 链轮
hook *n.* 钩,吊钩
protrude *v.* 突出
grit chamber 沉砂池
stringy *adj.* 纤维的
slide *n.* 滑,滑动,幻灯片
recess *n.* 凹槽
sluice *n.* 水闸,泄水管,水力冲泄
debris *n.* 碎片,残骸,悬浮泥沙,推移质
parshall *n.* 巴歇尔氏测流量装置
wetwell *n.* 湿井,吸水井
turbulence *n.* 骚乱,(液体或气体的)紊乱,紊流
eddy *n.* 旋转,漩涡
trapezoidal *adj.* 梯形的

dislodge　v. 移动，取出，清除
hopper　n. 斗仓，进料斗，加料斗
conveyor　n. 传送机，输送机，运输机
pneumatic　adj. 装满空气的，有气胎的，汽力的，气压的，气动的
　　　　　　n. 气胎
grinder　n. 研磨机，磨碎机
shred　n. 碎片，破布
　　　　v. 撕碎，切碎
air diffuser　气体扩散器
flume　n. 水槽，斜槽，渡槽，水道
grind　v. 磨(碎)，碾(碎)，折磨

Questions

1. What are the principal roles of coarse screens and fine screens?
2. What is the meaning of *screenings*?
3. What principal types of mechanically cleaned bar screens are there?
4. What factors should be considered in the design of screening installations?
5. For the optional shapes of screen, why is the wider width dimension located on the upstream side of the bar rack?
6. In what situations can the hand-cleaned coarse screens be used? Generally speaking, what is the function of hand-cleaned coarse screens installed together with mechanically cleaned screens?

Reading Material

Fine Screens, Microscreens And Screenings

Fine Screens

The applications for fine screens range over a broad spectrum; uses include preliminary treatment (following coarse bar screens), primary treatment (as a substitute for primary clarifiers), and treatment of combined sewer overflows. Fine screens can also be used to remove solids from primary effluent that could cause clogging problems in trickling filters.

Screens for Preliminary and Primary Treatment. Fine screens used for preliminary treatment are of the (1) static (fixed), (2) rotary drum, or (3) step type. Typically, the openings vary from 0.2 to 6 mm (0.01 to 0.25 in). In many cases, application of fine screens is limited to plants where headless through the screens is not a problem.

Fine screens may be used to replace primary treatment at small wastewater-treatment plants, up to 0.13 m³/s (3 Mgal/d) in design capacity. Typical removal rates of BOD and TSS are reported in Table 2. Stainless-steel mesh or special wedge-shaped bars are used as the screening medium. Provision is made for the continuous removal of the collected solids, supplemented by water sprays to keep the screening medium clean.

Headloss through the screens may range from about 0.8 to 1.4 m (2.5 to 4.5 ft).
Static Wedgewire Screens Static wedgewire screens customarily have 0.2 to 1.2 mm (0.01 to 0.06 in) clear openings and are designed for flowrates of about 400 to 1200 L/(m² · min) [10 to 30 gal/(ft² · min)] of screen area. Headloss ranges from 1.2 to 2 m (4 to 7 ft). The wedgewire medium consists of small, stainless-steel wedge-shaped shaped bars with the flat part of the wedge facing the flow. Appreciable floor area is required for installation and the screens must be cleaned once or twice daily with high-pressure hot water, steam, or degreaser to remove grease buildup. Static wedgewire screens are generally applicable to smaller plants or for industrial installations.

Typical data on the removal of BOD and TSS with fine screens used to replace primary sedimentation[a]

Table 2

Type of screen	Size of openings		Percent removed	
	in	mm	BOD	TSS
Fixed parabolic	0.0625	1.6	5~20	5~30
Rotary drum	0.01	0.25	25~50	25~45

[a] The actual removal achieved will depend on the nature of the wastewater-collection system and the wastewater travel time

Drum Screens For the drum-type screen, the screening or straining medium is mounted on a cylinder that rotates in a flow channel. The construction varies, principally with regard to the direction of flow through the screening medium. The wastewater flows either into one end of the drum and outward through the screen the solids collection on the interior surface, or into the top of the unit and passing through to the interior with solids collection on the exterior. Internally fed screens are applicable for flow ranges of 0.03 to 0.8 m³/s (0.7 to 19 Mgal/d) per screen, while externally fed screens are applicable for flowrates less than 0.13 m³/s (3 Mgal/d). Drum screens are available in various sizes, from 0.9 to 2 m (3 to 6.6 ft) in diameter and from 1.2 to 4 m (4 to 13.3 ft) in length.

Step Screens Step screens, although widely used in Europe, are a relatively new technology in fine screening in the United States. The design consists of two step-shaped sets of thin vertical plates, one fixed and one movable. The fixed and movable step plates alternate across the width of an open channel and together form a single screen face. The movable plates rotate in a vertical motion. Through this motion, solids captured on the screen face are automatically lifted up to the next fixed step landing, and are eventually transported to the top of the screen where they are discharged to a collection hopper. The circular pattern of the moving plates provides a self-cleaning feature for each step. Normal ranges of openings between the screen plates are 3 to 6 mm (0.12 or 0.24 in); however, openings as small as 1 mm (0.04 in) are available. Solids trapped on the screen also create a "filter mat" that enhances solids removal performance. In addition to wastewater screening, step screens can be used for removal of solids from primary sludge, or digested biosolids.

Fine Screens for Combined Sewer Overflows. Screens have also been developed specifically for the removal of floatable and other solids from combined sewer overflows. Two basic types used: horizontal reciprocating screens and tangential flow screens. The horizontal reciprocating screen is a rigid, weir-mounted screen configured of narrow stainless-steel bars that run the length of the device. The screening bars are parallel to the normal direction of flow and are designed in continuous runs with no intermediate supports to collect solids. As the water in the screen channel rises, wastewater begins to pass through the openings in the screen bars. Solids are trapped on the screen, and, as the level continues to rise in the channel due to the entrapped solids on the screen, a hydraulically driven rake assembly is automatically activated to remove the accumulated solids from the screen. The rake carriage travels back and forth across the screen, combing the entrapped solids. The combing tines of the rake assembly carry the solids to one end of the screen for disposal either into the wastewater channel that carries flow to the wastewater-treatment plant or to a solids-collection pit.

In the tangential flow screen, the technology relies on the natural motion of water to screen and trap solids. The separation process is effected using a fine-mesh cylindrical screen and requires no moving parts. As the wastewater flows into the separation chamber, a circular motion is generated that is designed to allow water to pass through the cylindrical screen while forcing solids to swirl toward the center of the chamber. The swirling water is regulated so that the tangential flow around the chamber is greater than the radial force attempting to push the solids outward. Thus, the accumulation of solids on the screen is minimized. The solids settle into a central sump where they can be removed. Floatables are trapped in the separation chamber until the flow stops, when they can be removed.

Microscreens

Microscreening involves the use of variable low-speed (up to 4r/min), continuously backwashed, rotating-drum screens operating under gravity-flow conditions. The filtering fabrics have openings of 10 to 35 μm and are fitted on the drum periphery. The wastewater enters the open end of the drum and flows outward though the rotating-drum screening cloth. The collected solids are backwashed by high-pressure jets into a trough located within the drum at the highest point of the drum. The principal applications for microscreens are to remove suspended solids from secondary effluent and from stabilization-pond effluent.

Typical suspended-solids removal achieved with microscreens ranges from 10 to 80 percent, with an average of 55 percent. Problems encountered with microscreens include incomplete solids removal and inability to handle solids fluctuations. Reducing the rotating speed of the drum and less frequent flushing of the screen have resulted in increased removal efficiencies but reduced capacity.

The functional design of a microscreen involves(1)characterizing the suspended solids with respect to the concentration and degree of flocculation, (2) selecting design parameters that will not only assure sufficient capacity to meet maximum hydraulic loadings with critical solids characteristics but also meet operating performance requirements over the expected range of hydraulic and solids loadings, and (3) providing backwash and cleaning facilities to maintain the capacity of the screen. Typical design information for microscreens is presented in Table 3. Because of the variable performance of microscreens, pilot-plant studies are recommended, especially if the units are to be used to remove solids from stabilization-pond effluent, which may contain significant amounts of algae.

Typical design information for microscreens used for screening secondary settled effluent   Table 3

Item	Typical value		Remarks
	U. S. customary units	SI units	
Screen size	20~35μm	20~35μm	Stainless-steel or polyester screen cloths are available in sizes ranging from 15 to 60μm
Hydraulic loading rate	75~150gal/(ft² · min)	3~6m³/(m² · min)	Based on submerged surface area of drum
Headloss though screen	3~6in	75~150mm	Bypass should be provided when headloss exceeds 200mm (8in)
Drum submergence	70%~75% of height; 60%~70% of area	70%~75% of height; 60%~70% of area	Varies depending on screen design
Drum diameter	8~16ft	2.5~5m	3m(10ft) is most commonly used size; smaller sizes increase backwash requirements
Drum speed	15ft/min at 3in headloss	4.5m/min at 75mm headloss	Maximum rotational speed is limited to 45m/min (150ft/min)
Backwash requirements	2% of throughput at 50lb$_f$/in²; 5% of throughput at 15 lb$_f$/in²	2% of throughput at 350kPa; 5% of throughput at 100kPa	

Screenings Characteristics and Quantities

Screenings are the material retained on bar racks and screens. The smaller the screen opening, the greater will be the quantity of collected screenings. While no precise definition of screenable material exists, and no recognized method of measuring quantities of screenings is available, screenings exhibit some common properties.

Screenings Retained on Coarse Screens. Coarse screenings, collected on coarse screens of about 12 mm (0.5 in) or greater spacing, consist of debris such as rocks, branches, pieces of lumber, leaves, paper, tree roots, plastics, and rags. Organic matter can collect as well. The accumulation of oil and grease can be a serious problem, especially in cold climates. The quantity and characteristics of screenings collected for disposal vary, depending on the type of bar screen, the size of the bar screen opening, the type of sewer system, and the geographic location. Typical data on the characteristics and quantities of coarse screenings to be expected at wastewater-treatment plants served by conventional gravity sewers are reported in Table 4.

**Typical information on the characteristics and quantities
of screenings removed from wastewater with coarse screens**　　　Table 4

Size of opening between bars, mm	Moisture content, %	Specific weight, kg/m³	Volume of screening			
			ft³/Mgal		L/1000m³	
			Range	Typical	Range	Typical
12.5	60~90	700~1100	5~10	7	37~74	50
25	50~80	600~1000	2~5	3	15~37	22
37.5	50~80	600~1000	1~2	1.5	7~15	11
50	50~80	600~1000	0.5~1.5	0.8	4~11	6

Note: mm×0.3937=in
kg/m³×8.3492=lb/1000gal

Combined storm and sanitary collection systems may produce volumes of screenings several times the amounts produced by separate systems. The quantities of screenings have also been observed to vary widely, ranging from large quantities during the "first flush" to diminishing amounts as the wet weather flows persist. The quantities of screenings removed from combined sewer flows are reported to range from 3.5 to 84 L/(1000m³) of flow (0.5 to 11.3ft³/Mgal).

Screenings Retained on Fine Screens. Fine screenings consist of materials that are retained on screens with openings less than 6 mm (0.25 in). The materials retained on fine screens include small rags, paper, plastic materials of various types, razor blades, grit, undecomposed food waste, feces, etc. Compared to coarse screenings, the specific weight of the fine screenings is slightly lower and the moisture content is slightly higher (see Table 5). Because putrescible matter, including fecal material, is contained within screenings, they must be handled and disposed of properly. Fine screenings contain substantial grease and scum, which require similar care, especially if odors are to be avoided.

**Typical information on the characteristics and quantities of
screenings removed from wastewater with fine bar and rotary-drum screens**　　　Table 5

Operation	Size of opening, mm	Moisture content, %	Specific weight, kg/m³	Volume of screening			
				ft³/Mgal		L/1000m³	
				Range	Typical	Range	Typical
Fine bar screen	12.5	80~90	900~1100	6~15	10	44~110	75
Rotary drum[a]	25	80~80	900~1000	4~8	6	30~60	45

[a] Following coarse screening.

Note: mm×0.3937=in
kg/m³×8.3492=lb/1000gal

Screenings Handling, Processing, and Disposal. In mechanically cleaned screen installations, screenings are discharged from the screening unit directly into a screenings grinder, a pneumatic ejector, or a container for disposal, or onto a conveyor for transport to a screenings compactor or collection hopper. Belt conveyors and pneumatic ejectors are generally the primary means of mechanically transporting screenings. Belt conveyors offer the advantages of simplicity of operation, low maintenance, freedom from clogging, and low cost. Belt conveyors give off odors and may have to be provided with covers. Pneumatic ejectors are less odorous and typically require less space; however, they are subject to clogging if large objects are present in the screenings.

Screenings compactors can be used to dewater and reduce the volume of screenings. Such devices, including hydraulic ram and screw compactors, receive screenings directly from the bar screens and are capable of transporting the compacted screenings to a receiving hopper. Compactors can reduce the water content of the screenings by up to 50 percent and the volume by up to 75 percent. As with pneumatic ejectors, large objects can cause jamming, but automatic controls can sense jams, automatically reverse the mechanism, and actuate alarms and shut down equipment.

Means of disposal of screenings include (1) removal by hauling to disposal areas (landfill) including codisposal with municipal solid wastes, (2) disposal by burial on the plant site (small installations only), (3) incineration either alone or in combination with sludge and grit (large installations only), and (4) discharge to grinders or macerators where they are ground and returned to the wastewater. The first method of disposal is most commonly used. In some states, screenings are required to be lime stabilized for the control of pathogenic organisms before disposal in landfills.

New Words and Phrases

trickling filter　滴滤池
internally　*adv.* 在内，在中心
tangential　*adj.* 切线的
entrap　*v.* 截留，诱陷
carriage　*n.* 滑架，小车，车架，拖架
tine　*n.* 尖头，尖，齿，叉
swirl　*n.* 旋涡，涡状形
　　　v. 使成旋涡，打旋
sump　*n.* 污水坑，水坑，池，集水池
fabric　*n.* 织品，织物，结构，建筑物，构造
periphery　*n.* 外围，周围
polyester　*n.* 聚酯

razor　*n.* 剃刀
blade　*n.* 刀刃，刀片
feces　*n.* 粪，屎，渣滓
putrescible　*adj.* 易腐烂的
　　　　　n. 会腐烂的物质
scum　*n.* 浮渣，浮垢，泡沫，糖渣，铁渣
　　　vt. 将浮渣去除掉
　　　vi. 产生泡沫，被浮渣覆盖
compactor　*n.* 压缩器，夯具
ram　*n.* 活塞，柱塞，夯，桩锤
screw　*n.* 螺丝钉，螺杆，螺孔，螺旋桨
macerator　*n.* 切碎机，浸渍器

Lesson 6

Coagulation and Flocculation: I

Naturally occurring silt particles suspended in water are difficult to remove because they are very small, often colloidal in size, and possess negative charges; thus they are prevented from coming together to form large particles that can more readily be settled out. However, the charged layers surrounding the particles form an energy barrier between the particles. The removal of these particles by settling requires reduction of this energy barrier by neutralizing the electric charges and by encouraging the particles to collide with each other. The charge neutralization is called coagulation, and the building of larger flocs from smaller particles is called flocculation.

One means of accomplishing this end is to add trivalent cations to the water. These ions would snuggle up to the negatively charged particle and, because they possess a stronger charge, displace the monovalent cations. The effect of this would be to reduce the net negative charge and thus lower the repulsive force seen in Figure 1. In this condition, the particles will not repel each other and, upon colliding, will stick together. A stable colloidal suspension has thus been made into an unstable colloidal suspension.

The usual source of trivalent cations in water treatment is alum (aluminum sulfate). Alum has an additional advantage in that some fraction of the aluminum may form aluminum oxides/hydroxides, represented simply as

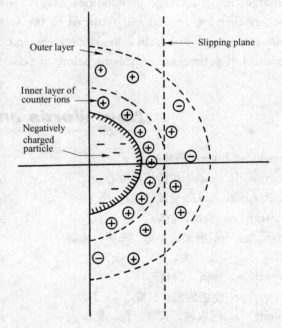

Figure 1 A colloidal particle is negatively charged and attracts positive counter ions to its surface

$$Al^{3+} + 3OH^- \rightarrow Al(OH)_3 \downarrow \tag{1}$$

These complexes are sticky and heavy and will greatly assist in the clarification of the water in the settling tank if the unstable colloidal particles can be made to come into contact with the floc. This process is enhanced through the operation known as flocculation.

LESSON 6

Fundamentals of Chemical Coagulation

Colloidal particles found in wastewater typical have a net negative surface charge. The size of colloids (about 0.01 to 1 μm) is such that the attractive body forces between particles are considerably less than the repelling forces of the electrical charge. Under these stable conditions, Brownian motion keeps the particles in suspension. Brownian motion (i.e., random movement) is brought about by the constant thermal bombardment of the colloidal particles by the relatively small water molecules that surround them. *Coagulation is the process of destabilizing colloidal particles so that particle growth can occur as a result of particle collisions.* The theory of chemical coagulation reactions is very complex. The simplified reactions used in this and other textbooks to describe coagulation and chemical precipitation processes can only be considered approximations as the reactions may not necessarily proceed as indicated.

Coagulation reactions are often incomplete, and numerous side reactions with other substances in wastewater may take place depending on the characteristics of the wastewater which will vary throughout the day as well as seasonally. To introduce the subject of chemical coagulation the following topics are discussed in this section: (1) basic definitions for coagulation and flocculation, (2) the nature of particles in wastewater, (3) the development and measurement of surface charge, (4) consideration of particle-particle interaction, (5) particle destabilization with potential determining ions and electrolytes, (6) particle destabilization and aggregation with polyelectrolytes, and (7) particle destabilization and removal with hydrolyzed metal ions. The following discussion is meant to serve as an introduction to the nature of the phenomena and processes involved in the coagulation process.

Basic Definitions

The term "chemical coagulation" as used in this text includes all of the reactions and mechanisms involved in the chemical destabilization of particles and in the formation of larger particles through perikinetic flocculation (aggregation of particles in the size range from 0.01 to 1 μm). *Coagulant and flocculant* are terms that will also be encountered in the literature on coagulation. In general, *a coagulant is the chemical that is added to destabilize the colloidal particles in wastewater so that floc formation can result. A flocculant is a chemical, typically organic, added to enhance the flocculation process.* Typical coagulants and flocculants include natural and synthetic organic polymers, metal salts such as alum or ferric sulfate, and prehydrolized metal salts such as polyaluminum chloride (PACl) and polyiron chloride (PICl). Flocculants, especially organic polymers, are also used to enhance the performance of granular medium filters and in the dewatering of digested biosolids. In these applications, the flocculant chemicals are often identified as filter aids.

The term "flocculation" is used to describe the process whereby the size of particles increases as a result of particle collisions. There are two types of flocculation: (1)

microflocculation (also known as *perikinetic flocculation*), in which particle aggregation is brought about by the random thermal motion of fluid molecules known as Brownian motion or movement and (2) macroflocculation (also known as *orthokinetic flocculation*), in which particle aggregation is brought about by inducing velocity gradients and mixing in the fluid containing the particles to be flocculated. Another form of macroflocculation is brought about by differential settling in which large particles overtake small particles to form larger particles. The purpose of flocculation is to produce particles, by means of aggregation, that can be removed by inexpensive particle-separation procedures such as gravity sedimentation and filtration. Macroflocculation is ineffectual until the colloidal particles reach a size of 1 to 10 μm through contacts produced by Brownian motion and gentle mixing.

Nature of Particles in Wastewater

The particles in wastewater may, for practical purposes, be classified as suspended and colloidal. Suspended particles are generally larger than 1.0 μm and can be removed by gravity sedimentation. In practice, the distinction between colloidal and suspended particles is blurred because the particles removed by gravity settling will depend on the design of the sedimentation facilities. Because colloidal particles cannot be removed by sedimentation in a reasonable period of time, chemical methods (i.e., the use of chemical coagulants and flocculant aids) must be used to help bring about the removal of these particles.

To understand the role that chemical coagulants and flocculant aids play in bringing about the removal of colloidal particles, it is important to understand the characteristics of the colloidal particles found in wastewater. Important factors that contribute to the characteristics of colloidal particles in wastewater include (1) particle size and number, (2) particle shape and flexibility, (3) surface properties including electrical characteristics, (4) particle-particle interactions, and (5) particle-solvent interactions. Particle size, particle shape and flexibility, and particle-solvent interactions are considered below. Because of their importance, the development and measurement of surface charge and particle-particle interactions are considered separately.

Particle Size and Number. The size of colloidal particles in wastewater is typically in the range from 0.01 to 1.0 μm. Some researchers have classified the size range for colloidal particles as varying from 0.001 to 1 μm. The number of colloidal particles in untreated wastewater and after primary sedimentation is typically in the range from 10^6 to 10^{12}/mL. It is important to note that the number of colloidal particles will vary depending on the location where the sample is taken within a treatment plant. The number of particles, as will be discussed later, is of importance with respect to the method to be used for their removal.

Particle Shape and Flexibility. Particle shapes found in wastewater can be described as spherical, semispherical, ellipsoids of various shapes (e.g., prolate and oblate), rods of various length and diameter (e.g., *E. coli*), disk and disklike, strings of various lengths, and random coils. Large organic molecules are often found in the form of coils, which may be compressed, uncoiled, or almost linear. The shape of some larger floc particles is often described as fractal. The particle shape will vary depending on the location within the treatment process that is being evaluated. The shape of the particles will affect the electrical properties, the particle-particle interactions, and particle-solvent interactions. Because of the many shapes of particles encountered in wastewater, the theoretical treatment of particle-particle interactions is an approximation at best.

Particle-Solvent Interactions. There are three general types of colloidal particles in liquids: hydrophobic or "water-hating", hydrophilic or "water-loving", and association colloids. The first two types are based on the attraction of the particle surface for water. Hydrophobic particles have relatively little attraction for water; while hydrophilic particles have a great attraction for water. It should be noted, however, that water can interact to some extent even with hydrophobic particles. Some water molecules will generally adsorb on the typical hydrophobic surface, but the reaction between water and hydrophilic colloids occurs to a much greater extent. The third type of colloid is known as an association colloidal, typically made up of surface-active agents such as soaps, synthetic detergents, and dyestuffs which form organized aggregates known as micelles.

Development and Measurement of Surface Charge

An important factor in the stability of colloids is the presence of a surface charge. It develops in a number of different ways, depending on the chemical composition of the medium (wastewater in this case) and the nature of the colloid. Surface charge develops most commonly through (1) isomorphous replacement, (2) structural imperfections, (3) preferential adsorption, and (4) ionization, as defined below. Regardless of how it develops, the surface charge, which promotes stability, must be overcome if these particles are to be aggregated (flocculated) into larger particles with enough mass to settle easily.

Isomorphous Replacement. Charge development through isomorphous replacement occurs in clay and other sail particles, in which ions in the lattice structure are replaced with ions from solution (e. g., the replacement of Si^{4+} with Al^{3+}).

Structural Imperfections. In clay and similar particles, charge development can occur because of broken bonds on the crystal edge and imperfections in the formation of the crystal.

Preferential Adsorption. When oil droplets, gas bubbles, or other chemically inert substances are dispersed in water, they will acquire a negative charge through the preferential adsorption of anions (particularly hydroxyl ions).

Ionization. In the case of substances such as proteins or microorganisms, surface charge is acquired through the ionization of carboxyl and amino groups. This ionization can be represented as follows, where R represents the bulk of the solid:

$$R_{NH_2}^{COO^-} \qquad R_{NH_3}^{COOH} \qquad R_{NH_2}^{COO^-} \qquad (2)$$

$$\text{at high pH} \qquad \text{at low pH} \qquad \text{at isoelectric point}$$

The Electrical Double Layer. When the colloid or particle surface becomes charged, some ions of the opposite charge (known as counterions) become attached to the surface (see Figure 2). They are held there through electrostatic and van der Waals forces of attraction strongly enough to overcome thermal agitation. Surrounding this fixed layer of ions is a diffuse layer of ions, which is prevented from forming a compact double layer by thermal agitation, as illustrated schematically on Figure 2. The electrical double layer consists of a compact layer (Stern) in which the potential drops from ψ_0 to ψ_s, and a diffuse layer in which the potential drops from ψ_0 to 0 in the bulk solution.

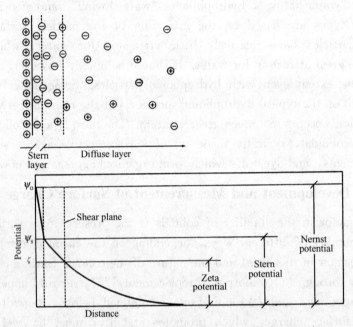

Figure 2 Stern model of electrical double Layer

Measurement of Surface Potential. If a particle is placed in an electrolyte solution, and an electric current is passed through the solution, the particle, depending on its surface charge, will he attracted to one or the other of the electrodes, dragging with it a cloud of ions. The potential at the surface of the cloud (called the surface of shear) is sometimes measured in wastewater-treatment operations. The measured value is often called the zeta potential. Theoretically, however, the zeta potential should correspond to the potential measured at the surface enclosing the fixed layer of ions attached to the particle, as shown on Figure 2. The use of the measured zeta potential value is limited because it will vary with the nature of the solution components.

New Words and Phrases

neutralize *v.* 使中和，压制
silt *n.* 淤泥，残渣，煤粉，泥沙
barrier *n.* 屏障，势垒，潜堰
collide *vi.* 碰撞，抵触

charge neutralization 电中和
floc *n.* 絮体
flocculation *n.* 絮凝
cation *n.* 阳离子

LESSON 6

trivalent   *adj.* 三价的
monovalent   *adj.* 单价的
repulsive force   排斥力
alum   *n.* 明矾，矾
aluminum sulfate   硫酸铝
oxide   *n.* 氧化物
hydroxide   *n.* 氢氧化物，羟化物
complex   *n.* 复合体，配合物，络合物
sticky   *adj.* 黏的，黏性的
slipping plane   滑动面
surface charge   表面电荷
Brownian motion   布朗运动
bombardment   *n.* 轰击
approximation   *n.* 接近，近似
side reaction   副反应
potential determining ions   决定电位离子
electrolyte   *n.* 电解质，电解液
polyelectrolyte   *n.* 聚合（高分子）电解质
aggregation   *n.* 聚合，集合体
hydrolyzed metal ions   水解金属离子
coagulant   *n.* 混凝剂
flocculant   *n.* 絮凝剂
destabilize   *vt.* 脱稳
synthetic organic polymer   合成有机聚合物
ferric   *adj.* 铁的，含铁的，［化］（正）铁的，三价铁的
prehydrolized   *adj.* 预水解的
polyaluminum chloride   聚合氯化铝
polyiron chloride   聚合氯化铁
granular   *adj.* 粒状的
microflocculation   *n.* 异向絮凝，微絮凝
macroflocculation   *n.* 同向絮凝
orthokinetic flocculation   同向絮凝（作用）
perikinetic flocculation   异向絮凝（作用）
overtake   *vt.* 赶上，追上

blur   *v.* 模糊，弄污
flexibility   *n.* 弹性，适应性，机动性，挠性
ellipsoid   *n.* 椭圆体
prolate   *adj.* 扁长的
oblate   *adj.* 扁平的，扁圆的
coil   *n.* 线团，卷曲，线圈，绕组
fractal   *n.* （分形学中）不规则碎片形
hydrophobic   *adj.* water-hating
hydrophilic   *adj.* water-loving
surface-active agent   表面活性剂
synthetic detergent   合成清洁剂
dyestuff   *n.* 染料
micelle   *n.* 胶束，胶囊，微胞，微团，胶态离子
composition   *n.* 成分，合成物
isomorphous replacement   同晶置换
structural imperfection   结构性缺陷
ionization   *n.* 离子化，电离
lattice structure   晶格结构
inert   *adj.* 惰性的
hydroxyl ion   *n.* 氢氧离子，羟离子
carboxyl   *n.* 羧基
amino   *adj.* 氨基的
isoelectric point   等点电
counterion   *n.* 带相反电荷的离子，抗衡离子，补偿离子
electrostatic forces   静电力
van der Waals forces   范德华力
thermal agitation   热搅动
diffuse layer   扩散层
compact layer（Stern）   压缩层
cloud of ions   电子云
zeta potential   ζ电位
Nernst potential   能斯脱电位

Questions

1. What is the difference between *coagulation* and *flocculation*?
2. What are the definitions of *coagulant* and *flocculant*?

3. What are the two types of flocculation?
4. What are the factors that contribute to the characteristics of colloidal particles in water?
5. For what reason does the surface charge develop?
6. What term can be used to describe the shape of some larger floc particles?
7. Please explain the meanings of hydrophobic and hydrophilic colloidal particles.
8. Please explain the Electrical Double Layer.
9. What is the meaning of zeta potential?

Reading Material

Coagulation and Flocculation: II

Particle-Particle Interactions

Particle-particle interactions are extremely important in bringing about aggregation by means of Brownian motion. The theory that has been developed to describe particle-particle interactions is based on the consideration of interaction between two charged flat plates and between two charged spheres. As neither of these developments is directly applicable to the particles found in wastewater, as described above, the analysis for two charged flat plates will be used for illustrative purposes. The interaction between two plates is illustrated on Figure 3. As shown on Figure 3, the two principal faces involved are the forces of repulsion, due to the electrical properties of the charged plates, and the van der Waals forces of attraction.

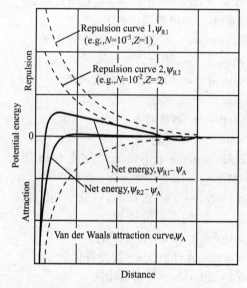

Figure 3 Definition sketch for particle-particle interactions based on the repulsion due to particle surface charge and van der Waals forces of attraction

It should be noted that the van der Waals forces of attraction do not come into play until the two plates are brought together in close proximity to each other.

The net total energy shown by the solid lines on Figure 3 is the difference between the forces of repulsion and attraction. The two conditions, with respect to the forces of repulsion, are illustrated on Figure 3. As shown for condition 1, the forces of attraction will predominate at short and long distances. The net energy curve for condition 1 contains a repulsive maximum that must be overcome if the particles, represented as the two plates, are to be held together by the van der Waals force of attraction. In condition

2, there is no energy barrier to overcome. Clearly, if colloidal particles are to be removed by microflocculation, the repulsive force must be reduced. Although floc particles can form at long distances as shown by the net energy curve for condition 1, the net force holding these particles together is weak and the floc particles that are formed can be ruptured easily.

Particle Destabilization with Potential-Determining Ions and Electrolytes

To bring about particle aggregation through microflocculation, steps must be taken to reduce particle charge or to overcome the effect of this charge. The effect of the charge can be overcome by(1)the addition of potential-determining ions, which will be taken up by or will react with the colloid surface to lessen the surface charge and(2)the addition of electrolytes, which have the effect of reducing the thickness of the diffuse electric layer and, thereby, reduce the zeta potential.

Use of Potential - Determining Ions. The addition of potential-determining ions to promote coagulation can be illustrated by the addition of strong acids or bases to reduce the charge of metal oxides or hydroxides to near zero so that coagulation can occur. The effect of adding potential-determining ions in a solution containing charged particles is illustrated on Figure 4. The magnitude of the effect will depend on the concentration of potential-determining ions added. The following ratios, known as the Shultz-Hardy rule, can be used to assess the effectiveness of potential-determining or counterions:

$$1 : \frac{1}{2^6} : \frac{1}{3^6} \quad \text{or} \quad 100 : 1.6 : 0.13 \quad (3)$$

It is interesting to note that depending on the concentration and nature of the counterions added, it is possible to reverse the charge of the double layer and develop a new stable particle.

The effect of adding counterions to a solution containing charged particles is illustrated on Figure 5. The upper curve on Figure 5 represents the surface charge of the particle as a function of the concentration of counterions added. The lines designated kT represent the thermal kinetic energy of the

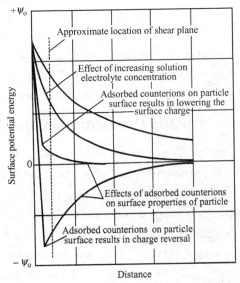

Figure 4 Definition sketch for the effects of the addition of counterions and electrolytes to solutions containing charged colloidal particles

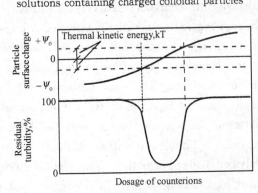

Figure 5 Definition sketch for the reversal of particle surface charge due to the addition of counterions

particle. The lower diagram is a plot of the turbidity that would result if the particles that have been destabilized and have undergone microflocculation were removed by settling. As shown, when the surface charge (either positive or negative) is greater than the thermal kinetic energy of the particles, the particles will not flocculate and the original turbidity is observed.

Additional details on the use of counterions may be found in Shaw (1966). The use of potential determining ions is not feasible in either water or wastewater treatment because of the massive concentration of ions that must be added to bring about sufficient compression of the electrical double layer to effect perikinetic flocculatin.

Use of Electrolytes. Electrolytes can also be added to coagulate colloidal suspensions. Increased concentration of a given electrolyte will cause a decrease in zeta potential and a corresponding decrease in repulsive forces as illustrated in condition 2 on Figure 3 and on Figure 4. The concentration of an electrolyte that is needed to destabilize a colloidal suspension is known as the *critical coagulation concentration* (CCC). Increasing the concentration of an indifferent electrolyte will not result in the restabitization of the colloidal particles. As with the addition of potential-determining ions, the use of electrolytes is also not feasible in wastewater treatment. As discussed subsequently, a change in the particle charge will occur when chemicals are added to adjust the pH of the wastewater to optimize the performance of hydrolyzed metal ions used as coagulants.

Particle Destabilization and Aggregation with Polyelectrolytes

Polyelectrolytes may be divided into two categories: natural and synthetic. Important natural polyelectmlytes include polymers of biological origin and those derived from starch products such as cellulose derivatives and alginates. Synthetic polyelectrolytes consist of simple monomers that are polymerized into high-molecular-weight substances. Depending on whether their charge, when placed in water, is negative, positive, or neutral, these polyelectrolytes are classified as anionic, cationic, and nonionic, respectively. The action of polyelectrolytes may be divided into the following three general categories.

Charge Neutralization. In the first category, polyelectrolytes act as coagulants that neutralize or lower the charge of the wastewater particles. Because wastewater particles normally are charged negatively, cationic polyelectrolytes are used for this purpose. In this application, the cationic polyelectrolytes are considered to be primary coagulants. To effect charge neutralization, the polyelectrolyte must be adsorbed to the particle. Because of the large number of particles found in wastewater, the mixing intensity must be sufficient to bring about the adsorption of the polymer onto the colloidal particles. With inadequate mixing, the polymer will eventually fold back on itself and its effectiveness in reducing the surface charge will be diminished. Further, if the number of colloidal particles is limited, it will be difficult to remove them with low polyelectrolyte dosages.

Polymer Bridge Formation. The second mode of action of polyelectrolytes is interparticle bridging (see Figure 6). In this case, polymers that are anionic and nonionic (usually anionic to a slight extent when placed in water) become attached at a number of adsorption sites to the surface of the particles found in the wastewater. A bridge is formed when two or more particles become adsorbed along the length of the polymer. Bridged particles become intertwined with other bridged particles during the flocculation process. The size of the resulting three-dimensional particles grows until they can be removed easily by sedimentation. Where particle removal is to be achieved by the formation of particle-polymer bridges, the initial mixing of the polymer and the wastewater containing the particles to be removed must be accomplished in a matter of seconds. Instantaneous initial mixing is usually not required as the polymers are already formed, which is not the case with the polymers formed by metal salts. As noted above, the mixing intensity must be sufficient to bring about the adsorption of the polymer onto the colloidal particles. If inadequate mixing is provided, the polymer will eventually fold back on itself, in which case it is not possible to form polymer bridges.

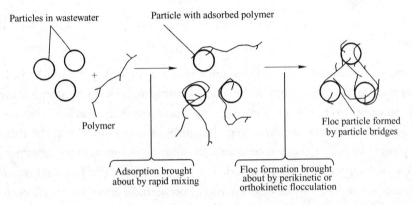

Figure 6 Definition sketch for interparticle bridging with organic polymers

Charge Neutralization and Polymer Bridge Formation. The third type of polyelectrolyte action may be classified as a charge neutralization and bridging phenomenon, which results from using cationic polyelectrolytes of extremely high molecular weight. Besides lowering the surface charge on the particle, these polyelectrolytes also form particle bridges as described above.

Particle Destabilization and Removal with Hydrolyzed Metal Ions

In contrast with the aggregation brought about by the addition of chemicals that act as counterions, electrolytes, and polymers, aggregation brought about by the addition of alum or ferric sulfate is a more complex process. To understand particle destabilization and the removals achieved with hydrolyzed metal ions, it will be instructive to consider first the formation of metal ion hydrolysis products. Operating ranges for action of metal salts and the importance of initial mixing are also considered in light of the formation of these particles.

Formation of Hydrolysis Products. In the past, it was thought that free Al^{3+} and Fe^{3+} were responsible for the effects observed during particle aggregation; it is now known, however, that their hydrolysis products are responsible (*Stumm and Morgan*, 1962; *Stumm and O'Melia*, 1968). Although the effect of these hydrolysis products is only now appreciated, it is interesting to note that their chemistry was first elucidated in the early 1900s by Pfeiffer (1902~1907), Bjerrum (1906~1920), and Werner (1907)

(Thomas, 1934). In the early 1900s, Pfeiffer proposed that the hydrolysis of trivalent metal salts, such as chromium, aluminum, and iron, could be represented as

$$\begin{bmatrix} H_2O & OH_2 \\ H_2O-Me-OH_2 \\ H_2O & OH_2 \end{bmatrix}^{3+} \rightleftharpoons \begin{bmatrix} H_2O & OH \\ H_2O-Me-OH_2 \\ H_2O & OH_2 \end{bmatrix}^{2+} + H^+ \quad (4)$$

with the extent of the dissociation depending on the anion associated with the metal and on the physical and chemical characteristics of the solution. Further, it was proposed that, upon the addition of sufficient base, the dissociation can proceed to produce a negative ion (Thomas, 1934), such as

$$\begin{bmatrix} H_2O & OH \\ H_2O-Me-OH \\ HO & OH \end{bmatrix}^- \quad (5)$$

It should be noted that the complex compounds given in Eqs. (4) and (5) are known as *coordination compounds*, which are defined as a central metal ion (or atom) attached to a group of surrounding molecules or ions by coordinate covalent bonds. The surrounding molecules or ions are known as *ligands*, and the atoms attached directly to the metal ion are called ligand donor atoms. Ligand compounds of interest in wastewater treatment include carbonate (CO_3^{2-}), chloride (Cl^-), hydroxide (OH^-), ammonia (NH_3), and water (H_2O).

In addition, a number of the coordination compounds are also *amphoteric* in that they can exist both in strong acids and in strong bases. For example, aluminum hydroxide behaves as follows in acidic and basic solutions:

In acid: $Al(OH)_3(s) + 6H_3O^+ (aq) \rightleftharpoons Al^{3+}(aq) + 6H_2O$ \quad (6)

In base: $Al(OH)_3(s) + OH^-(aq) \rightleftharpoons Al(OH)_4^-(aq)$ \quad (7)

As shown in Eq. (6), $Al(OH)_3$ will dissolve in the presence of excess acid to form aqueous Al^{3+}. In the presence of excess hydroxide, $Al(OH)_3$ will dissolve to form the aluminate ion, $Al(OH)_4^-$. The acid and base properties of the hydroxides and the nature of the covalent bonds will depend on the position of the element on the periodic table. Further, it should be noted some basic hydroxides will dissolve in strong acid, but not in a strong base.

$$[Al(H_2O)_6]^{3+} \xrightarrow{OH^-} [Al(OH)(H_2O)_5]^{2+} \xrightarrow{OH^-} [Al(OH)_2(H_2O)_4]^+$$
mononuclear species → mononuclear species → mononuclear species

$$\xrightarrow{OH^-}_{OH^-}$$

$$[Al_6(OH)_{15}]^{3+}(aq) \quad \text{or} \quad [Al_8(OH)_{20}]^{4+}(aq) \xrightarrow{OH^-}$$
polynuclear species   polynuclear species

$$[Al(OH)_3(H_2O)_3](s) \xrightarrow{OH^-} [Al(OH)_4(H_2O)_2]^- \quad (8)$$
mononuclear species precipitate   mononuclear species aluminateion

Over the past 50 years, it has been observed that the intermediate hydrolysis reactions of Al(Ⅲ) are much more complex than would be predicted on the basis of a model in which a base is added to the solution. At the present time the complete chemistry for the formation of hydrolysis reactions and products is not well understood (Letterman et al., 1999). A hypothetical model [see Eq. (8)], proposed by Stumm (Fair et al., 1968) for Al(Ⅲ), is useful for the purpose of illustrating the complex reactions involved. A number of alternative formation sequences have also been proposed (Letterman, 1991).

Before the reaction proceeds to the point where a negative aluminate ion is produced, polymerization as depicted in the following formula will usually take place.

$$2Me(H_2O_5)OH^{2+} \rightleftharpoons \left[(H_2O)_4 Me \begin{array}{c} OH \\ \diagup \diagdown \\ \diagdown \diagup \\ OH \end{array} Me(H_2O)_4 \right]^{4+} + 2H_2O \qquad (9)$$

As illustrated by Eqs. (8) and (9), the possible combinations of the various hydrolysis products are endless, and their enumeration is not the purpose here. What is important, however, is the realization that one or more of the hydrolysis products and/or polymers may be responsible for the observed action of aluminum or iron.

Further, because the hydrolysis reactions follow a stepwise process, the effectiveness of aluminum and iron will vary with time. For example, an alum slurry that has been prepared and stored will behave differently from a freshly prepared solution when it is added to a wastewater.

Action of Hydrolyzed metal Ions. The action of hydrolyzed metal ions in bringing about the destabilization and removal of colloidal particles may be divided into the following three categories:

1. Adsorption and charge neutralization
2. Adsorption and interparticle bridging
3. Enmeshment in sweep floc

Adsorption and charge neutralization involves the adsorption of mononuclear and polynuclear metal hydrolysis species [see Eq. (6)] on the colloidal particles found in wastewater. It should be noted that it is also possible to get charge reversal with metal salts, as described previously with the addition of counterions (see Figure 5). Adsorption and interparticle bridging involves the adsorption of polynuclear metal hydrolysis species and polymer species [see Eqs. (6) and (7)] which, in turn, will ultimately form particle-polymer bridges, as described previously. As the coagulant requirement for adsorption and charge neutralization is satisfied, metal hydroxide precipitates and soluble metal hydrolysis products will form as defined by Eq. (6). If a sufficient concentration of metal salt is added, large amounts of metal hydroxide floc will form. Following macroflocculation, large floc particles will be formed that will settle readily. In turn, as these floc particles settle, they sweep through the water containing colloidal particles. The colloidal particles that become enmeshed in the floc will thus be removed from the wastewater. In most wastewater applications, the sweep floc mode of operation is used most commonly where particles are to be removed by sedimentation.

Solubility of Metal Salts. To further appreciate the action of the hydrolyzed metal ions, it will be useful to consider the solubility of the metal salts. The solubility of the various alum [Al(Ⅲ)] and iron [Fe(Ⅲ)] species is illustrated on Figure 7a and b, respectively, in which the log molar concentrations have been plotted versus pH. In preparing these diagrams, only the mononuclear species for alum and iron have been plotted. The formation of some of the mononuclear species is illustrated in Eq. (8). It should be noted that Hayden and Rubin (1974) compared experimental and predicted values and concluded that $Al(OH)_2^+$ is not an important mononuclear species. Accordingly, mononuclear species $Al(OH)_2^+$ has not been included in the development of Figure 7a. The solid lines trace the approximate total concentration of residual soluble alum (see Figure 7a) and iron (see Figure 7b) after precipitation. Aluminum hydroxide and ferric hydroxide are precipitated within the shaded areas, and polynuclear and polymeric species are formed outside at higher and lower pH values. As shown, the operating region for alum precipitation is from a pH range of 5 to about 7, with minimum solubility occurring at a pH of 6.0, and from about 7 to 9 for iron precipitation, with minimum solubility occurring at a pH of 8.0.

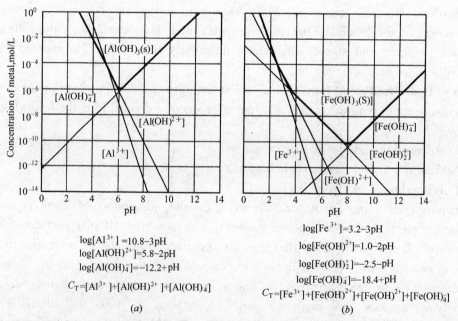

Figure 7 Solubility diagram for alum [Al(Ⅲ)] and iron [Fe(Ⅲ)]. It should be noted that only the mononuclear species have been plotted. The polynuclear species are extremely dependent on the chemistry of the wastewater. The mononuclear species $Al(OH)_2^+$ has not been included in the development of Figure. 7a. Further, because of the wide variation in the solubility and formation constants for the various metal hydroxides, the curves presented in this figure should only be used as a reference guide

Operating Regions for Action of Metal Salts. Because the chemistry of the various reactions is so complex, there is no complete theory to explain the action of hydrolyzed metal ions.

To quantify qualitatively the application of alum as a function of pH, taking into account the action of alum as described above, Amirtharajah and Mills (1982) developed a diagram for water treatment applications. On that diagram, the approximate regions in which the different phenomena associated with particle removal in conventional sedimentation and filtration processes are operative are plotted as a function of the alum dose and the pH of the treated effluent after alum has been added. For example, optimum particle removal by sweep floc occurs in the pH range of 7 to 8 with an alum dose of 20 to 60 mg/L. Generally, for many wastewater effluents that have high pH values (e.g., 7.3 to 8.5), low alum dosages in the range of 5 to 10 mg/L will not be effective. With proper pH control it is possible to operate with extremely low alum dosages. Because the characteristics of wastewater will vary from treatment plant to treatment plant, bench-scale and pilot-plant tests must be conducted to establish the appropriate chemical dosages.

Importance of Initial Chemical Mixing with Metal Salts. Perhaps the least appreciated fact about chemical addition of metal salts is the important of the rapid initial mixing of the chemicals with the wastewater to be treated. In a 1967 article, Hudson and Wolfner (1967) noted that "coagulants hydrolyze and begin to polymerize in a fraction of second after being added to water." Hahn and Stumm (1968) studied the coagulation of silica dispersions with Al(Ⅲ). They reported that the time required for the formation of mono-and polynuclear hydroxide species appears to be extremely short, on the order of 10^{-3} s. The time of formation for the polymer species was on the order of 10^{-2} s. Further, they found that the rate-limiting step in the coagulation process was the time required for the colloidal transport step brought about by Brownian motion (i.e., perikinetic flocculation), which was estimated to be on the order of 1.5×10^{-3} to 3.3×10^{-3} s. Clearly, based on the literature and actual field evaluations, the instantaneous rapid and intense mixing of metal salts is of critical importance, especially where the metal salts are to be used as coagulants to lower the surface charge of the colloidal particles. It should be noted that although achieving extremely low mixing times in large treatment plants is often difficult, low mixing times can be achieved by using multiple mixers.

New Words and Phrases

proximity *n.* 接近，亲近
solid line 实线
rupture *v. & n.* 破裂
Shultz-Hardy rule 苏采-哈代原则
restabitization *n.* 再稳定
starch *n.* 淀粉
derivative *adj.* 引出的，系出的
           n. 衍生物，派生词，导数，微商
alginate *n.* 藻酸盐

monomer *n.* 单体
intertwine *v.* （使）纠缠，（使）缠绕
instantaneous *adj.* 瞬间的
elucidate *vt.* 阐明，说明
dissociation *n.* 分裂，离解，溶解
coordination compound 配位化合物
covalent bond 共价键
ligand *n.* 配合基［体］，配位体
donor *n.* 施主，原料物质，供体

amphoteric   adj. 两性的
aluminate   n. 铝酸盐
periodic table   （元素）周期表
intermediate hydrolysis   中间水解
hypothetical   adj. 假设的，假定的
polymerization   n. 聚合
enumeration   n. 列举
stepwise   adj. 逐步的
slurry   n. 泥浆，浆

sweep floc   扫沉絮体，沉淀型絮体
enmesh   vt. 使绊住，使陷入
precipitate   n. 沉淀物，沉淀
polymeric   adj. 聚合的，聚合体的
bench-scale   adj. 小型的（台架规模的）
pilot-plant   n. 中试厂
dosage   n. 剂量，配药，用量
intense   adj. 强烈的

LESSON 7

Gravity Separation Theory: I

The removal of suspended and colloidal materials from water by gravity separation is one of the most widely used unit operations in water treatment. A summary of gravitational phenomena is presented in Table 1. Sedimentation is the term applied to the separation of suspended particles that are heavier than water, by gravitational settling. The terms of *sedimentation* and *settling* are used interchangeably. A sedimentation basin may also be referred to as a sedimentation tank, clarifier, settling basin, or settling tank. Accelerated gravity settling involves the removal of particles in suspension by gravity settling in an accelerated flow field. The fundamentals of gravity separation are introduced in this section.

Types of gravitational phenomena utilized in wastewater treatment — Table 1

Type of separation phenomenon	Description	Application/occurrence
Discrete particle Settling	Refers to the settling of particles in a suspension of low solids concentration by gravity in a constant acceleration field. Particles settle as individual entities, and there is no significant interaction with neighboring particles	Removal of grit and sand particles from wastewater
Flocculent settling	Refers to a rather dilute suspension of particles that coalesce, or flocculate, during the settling operation. By coalescing, the particles increase in mass and settle at a faster rate	Removal of a portion of the TSS in untreated wastewater in primary settling facilities, and in upper portions of secondary settling facilities. Also removes chemical floc in settling tanks
Ballasted flocculent Settling	Refers to the addition of an inert ballasting agent and a polymer to a partially flocculated suspension to promote rapid settling and improved solids reduction. A portion of the recovered ballasting agent is recycled to the process	Removal of a portion of the TSS in untreated wastewater, wastewater from combined systems, and industrial wastewater. Also reduces BOD and phosphorus
Hindered settling (also called zone settling)	Refers to suspensions of intermediate concentration, in which inter-particle forces are sufficient to hinder the settling of neighboring particles. The particles tend to remain in fixed positions with respect to each other, and the mass of particles settles as a unit. A solids-liquid interface develops at the top of the settling mass	Occurs in secondary settling facilities used in conjunction with biological treatment facilities

Table 1(Continued)

Type of separation phenomenon	Description	Application/occurrence
Compression settling	Refers to settling in which the particles are of such concentration that a structure is formed, and further settling can occur only by compression of the structure. Compression takes place from the weight of the particles, which are constantly being added to the structure by sedimentation from the supernatant liquid	Usually occurs in the lower layers of a deep solids or biosolids mass, such as in the bottom of deep secondary settling facilities and in solids-thickening facilities
Accelerated gravity Settling	Removal of particles in suspension by gravity settling in an acceleration field	Removal of grit and sand particles from wastewater
Flotation	Removal of particles in suspension that are lighter that water by air or gas flotation	Removal of greases and oils, light material that floats, thickening of solids suspensions

Description

Sedimentation is used for the removal of grit, TSS in primary settling basins, biological floc removal in the activated-sludge settling basin, and chemical floc removal when the chemical coagulation process is used. Sedimentation is also used for solids concentration in sludge thickeners. In most cases, the primary purpose is to produce a clarified effluent, but it is also necessary to produce sludge with a solids concentration that can be handled and treated easily.

On the basis of the concentration and the tendency of particles to interact, four types of gravitational settling can occur: (1) discrete particle, (2) flocculent, (3) hindered (also called *zone*), and (4) compression. Because of the fundamental importance of the separation processes in the treatment of wastewater, the analysis of each type of separation process is discussed separately. In addition, tube settlers, used to enhance the performance of sedimentation facilities, are also described. Other gravitational separation processes include high-rate clarification, accelerated gravity settling, and flotation and are discussed in subsequent sections.

Particle Settling Theory

The settling of discrete, nonflocculating particles can be analyzed by means of the classic laws of sedimentation formed by Newton and Stokes. Newton's law yields the terminal particle velocity by equating the gravitational force of the particle to the frictional resistance, or drag. The gravitational force is given by

$$F_G = (\rho_p - \rho_w) \cdot g V_p \tag{1}$$

where F_G = gravitational force, MLT^{-2} (kg·m/s^2)

ρ_p = density of particle, ML^{-3} (kg/m^3)

ρ_w = density of water, ML^{-3} (kg/m^3)

g = acceleration due to gravity, LT^{-2} (9.81m/s^2)

V_p = volume of particle, $L^3 (m^3)$

The frictional drag force depends on the particle velocity, fluid density, fluid viscosity, particle diameter, and the drag coefficient C_d (dimensionless), and is given by Eq. (2).

$$F_d = \frac{C_d A_p \rho_w v_p^2}{2} \quad (2)$$

where F_d = frictional drag force, MLT^{-2} (kg · m/s^2)

C_d = drag coefficient (unitless)

A_p = cross-sectional or projected area of particles in direction of flow, $L^2 (m^2)$

v_p = particle settling velocity, LT^{-1} (m/s)

Equating the gravitational force to the frictional drag force for spherical particles yields Newton's law:

$$v_{p(t)} = \sqrt{\frac{4g}{3C_d}\left(\frac{\rho_p - \rho_w}{\rho_w}\right) \cdot d_p} \approx \sqrt{\frac{4g}{3C_d}(sg_p - 1) \cdot d_p} \quad (3)$$

where $v_{p(t)}$ = terminal velocity of particle, LT^{-1} (m/s)

d_p = diameter of particle, L(m)

sg_p = specific gravity of the particle

The coefficient of drag C_d takes on different values depending on whether the flow regime surrounding the particle is laminar or turbulent. The drag coefficient for various particles is shown on Figure 1 as a function of the Reynolds number. As shown on Figure 1, there are three more or less distinct regions, depending on the Reynolds number: laminar ($N_R < 1$), transitional ($N_R = 1$ to 2000), and turbulent ($N_R > 2000$). Although particle shape affects the value of the drag coefficient, for particles that are approximately spherical, the curve on Figure 1 is approximated by the following equation (upper limit of $N_R = 10^4$):

$$C_d = \frac{24}{N_R} + \frac{3}{\sqrt{N_R}} + 0.34 \quad (4)$$

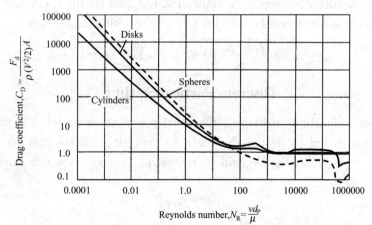

Figure 1 Coefficient of drag as a function of Reynolds number

The Reynolds number N_R for settling particles is defined as

$$N_R = \frac{v_p d_p \rho_w}{\mu} = \frac{v_p d_p}{\nu} \quad (5)$$

where μ = dynamic viscosity, MTL^{-2} (N · s/m^2)

ν = kinematic viscosity, L^2T^{-1} (m²/s)

Other terms are as defined above.

Equation (3) must be modified for nonspherical particles. An application that has been proposed is to rewrite Eq. (3) as follows:

$$v_{r(t)} = \sqrt{\frac{4g}{3C_d\phi}\left(\frac{\rho_p-\rho_w}{\rho_w}\right) \cdot d_p} \approx \sqrt{\frac{4g}{3C_d\phi}(sg_p-1) \cdot d_p} \qquad (6)$$

where ϕ is a shape factor and the other terms are as defined previously. The value of the shape factor is 1.0 for spheres, 2.0 for sand grains, and up to and greater than 20 for fractal floc. The shape factor is especially important in wastewater treatment where few, if any, particles are spherical. The shape factor must also be accounted for in computing N_R.

Settling in the Laminar Region. For Reynolds numbers less than about 1.0, viscosity is the predominant force governing the settling process, and the first term in Eq. (4) predominates. Assuming spherical particles, substitution of the first term of the drag coefficient equation [Eq. (4)] into Eq. (3) yields Stokes' laws:

$$v_p = \frac{g(\rho_p-\rho_w)}{18\mu} \approx \frac{g(sg_p-1) \cdot d_p^2}{18v} \qquad (7)$$

Terms are as defined previously.

For laminar-flow conditions, Stokes found the drag force to be

$$F_D = 3\pi\mu v_p d_p \qquad (8)$$

Settling in the Transition Region. In the transition region, the complete form of the drag equation [Eq. (1)] must be used to determine the settling velocity. Because of the nature of the drag equation, finding the settling velocity is an iterative process.

Settling in the Turbulent Region. In the turbulent region, inertial forces are predominant, and the effect of the first two terms in the drag coefficient equation [Eq. (4)] is reduced. For settling in the turbulent region, a value of 0.4 is used for the coefficient of drag. If a value of 0.4 is substituted into Eq. (6) for C_d, the resulting equation is:

$$v_p = \sqrt{3.33g\left(\frac{\rho_p-\rho_w}{\rho_w}\right) \cdot d_p} \approx \sqrt{3.33g(sg_p-1) \cdot d_p} \qquad (9)$$

Discrete Particle Settling

In the design of sedimentation basins, the usual procedure is to select a particle with a terminal velocity v_c and to design the basin so that all particles that have a terminal velocity equal to or greater than v_c will be removed. The rate at which clarified water is produced is equal to

$$Q = Av_c \qquad (10)$$

where Q = flowrate, L^3T^{-1} (m³/s)

A = surface of the sedimentation basin, L^2 (m²)

v_c = particle settling velocity, LT^{-1} (m/s)

Rearranging Eq. (10) yields

$$v_c = \frac{Q}{A} = \text{overflow rate, } LT^{-1} \text{ [m}^3/(\text{m}^2 \cdot \text{d})]$$

Thus, the critical velocity is equivalent to the overflow rate or surface loading rate. A common basis of design for discrete particle settling recognizes that the flow capacity is independent of the depth.

For continuous-flow sedimentation, the length of the basin and the time a unit volume of water is in the basin (detention time) should be such that all particles with the design velocity v_c will settle to the bottom of the tank. The design velocity, detention time, and basin depth are related as follows:

$$v_c = \frac{\text{depth}}{\text{detention time}} \tag{11}$$

In actual practice, design factors must be adjusted to allow for the effects of inlet and outlet turbulence, short-circuiting, sludge storage, and velocity gradients due to the operation of sludge-removal equipment. In the above discussion ideal settling conditions have been assumed.

Idealized discrete particle settling in three different types of settling basins is illustrated on Figure 2. Particles that have a velocity of fall less than v_c will not all be removed during the time provided for settling. Assuming that the particles of various sizes are uniformly distributed over the entire depth of the basin at the inlet, it can be seen from an analysis of the particle trajectory on Figure 3 those particles with a settling velocity less than v_c will be removed in the ratio

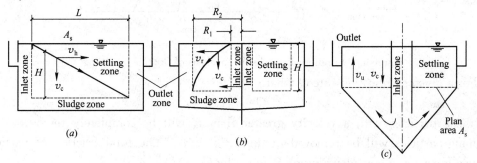

Figure 2 Definition sketch for the idealized settling of discrete particles in three different types of settling basins: (a) rectangular, (b) circular, and (c) upflow

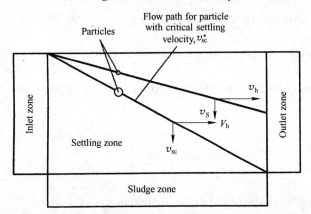

Figure 3 Definition sketch for the analysis of ideal discrete particle settling

$$X_r = \frac{v_p}{v_c} \qquad (12)$$

where X_r is the fraction of the particles with settling velocity v_p that are removed.

In most suspensions encountered in wastewater treatment, a large gradation of particle sizes will be found. To determine the efficiency of removal for a given settling time, it is necessary to consider the entire range of settling velocities present in the system. The settling velocities of the particles can be obtained by use of a settling column test. The particle settling data are used to construct a velocity settling curve as shown on Figure 4.

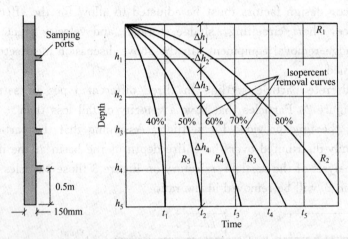

Figure 4 Definition sketch for the analysis of flocculent settling

For a given clarification rate Q where

$$Q = v_c A \qquad (13)$$

only those particles with a velocity greater than v_c will be completely removed. The remaining particles will be removed in the ratio v_p/v_c. The total fraction of particles removed for a continuous distribution is given by Eq. (14).

$$\text{Fraction removed} = (1 - X_c) + \int_0^{x_c} \frac{v_p}{v_c} \mathrm{d}x \qquad (14)$$

where $1 - X_c$ = fraction of particles with velocity v_p greater than v_c

$\int_0^{x_c} \frac{v_p}{v_c} \mathrm{d}x$ = fraction of particles removed with v_p less than v_c

For discrete particles within a given settling velocity range, the following expression may be used

$$\text{Total fraction removed} = \frac{\sum_{i=1}^{n} \frac{v_{n_i}}{v_c}(n_i)}{\sum_{i=1}^{n} n_i} \qquad (15)$$

Where v_n = average velocity of particles in the ith velocity range

n_i = number of particles in the ith velocity range

New Words and Phrases

sedimentation *n.* 沉淀，沉降
accelerated gravity settling 加速重力沉降
ballasted flocculent settling 加重絮凝沉淀
tube settler 斜管沉淀池
frictional *adj.* 摩擦的，摩擦力的
drag coefficient 阻力系数
flocculent settling 絮凝沉降
coalesce *v.* 凝聚，聚结，联合，接合
ballasting agent 加重剂
hindered settling 干扰沉降，拥挤沉降
compression settling 压缩沉降
specific gravity 比重

laminar *adj.* 层(状、流)的
turbulent *adj.* 紊流的
transitional *adj.* 过渡的
kinematic *adj.* 运动学的，运动学上的
Reynolds number 雷诺数
iterative *adj.* 重复的，反复的，迭代的
inertial forces 惯性力
overflow rate 溢流率
surface loading 表面负荷
discrete particle settling 离散颗粒沉降
detention time 滞留时间，停留时间
trajectory *n.* [物] 轨线
settling column 沉降柱

Questions

1. What types of gravitational settling can occur on the basis of the concentration and the tendency of particles to interact?
2. Try to deduce the Stokes' laws.
3. What is the basis of design for discrete particle settling?
4. Try to express the equation of the total fraction of particles removed for a continuous distribution and explain the meanings of the equation.
5. Please describe the formula of surface-loading rate and explain its meaning.

Reading Material

Gravity Separation Theory: II

Flocculent Particle Settling

Particles in relatively dilute solutions will not act as discrete particles but will coalesce during sedimentation. As coalescence or flocculation occurs, the mass of the particle increases, and it settles faster. The extent to which flocculation occurs is dependent on the opportunity for contact, which varies with overflow rate, depth of the basin, velocity gradients in the system, concentration of particles, and range of particle sizes. The effects of these variables can be determined only by sedimentation tests.

The settling characteristics of a suspension of flocculent particles can be obtained by using a settling column test. Such a column can be of any diameter but should be equal in height to the depth of the proposed tank. The solution containing the suspended matter should be introduced into the column in such a way that a uniform distribution of particle sizes occurs from top to bottom. Care should be taken to ensure that a uniform temperature is maintained throughout the test to eliminate convection currents. Settling should take place under quiescent conditions. The duration of the test should be equivalent to the settling time in the proposed tank.

At the conclusion of the settling time, the settled matter that has accumulated at the bottom of the column is drawn off, the remaining liquid is mixed, and the TSS of the liquid is measured. The TSS of the liquid is then compared to the sample TSS before settling to obtain the percent removal.

The more traditional method of determining settling characteristics of a suspension is to use a column similar to the one described above but with sampling ports inserted at approximately 0.5 m (1.5 ft) intervals. At various time intervals, samples are withdrawn from the ports and analyzed for suspended solids. The percent removal is computed for each sample analyzed and is plotted as a number against time and depth, as elevations are plotted on a survey grid. Curves of equal percent removal are drown as shown on Figure 4. From the curves shown on Figure 4, the overflow rate for various settling is determined by noting the value where the curve intersects the x axis. The settling velocity v_c is

$$v_c = \frac{H}{t_c} \tag{16}$$

where H = height of the settling column, L(m)

t_c = time required for a given degree of removal to be achieved, T (min)

The fraction of particles removed is given by

$$R, \% = \sum_{h=1}^{n} \left(\frac{\Delta h_n}{H}\right)\left(\frac{R_n + R_{n+1}}{2}\right) \tag{17}$$

where R = TSS removal, %

n = number of equal percent removal curve

Δh_n = distance between curves of equal percent removal, L (m)

H = total height of settling column, L (m)

R_n = equal percent removal curve number n

R_{n+1} = equal percent removal curve number $n+1$

The advantage of the more traditional method is that it is possible to obtain removal data at various depths of settling.

Inclined Plate and Tube Settling

Inclined plate and tube settlers are shallow settling devices consisting of stacked offset trays or bundles of small plastic tubes of various geometries (see Figure 5a) that are used to enhance the settling characteristics of sedimentation basins. They are based on the theory that settling depends on the settling area rather than detention time. Although they are used predominantly in water-treatment applications, plate and tube settles are used in wastewater-treatment for primary, secondary, and tertiary sedimentation. In primary sedimentation applications, however, fine screening should be provided ahead of the settling operation to prevent plugging of the plates or tubes.

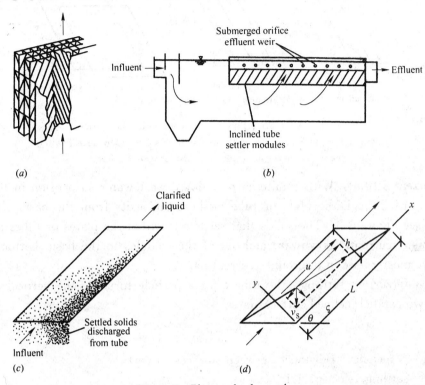

Figure 5 Plate and tube settlers
(a)module of inclined tubes, (b)tudes installed in a rectangular sedimentation tank,
(c)operation, and(d)definition sketch for the analysis of settling in a tube settler

To be self-cleaning, plate or tube settlers are usually set at an angle between 45° and 60° above the horizontal. When the angle is increased above 60°, the efficiency decreases. If the plates and tubes are inclined at angles less than 45°, solids will tend to accumulate within the plates or tubes. Nominal spacing between plates is 50 mm (2 in), with an inclined length of 1 to 2 m (3 to 6 ft). To control biological growths and the production of odors (the principal problems encountered with their use), the accumulated solids must be flushed out periodically (usually with a high-pressure water). The need for flushing poses a problem with the use of plate and tube settlers when the characteristics of the solids to be removed vary from day to day.

The main objective in inclined settler development has been to obtain settling efficiencies close to theoretical limits. Attention must be given to providing equal flow distribution to each settler, producing good flow distribution within each settler, and collecting settled solids while preventing resuspension.

Inclined settling systems are generally constructed for use in one of three ways with respect to the direction of liquid flow relative to the direction of particle settlement: (a) countercurrent, (b) cocurrent, and (c) cross-flow. The flow patterns are shown schematically on Figure 6.

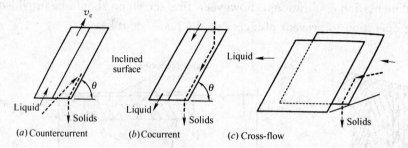

Figure 6 Alternative flow patterns through tube settlers
(a) countercurrent with respect to the movement of solids, (b) cocurrent with
the respect to the movement of solids, and (c) cross-flow.

Countercurrent Settling. With countercurrent flow, wastewater suspension in the basin passes upward through the plate or tube modules and exits from the basin above the modules (see Figure 6a). The solids that settle out within the plates or tubes move by gravity countercurrently downward and out of the modules to the basin bottom. Tube settlers are mostly used in the countercurrent mode.

In countercurrent settling, the time t for a particle to settle the vertical distance between two parallel inclined surfaces is:

$$t = \frac{w}{v\cos\theta} \tag{18}$$

where w = perpendicular distance between surfaces, L(m)
v = settling velocity, LT^{-1} (m/s)
θ = angle of the surface inclination from the horizontal

The length of surface L_p needed to provide this time, if the liquid velocity between the surfaces is v_θ, is

$$L_p = \frac{w(v_\theta - v\sin\theta)}{v\cos\theta} \tag{19}$$

By rearranging this equation, all particles with a settling velocity v and greater are removed if

$$v \geqslant \frac{v_\theta w}{L_p \cos\theta + w\sin\theta} \tag{20}$$

When many plates or tubes are used

$$v_\theta = \frac{Q}{Nwb} \tag{21}$$

where Q = flowrate, $L^3 T^{-1}$ (m³/s)
N = number of channels made by $N+1$ plates or tubes
b = dimension of the surface at right angles to w and Q, L (m)
w = perpendicular distance between surfaces, L (m)
v_θ = the liquid velocity between the surfaces, LT^{-1} (m/s)

Cocurrent Settling. In cocurrent settling, the solids suspension is introduced above the inclined surfaces and the flow is down through the tubes or plates (see Figure 6b). The time for a particle to settle the vertical distance between two surfaces is the same as for countercurrent settling. The length of surface needed, L_p, however, has to be based on downward and not upward liquid flow, as follows:

$$L_p = w\frac{(v_\theta + v\sin\theta)}{v\cos\theta} \qquad (22)$$

Consequently, the condition for removal of particles is given by

$$v \geqslant \frac{v_\theta w}{L_p\cos\theta - w\sin\theta} \qquad (23)$$

Cross-Flow Settling. In cross-flow settling, the liquid flow is horizontal and dose not interact with the vertical settling velocity (see Figure 6c). The length of the surface L_p is determined by

$$L_p = \frac{w v_\theta}{v\cos\theta} \qquad (24)$$

and

$$v \geqslant \frac{v_\theta w}{L_p\cos\theta} \qquad (25)$$

Hindered (Zone) Settling

In systems that contain a high concentration of suspended solids, both hindered or zone settling and compression settling usually occur in addition to discrete (free) and flocculent settling. The settling phenomenon that occurs when a concentrated suspension, initially of uniform concentration throughout, is placed in a graduated cylinder, is illustrated on Figure 7. Because of the high concentration of particles, the liquid tends to move up through the interstices of the contacting particles. As a result, the contacting particles tend to settle as a zone or "blanket", maintaining the same relative position with respect to each other. The phenomenon is known as hindered settling. As the particles settle, a relatively clear layer of water is produced above the particles in the settling region. The scattered, relatively light particles remaining usually settles as discrete or flocculent particles, as discussed previously. In most cases, an identifiable interface develops between the upper region and

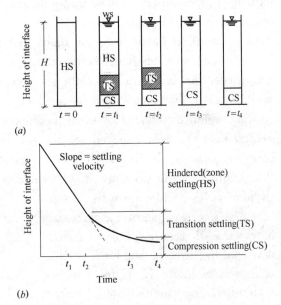

Figure 7 Definition sketch for hindered (zone) settling
(a) settling column in which the suspension is transitioning through various phases of settling and
(b) the corresponding interface settling curve

the hindered settling region on Figure 7. The rate of settling in the hindered settling region is a function of the concentration of solids and their characteristics.

As settling continues, a compressed layer of particles begins to form on the bottom of the cylinder in the compression settling region. The particles apparently form a structure in which there is close physical contact between the particles. As the compression layer forms, regions containing successively lower concentrations of solids than those in the compression region extend upward in the cylinder. Thus, in actuality the hindered settling region contains a gradation in solids concentration from that found at the interface of the settling region to that found in the compression settling region.

Because of the variability encountered, settling tests are usually required to determine the settling characteristics of suspensions where hindered and compression settling are important considerations. On the basis of data derived from column settling tests, two different design approaches can be used to obtain the required area for the settling/thickening facilities. In the first approach, the data derived from one or more batch settling tests are used. In the second approach, known as the solids flux method, data from a series of settling tests conducted at different solids concentrations are used. Both methods are described in the following discussion. It should be noted that both methods have been used where existing plants are to be expanded or modified. These methods are, however, seldom used in the design of small treatment plants.

Area Requirement Based on Single-Batch Test Results. For purposes of design, the final overflow rate selected should be based on a consideration of the following factors: (1) the area needed for clarification, (2) the area needed for thickening, and (3) the rate of sludge withdrawal. Column settling tests can be used to determine the area needed for the free settling region directly. However, because the area required for thickening is usually greater than the area required for the settling, the rate of free settling rarely is the controlling factor. In the case of the activated-sludge process where stray, light fluffy floc particles may be present, it is conceivable that the free flocculent settling velocity of these particles could control the design.

The area requirement for thickening is determined according to a method developed by Talmadge and Fitch (1955). A column of height H_0 is filled with a suspension of solids of uniform concentration C_0. The position of the interface as time elapses and the suspension settles is given on Figure 8. The rate at which the interface subsides is then equal to the slope of the curve at that point in time. According to the procedure, the area required for thickening is given by Eq. (26):

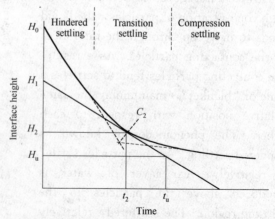

Figure 8 Graphical analysis of hindered (zone) interface settling curves.

LESSON 7

$$A = \frac{Qt_u}{H_0} \tag{26}$$

where A = area required for sludge thickening, $L^2 (m^2)$
Q = flowrate into tank, $L^3 T^{-1} (m^3/s)$
H_0 = initial height of interface in column, L (m)
t_u = time to reach desired underflow concentration, T (s)

The critical concentration controlling the solids handling capability of the tank occurs at a height H_2 where the concentration is C_2. This point is determined by extending the tangents to the hindered settling and compression regions of the subsidence curve to the point of intersection and bisecting the angle thus formed, as shown on Figure 8. The time t_u can be determined as follows:

1. Construct a horizontal line at the depth H_u that corresponds to the depth at which the solids are at the desired underflow concentration C_u. The value of H_u is determined using the following expression:

$$H_u = \frac{C_0 H_0}{C_u} \tag{27}$$

2. Construct a tangent to the settling curve at the point indicated by C_2.
3. Construct a vertical line from the point of intersection of the two lines drawn in steps 1 and 2 to the time axis to determine the value of t_u.

With this value of t_u the area required for the thickening is computed using Eq. (26). The area required for clarification is then determined. The larger of the two areas is the controlling value.

Area Requirement Based on Solids Flux Analysis. An alternative method of determining the area required for hindered settling is based on an analysis of the solids (mass) flux (Coe and Clevenger, 1916). In the solids flux method of analysis it is assumed that a settling basin is operated at steady state. Within the tank, the downward flux of solids is brought about by gravity (hindered) settling and by bulk transport due to the underflow that is being pumped out and recycled. The solids flux method of analysis is used to assess the performance of existing facilities and to obtain information for the design of new facilities to treat the same wastewater.

Compression Settling

The volume required for the sludge in the compression region can also be determined by settling tests. The rate of consolidation has been found to be proportional to the difference in the depth at time t and the depth to which the sludge will settle after a long period of time. The long-term consolidation can be modeled as a first-order decay function, as given by Eq. (28).

$$H_t - H_\infty = (H_2 - H_\infty) \cdot e^{-i(t-t_2)} \tag{28}$$

where H_t = sludge height at time t, L
H_∞ = sludge depth after long settling period, on the order of 24h, L
H_2 = sludge height at time t_2, L
i = constant for a given suspension

Stirring serves to compact solids in the compression region by breaking up the floc and permitting water to escape. Rakes are often used on sedimentation equipment to manipulate the solids and thus produce better compaction.

Gravity Separation in an Accelerated Flow Field

Sedimentation, as described previously, occurs under the force of gravity in a constant acceleration field. The removal of settleable particles can also be accomplished by taking advantage of a changing acceleration field. A number of devices that take advantage of both gravitational and centrifugal forces and induced velocities have been developed for the removal of grit from wastewater. The principles involved are illustrated on Figure 9. In appearance, the separator looks like a large diameter cylinder with a conical bottom. Wastewater, from which grit is to be separated, is introduced tangentially near the top and exits through the opening in the top of the unit. The liquid is removed at the top. Grit is removed through an opening in the bottom of the unit.

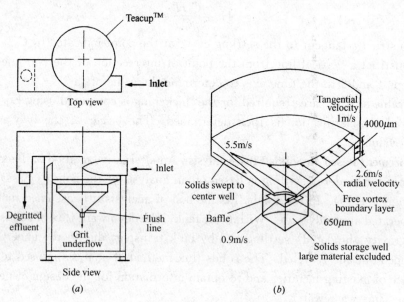

Figure 9 Accelerated gravity separator
(a) outline sketch and (b) definition sketch

New Words and Phrases

convection current　对流，运流
quiescent　*adj.* 静止的
draw off　*v.* 撤退，排除（水）
sampling port　取样口
inclined plate settler　斜板沉淀器
inclined tube settler　斜管沉淀器
countercurrent　*n.*（沉淀理论中的）上向流

cocurrent　*n.*（沉淀理论中的）下向流
cross-flow　*n.*（沉淀理论中的）横向流
zone settling　成层沉降
graduated cylinder　量筒
interstice　*n.* 空隙，裂缝
scattered　*adj.* 离散的，分散的
column settling test　沉降柱试验

solids flux 固体通量
fluffy *adj.* 绒毛似的，蓬松的，松散的
stray *adj.* 分散的，杂散的；迷路的
elapse *vi.* (时间)过去，消逝
subside *v.* 下沉，沉淀
tangent *n.* 切线
subsidence curve 沉降曲线

intersection *n.* [数] 交叉点
bisect *v.* 切成两分，对(截)开
consolidation *n.* 压实，合并
decay *v. & n.* 腐朽，腐烂，衰减
on the order of 约为，大约
induced velocity 诱导速度

LESSON 8
Filtration

As the sand filter removes the impurities, the sand grains get dirty and must be cleaned. The process of rapid sand filtration therefore involves two operations: filtration and backwashing. Figure 1 shows a cutaway of a slightly simplified version of the rapid sand filter. Water from the settling basins enters the filter and seeps through the sand and gravel bed, through a false floor, and out into a clear well that stores the finished water. Valves A and C are open during filtration.

The cleaning process is done by reversing the flow of water through the filter. The operator first shuts off the

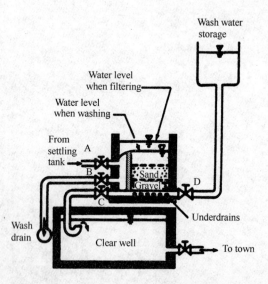

Figure 1 Rapid sand filter

flow of water to the filter, closes valves A and C, then opens valves D and B, which allow wash water (clean water stored in an elevated tank or pumped from the clear well) to enter below the filter bed. This rush of water forces the sand and gravel bed to expand and jolts individual sand particles into motion, rubbing against their neighbors. The light colloidal material trapped within the filter is released and escapes with the wash water. After 10 to 30 minutes of washing, the wash water is shut off and filtration is resumed.

Filter beds might contain filtration media other than sand. Crushed coal, for example, is often used in combination with sand to produce a dual media filter which can achieve greater removal efficiencies.

Introduction to Depth Filtration

Depth filtration involves the removal of particulate material suspended in a liquid by passing the liquid through a filter bed comprised of a granular or compressible filter medium. Although depth filtration is one of the principal unit operations used in the treatment of potable water, the filtration of effluents from wastewater - treatment processes is becoming more common. Depth filtration is now used to achieve supplemental removals of suspended solids (including particulate BOD) from wastewater effluents of biological and chemical treatment processes to reduce the mass discharge of solids and, perhaps more importantly, as a conditioning step that will allow for the effective disinfection of the filtered effluent. Depth filtration is also used as a pretreatment step for membrane filtration. Single and two-stage filtration is also used to remove chemically precipitated phosphorus.

Historically, the first depth filtration process developed for the treatment of wastewater was the slow sand filter [typical filtration rates of 30 to 60 L/(m^2 · d) [(0.75 to 1.5 gal/(ft^2 · d))], Frankland (1870), and Dunbar (1908)]. The rapid sand filter (typical filtration rates of 80 to 200 L/(m^2 · min)) [(2.0 to 5.0 gal/(ft^2 · min))], the subject of this section, was developed to treat larger volumes of water in a facility with a smaller footprint. To introduce the subject of depth filtration, the purpose of this section is to present (1) a general introduction to the depth filtration process, (2) an introduction to filter clean-water hydraulics, and (3) an analysis of the filtration process. The types of filters that are available and issues associated with their selection and design, including a discussion of the need for pilot-plant studies, are considered in the following section.

Description of the Filtration Process

Before discussing the available filter technologies, it will be useful to first describe the basics of the depth filtration including (1) the physical features of a conventional granular medium-depth filter, (2) filter-medium characteristics, (3) the filtration process in which suspended material is removed from the liquid, (4) the operative particle-removal mechanisms that bring about the removal of suspended material within the filter, and (5) the backwash process, in which the material that has been retained within the filter is removed.

Physical Features of a Depth Filter. The general features of a conventional rapid granular medium-depth filter are illustrated on Figure 2. As shown, the filtering medium (sand in this case) is supported on a gravel layer, which, in turn, rests on the filter underdrain system. The water to be filtered enters the filter from an inlet channel. Filtered water is collected in the underdrain system, which is also used to reverse the flow to backwash the filter. Filtered water typically is disinfected before being discharged to the environment. If the filtered water is to be reused, it can be discharged to a storage reservoir or to the reclaimed water distribution system. The hydraulic control of the filter is described in a subsequent section.

Filter-Medium Characteristics. Grain size is the principal filter-medium characteristic that affects the filtration operation. Grain size affects both the clear-water headloss and the buildup of headloss during the filter run. If too small a filtering medium is selected, much of the driving force will be wasted in overcoming the frictional resistance of the filter bed. On the other hand, if the size of the medium is too large, many of the small particles in the influent will pass directly through the bed. The size distribution of the filter material is usually determined by sieve analysis using a series of decreasing sieve sizes. The designation and size of opening for U.S. sieve sizes are given in Table 1. The results of a sieve analysis are usually analyzed by plotting the cumulative percent passing a

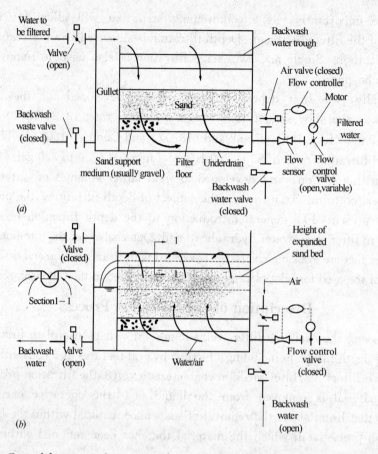

Figure 2 General features and operation of a conventional rapid granular medium-depth filter
(a) flow during filtration cycle, and (b) flow during backwash cycle

Designation and size of opening of U. S. sieve sizes   Table 1

Sieve size or number	Size of opening		Sieve size or number	Size of opening	
	in	mm		in	mm
3/8in	0.375[a]	9.51[a]	25	0.0280[a]	0.710[a]
1/4in	0.250[a]	6.35[a]	30	0.0234	0.595
4	0.187	4.76	35	0.0197[a]	0.500[a]
6	0.132	3.36	40	0.0165	0.420
8	0.0937	2.38	45	0.0138[a]	0.350[a]
10	0.0787[a]	2.00[a]	50	0.0117	0.297
12	0.0661	1.68	60	0.0098[a]	0.250[a]
14	0.0555[a]	1.41[a]	70	0.0083	0.210
16	0.0469	1.19	80	0.0070[a]	0.177[a]
18	0.0394[a]	1.00[a]	100	0.0059	0.149
20	0.0331	0.841			

[a] Size does not follow the ratio $(2)^{0.5}$.

given sieve size on arithmetic-log or probability-log paper.

The effective size of a filtering medium is defined as the 10 percent size based on mass and is designated as d_{10}. For sand, it has been found that the 10 percent size by weight corresponds to the 50 percent size by count. The uniformity coefficient (UC) is defined as the ratio of the 60 percent size to the 10 percent size ($UC = d_{60}/d_{10}$). Sometimes it is advantageous to specify the 99 percent passing size and the 1 percent passing size to define the gradation curve for each filter medium more accurately. Additional information on filter-medium characteristics is presented in the following section dealing with the design of filters.

The Filtration Process. During filtration in a conventional downflow depth filter, wastewater containing suspended matter is applied to the top of the filter bed (Figure 2a). As the water passes through the filter bed, the suspended matter in the wastewater is removed by a variety of removal mechanisms as described below. With the passage of time, as material accumulates within the interstices of the granular medium, the headloss through the filter starts to build up beyond the initial value, as shown on Figure 3.

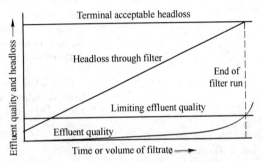

Figure 3 Definition sketch for length of filter run based on headloss and effluent turbidity

After some period of time, the operating headloss or effluent turbidity reaches a predetermined headloss or turbidity value, and the filter must be cleaned. Under ideal conditions, the time required for the headloss buildup to reach the preselected terminal value should correspond to the time when the suspended solids in the effluent reach the preselected terminal value for acceptable quality. In actual practice, one or the other event will govern the backwash cycle.

Particle Removal Mechanisms. The principal particle removal mechanisms, believed to contribute to the removal of material within a granular-medium filter, are identified and described in Table 2. The major removal mechanisms (the first six listed in Table 2) are illustrated pictorially on Figure 4. Straining has been identified as the principal mechanism that is operative in the removal of suspended solids during the filtration of settled secondary effluent from biological treatment processes. Other mechanisms including impaction, interception, and adhesion are also operative even though their effects are small and, for the most part, masked by the straining action.

Principal mechanisms and phenomena contributing to removal of material within a granular medium-depth filter   Table 2

Mechanism/ phenomenon	Description
1. Straining	
a. Mechanical	Particles larger than the pore space of the filtering medium are strained out mechanically

Table 2(Continued)

Mechanism/phenomenon	Description
b. Chance contact	Particles smaller than the pore space are trapped within the filter by chance contact
2. Sedimentation	Particles settle on the filtering medium within the filter
3. Impaction	Heavy particles will not follow the flow streamlines
4. Interception	Many particles that move along in the streamline are removed when they come in contact with the surface of the filtering medium
5. Adhesion	Particles become attached to the surface of the filtering medium as they pass by. Because of the force of the flowing water, some material is sheared away before it becomes firmly attached and is pushed deeper into the filter bed. As the bed becomes clogged, the surface shear force increases to a point at which no additional material can be removed. Some material may break through the bottom of the filter, causing the sudden appearance of turbidity in the effluent
6. Flocculation	Flocculation can occur within the interstices of the filter medium. The larger particles formed by the velocity gradients within the filter are then removed by one or more of the above removal mechanisms

7. Chemical adsorption
  a. Bonding
  b. Chemical interaction
8. Physical adsorption
  a. Electrostatic forces
  b. Electrokinetic forces
  c. van der Waals forces
	Once a particle has been brought in contact with the surface of the filtering medium or with other particles, either one of these mechanisms, chemical or physical adsorption or both, may be responsible for holding it there

9. Biological growth	Biological growth within the filter will reduce the pore volume and may enhance the removal of particles with any of the above removal mechanisms (1 through 5)

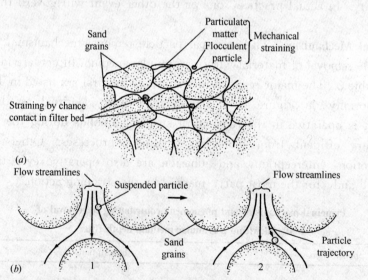

Figure 4 Removal of suspended particulate matter within a granular filter(1)
(a)by straining, (b)by sedimentation or inertial impaction

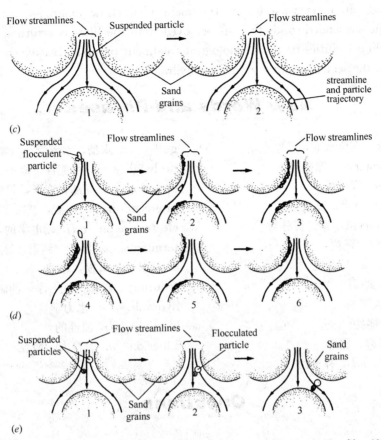

Figure 4　Removal of suspended particulate matter within a granular filter(2)
(c)by interception, (d)by adhesion, (e)by flocculation.

　　The removal of the smaller particles found in wastewater (see Figure 4) must be accomplished in two steps involving (1)the transport of the particles to or near the surface where they will be removed and(2) the removal of the particles by one or more of the operative removal mechanisms. This two-step process has been identified as transport and attachment (O'Melia and Stumm, 1967).

　　Backwash Process. The end of the filter run (filtration phase) is reached when the suspended solids in the effluent start to increase (break through) beyond an acceptable level, or when a limiting headloss occurs across the filter bed (see Figure 3). Once either of these conditions is reached, the filtration phase is terminated, and the filter must be cleaned (backwashed) to remove the material (suspended solids) that has accumulated within the granular filter bed. Backwashing is accomplished by reversing the flow through the filter (see Figure 2b). A sufficient flow of washwater is applied until the granular filtering medium is fluidized (expanded), causing the particles of the filtering medium to abrade against each other.

　　The suspended matter arrested within the filter is removed by the shear forces created by backwash water as it moves up through the expanded bed. The material that has accumulated within the bed is then washed away. Surface washing with water and air scouring are often used in conjunction with the water backwash to enhance the cleaning of the filter bed. In most wastewater-treatment plant flow diagrams, the washwater containing the suspended solids that are removed from the filter is returned either to the primary settling facilities or to the biological treatment process. Backwash hydraulics is considered in the section dealing with filter hydraulics.

New Words and Phrases

elevated tank　高位水池，高架水箱
frictional resistance　摩擦阻力
sieve analysis　筛分析
arithmetic　*n.* 算术，算法
cumulative percent　累计百分数
grain　*n.* 细粒，颗粒
backwashing　*n.* 反冲洗
cutaway　*n.* 剖面图
false　*adj.* 人工的
jolt　*v.* & *n.* 摇晃
crush　*vt.* 压碎，碾碎
supplemental　*adj.* 补充的

gullet　*n.* 水槽，水落管，海峡
probability　*n.* 可能性，概率
straining　*n.* 筛滤，变形，隔滤
interception　*n.* 拦截，截留
electrokinetic　*adj.* 动电学的，电动的
terminate　*v.* 停止，结束，终止
abrade　*v.* 磨损，摩擦
scouring　*n.* 擦［洗］净，冲刷，洗涤
hydraulics　*n.* 水力学
inertial　*adj.* 惯性的
adhesion　*n.* 附着力，胶粘

Questions

1. What operations does the process of rapid sand filtration involve?
2. How much are the typical filtration rates in slow and rapid sand filter?
3. By what method can the size distribution of the filter material be determined?
4. What is the meaning of d_{10}?
5. What is the meaning of the uniformity coefficient (UC)?
6. What is the process of removal of the smaller particles found in water?
7. In a granular-medium filter, what are the principal particle removal mechanisms?

Reading Material

Rapid Filters

The first filters built for water purification used very fine sand as the filter media. Because of the tiny size of the pore spaces in the fine sand, water takes a long time to flow through the filter bed, and when the surface becomes clogged with suspended particles, it becomes necessary to manually scrape the sand surface to clean the filter. These units, called *slow sand filters*, take up a considerable amount of land area because of the slow filtration rates. Slow sand filters are still used in several existing treatment plants. They are effective and relatively inexpensive to operate.

In modern water treatment plants, the *rapid filter* has largely replaced the slow sand filter. As its name implies, the water flows through the filter bed much faster (about 30 times as fast) than it flows through the slow sand filter. This naturally makes it necessary to clean the filter much more frequently. But instead of manual cleaning by scraping of the surface, rapid filters are cleaned by reversing the direction of flow through the bed. This is shown schematically in Figure 5.

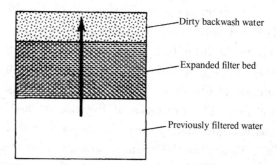

Figure 5 Schematic diagram of the backwash or cleaning cycle of a rapid filter

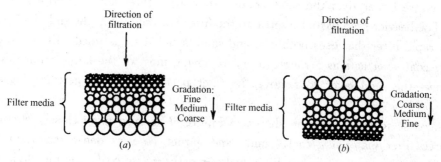

Figure 6

(a) Typical gradation of a rapid sand bed. Solids removal occurs primarily by straining action at the top of the sand bed;

(b) Typical coarse-to-fine gradation in a *mixed-media* filter

It is preferable to the sand bed because it provides in-depth filtration

During filtration, the water flows downward through the bed under the force of gravity. When the filter is washed, clean water is forced upward, expanding the filter bed slightly and carrying away the accumulated impurities. This process is called *backwashing*. Cleaning by a backwash operation is a key characteristic of a rapid filter.

Many rapid filters currently in operation use sand as the filter medium and are called *rapid filters*. But the sand grains (are pore spaces) are larger than those in the older, slow sand filters. In a rapid sand filter, the effective size of the sand is about 0.5mm and the uniformity coefficient is 1.5. A difficulty that arises when using only sand in the rapid filter is that, after backwashing, the larger sand grains settle to the bottom first, leaving the smaller sand grains at the filter surface. This pattern of filter medium gradation is shown in Figure 6a.

Because of this small-to-larger gradation of sand grains in the direction of flow, most of the filtering action takes place in the top layer of the bed. This results in inefficient use of the filter. The filter run time (period of time between backwashes) is reduced, and frequent backwashes are required. Also, if some of the suspended material happens to penetrate the upper layer of fine sand, it is then likely to pass through the entire filter bed.

A preferable size distribution of the filter material is shown in Figure 6b. The larger-to-small particle gradation allows the suspended particles to reach greater depths within the filter bed. This *in-depth filtration*, as it is called, provides more storage space for the solids, offers less resistance to flow, and allows longer filter runs. The process of filtration becomes more than just a physical straining action at the surface of the bed. The processes of flocculation and sedimentation also occur within the pore spaces, and some material is adsorbed onto the surfaces of the filter medium.

To achieve the optimum gradation for in-depth filtration, it is necessary to use two or more different filter material. For example, if a coarse layer or anthracite coal is placed above the sand, the coal grains will always remain on top after backwashing occurs. This is because the coal has a much lower density than the sand. Even though the coal grains are larger than the sand grains, they are lighter and therefore settle more slowly. The heavier sand particles settle to the filter bottom first at the end of a backwash cycle. A rapid filter that uses both coal and sand is called a dual-media filter. In effect, the upper coal layer acts as a rough filter, removing most of the large impurities first. This allows the sand layer to remove the finer particles without getting clogged too quickly.

The coarse-to-fine gradation shown in Figure 6b is even more closely obtained by using three filter materials: coal, sand, and garnet (a very dense material). After backwashing, the top layer of the filter bed is mostly coarse coal, the middle is mostly medium sand, and the bottom layer is mostly very fine grain of garnet. This is called a mixed-media filter. Filter material ranges in size from about 2 mm at the top to about 0.2 mm at the bottom. In recent years, dual-and mixed-media filters have been used to replace existing rapid sand filters in many treatment plants.

Filter Design

Rapid filters, whether of sand, dual media, or mixed media, are usually built in boxlike concrete structures, as illustrated in Figure 7. Multiple filter boxes or units are arranged on both sides of a central *piping gallery*, and a *clear well* used for storing filtered water is often located under the filters. Since only one unit is backwashed at a time, the filtration process can occur continuously as water flows through the treatment plant.

A typical rapid filter box is about 3 m, or 10 ft, deep, but the filter bed itself is only about 0.75 m, or 2.5 ft, deep. Located above the surface of the filter bed are *wash-water troughs*, which carry away the dirty backwash water as it flows upward through the bed and over the edge of the troughs. The filter medium is generally supported on a layer of coarse gravel. Below the gravel, which only serves to support the filter bed and does not contribute to the filtering action, is a special filter bottom or *underdrain system*.

LESSON 8

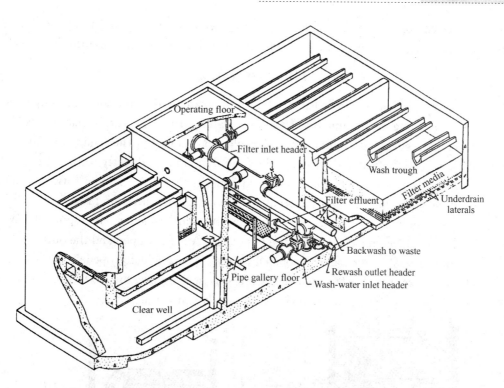

Figure 7 Perspective view of a typical rapid filter facility. The filtered water is temporarily stored in the clear well. Multiple filter boxes provide operational flexibility; only one filter is backwashed at a time

The underdrains collect the filtered water and uniformly distribute the wash water across the filter bottom during the backwash cycle. They may consist of a grid of perforated pipes leading to a commom header pipe that carries the water into the clear well. In many filters, the underdrains consist of specially manufactured porous tile blocks or steel plates with nozzles to help to distribute the backwash water. A cross-section of a typical filter unit is shown in Figure 8.

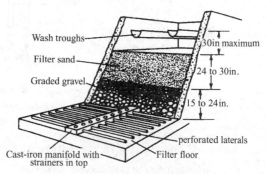

Figure 8 Cross-sectional view of a typical sand filter box

The effectiveness of filtration and the length of a filter run depend on the filtration rate. Lower filtration rates generally allow longer filter runs and produce higher quality water, but they require larger filters. Filtration rate is often expressed as the flow rate of water divided by the surface area of the filter. In customary units, this is usually in terms of gallons per minute per square foot (gpm/ft^2 or $gal/ft^2/min$). in SI metric units, it is liters per square meter per second $[L/(m^2 \cdot s)]$. Rapid sand filters are usually designed to operate at an average rate of about 1.4 $[L/(m^2 \cdot s)]$ or 2 gpm/ft^2, whereas mixed-media filters can operate effectively at an average rate of about 3.5 [L/(m² · s)] or 5 gpm/ft². The filtration rate is proportional to the velocity flow through the filter bed.

Filter Operation

Rapid filtration is usually preceded by coagulation and sedimentation. In some cases, however, depending on the quality of the raw water, *direct filtration* may be used. In direct filtration, coagulation mixing and flocculation occur, but the sedimentation step is omitted. Instead, the water flows from the flocculation basin directly to the filters. This provides a saving in treatment plant area and construction cost. (Some filtration plants also use ozone and a process called flocculation to aid the clarification process.)

A cross-sectional view of a typical rapid filter unit is shown in Figure 9. When filtration begins through a clean bed, the inlet valve A is fully open and the outlet valve B is throttled (that is, only partially open). Valve B is gradually opened farther by an automatic *filter rate controller*, which operates by sensing pressure difference caused by changes in flow rate. The control device is usually a venturi meter.

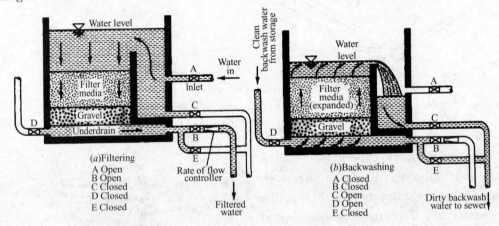

Figure 9 Schematic diagrams of a rapid filter in the
(a) filtering cycle and (b) backwash cycle of operation. Valves A, B, C, D,
and E control the flow. Valve E is opened briefly when filtering starts

As solids accumulate in the filter, the resistance to flow through the bed increases and the filtration rate tends to decrease. The reduced flow is sensed by the rate controller, which causes valve B compensates for the continually increasing resistance to flow in the filter bed. In this way, the rate of flow through the filter does not vary. This type of operation is called *constant-rate filtration*. During constant-rate filtration, the water level in the filter box remains about 1 m (3 ft) above the top of the bed.

Eventually, the filter bed gets clogged to the extent that valve B must be wide open to maintain the desired filtration rate. At this point it becomes necessary to clean or backwash the filter. To do this, valves A and B are closed and valves C and D are opened. Water from the backwash storage tank then flows upward through the filter bed, expending it slightly and carrying away the accumulated solids. The dirty backwash water flows into the wash-water troughs and then is either recycled or drained into a municipal sewerage system.

Filter backwash water may contain very levels of harmful microbes, such as *Cryptosporidium* (which has caused 12 waterborne disease out breaks in the United States since 1984). Improper backwash recycling procedures have been identified as possible causes for several of those disease outbreaks. Under the SDWA, a *Filter Backwash Recycling Rule* has been promulgated to protect public health. The rule requires that backwash water be returned to the headworks of the water treatment facility so that it undergoes all of the conventional treatment processes. Appropriate record keeping of recycle flow rates is also required.

Rapid filters are generally backwashed at a rate of about 10 L/(m² · s)(15 gpd/ft²) for about 10 min. After the backwash flow stops, the filter material settles back in the bed and the filtration cycle begins again. For the first 5 min of filtering, however, the filtered water is discarded through valve E to ensure that any remaining solids will not be carried into the clear well.

In recent years, a mode of operation called *declining-rate filtration* has been applied in some water treatment plants. In this mode of operation, rate-of-flow controllers are not used. The filtration rate is allowed to gradually decline from a maximum valve when the bed is clogged. As the filter becomes clogged with accumulated solids, the water level gradually rises in the filter box. When the water level reaches a predetermined height, the filter is automatically backwashed.

Both declining-rate filtration and constant-rate filtration produce water of excellent quality. The crystal clear effluents from properly designed and operated rapid filters generally have turbidity levels less than 0.2 NTU.

New Words and Phrases

anthracite   *n.* 无烟煤
garnet   *n.* 石榴石，深红色
perspective view   透视图
piping gallery   管廊
lateral   *n.* 侧部，支管线，边音
      adj. 横(向)的，侧面的

tile   *n.* 瓦片，瓷砖
nozzle   *n.* 管口，喷嘴
strainer   *n.* 滤网，松紧扣，过滤器
venturi   *n.* 文氏管，文丘里管(一种流体流
      量测定装置，亦作 venturitube)
promulgate   *vt.* 发布，公布，传播

LESSON 9

Adsorption: I

Adsorption is the process of accumulating substances that are in solution on a suitable interface. Adsorption is a mass transfer operation in that a constituent in the liquid phase is transferred to the solid phase. The *adsorbate* is the substance that is being removed from the liquid phase at the interface. The *adsorbent* is the solid, liquid, or gas phase onto which the adsorbate accumulates. Although adsorption is used at the air-liquid interface in the flotation process, only the case of adsorption at the liquid-solid interface will be considered in this discussion. The adsorption process has not been used extensively in wastewater treatment, but demands for a better quality of treated wastewater effluent, including toxicity reduction, have led to an intensive examination and use of the process of adsorption on activated carbon. Activated carbon treatment of wastewater is usually thought of as a polishing process for water that has already received normal biological treatment. The carbon in this case is used to remove a portion of the remaining dissolved organic matter. The purpose of this section is to introduce the basic concepts of adsorption and to consider carbon adsorption.

Types of Adsorbents

The principal types of adsorbents include activated carbon, synthetic polymeric, and silica-based adsorbents, although synthetic polymeric and silica-based adsorbents are seldom used for water adsorption because of their high cost. Because activated carbon is used most commonly in advanced water-treatment applications, the focus of the following discussion is on activated carbon. The nature of activated carbon, the use of granular carbon and powdered carbon for water treatment, and carbon regeneration and reactivation are discussed below.

Activated Carbon. Activated carbon is prepared by first making a char from organic materials such as almond, coconut, and walnut hulls; other materials including woods, bone, and coal have also been used. The char is produced by heating the base material to a red heat (less than about 700℃) in a retort to drive off the hydrocarbons, but with an insufficient supply of oxygen to sustain combustion. The carbonization or char-producing process is essentially a pyrolysis process. The char particle is then *activated* by exposure to oxidizing gases such as steam and CO_2 at high temperatures, in the range from 800 to 900℃. These gases develop a porous structure in the char and thus create a large internal surface area. The resulting pore sizes are defined as follows:

　　Macropores　　>25 nm
　　Mesopores　　>1 nm and <25 nm

LESSON 9

Micropores   <1 nm

The surface properties that result are a function of both the initial material used and the preparation procedure, so that many variations are possible. The type of base material from which the activated carbon is derived may also affect the pore-size distribution and the regeneration characteristics. After activation, the carbon can be separated into, or prepared in, different sizes with different adsorption capacity. The two size classifications are *powdered activated carbon* (PAC), which typically has a diameter of less than 0.074 mm (200 sieve), and *granular activated carbon* (GAC), which has a diameter greater than 0.1 mm (~140 sieve). The characteristics of granular and powdered activated carbon are summarized in Table 1.

Comparison of granular and powdered activated carbon   Table 1

Parameter	Unit	Type of activated carbon[a]	
		GAC	PAC
Total surface area	m^2/g	700~1300	800~1800
Bulk density	kg/m^3	400~500	360~740
Particle density, wetted in water	kg/L	1.0~1.5	1.3~1.4
Particle size range	mm(μm)	0.1~2.36	(5~50)
Effective size	mm	0.6~0.9	na
Uniformity coefficient	UC	≤1.9	na
Mean pore radius		16~30	20~40
Iodine number		600~1100	800~1200
Abrasion number	minimum	75~85	70~80
Ash	%	≤8	≤6
Moisture as packed	%	2~8	3~10

[a] Specific values will depend on the source material used for the production of the activated carbon.

Carbon Regeneration and Reactivation. Economical application of activated carbon depends on an efficient means of regenerating and reactivating the carbon after its adsorptive capacity has been reached. *Regeneration* is the term used to describe all of the processes that are used to recover the adsorptive capacity of the spent carbon, exclusive of reactivation, including: (1) chemicals to oxidize the adsorbed material, (2) steam to drive off the adsorbed material, (3) solvents, and (4) biological conversion processes. Typically some of the adsorptive capacity of the carbon (about 4 to 10 percent) is also lost in the regeneration process, depending on the compounds been adsorbed and the regeneration method used. In some applications, the capacity of the carbon following regeneration has remained essentially the same for years. A major problem with the use of powdered activated carbon is that the methodology for its regeneration is not well defined. The use of powdered activated carbon produced from recycled solid wastes may obviate the need to regenerate the spent carbon, and may be more economical.

Reactivation of granular carbon involves essentially the same process used to create the activated carbon from virgin material. Spent carbon is reactivated in a furnace by oxidizing the adsorbed organic material and, thus, removing it from the carbon surface. The following series of events occur in the reactivation of spent activated carbon: (1) the carbon is heated to drive off the absorbed organic material (i. e., absorbate), (2) in the process of driving off the absorbed material some new compounds are formed that remain on the surface of the carbon, and (3) the final step in the reactivation process is to burn off the new compounds that were formed when the absorbed material was burned off. With effective process control, the adsorptive capacity of reactivated carbon will be essentially the same as that of the virgin carbon. For planning purposes, it is often assumed that a loss of 2 to 5 percent will occur in the reactivation process. It is important to note that most other losses of carbon occur through attrition due to mishandling. For example, right angle bends in piping cause attrition through abrasion and impact. The type of pumping facilities used will also affect the amount of attrition. In general, a 4 to 8 percent loss of carbon is assumed, due to handling. Replacement carbon must be available to make up the loss.

Fundamentals of Adsorption

The adsorption process, as illustrated on Figure 1, takes place in four more or less definable steps: (1) bulk solution transport, (2) film diffusion transport, (3) pore transport, and (4) adsorption (or sorption). *Bulk solution transport* involves the movement of the organic material to be adsorbed through the bulk liquid to the boundary layer of fixed film of liquid surrounding the adsorbent, typically by advection and dispersion in carbon contactors. *Film diffusion transport* involves the transport by diffusion of the organic material through the stagnant liquid film to the entrance of the pores of the adsorbent. *Pore transport* involves the transport of the material to be adsorbed through the pores by a combination of molecular diffusion through the pore liquid and/or by diffusion along the surface of the adsorbent. Adsorption involves the attachment of the material to be adsorbed to adsorbent at an available adsorption site. Adsorption can occur on the outer surface of the adsorbent and in the macropores, mesopores, micropores, and submicropores, but the surface area of the macro-and mesopores is small compared with the surface area of the micropores and submicropores and the amount of material adsorbed there is usually considered negligible. Adsorption forces include:

- ◆ Coulombic-unlike charges
- ◆ Point charge and a dipole
- ◆ Dipole-dipole interactions
- ◆ Point charge neutral species
- ◆ London or van der Waals forces
- ◆ Covalent bonding with reaction
- ◆ Hydrogen bonding

LESSON 9

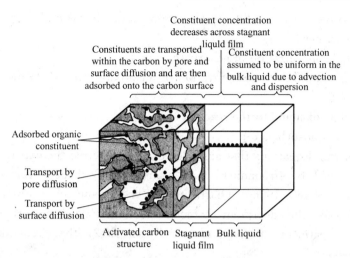

Figure 1 Definition sketch for the adsorption of an organic constituent with activated carbon

Because it is difficult to differentiate between chemical and physical adsorption, the term *sorption* is often used to describe the attachment of the organic material to the activated carbon.

Because the adsorption process occurs in a series of steps, the slowest step in the series is identified as the *rate limiting step*. In general, if physical adsorption is the principal method of adsorption, one of the diffusion transport steps will be the rate limiting, because the rate of physical adsorption is rapid. Where chemical adsorption is the principal method of adsorption, the adsorption step has often been observed to be rate limiting. When the rate of sorption equals the rate of desorption, equilibrium has been achieved and the capacity of the carbon has been reached. The theoretical adsorption capacity of the carbon for a particular contaminant can be determined by developing its adsorption isotherm as described below.

Development of Adsorption Isotherms. The quantity of adsorbate that can be taken up by an adsorbent is a function of both the characteristics and concentration of adsorbate and the temperature. The characteristics of the adsorbate that are of importance include: solubility, molecular structure, molecular weight, polarity, and hydrocarbon saturation. Generally, the amount of material adsorbed is determined as a function of the concentration at a content temperature, and the resulting function is called an adsorption isotherm. Adsorption isotherms are developed by exposing a given amount of absorbate in a fixed volume of liquid to varying amounts of activated carbon. Typically, more than ten containers are used, and the minimum time allowed for the samples to equilibrate where powdered activated carbon is used is seven days. If granular activated carbon is used, it is usually powdered to minimize adsorption times. At the end of the test period, the amount of absorbate remaining in solution is measured. The absorbent phase concentration after equilibrium is computed using Eq. (1). The absorbent phase concentration data computed using Eq. (1) are then used to develop adsorption isotherms as described below.

$$q_e = \frac{(C_0 - C_e) \cdot V}{m} \tag{1}$$

where q_e = adsorbent (i. e., solid) phase concentration after equilibrium, mg adsorbate/g adsorbent

C_0 = initial concentration of adsorbate, mg/L

C_e = final equilibrium concentration of adsorbate after absorption has occurred, mg/L

V = volume of liquid in the reactor, L

m = mass of adsorbent, g

Freundlich Isotherm. Equations that are often used to describe the experimental isotherm data were developed by Freundlich, Langmuir, and Bruhauer, Emmet, and Teller (BET isotherm) (Shaw, 1966). Of the three, the Freundlich isotherm is used most commonly to describe the adsorption characteristics of the activated carbon used in water and wastewater treatment. Derived empirically in 1912, the Freundlich isotherm is defined as follows:

$$\frac{x}{m} = K_f C_e^{1/n} \qquad (2)$$

where x/m = mass of adsorbate adsorbed per unit mass of adsorbent, mg adsorbate/g activated carbon

K_f = Freundlich capacity factor, (mg absorbate/g activated carbon)(L water/mg adsorbate)$^{1/n}$

C_e = equilibrium concentration of adsorbate in solution after adsorption, mg/L

$1/n$ = Freundlich intensity parameter

The constants in the Freundlich isotherm can be determined by plotting log (x/m) versus log C_e and making use of Eq. (2) rewritten as:

$$\log\left(\frac{x}{m}\right) = \log K_f + \frac{1}{n} \log C_e \qquad (3)$$

The U. S. EPA has developed adsorption isotherms for a variety of toxic compounds. The variation in the Freundlich capacity factor for the various compounds is extremely wide (e.g., 14000 for PCB to 6.8×10^{-5} for N-Dimethylnitrosamine). Because of the wide variation, the Freundlich capacity factor must be determined for each new compound.

Langmuir Isotherm. Derived from rational considerations, the Langmuir adsorption isotherm is defined as:

$$\frac{x}{m} = \frac{abC_e}{1+bC_e} \qquad (4)$$

where x/m = mass of adsorbate adsorbed per unit mass of adsorbent, mg adsorbate/g activated carbon

a, b = empirical constants

C_e = equilibrium concentration of adsorbate in solution after adsorption, mg/L

The Langmuir adsorption isotherm was developed by assuming: (1) a fixed number of accessible sites are available on the adsorbent surface, all of which have the same energy, and (2) adsorption is reversible. Equilibrium is reached when the rate of adsorption of molecules onto the surface is the same as the rate of desorption of molecules from the surface. The rate at which adsorption proceeds is proportional to the driving force, which is the difference between the amount adsorbed at a particular concentration and the amount that can be adsorbed at that concentration. At the equilibrium concentration, this difference is zero.

Correspondence of experimental data to the Langmuir equation does not mean that the stated assumptions are valid for the particular system being studied, because departures from the assumptions can have a canceling effect. The constants in the Langmuir isotherm can be determined by plotting $C_e/(x/m)$ versus C_e and making use of Eq. (4) rewritten as:

$$\frac{C_e}{(x/m)} = \frac{1}{ab} + \frac{1}{a} C_e \tag{5}$$

New Words and Phrases

adsorption   *n.* 吸附
adsorbate   *n.* 被吸附物
adsorbent   *adj.* 吸附的
             n. 吸附剂
activated carbon   活性炭
polishing process   精处理法
regeneration   *n.* 再生
char   *n.* (木)炭，茶
almond   *n.* [植] 杏树
coconut   *n.* 椰子
walnut   *n.* 胡桃，胡桃木
hull   *n.* (果实等的)外壳，船体
red heat   赤热，赤热状态
retort   *n.* 曲颈甑，曲颈瓶，蒸器
carbonization   *n.* 碳化，干馏，碳化物
pyrolysis   *n.* 高温分解
meso-   [词头] 中间的，中等的
powdered activated carbon (**PAC**):
   粉末活性炭
granular activated carbon (**GAC**):
   粒状活性炭
bulk density   堆积密度，松密度
iodine number   碘值

abrasion   *n.* 磨损
spent   *adj.* 用尽的，失去效能的
obviate   *vt.* 消除，排除(危险、障碍等)
virgin   *adj.* 原始的，美国著名游戏软件
        公司
furnace   *n.* 炉子，熔炉
attrition   *n.* 磨耗，磨损
mishandling   *n.* 违规操作
impact   *n.* 碰撞，影响
sorption   *n.* 吸着 [作用]
advection   *n.* 水平对流
dispersion   *n.* 弥散、扩散(现象)
contactor   *n.* 接触器
diffusion   *n.* 扩散，传播
stagnant   *adj.* 停滞的
coulombic   *adj.* 库仑的，库仑定律的
dipole   *n.* 双极子，偶极
hydrogen bonding   氢键结合
adsorption isotherm   吸附等温线
polarity   *n.* 极性
PCB   多氯联苯
dimethylnitrosamine   *n.* 二甲基亚硝胺
valid   *adj.* 有效的，正确的

Questions

1. What is the process of adsorption?
2. What are the definitions of *adsorbate* and *adsorbent*?

3. What is the meaning of regeneration of the spent carbon? What methods can be used to carbon regeneration?
4. What is the meaning of sorption?
5. What is the *rate-limiting step* in the adsorption process?
6. What is the definition of adsorption isotherm?
7. What are the assuming conditions of Langmuir adsorption isotherm?

Reading Material

Adsorption: II

Activated Carbon Adsorption Kinetics

As noted previously, both granular carbon (in downflow and upflow columns) and powdered activated carbon are used for water and wastewater treatment. The analysis procedures for both types are described briefly in the following discussion.

Mass Transfer Zone. The area of the GAC bed in which sorption occurs is called the mass transfer zone (MTZ) (see Figure 2). After the water containing the constituent to be removed passes through a region of the bed whose depth is equal to the MTZ, the concentration of the contaminant in the water will have been reduced to its minimum value. No further adsorption will occur within the bed below the MTZ. As the top layers of carbon granules become saturated with organic material, the MTZ will move down in

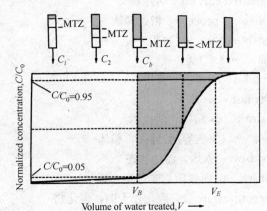

Figure 2 Typical breakthrough curve activated carbon showing movement of mass transfer zone (MTZ) with throughput volume

the bed until breakthrough occurs. Typically, breakthrough is said to have occurred when the effluent concentration reaches 5 percent of the influent value. Exhaustion of the adsorption bed is assumed to have occurred when the effluent concentration is equal to 95 percent of the influent concentration. The length of the MTZ is typically a function of the hydraulic loading rate applied to the column and the characteristics of the activated carbon. In the extreme, if the loading rate is too great the height of the MTZ will be larger than the GAC bed depth, and the adsorbable constituent will not be removed completely by the carbon. At complete exhaustion, the effluent concentration is equal to the influent concentration.

In addition to the applied hydraulic loading rate, the shape of the breakthrough curve will also depend on whether the applied liquid contains nonadsorbable and biodegradable constituents. The impact of the presence of nonadsorbable and biodegradable organic constituents on the shape of the breakthrough curve is illustrated on Figure 3. As shown on Figure 3, if the liquid contains nonadsorbable constituents, the nonadasorbable constituents will appear in the effluent as soon as the carbon column is put into operation. If adsorbable and biodegradable constituents are present in the applied liquid, the breakthrough curve will not reach a C/C_0 value of 1.0, but will be depressed, and the observed C/C_0 value will depend on the biodegradability of the influent constituents, because biological activity continues even though the adsorption capacity has been utilized. If the liquid contains nonadsorbable and biodegradable constituents, the observed breakthrough curve will not start at zero and will not terminate at a value of 1.0. The above effects are observed quite commonly in wastewater adsorption applications, especially with respect to the removal of COD.

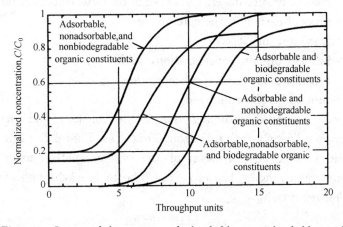

Figure 3 Impact of the presence of adsorbable, nonadsorbable, and biodegradable organic constituents on the shape of the activated carbon

Carbon Adsorption Capacity. The adsorptive capacity of a given carbon is estimated from isotherm data as follows. If isotherm data are plotted, the resulting isotherm will be as shown on Figure 4. Referring to Figure 4, the adsorptive capacity of the carbon can be estimated by extending a vertical line from the point on the horizontal axis corresponding to the initial concentration C_0, and extrapolating the isotherm to intersect this line. The $q_e = (x/m)_{C_0}$ value at the point of intersection can be read from the vertical axis. The $(q_e)_{C_0}$ value represents the amount of constituent adsorbed per unit weight of carbon when the carbon is at equilibrium with

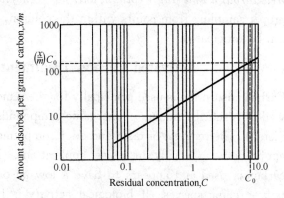

Figure 4 Typical activated carbon adsorption isotherm

the initial concentration of constituent C_0. The equilibrium condition generally exists in the upper section of a carbon bed during column treatment, and it therefore represents the ultimate capacity of the carbon for a particular waste.

Breakthrough Adsorption Capacity. In the field, the breakthrough adsorption capacity $(x/m)_b$ of the GAC in a full-scale column is some percentage of the theoretical adsorption capacity found from the isotherm. The $(x/m)_b$ of a single column can be assumed to be approximately 25 to 50 percent of the theoretical capacity, $(x/m)_0$. The value of $(x/m)_b$ can be determined using the small-scale column test described later in this section. Once $(x/m)_b$ is known, the time to breakthrough can be approximated by solving the following equation for t_b.

$$\left(\frac{x}{m}\right)_b = \frac{x_b}{m_{GAC}} = Q\left(C_0 - \frac{C_b}{2}\right)\frac{t_b}{m_{GAC}} \tag{6}$$

Where $(x/m)_b$ = field breakthrough adsorption capacity, g/g

x_b = mass of organic material adsorbed in the GAC column at breakthrough, g

m_{GAC} = mass of carbon in the column, g

Q = flowrate, m³/d

C_0 = influent organic concentration, g/m³

C_b = breakthrough organic concentration, g/m³

t_b = time to breakthrough, d

Equation (6) was developed assuming that C_0 is constant and that the effluent concentration increases linearly with time from 0 to C_b (see Figure 2). The term $(C_0 - C_b/2)$ represents the average concentration of the organic matter adsorbed up to the breakthrough point. Rearranging Eq. (6), the time to breakthrough can be calculated using the following relationship:

$$t_b = \frac{(x/m)_b m_{GAC}}{Q(C_0 - C_b/2)} \tag{7}$$

However, as noted previously, because of the breakthrough phenomenon (see Figure 4), the usual practice is either to use *two or more columns in series and rotate them as they become exhausted*, or to use *multiple columns in parallel so that breakthrough in a single column will not significantly affect the effluent quality*. With proper sampling from points within the column, constituent (e.g., TOC) breakthrough can be anticipated.

Activated Carbon Treatment Process Applications

Carbon adsorption is used principally for the removal of refractory organic compounds, as well as residual amounts of inorganic compounds such as nitrogen, sulfides, and heavy metals. The removal of taste and odor compounds from wastewater is another important application, especially in reuse applications. Both powdered and granular activated carbon is used and appears to have a low adsorption affinity for low molecular weight polar organic species. If biological activity is low in the carbon contactor or in other biological unit processes, these species are difficult to remove with activated carbon. Under normal conditions, after treatment with carbon, the effluent BOD ranges from 2 to 7 mg/L, and the effluent COD ranges from 10 to 20 mg/L. Under optimum conditions, it appears that the effluent COD can be reduced to less than 10 mg/L.

Treatment with Granular Activated Carbon (GAC). Treatment with GAC involves passing a liquid to be treated through a bed of activated carbon held in a reactor (sometimes called a contactor). Several types of activated carbon contactors are used for advanced water treatment. Typical systems may be either pressure or gravity type, and may be downflow or upflow fixed-bed units having two or three columns in series, or expanded bed upflow-countercurrent type. Typical schematic diagrams of carbon contactors are shown on Figure 5.

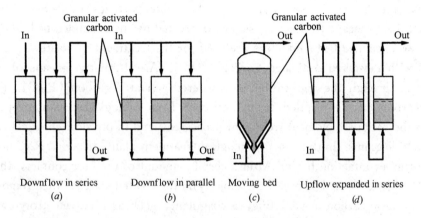

Figure 5 Types of activated carbon contactors
(a)downflow in series, (b)downflow in parallel
(c)moving ded, and(d)upflow expended in series

Fixed-Bed A fixed-bed column is used most commonly for contacting water with GAC. Fixed-bed columns can be operated singly, in series, or in parallel. Granular-medium filters are commonly used upstream of the activated carbon contactors to remove the organics associated with the suspended solids present in secondary effluent. The water to be treated is applied to the top of the column and withdrawn at the bottom. The carbon is held in place with an underdrain system at the bottom of the column. Provision for backwashing and surface washing is often provided in water applications to limit the headloss buildup due to the removal of particulate suspended solids within the carbon column. Unfortunately, backwashing has the effect of destroying the adsorption front as discussed later.

The advantage of a downflow design is that adsorption of organics and filtration of suspended solids are accomplished in a single step. Although upflow fixed-bed reactors have been used, downflow beds are used more commonly to lessen the chance of accumulating particulate material in the bottom of the bed, where the particulate material would be difficult to remove by backwashing. If soluble organic removal is not maintained at a high level, more frequent regeneration of the carbon may be required. Lack of consistency in pH, temperature, and flowrate may also affect performance of carbon contactors.

Expanded-Bed Expanded-bed, moving-bed, and pulsed-bed carbon contactors have also been developed to overcome the problems associated with headloss buildup. In the expanded-bed system, the influent is introduced at the bottom of the column and the activated carbon is allowed to expand, much as a filter bed expands during backwash. When the adsorptive capacity of the carbon at the bottom of the column is exhausted, the bottom portion of carbon is removed, and an equivalent amount of regenerated or virgin carbon is added to the top of the column. In such a system, headloss does not build up with time after the operating point has been reached. In general, expanded-bed upflow contactors may have more carbon fines in the effluent than downflow contactors because bed expansion leads to the creation of fines as the carbon particles collide and abrade, and allows the fines to escape through passageways created by the expanded bed. At present, few, if any, expanded bed contactors are used for the treatment of wastewater.

Treatment with Powdered Activated Carbon (PAC). An alternative means of achieving adsorption is through the application of powdered activated carbon (PAC). Powdered activated carbon can be applied to the effluent from biological treatment processes, directly to the various biological treatment processes, and in physical-chemical treatment process flow diagrams. In the case of biological treatment plant effluent, PAC is added to the effluent in a contacting basin. After a certain amount of time for contact, the carbon is allowed to settle to the bottom of the tank, and the treated water is then removed from the tank. Because carbon is very fine, a coagulant, such as a polyelectrolyte, may be needed to aid the removal of the carbon particles, or filtration through rapid sand filters may be required. The addition of PAC directly to the aeration basin of an activated-sludge treatment process has proved to be effective in the removal of a number of soluble refractory organics. In physical-chemical treatment processes, PAC is used in conjunction with chemicals used for the precipitation of specific constituents.

Analysis and Design of Granular Activated Carbon Contactor

The sizing of carbon contactors is based on four factors: contact time, hydraulic loading rate, carbon depth, and number of contactors. Typical design information for the first three factors is presented in Table 2. A minimum of two parallel carbon contractors is recommended for design. Multiple units permit one or more units to remain in operation while one unit is taken out of service for removal and regeneration of spent carbon, or for maintenance.

Typical design values for GAC contactors[a] — Table 2

Parameter	Symbol	Unit	Value
Volumetric flowrate	V	m^3/h	50~400
Bed volume	V_b	m^3	10~50
Cross-sectional area	A_b	m^2	5~30
Length	D	m	1.8~4
Void fraction	α	m^3/m^3	0.38~0.42
GAC density	ρ	kg/m^3	350~550

Table 2(Continued)

Parameter	Symbol	Unit	Value
Approach velocity	V_f	m/h	5~15
Effective contact time	t	min	2~10
Empty bed contact time	EBCT	min	5~30
Operation time	t	d	100~600
Throughput volume	V_L	m³	10~100
Specific throughput	V_{sp}	m³/kg	50~200
Bed volumes	BV	m³/m³	2000~20000

[a] Adapted from Sontheimer et al. (1998).

For the case where the mass transfer rate is fast and the mass transfer zone is a sharp wave front, a steady-state mass balance around a carbon contactor (see Figure 6) reactor yields:

Accumulation=inflow−outflow−amount absorbed

$$0 = QC_0 t - QC_e t - m_{GAC} q_e \qquad (8)$$

where Q = volumetric flowrate, L/h

C_0 = initial concentration of adsorbate, mg/L

t = time, h

C_e = final equilibrium concentration of adsorbate, mg/L

m_{GAC} = mass of adsorbent, g

q_e = adsorbent phase concentration after equilibrium, mg adsorbate/g adsorbent

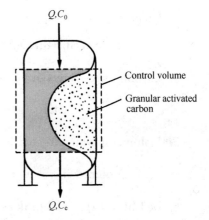

Figure 6 Definition sketch for the analysis of activated-carbon adsorption.

From Eq. (8), the adsorbent usage rate is defined as

$$\frac{m_{GAC}}{Qt} = \frac{C_0 - C_e}{q_e} \qquad (9)$$

If it is assumed that the mass of the adsorbate in the pore space is small compared to the amount adsorbed, then the term $QC_e t$ in Eq. (8) can be neglected without serious error and the absorbent usage rate is given by:

$$\frac{m_{GAC}}{Qt} \approx \frac{C_0}{q_e} \qquad (10)$$

To quantify the operational performance of GAC contactors, the following terms have been developed and are used commonly.

1. Empty-bed contact time (EBCT):

$$EBCT = \frac{V_b}{Q} = \frac{A_b D}{v_f A_b} = \frac{D}{v_f} \qquad (11)$$

Where EBCT = empty bed contact time, h

V_b = volume of GAC in contractor, m³

Q = volumetric flowrate, m³/h

A_b = cross-sectional area of GAC filter bed, m²

D = length of GAC in contactor, m

v_f = linear approach velocity, m/h

2. Activated carbon density:
The density of the activated carbon is defined as

$$\rho_{GAC} = \frac{m_{GAC}}{V_b} \quad (12)$$

where ρ_{GAC} = density of granular activated carbon, g/L
m_{GAC} = mass of granular activated carbon, g
V_b = volume of GAC filter bed, L

3. Specific throughput, expressed as m³ of water treated per gram of carbon:

$$\text{Specific throughput, m}^3/\text{g} = \frac{Qt}{m_{GAC}} = \frac{V_b t}{EBCT \times m_{GAC}} \quad (13)$$

Using Eq. (12), Eq. (13) can be written as

$$\text{Specific throughput} = \frac{V_b t}{EBCT(\rho_{GAC} \times V_b)} = \frac{t}{EBCT \, \rho_{GAC}} \quad (14)$$

4. Carbon usage rate (CUR) expressed as gram of carbon per m³ of water treated:

$$\text{CUR, g/m}^3 = \frac{m_{GAC}}{Qt} = \frac{1}{\text{Specific throughput}} \quad (15)$$

5. Volume of water treated for a given EBCT, expressed is liters, L:

$$\text{Volume of water treated, L} = \frac{\text{Mass of GAC for given EBCT}}{\text{GAC usage rate}} \quad (16)$$

6. Bed life, expressed in days, d:

$$\text{Bed life, d} = \frac{\text{Volume of water treated for given BBCT}}{Q} \quad (17)$$

Small-Scale Column Tests

Over the years, a number of small-scale column tests have been developed to simulate the results obtained with full-scale reactors. One of the early column tests was the *high-pressure minicolumn* (HPMC) technique developed by Rosene et al. (1983), and later modified by Bilello and Beaudet (1983). In the HPMC test procedure, a high-pressure liquid chromatography column loaded with activated carbon is used. Typically the HPMC test procedure is used to determine the capacity of activated carbon for the adsorption of volatile organic compounds. The principal advantage of the HPMC test procedure is that it allows for the rapid determination of the GAC adsorptive capacity under conditions similar to those encountered in the field.

An alternative procedure known as the *rapid small-scale column* test (RSSCT) has been developed by Crittenden et al. (1991). The test procedure allows for the scaling of data obtained from small columns (see Figure 7) to predict the performance of pilot or full-scale carbon columns. In developing the procedure, mathematical models were used to define the relationships between the breakthrough curve for small and large columns. In adsorption columns, the mass transfer mechanisms that are responsible for the spreading of the mass transfer zone are (1) dispersion, (2) film diffusion, and (3) interparticle diffusion. Two different design relationships were developed, one for constant diffusivity

LESSON 9

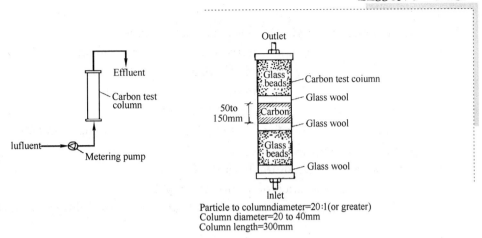

Figure 7 Small-scale column used to develop data for piot-or full-scale carbon columns

and one for proportional diffusivity. In the constant diffusivity model, it is assumed that dispersion is negligible because the hydraulic loading rate is high in the RSSCT, and that mass transfer occurs as a result of film diffusion. Further, it is assumed that the interparticle diffusivity is the same for both the small and large columns. In the proportional diffusivity model, it is assumed that dispersion is negligible because the hydraulic loading rate is high in the RSSCT, and that mass transfer occurs as a result of interparticle diffusion. The relationships between the two cases can be generalized as follows:

$$\frac{EBCT_{SC}}{EBCT_{LC}} = \left[\frac{d_{SC}}{d_{LC}}\right]^{2-x} = \frac{t_{SC}}{t_{LC}} \qquad (18)$$

$$\frac{V_{SC}}{V_{LC}} = \frac{d_{LC}}{d_{SC}} \qquad (19)$$

where d_{SC} = diameter of particle in short column, mm
d_{LC} = diameter of particle in long column, mm
t_{SC} = time in short column, min
t_{LC} = time in long column, min
V_{SC} = superficial velocity in short column, m/h
V_{LC} = superficial velocity in long column, m/h

For constant and proportional diffusivity, the value of x in the exponent in Eq. (18) is 0 and 1, respectively.

Analysis and Design of Powdered Activated Carbon Contactor

For a powdered activated carbon (PAC) application, the isotherm adsorption data can be used in conjunction with a materials mass balance analysis to obtain an approximate estimate of the amount of carbon that must be added as illustrated below. Here again, because of many unknown factors involved, column and bench scale tests are recommended to develop the necessary design data.

If a mass balance is written around the contactor (i.e., batch reactor) after equilibrium has been reached, the resulting expression is:

$$\begin{matrix} \text{Amount} & \text{initial amount} & \text{final amount} \\ \text{adsorbed} = & \text{of absorbate} - & \text{of absorbate} \\ & \text{present} & \text{present} \end{matrix} \qquad (20)$$

$$q_e m = VC_0 - VC_e \qquad (21)$$

where q_e = adsorbent phase concentration after equilibrium, mg adsorbate/g adsorbent
m = mass of adsorbent, g
V = volume of liquid in the reactor, L
C_0 = initial concentration of adsorbate, mg/L
C_e = final equilibrium concentration of adsorbate after absorption has occurred, mg/L

It should be noted that q_e is in equilibrium with C. If Eq. (21) is solved for q_e, the following expression is obtained.

$$q_e = \frac{V(C_0 - C_e)}{m} \qquad (22)$$

If Eq. (22) is rewritten as follows:

$$\frac{V}{m} = \frac{q_e}{C_0 - C_e} \qquad (23)$$

The term V/m is defined as the *specific volume* and represents the volume of liquid that can be treated with a given amount of carbon. The reciprocal value of the specific volume corresponds to the dose of adsorbent that must be used.

Activated Sludge with Powdered Activated Carbon Treatment

A proprietary process, "PACT", combines the use of powdered activated carbon with the activated-sludge process (see Figure 8). In this process, when the activated carbon is added directly to the aeration tank, biological oxidation and physical adsorption occur simultaneously. A feature of this process is that it can be integrated into existing activated sludge systems at nominal capital cost. The addition of powdered activated

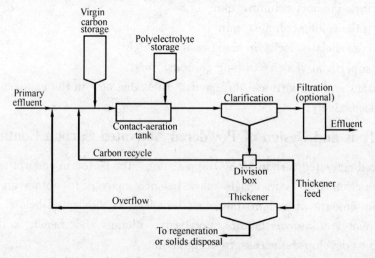

Figure 8 Definition sketch for the application of powdered activated carbon

carbon has several process advantages, including(1)system stability during shock loads, (2)reduction of refractory priority pollutants, (3)color and ammonia removal, and(4) improved sludge settleability. In some industrial waste applications, where nitrification is inhibited by toxic organics, the application of powdered activated carbon may reduce or limit this inhibition.

The dosage of powdered activated carbon and the mixed liquor-powdered activated carbon suspended solids concentration are related to the SRT as follows:

$$X_p = \frac{X_i SRT}{\tau} \qquad (24)$$

where X_p = equilibrium powdered activated carbon-MLSS content, mg/L
        X_i = powdered activated carbon dosage, mg/L
    SRT = solids retention time, d
      τ = hydraulic retention time, d

Carbon dosages typically range from 20 to 200 mg/L. With higher SRT values, the organic removal per unit of carbon is enhanced, thereby improving the process efficiency. Reasons cited for this phenomenon include (1)additional biodegradation due to decreased toxicity, (2)degradation of normally nondegradable substances due to increased exposure time to the biomass through adsorption on the carbon, and (3)replacement of low-molecular-weight compounds with high-molecular-weight compounds, resulting in improved adsorption efficiency and lower toxicity.

New Words and Phrases

extrapolate *v.* 推断，[数] 外推
refractory *adj.* 难控制的，难熔的，难降解的
affinity *n.* 亲和力
in conjunction with *adv.* 与…协力
void fraction 空隙率，孔隙率
throughput *n.* 产量，生产能力
chromatography *n.* 层析，色谱(法)

scaling *n.* 缩放比例
diffusivity *n.* 扩散能力，扩散率
superficial velocity 表观速度，空塔速度
batch reactor 序批式反应器，间歇式反应器
shock load 冲击负荷
biomass *n.* (单位面积或体积内)生物量

LESSON 10

Chemical Oxidation

Chemical oxidation in wastewater treatment typically involves the use of oxidizing agents such as ozone (O_3), hydrogen peroxide (H_2O_2), permanganate (MnO_4), chloride dioxide (ClO_2), chlorine (Cl_2) or ($HOCl$), and oxygen (O_2), to bring about changes in the chemical composition of a compound or a group of compounds. Included in the following discussion is an introduction of the fundamental concepts involved in chemical oxidation, an overview of the uses of chemical oxidation in wastewater treatment, and a discussion of the use of chemical oxidation for the reduction of BOD and COD, the oxidation of ammonia, and oxidation of nonbiodegradable organic compounds. Advanced oxidation process (AOPs) in which the free hydroxyl radical ($HO°$) is used as a strong oxidant to destroy specific organic constituents and compounds that cannot be oxidized by conventional oxidants such as ozone and chlorine are discussed in some papers, which deals with advanced treatment methods.

Fundamentals of Chemical Oxidation

The purpose of the following discussion is to introduce the basic concepts involved in chemical oxidation reactions. The topics to be discussed include (1) oxidation-reduction reactions, (2) half reaction potentials, (3) reaction potentials, (4) equilibrium constants for redox equations, and (5) rate of oxidation-reduction reactions.

Oxidation-Reduction Reactions. Oxidation-reduction reactions (known as redox equations) take place between an *oxidizing agent* and a *reducing agent*. In oxidation-reduction reactions both electrons are exchanged as are the oxidation states of the constituents involved in the reaction. While an oxidizing agent causes the oxidation to occur, it is reduced in the process. Similarly, a reducing agent that causes a reduction to occur is oxidized in the process. For example, consider the following reduction:

$$Cu^{2+} + Zn \rightleftharpoons Cu + Zn^{2+} \tag{1}$$

In the above reaction copper (Cu) changes from a $+2$ to zero oxidation state and the zinc (Zn) changes from zero to a $+2$ state. Because of the electrons gain or loss, oxidation-reduction reactions can be separated into two half reactions. The oxidation half reaction involves the loss of electrons while the reduction half reaction involves the gain of electrons. The two half reactions that comprise Eq. (1) are as follows:

$$Zn - 2e^- \rightleftharpoons Zn^{2+} \quad (\text{oxidation}) \tag{2}$$

$$Cu^{2+} + 2e^- \rightleftharpoons Cu \quad (\text{reduction}) \tag{3}$$

Referring to the above equations, there is a two-electron change.

Half-Reaction Potentials. Because of the almost infinite number of possible reactions, there are no summary tables of equilibrium constants for oxidation-reduction reactions. What is done instead is the chemical and thermodynamic characteristics of the half reactions, such as those given by Eqs. (2) and (3), are determined and tabulated so that any combination of reactions can be studied. Of the many properties that can be used to characterize oxidation-reduction reactions, the electrical potential (i. e., voltage) or emf of the half reaction is used most commonly. Thus, every half reaction involving an oxidation or reduction has a *standard potential* $E°$ associated with it. The potentials for the half reactions given by Eqs. (2) and (3) are as follows:

$$Cu^{2+} + 2e^- \rightleftharpoons Cu \quad E° = 0.34 \text{ volt} \tag{4}$$

$$Zn - 2e^- \rightleftharpoons Zn^{2+} \quad E° = 0.763 \text{ volt} \tag{5}$$

The half-reaction potential is a measure of the tendency of a reaction to proceed to the right. Half reactions with large positive potential, $E°$, tend to proceed to the right as written. Conversely, half reactions with large negative potential, $E°$, tend to proceed to the left.

Reaction Potentials. The half-reaction potentials, discussed above, can be used to predict whether a reaction comprised of two half reactions will proceed as written. The tendency of a reaction to proceed is obtained by determining the $E°_{reaction}$ for the entire reaction as given by the following expression.

$$E°_{reaction} = E°_{reduction} - E°_{oxidation} \tag{6}$$

Where $E°_{reaction}$ = potential of the overall reaction

$E°_{reduction}$ = potential of the reduction half reaction

$E°_{oxidation}$ = potential of the oxidation half reaction

For example, for the reaction between copper and zinc [see Eq. (1)] the $E°_{reaction}$ of the reaction is determined as follows:

$$E°_{reaction} = E°_{Cu^{2+},Cu} - E°_{Zn^{2+},Zn} \tag{7}$$

$$E°_{reaction} = 0.34 - (-0.763) = 1.103 \text{ volts} \tag{8}$$

The positive value for the $E°_{reaction}$ is taken as an indication that the reaction will proceed as written. The magnitude of the value, as will be illustrated subsequently, can be taken as a measure of the extent to which the reaction as written will proceed. For example, if Eq. (1) had been written as follows:

$$Cu + Zn^{2+} \rightleftharpoons Cu^{2+} + Zn \tag{9}$$

The corresponding $E°_{reaction}$ for this reaction is

$$E°_{reaction} = E°_{Zn^{2+},Zn} - E°_{Cu^{2+},Cu} \tag{10}$$

$$E°_{reaction} = -0.763 - 0.34 = -1.103 \text{ volts} \tag{11}$$

Because the $E°_{reaction}$ for the reaction is negative, the reaction will proceed in the opposite direction from what is written.

Equilibrium Constants for Redox Equation. The equilibrium constant for oxidation-reduction reactions is calculated using the Nernst equation as defined below.

$$\ln K = \frac{nFE°_{reaction}}{RT} \tag{12a}$$

$$\log K = \frac{nFE°_{reaction}}{2.303RT} \tag{12b}$$

where K = equilibrium constant

n = number of electrons exchanged in the overall reaction

F = Faraday's constant

= 96485 a·s/g eq = 96485 C/g eq (Note: C = coulomb)

$E^\circ_{reaction}$ = reaction potential

R = universal gas constant

= 8.3144 J (abs)/(mole·K)

T = temperature, K (273.15 + ℃)

Rate of Oxidation-Reduction Reactions. As noted previously, the half-reaction potentials can be used to predict whether a reaction will proceed as written. Unfortunately, the reaction potential provides no information about the rate at which the reaction will proceed. Chemical oxidation reactions often require the presence of one or more catalysts for the reaction to proceed or to increase the rate of reaction. Transition metal cations, enzymes, pH adjustment, and a variety of proprietary substances have been used as catalysts.

Applications. In the past, chemical oxidation was used most commonly to (1) reduce the concentration of residual organics, (2) control odors, (3) remove ammonia, and (4) reduce the bacterial and viral content of wastewater. Chemical oxidation is especially effective for the elimination of odorous compounds (e.g., oxidation of sulfides and mercaptans). Now chemical oxidation is commonly used to (1) improve the treatability of nonbiodegradable (refractory) organic compounds, (2) eliminate the inhibitory effects of certain organic and inorganic compounds to microbial growth, and (3) reduce or eliminate the toxicity of certain organic and inorganic compounds to microbial growth and aquatic flora. The chemical oxidation of BOD and COD, ammonia, and refractory organic compounds is considered in this section.

Chemical Oxidation of BOD and COD

The overall reaction for the oxidation of organic molecules comprising BOD, for example, with chlorine, ozone, and hydrogen peroxide, can be represented as follows:

$$\text{Organic molecule (e.g., BOD)} \xrightarrow[H_2O_2]{Cl, O_3} \text{Intermediate oxygenated molecules} \xrightarrow[H_2O_2]{Cl, O_3} \text{Simple end products (e.g., } CO_2, H_2O, \text{etc.)} \quad (13)$$

Multiple arrows in the direction of the reaction are used to signify that a number of steps are involved in the overall reaction sequence. The use of oxidizing agents such as oxygen, chlorine, ozone, and hydrogen peroxide is termed "simple oxidation". In general the overall reaction rates are usually too slow to be applicable generally for wastewater treatment. Advanced oxidation processes (AOPs), which typically involve the use of the hydroxyl radical for the oxidation of complex organic molecules, are considered in other literatures.

Chemical Oxidation of Nonbiodegradable Organic Compounds. Typical chemical dosages for both chlorine and ozone for the oxidation of the organics in wastewater are reported in Table 1. As shown in Table 1, the dosages increase with the degree of treatment, which is reasonable when it is considered that the organic compounds that remain after biological treatment are typically composed of low-molecular-weight polar organic compounds and complex organic compounds built around the benzene ring structure. Because of the complexities associated with composition of wastewater, chemical dosages for the removal of refractory organic compounds cannot be derived from the chemical stoichiometry, assuming that it is known. Pilot-plant studies must be conducted when either chlorine, chlorine dioxide, or ozone is to be used for the oxidation of refractory organics to assess both the efficacy and required dosages.

Typical chemical dosages for the oxidation of organics in wastewater Table 1

Chemical	Use	Dosage kg/kg destroyed	
		Range	Typical
Chlorine	BOD reduction		
	Settled wastewater	0.5~2.5	1.75
	Secondary efffluent	1.0~3.2	2.0
Ozone	COD reduction		
	Settled wastewater	2.0~4.0	3.0
	Secondary efffluent	3.0~8.0	6.0

Chemical Oxidation of Ammonia

The chemical process in which chlorine is used to oxidize the ammonia nitrogen in solution to nitrogen gas and other stable compounds is known as breakpoint chlorination. Perhaps the most important advantage of this process is that, with proper control, all the ammonia nitrogen in the wastewater can be oxidized. However, because the process has a number of disadvantages including the buildup of acid (HCl) which will react with the alkalinity, the buildup of total dissolved solids, and the formation of unwanted chloro-organic compounds, ammonia oxidation is seldom used today.

Application. The breakpoint chlorination process can be used for the removal of ammonia nitrogen from treatment-plant effluents, either alone or in combination with other processes. To avoid the large chlorine dosages required when used alone, break-point chlorination can be used following biological nitrification to achieve low levels of ammonia in the effluent.

To optimize the performance of this process and to minimize equipment and facility costs, flow equalization is usually required. Also, because of the potential toxicity problems that may develop if chlorinated compounds are discharged to the environment, it is usually necessary to dechlorinate the effluent.

New Words and Phrases

chemical oxidation 化学氧化
hydrogen peroxide (H_2O_2) 过氧化氢
free hydroxyl radical 自由羟基
Advanced oxidation process (AOPs)

	高级氧化工艺	permanganate　*n.* 高锰酸盐
oxidation-reduction reaction	氧化还原反应	redox　*n.* 氧化还原作用
		half reaction potential　半反应电势
oxidizing agent　氧化剂		thermodynamic　*adj.* 热力学的
reducing agent　还原剂		emf *abbr.* (electromotive force)　电动势
standard potential　标准电势		catalyst　*n.* 催化剂
transition metal　过渡金属		enzyme　*n.* 酶
aquatic flora　水生植物区系，水生植物志		sulfide　*n.* 硫化物
end product　终产物		mercaptan　*n.* 硫醇
benzene ring　苯环		inhibitory　*adj.* 抑制的
chloro-organic compound　氯化有机化合物		efficacy　*n.* 功效，效验
		chlor(o)-　氯化

Questions

1. What function does the half-reaction potential have?
2. What matter can be used as catalyst?
3. Where can the chemical oxidation be used?
4. Please describe the overall reaction for the oxidation of organic molecules comprising BOD.
5. Why do the dosages for both chlorine and ozone for the oxidation of the organics in wastewater increase with the degree of treatment?
6. What is the characteristic of breakpoint chlorination?

Reading Material

Disinfection

The unit processes described in the previous sections—coagulation, sedimentation, and filtration—together compose a type of treatment called *clarification*. Clarification removes many microorganisms from the water along with the suspended solids. But clarification by itself is not sufficient to ensure the complete removal of pathogenic bacteria or viruses. A potable water must be more than crystal clear—it must be completely free of disease-causing microorganisms. To accomplish this, the final treatment process in water treatment plants is *disinfection*, which destroys or inactivates the pathogens.

Chlorination

Chlorine is the most commonly used substance for disinfection in the United States. The addition of chlorine or chlorine compounds to water is called *chlorination*. Chlorination is considered to be the single most important process for preventing the spread of waterborne disease.

Molecular chlorine, Cl_2, is a greenish-yellow gas at ordinary room temperature and pressure. In gaseous form it is very toxic, and even in low concentrations it is a severe irritant. But when the chlorine is dissolved in low concentrations in clean water, it is not harmful, and if it is properly applied, objectionable tastes and odors due to the chlorine and its by-products are not noticeable to the average person.

Although chlorine is effective in destroying pathogens and preventing the spread of communicable disease, there may be an indirect noninfectious health problem caused by the chlorination process. Natural waters often contain trace amounts of organic compounds, primarily from natural sources such as decaying vegetation. These substances can react with the chlorine to form compounds called *trihalomethanes* (THMs), which may cause cancer in humans. Chloroform is an example of a THM compound.

The EPA has set standards that limit the maximum amount of THM compounds in drinking water. One way to prevent THM formation is to make sure that the chlorine is added to the water only after clarification and the removal of most of the organics. Also, alternative methods of disinfection are available that do not use chlorine. These are discussed later in this section.

Chlorination Chemistry. When chlorine is dissolved in pure water, it reacts with the H^+ ions and the OH^- ions in the water. Two of the products of this reaction are *hypochlorous acid*, $HOCl$, and the *hypochlorite ion*, OCl^-. These are the actual disinfecting agents. If microorganisms are present in the water, $HOCl$ and OCl^- penetrate the microbe cells and react with certain enzymes. This reaction disrupts the organisms' metabolism and kills them.

Hypochlorous acid is a more effective disinfectant than the hypochlorite ion because it diffuses faster through the microbe cell wall. The relative concentrations of $HOCl$ and OCl^- depend on the pH of the water. The lower the pH, the more $HOCl$ there is relative to the OCl^-. In general, then, the lower the pH of the water, the more effective is the chlorination-disinfection process.

When chlorine is first added to water containing some impurities, the chlorine immediately reacts with the dissolved inorganic or organic substances and is then unavailable for disinfection. The amount of chlorine used up in this initial reaction is called the *chlorine demand* of the water. If dissolved ammonia, NH_3, is present in the water, the chlorine reacts with it to form compounds called *chloramines*. Only after the chlorine demand is satisfied and the reaction with all the dissolved ammonia is complete is the chlorine actually available in the form of $HOCl$ and OCl^-.

Chlorine in the form of $HOCl$ and OCl^- is called *free available chlorine*, whereas chloramines are referred to as *combined chlorine*. Free chlorine is often the preferred form for disinfection of drinking water. It works faster than combined chlorine, and it does not cause objectionable tastes and odors. Combined chlorine is also effective as a disinfectant, but it is slower acting and it may cause the typical swimming-pool odor of chlorinated water. Its advantage is that it lasts longer and can maintain sanitary protection throughout the water distribution system.

A process called *breakpoint chlorination* is sometimes used to ensure the presence of free chlorine in public water supplies. To do this, it is necessary to add enough chlorine to the water to satisfy the chlorine demand and to react with all the dissolved ammonia. When this occurs, it is said that the chlorine breakpoint has been reached. Chlorine added beyond the breakpoint will be available as a free chlorine residual in direct proportion to the amount of chlorine added. This is illustrated in Figure 1. The chlorine demand and the breakpoint dose vary, depending on the water quality. Sometimes, chlorine doses up to 10 mg/L are needed to obtain a free chlorine residual of 0.5 mg/L.

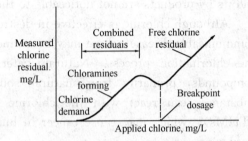

Figure 1 Breakpoint chlorination curve

Chlorination Methods. Chlorine is commercially available in gaseous form or in the form of solid and liquid compounds called *hypochlorites*. For the disinfection of relatively large volumes of water, the gaseous form of chlorine is generally the most economical, but for smaller volumes, the use of hypochlorite compounds is more common.

Gaseous chlorine is stored and shipped in pressurized steel cylinders. Under pressure, the chlorine is actually in liquid form in the cylinder; when it is released from the cylinder, it vaporizes into a gas. The cylinders may range in capacity from 45 kg (100 lb) to about 1000 kg (1 ton). Very large water (or wastewater) treatment plants may use special railroad tank cars filled with chlorine.

A device called an *all-vacuum chlorinator* is considered to provide the safest type of chlorine feed installation. It is mounted directly on the chlorine cylinder. The gaseous chlorine is always under a partial vacuum in the line that carries it to the point of application; chlorine leaks cannot occur in that line. A typical vacuum chlorine feed system is shown in Figure 2. The vacuum is formed by water flowing through the ejector unit at high velocity. There are other types of chlorinators, some of which have the chlorine or concentrated chlorine solutions conveyed relatively long distances under pressure. These present somewhat greater risks of chlorine leaks. In any chlorine feed installation, safety factors are very important because of the toxicity of the gas.

Hypochlorites are usually applied to water in liquid form by means of small pumps, such as the one illustrated in Figure 3. These are *positive-displacement-type* pumps, which deliver a specific amount of liquid on each stroke of a piston or flexible diaphragm.

Two types of hypochlorite compounds are available for disinfection: *sodium hypochlorite* and *calcium hypochlorite*. Sodium hypochlorite is available only in liquid form and contains up to 15 percent available chlorine. It is usually diluted with water before being applied as a disinfectant. (Common laundry bleach is a 5 percent solution of

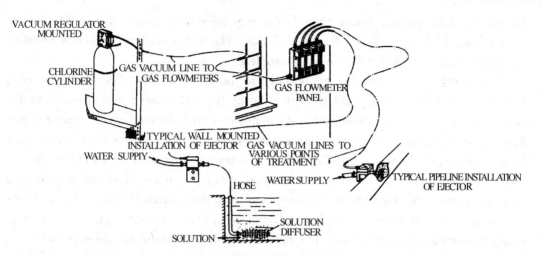

Figure 2 Typical vacuum-feed chlorination system. There is little risk of a chlorine gas leak because the chlorine feed line is at less than atmospheric pressure

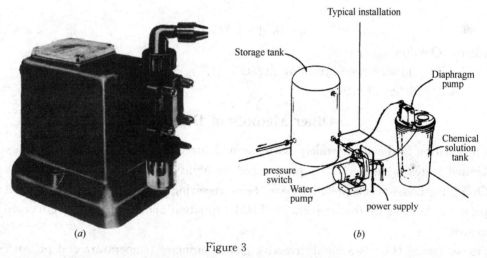

Figure 3
(a) Typical hypochlorinator or solution metering pump and (b) a typical hypochlorinator installation

sodium hypochlorite.) Calcium hypochlorite is a dry compound, available in granular or tablet form; it is readily soluble in water. Calcium hypochlorite solutions are more stable than solutions of sodium hypochlorite, which deteriorate over time.

In addition to pH, the effectiveness of chlorine and chlorine compounds in destroying bacteria depends on the chlorine concentration and the *contact time*. Contact time is the time period during which the free or combined chlorine is acting on the microorganisms. At pH values close to 7 (neutral conditions), a free chlorine residual of 0.2 mg/L with a 10-min contact time has about the same disinfecting power as 1.5 mg/L of combined chlorine residual with a 1-h contact time.

The effectiveness of chlorination can be determined by the coliform test or by a more convenient test for chlorine residual in the treated water. The method approved for chlorine residual testing, under the SDWA regulations, is called the *DPD chlorine residual test*. Field test kits are readily available. The test procedure, which is based on a color comparison, takes only 5 min to complete.

In the DPD test, a chemical dye is added to the water sample. The dye turns red if chlorine residual is present, and the intensity of the red color is proportional to the chlorine concentration. It is assumed that the presence of a chlorine residual ensures that there are no surviving pathogenic organisms in the water. It is possible to measure either the total residual, the free residual, or the combined residual with the DPD test kit.

It is often necessary to compute the total weight or mass of chlorine used at a treatment plant to be able to order chlorine supplies at the appropriate time. Also, it may be necessary to determine the applied chlorine dosage or concentration if the mass or weight consumed is known. The following relationships are useful for these purposes:

$$kg/d = Q \times C \quad (14a)$$

where Q = flow rate, ML/d
  C = chlorine concentration, mg/L

or

$$lb/d = 8.34 \times Q \times C \quad (14b)$$

where Q = flow rate, mgd
  C = chlorine concentration, mg/L
  8.34 = lb/gal of water

Other Methods of Disinfection

Chlorination is the most widely used method for disinfection of water supplies in the United States because of its economy and its ability to maintain a protective residual. Other methods of disinfection have been receiving more attention in recent years, primarily because of the problem of THM formation and the potential effect on public health.

Ozone. Ozone (O_3) is a highly reactive gas at ordinary temperature and pressures, and acts as a very potent disinfectant when mixed with water. It has been used for over 90 years in European countries as an alternative to chlorine, which sometimes leaves a noticeable taste and odor in drinking water. Ozone can be produced by passing a very high voltage electric current through air or oxygen. However, because it is very unstable and cannot be stored, it must be manufactured on site, where it is used. And because it does not leave a measurable residual in water after the initial contact time, some chlorine (although in relatively smaller amounts) must be used to ensure continued disinfection as the water flows throughout the network of water distribution pipes.

In addition to the ability of ozone to act as a disinfectant without causing taste and odor problems, it does not react to form THM (trihalomethane) compounds. Ozone is also a stronger disinfectant than chlorine and is able to inactivate most viruses in addition to bacteria. (It is approved by the EPA for disinfection.) It can assist as a coagulant when used with alum, thus reducing the amount of chemicals needed to adjust the final pH of the water to make it noncorrosive. Because it greatly aids the coagulation process, ozone can also facilitate the application of a direct filtration process and eliminate the need for large sedimentation basins.

Despite these advantages, the high cost of its production and application compared to that for chlorine has discouraged widespread use of ozone for disinfection in the United States. There are some notable exceptions to this. For example, ozone is used at the 1900ML/d (500-mgd) Los Angeles water treatment plant. It is also used for clarification and disinfection at the 570ML/d (150-mgd) water treatment plant in Haworth, New Jersey. Both these plants also use the direct filtration process. A flow diagram showing major treatment steps at the Haworth plant is shown in Figure 4.

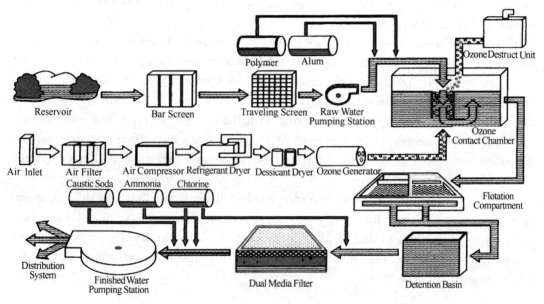

Figure 4 A flow diagram of the ozone water purification process at United Water Resources Haworth water treatment plant. Major steps in the process include:

Step 1: Raw reservoir water is drawn in to the treatment process by intake pumps. As the water enters the plant, bar screens remove large particles, and small amounts of chemical coagulants are added to help remove small particles and clarify the water.

Step 2: Outside air from which ozone is generated is first filtered, cooled, and dried.

Step 3: The treated air passes over many glass tubes, each individually fused with an electric filament; a lightning-like electrical charge transforms oxygen in the air to a mixture of ozone and oxygen.

Step 4: In the ozone contact chamber, small ozone bubbles move upward as water flows downward in a counter current. The rising bubbles help to mix the coagulants and water, carry small particles upward, and destroy bacteria and viruses. Any remaining ozone is converted back into oxygen by a catalytic converter in the ozone destruction unit.

Step 5: The ozone-treated water flows to flotation compartments, where skimmers remove the floating materials.

Step 6: The skimmed water flows into detention basins, where additional particles settle out.

Step 7: The water flows by gravity down through dual-media granular filters.

Step 8: Small amounts of chlorine are added to ensure continued disinfection of the water in the distribution system, and other chemicals are added to eliminate corrosion and the likelihood of lead dissolving into the water from household plumbing.

Step 9: Large electrically powered pumps push up to 200 mgd of the treated water into the distribution system.

Ozone is more effective than chlorine as a disinfectant when used to prevent outbreaks of cryptosporidiosis. Water treatment facilities in Milwaukee, Wisconsin, were recently upgraded for just this purpose.

Note: *Cryptosporidium* is a protozoan parasite that can move through the aquatic environment in the form of microscopic egg-shaped capsules called *oocysts*. Oocysts, the dormant stage of organism, are typically 1/20 the thickness of the strand of human of hair (about 5 μm) and are resistant to ordinary filtration and chlorination. Drinking water contaminated with these pathogens causes gastrointestinal illness (severe cramps and diarrhea) in humans. The effects can be fatal, particularly for people with weakened immune systems. Cryptosporidia capable of infecting humans can come from cattle manure that washes off the land into lakes and streams, or from human waste if it is not treated before entering surface water.

Ultraviolet Radiation. Ultraviolet (UV) light can be used for disinfection. Ultraviolet light is electromagnetic radiation just beyond the blue end of the light spectrum, outside the range of visible light. It has a much higher energy level than visible light, and in large doses it destroys bacteria and viruses. The UV energy is absorbed by genetic material in the microorganisms, interfering with their ability to reproduce and survive. UV light can be generated by a variety of lamps; submerged, low-pressure mercury lamps are best suited for use in disinfection systems because they generate a large fraction of UV energy that gets absorbed.

Ultraviolet disinfection systems do not involve chemical handling, as do chlorine or ozone systems, thereby minimizing chemical safety concerns. Like ozone, though, UV radiation leaves no measurable residual in the water. Advances in UV germicidal lamp technology are making UV disinfection a more reliable and economical option for disinfection.

New Words and Phrases

inactivate   v. 灭活
irritant   n. 刺激物
    adj. 刺激的
noninfectious   adj. 无传染性的
decaying vegetation   腐殖质
trihalomethane   三卤甲烷
chloroform   n. 氯仿
hypochlorous acid   n. 次氯酸
hypochlorite   n. 次氯酸盐
chloramine   n. [化]氯胺
hose   n. 软管,水龙带
diffuser   n. 分散器
ejector (jet pump)   n. 射流泵
positive-displacement-type pump   容积式泵
piston   n. [机]活塞,瓣
diaphragm   n. 隔膜,照相机镜头上的光圈 振动膜
protozoan   n. 原生动物
dessicant   n. 干燥剂
caustic soda   n. 苛性钠
intake pump   n. 取水泵
filament   n. 细丝,灯丝
catalytic converter   n. 催化转化器
likelihood   n. 可能,可能性
genetic   adj. 遗传的,起源的
germicidal   adj. 杀菌的,有杀菌力的

Ion Exchange

Ion exchange is a unit process in which ions of a given species are displaced from an insoluble exchange material by ions of a different species in solution. The most widespread use of this process is in domestic water softening, where sodium ions from a cationic-exchange resin replace the calcium and magnesium ions in the treated water, thus reducing the hardness. Ion exchange has been used in water and wastewater applications for the removal of nitrogen, heavy metals, and total dissolved solids.

Ion-exchange processes can be operated in a batch or continuous mode. In a batch process, the resin is stirred with the water to be treated in a reactor until the reaction is complete. The spent resin is removed by settling and subsequently is regenerated and reused. In a continuous process, the exchange material is placed in a bed or a packed column, and the water to be treated is passed through it. Continuous ion exchangers are usually of the downflow, packed-bed column type. Water enters the top of the column under pressure, passes downward through the resin bed, and is removed at the bottom. When the resin capacity is exhausted, the column is backwashed to remove trapped solids and is then regenerated.

Ion-Exchange Materials

Naturally occurring ion-exchange materials, known as zeolites, are used for water softening and ammonium ion removal. Zeolites used for water softening are complex aluminosilicates with sodium as the mobile ion. Ammonium exchange is accomplished using a naturally occurring zeolite clinoptilolite. Synthetic aluminosilicates are manufactured, but most synthetic ion-exchange materials are resins or phenolic polymers. Five types of synthetic ion-exchange resins are in use: (1) strong-acid cation, (2) weak-acid cation, (3) strong-base anion, (4) weak-base anion, and (5) heavy-metal selective chelating resins. The properties of these resins are summarized in Table 1.

Table 1

Classification of ion-exchange resins[a]

Type of resin	Characteristics
Strong-acid cation resins	Strong-acid resins behave in a manner similar to a strong acid, and are highly ionized in both the acid ($R\text{-}SO_3H$) and salt ($R\text{-}SO_3Na$) form, over the entire pH range
Weak-acid cation resins	Weak-acid cation exchangers have a weak-acid functional group (-COOH), typically a carboxylic group. These resins behave like weak organic acids that are weakly dissociated

Table 1(Continued)

Type of resin	Characteristics
Strong-base anion resins	Strong-base resins are highly ionized, having strong-base functional groups such as (OH), and can be used over the entire pH range. These resins are used in the hydroxide (OH) form for water deionization
Weak-base anion resins	Weak-base resins have weak-base functional groups in which the degree of ionization is dependent on pH
Heavy-metal selective chelating resins	Chelating resins behave like weak-acid cation resins but exhibit a high degree of selectivity for heavy-metal cations. The functional group in most of these resins is EDTA, and the resin structure in the sodium form is R-EDTA-Na

^aAdapted in part from Eckenfelder (2000).

Most synthetic ion-exchange resins are manufactured by a process in which styrene and divinylbenzene are copolymerized. The styrene serves as the basic matrix of the resin, and divinylbenzene is used to cross-link the polymers to produce an insoluble tough resin. Important properties of ion-exchange resins include exchange capacity, particle size, and stability. The exchange capacity of a resin is defined as the quantity of an exchangeable ion that can be taken up. The exchange capacity of resins is expressed as eq/L or eq/kg (meq/L or meq/g). The particle size of a resin is important with respect to the hydraulics of the ion-exchange column and the kinetics of ion exchange. In general, the rate of exchange is proportional to the inverse of the square of the particle diameter. The stability of a resin is important to the long-term performance of the resin. Excessive osmotic swelling and shrinking, chemical degradation, and structural changes in the resin caused by physical stresses are important factors that may limit the useful life of a resin.

Typical Ion-Exchange Reactions

Typical ion-exchange reactions for natural and synthetic ion-exchange materials are given below.

For natural zeolites (Z):

$$ZNa_2 + \begin{bmatrix} Ca^{2+} \\ Mg^{2+} \\ Fe^{2+} \end{bmatrix} \rightleftharpoons Z\begin{bmatrix} Ca^{2+} \\ Mg^{2+} \\ Fe^{2+} \end{bmatrix} + 2Na^+ \tag{1}$$

For synthetic resins (R):

Strong-acid cation exchange:

$$RSO_3H + Na^+ \rightleftharpoons RSO_3Na + H^+ \tag{2}$$

$$2RSO_3Na + Ca^{2+} \rightleftharpoons (RSO_3)_2Ca + 2Na^+ \tag{3}$$

Weak-acid cation exchange:

$$RCCOOH + Na^+ \rightleftharpoons RCOONa + H^+ \tag{4}$$

$$2RCOONa + Ca^{2+} \rightleftharpoons (RCOO)_2Ca + 2Na^+ \tag{5}$$

Strong-base anion exchange:
$$RR'_3NOH + Cl^- \rightleftharpoons RR'_3NCl + OH^- \quad (6)$$

Weak-base anion exchange:
$$RNH_3OH + Cl^- \rightleftharpoons RNH_3Cl + OH^- \quad (7)$$
$$2RNH_3Cl + SO_4^{2-} \rightleftharpoons (RNH_3)_2SO_4 + 2Cl^- \quad (8)$$

Exchange Capacity of Ion-Exchange Resins

Reported exchange capacities vary with the type and concentration of regenerant used to restore the resin. Typical synthetic resin exchange capacities are in the range of 2 to 10 eq/kg of resin; zeolite cation exchangers have exchange capacities of 0.05 to 0.1 eq/kg. Exchange capacity is measured by placing the resin in a known form. A cationic resin would be washed with a strong acid to place all of the exchange sites on the resin in the H^+ form or washed with a strong NaCl brine to place all of the exchange sites in the Na^+ form. A solution of known concentration of an exchangeable ion (e.g., Ca^{2+}) can then be added until exchange is complete and the amount of exchange capacity can be measured, or in the acid case, the resin is titrated with a strong base.

Exchange capacities for resins often are expressed in terms of grams $CaCO_3$ per cubic meter of resin (g/m^3) or gram equivalents per cubic meter ($g\ eq/m^3$). Conversion between these two units is accomplished using the following expression:

$$\frac{1\ eq}{m^3} = \frac{(1\ eq)(50\ g\ CaCO_3/eq)}{m^3} = 50\ g\ CaCO_3/m^3 \quad (9)$$

Ion-Exchange Chemistry

The chemistry of the ion-exchange process may be represented by the following equilibrium expression for the reaction of constituent A on a cation-exchange resin and constituent B in solution.

$$nR^-A^+ + B^{+n} \rightleftharpoons R_n^-B^{+n} + nA^+ \quad (10)$$

Where R^- is the anionic group attached to an ion-exchange resin and A and B are cations in solution. The generalized form of the equilibrium expression for the above reaction is

$$\frac{[A^+]_s^n[R_n^-B^{+n}]_R}{[R^-A^+]_R^n[B^{+n}]_s} = K_{A^+ \rightarrow B^{+n}} \quad (11)$$

where $K_{A^+ \rightarrow B^{+n}}$ = selectivity coefficient
$[A^+]_s$ = concentration of A in solution
$[R^-A^+]_R$ = concentration A on the exchange resin

The reactions for the removal of sodium (Na^+) and calcium (Ca^{2+}) ions from water using a strong-acid synthetic cationic-exchange resin R, and the regeneration of the exhausted resins with hydrochloric acid (HCl) and sodium chloride (NaCl) are as follows:

Reaction:

$$R^-H^+ + Na^+ \rightleftharpoons R^-Na^+ + H^+ \tag{12}$$

$$2R^-Na^+ + Ca^{2+} \rightleftharpoons R_2^-Ca^{2+} + 2Na^+ \tag{13}$$

Regeneration:

$$R^-Na^+ + HCl \rightleftharpoons R^-H^+ + NaCl \tag{14}$$

$$R_2^-Ca^+ + 2NaCl \rightleftharpoons 2R^-Na^+ + CaCl_2 \tag{15}$$

The corresponding equilibrium expressions for sodium and calcium are as follows:
For sodium:

$$\frac{[H^+][R^-Na^+]}{[R^-H^+][Na^+]} = K_{H \to Na} \tag{16}$$

For calcium:

$$\frac{[Na^+]^2[R^-Ca^{2+}]}{[R^-Na^+]^2[Ca^+]} = K_{Na \to Ca} \tag{17}$$

The selectivity coefficient depends primarily on the nature and valence of the ion, the type of resin and its saturation, and the ion concentration in wastewater and typically is valid over a narrow pH range. In fact, for a given series of similar ions, exchange resins have been found to exhibit an order of selectivity or affinity for the ions.

For synthetic cationic and anionic exchange resins, typical series are

$$Li^+ < H^+ < Na^+ < NH_4 < K^+ < Rb^+ < Ag^+ \tag{18}$$

$$Mg^{2+} < Zn^{2+} < Co^{2+} < Cu^{2+} < Ca^{2+} < Sr^{2+} < Ba^{2+} \tag{19}$$

$$OH^- < F^- < HCO^- < Cl^- < Br^- < NO_3^- < ClO_4^- \tag{20}$$

In practice, the selectivity coefficients are determined by measurement in the laboratory and are valid only in the conditions under which they were measured. At low concentrations, the value of the selectivity coefficient for the exchange of monovalent ions by divalent ions is, in general, larger than the exchange of monovalent ions by monovalent ions. This fact has, in many cases, limited the use of synthetic resins for the removal of certain substances in wastewater, such as ammonia in the form of the ammonium ion. There are, however, certain natural zeolites that favor NH_4^+ or Cu^{2+}.

Anderson (1975) in a classic paper developed a method that can be used to evaluate the effectiveness of a proposed ion-exchange process using strong ionic resins. In the development proposed by Anderson, it is assumed that at 100 percent leakage, the effluent concentration of a constituent is equal to the influent concentration (i.e., equilibrium has been reached). The equilibrium condition can be assumed to be either the limiting operating exchange capacity of the resin or the capacity corresponding to the maximum regeneration level that can be attained. Using this assumption, Eq. (11) is converted from concentration units to units of equivalent fractions by making the following substitutions:

$$X_{A^+} = \frac{[A^+]_S}{C} \text{ and } X_{B^+} = \frac{[B^+]_S}{C} \tag{21}$$

$$X_{A^+} + X_{B^+} = 1 \tag{22}$$

where X_A^+ and X_B^+ are the equivalent fractions of A and B in solution and C is the total cationic or anionic concentration in solution.

$$\overline{X}_{A^+} = \frac{[R^-A^+]_R}{\overline{C}} \text{ and } \overline{X}_{B^+} = \frac{[R^-B^+]_R}{\overline{C}} \tag{23}$$

$$\overline{X}_{A^+} + \overline{X}_{B^+} = 1 \tag{24}$$

where $\overline{X}_{A^+}$ and $\overline{X}_{B^+}$ are the equivalent fractions of A and B in the resin and $\overline{C}$ is the total ionic concentration in the resin (i.e., the total resin capacity in eq/L). Substituting the above terms into Eq. (11) and simplifying results in the following expression:

$$\frac{\overline{X}_{B^+} \cdot X_{A^+}}{\overline{X}_{A^+} \cdot X_{B^+}} = K_{A^+ \to B^+} \tag{25}$$

Substituting for X_A and $\overline{X}_A$ in Eq. (25) results in

$$\frac{\overline{X}_{B^+}}{1 - \overline{X}_{B^+}} = [K_{A^+ \to B^+}] \cdot \left[\frac{X_{B^+}}{1 - X_{B^+}}\right] \tag{26}$$

It should be noted that Eq. (26) is only valid for exchanges between monovalent ions on fully ionized exchange resins. The distribution of a single monovalent ion A between the solution and the resin for different values of the selectivity coefficient is presented on Figure 1. The distribution curves can be used to assess the effectiveness of a resin for the removal of a given ion, based on the selectivity coefficient.

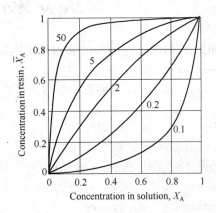

Figure 1 Distribution curves for a single monovalent ion A between the solution and the resin for different values of the selectivity

The following three attributes of Eq. (26) were identified by Anderson (1975).

1. The term $\overline{X}_B/(1-\overline{X}_B)$ corresponds to the state of the resin in an exchange column when the influent and effluent concentrations are the same.

2. The term $\overline{X}_B$ corresponds to the extent to which the resin can be converted to the B^+ form when the resin is in equilibrium with a solution of composition X_B.

3. The term $\overline{X}_B$ also corresponds to the maximum extent of regeneration that can be achieved with a regenerant composition of X_B.

The corresponding equation for exchanges between monovalent and divalent ions on a fully ionized exchange resin is

$$\frac{\overline{X}_{B^{2+}}}{(1-\overline{X}_B{}^{2+})^2} = [K_{A^+ \to B^{2+}}] \cdot \left[\frac{\overline{C}}{C}\right] \cdot \frac{X_{B^{2+}}}{(1-X_B{}^{2+})^2} \tag{27}$$

Operational Considerations

To make ion exchange economical for advanced wastewater treatment, it would be desirable to use regenerants and restorants that would remove both the inorganic anions and the organic material from the spent resin. Chemical and physical restorants found to be successful in the removal of organic material from resins include sodium hydroxide, hydrochloric acid, methanol, and bentonite. To date, ion exchange has had limited application because of the extensive pretreatment required, concerns about the life of the ion-exchange resins, and the complex regeneration system required.

High concentrations of influent TSS can plug the ion-exchange beds, causing high headlosses and inefficient operation. Resin binding can be caused by residual organics found in biological treatment effluents. Some form of chemical treatment and clarification is required before ion-exchange demineralization. This problem has been solved partially by prefiltering the wastewater or by using scavenger exchange resins before application to the exchange column.

New Words and Phrases

cationic-exchange resin　阳离子交换树脂
resin　n. 树脂
zeolite　n. 沸石, 与沸石类似的天然的或人工的硅酸盐
aluminosilicate　n. 硅酸铝
clinoptilolite　n. 斜发沸石
phenolic　adj. 酚的, 石碳酸的
chelate　adj. 有螯的, 螯合的
carboxylic　adj. 羧基的
styrene　n. 苯乙烯
divinylbenzene　n. 二乙烯苯
copolymerize　v. (使)共聚合
matrix　n. 基体, 基质
tough　adj. 强硬的, 坚韧的

osmotic　adj. 渗透的, 渗透性的
swell　v. (使)膨胀, 增大
shrink　v. 收缩, (使)皱缩, 缩短
regenerant　n. 再生剂
divalent　adj. 二价的
leakage　n. 泄漏, 渗漏
equivalent fractions　当量份数
restorant　n. 恢复剂
methanol　n. 甲醇
bentonite　n. 斑脱土(火山灰分解成的一种黏土), 膨润土
to date　adv. 到此为止
bind　v. 约束, 凝固
scavenger　n. 清洗剂, 净化剂

Questions

1. What is the definition of ion exchange?
2. How many types of synthetic ion-exchange materials are there? What are they?
3. What terms can be used to express the exchange capacities for resins?
4. What factors do the selectivity coefficient depend on?
5. What materials can be used to remove organic material from resins?

LESSON 11

Reading Material

Application of Ion Exchange

As noted previously, ion exchange has been used in wastewater applications for the removal of nitrogen, heavy metals, and total dissolved solids.

For Nitrogen Control. For nitrogen control, the ions typically removed from the waste stream are ammonium, NH_4^+, and nitrate, NO_3^-. The ion that the ammonium displaces varies with the nature of the solution used to regenerate the bed. Although both natural and synthetic ion-exchange resins are available, synthetic resins are used more widely because of their durability. Some natural resins (zeolites) have found application in the removal of ammonia from wastewater. *Clinoptilolite*, a naturally occurring zeolite, has proved to be one of the best natural exchange resins. In addition to having a greater affinity for ammonium ions than other ion-exchange materials, it is relatively inexpensive when compared to synthetic media. One of the novel features of this zeolite is the regeneration system employed. Upon exhaustion, the zeolite is regenerated with lime $Ca(OH)_2$, and the ammonium ion removed from the zeolite is converted to ammonia because of the high pH. A flow diagram for this process is shown on Figure 2. The stripped liquid is collected in a storage tank for subsequent reuse. A problem that must be solved is the formation of calcium carbonate precipitates within the zeolite exchange bed and in the stripping tower and piping appurtenances. As indicated, the zeolite bed is equipped with backwash facilities to remove the carbonate deposits that form within the filter.

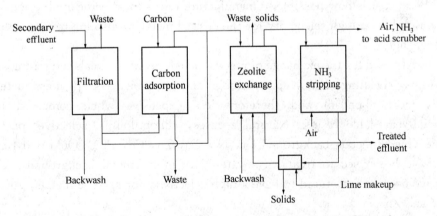

Figure 2 Typical flow diagram for the removal of ammonia by zeolite exchange
Note: The ammonia removed is removed in ammonia scrubber.

When using conventional synthetic ion-exchange resins for the removal of nitrate, two problems are encountered. First, while most resins have a greater affinity for nitrate over chloride or bicarbonate, they have a significantly lower affinity for nitrate as compared to sulfate, which limits the useful capacity of the resin for the removal of nitrate. Second, because of the lower affinity for nitrate over sulfate, a phenomenon known as *nitrate dumping* can occur. Nitrate dumping occurs when an ion-exchange column is operated past the nitrate breakthrough, at which point the sulfate in the feedwater will displace the nitrate on the resin, causing a release of nitrate. To overcome the problems associated with low affinity and nitrate breakthrough, new types of resins have been developed in which the affinities for nitrate and sulfate have been exchanged. When significant amounts of sulfate are present (i.e., typically greater than 25 percent of the total of the sum of the sulfate and nitrate expressed in meq/L), the use of nitrate-selective resins is advantageous. Because the performance of nitrate-selective resins will vary with the composition of the treated wastewater, pilot testing will usually be required.

Removal of Heavy Metals. Metal removal may be required as a pretreatment before discharge into a municipal sewer system. Because of the potential accumulation and toxicity of these metals, it is desirable to remove them from wastewater effluents before release to the environment. Ion exchange is one of the most common forms of treatment used for the removal of metals. Facilities and activities that may discharge wastewater containing high concentrations of metals include metal processing, electronics industries (semiconductors, printed circuit boards), metal plating and finishing, pharmaceuticals and laboratories, and vehicle service shops. High metal concentrations can also be found in leachate from landfills, and stormwater runoff.

Where industries produce effluents with widely fluctuating metal concentrations, flow equalization may be required to make ion exchange feasible, making process design difficult. The economic feasibility of using ion-exchange processes for metal removal greatly improves when the process is used for the removal and recovery of valuable metals. Because it is now possible to manufacture resins for specific applications, the use of resins that have a high selectivity for the desired metal(s) also improves the economics of ion exchange.

Materials used for the exchange of metals include zeolites, weak and strong anion and cation resins, chelating resins, and microbial and plant biomass. Biomass materials are generally more abundant and therefore less expensive when compared to other commercially available resins. Natural zeolites, clinoptilolite (selective for Cs) and chabazite (mixed metals background Cr, Ni, Cu, Zn, Cd, Pb) (Ouki and Kavannagh 1999), have been used to treat wastewater with mixed metal backgrounds. Chelating resins have been manufactured to have a high selectivity for specific metals, such as Cu, Ni, Cd, and Zn.

Ion-exchange processes are highly pH-dependent. Solution pH has a significant impact on the metal species present and the interaction between exchanging ions and the resin. Most metals bind better at higher pH, due to less competition from protons for adsorption sites. Operating and wastewater conditions determine selectivity of resin, pH, temperature, other ionic species, and chemical background. The presence of oxidants, particles, solvents, and polymers may affect the performance of ion-exchange resins. The quantity and quality of regenerate produced and subsequently requiring management must also be considered.

Removal of Total Dissolved Solids. For the reduction of the total dissolved solids, both anionic- and cationic-exchange resins must be used (see Figure 3). The wastewater is first passed through a cation exchanger where the positively charged ions are replaced by hydrogen ions. The cation-exchanger effluent is then passed over an anionic-exchange resin where the anions are replaced by hydroxide ions. Thus, the dissolved solids are replaced by hydrogen and hydroxide ions that react to form water molecules.

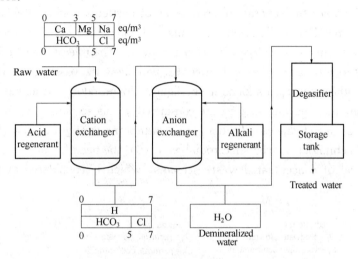

Figure 3   Typical flow diagram for the removal of hardness and for the complete demineralization of water using ion-exchange resins

Total dissolved solids removal can take place in separate exchange columns arranged in series, or both resins can be mixed in a single reactor. Wastewater application rates range from 0.20 to 0.40 $m^3/(m^2 \cdot min)$ [5 to 10 $gal/(ft^2 \cdot min)$]. Typical bed depths are 0.75 to 2.0 m (2.5 to 6.5 ft). In reuse applications, treatment of a portion of the wastewater by ion exchange, followed by blending with wastewater not treated by ion exchange, would possibly reduce the dissolved solids to acceptable levels. In some situations, it appears that ion exchange may be as competitive, if not more so, with reverse osmosis.

New Words and Phrases

calcium carbonate precipitate   碳酸钙沉淀物
stripping tower   汽提塔
semiconductor   *n.* 半导体
printed circuit board   印刷电路板
metal plating and finishing   金属电镀与表面精整
pharmaceutical   *n.* 医药品
leachate   *n.* 沥出液，沥滤液
stormwater runoff   暴雨径流
chabazite   *n.* 菱沸石
proton   *n.* 质子
solvent   *n.* 溶媒，溶剂

LESSON 12

Membrane Filtration Processes

Filtration involves the separation (removal) of particulate and colloidal matter from a liquid. In membrane filtration the range of particle sizes is extended to include dissolved constituents (typically 0.0001 to 1.0 μm). The role of the membrane, as shown on Figure 1, is to serve as a selective barrier that will allow the passage of certain constituents and will retain other constituents found in the liquid. To introduce membrane technologies and their application, the following subjects are considered in this section: (1) membrane process terminology, (2) membrane classification, (3) membrane configurations, (4) application of membrane technologies, (5) electrodialysis, (6) the need for pilot-plant studies, and (7) the disposal of concentrated waste streams, which is considered at the end of this section.

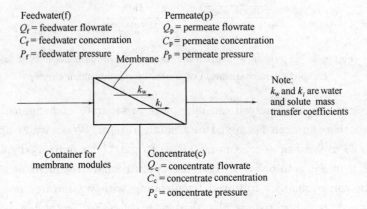

Figure 1 Definition sketch for a membrane process

Membrane Process Terminology

Terms commonly encountered when considering the application of membrane processes are summarized in Table 1. Referring to Figure 1 and Table 1, the influent to the membrane module is known as the *feed stream* (also known as feedwater). The liquid that passes through the semipermeable membrane is known as *permeate* (also known as the product stream or permeating stream) and the liquid containing the retained constituents is known as the *concentrate* (also known as the retentate, reject, retained phase, or waste stream). The rate at which the permeate flows through the membrane is known as the rate of *flux*, typically expressed as kg/(m² · d) [gal/(ft² · d)].

Terminology used to describe membrane processes — Table 1

Term	Description
Brine	Concentrate stream containing total dissolved solids greater than 36000 mg/L
Concentration, retentate, retained phase, reject, residual stream	The portion of the feed stream that does not pass through the membrane that contains higher TDS than the feed stream
Feed stream, feedwater	Input stream to the membrane array
Flux	Mass or volume rate of transfer through the membrane surface
Fouling	Deposition of existing solid material in the element on the feed stream of the membrane. Fouling can be either reversible or irreversible
Lumen	The interior of a hollow fiber membrane
Mass transfer coefficient (MTC)	Mass or volume unit transfer through membrane based on driving force
Membrane element	A single membrane unit containing a bound group of spiral-wound or hollow fine-fiber membranes to provide a nominal surface area
Module	A complete unit comprised of the membranes, the pressure support structure for the membranes, the feed inlet and outlet permeate and retentate ports, and an overall support structure
Molecular weight cutoff (MWCO)	The molecular weight of the smallest material rejected by the membrane, usually expressed in Daltons (D)
Permeate, product, permeating stream	The portion of the feed stream that passes through the membrane that contains lower TDS than the feed stream
Reject ion	Percent solute concentration reduction of permeate stream relative to feed stream
Pressure vessel	A single tube that contains several membrane elements in series
Scaling	Precipitation of solids in the element due to solute concentration on the feed stream of the membrane
Size exclusion	Removal of particles by sieving
Solvent	Liquid containing dissolved constituents (TDS), usually water
Solute	Dissolved constituents (TDS) in raw, feed, permeate, and concentrate streams
Stage or bank	Pressure vessels arranged in parallel
System arrays	Number of arrays needed to produce the required plant flow
Train or array	Multiple interconnected stages in series

Membrane Process Classification

Membrane processes include microfiltration (MF), ultrafiltration (UF), nanofiltration (NF), reverse osmosis (RO), dialysis, and electrodialysis (ED). Membrane processes can be classified in a number of different ways including (1) the type of material from which the membrane is made, (2) the nature of the driving force, (3) the separation mechanism, and (4) the nominal size of the separation achieved. Each of these methods of classifying membrane processes is considered in the following discussion. The general characteristics of membrane processes including typical operating ranges are reported in Table 2. The focus of the following discussion is on pressure-driven membrane processes. Electrodialysis is considered separately following the discussion of the application of pressure-driven membranes.

General characteristics membrane processes　　　　　　　　　Table 2

Membrane process	Membrane driving force	Typical separation mechanism	Operating structure (pore size)	Typical operating range, μm	Permeate description	Typical constituents removed
Microfiltration	Hydrostatic pressure difference	Sieve	Macropore (>50 nm)	0.08~2.0	Water + dissolved solutes	TSS, turbidity, protozoan oocysts and cysts, some bacteria and viruses
Ultrafiltration	Hydrostatic pressure difference	Sieve	Mescopores (2~50nm)	0.005~0.2	Water + small molecules	Macromolecules, colloids, most bacteria, some viruses, proteins
Nanofiltration	Hydrostatic pressure difference	Sieve + solution/diffusion + exclusion	Micropores (<2nm)	0.001~0.01	Water + very small molecules, ionic solutes	Small molecules, some harness, viruses
Reverse osmosis	Hydrostatic pressure difference	Solution/diffusion + exclusion	Dense (<2nm)	0.0001~0.001	Water + very small molecules, ionic solutes	Very small molecules, color, harness, sulfates, nitrate, sodium, other ions
Dialysis	Concentration difference	Diffusion	Mesopores (2~50nm)	—	Water + small molecules	Macromolecules, colloids, most bacteria, some viruses, proteins
Electrodialysis	Electromotive force	Ion exchange with selective membranes	Micropores (<2nm)	—	Water + ionic solutes	Ionized salt ions

Membrane Materials. Membranes used for the treatment of water and wastewater typically consist of a thin skin having a thickness of about 0.20 to 0.25 μm supported by a more porous structure of about 100 μm in thickness. Most commercial membranes are produced as flat sheets, fine hollow fibers, or in tubular form. The flat sheets are of two types, asymmetric and composite. Asymmetric membranes are cast in one process and consist of a very thin (less than 1 μm) layer and a thicker (up to 100 μm) porous layer that adds support and is capable of high water flux. Thin-film composite (TFC) membranes are made by bonding a thin cellulose acetate, polyamide, or other active layer (typically 0.15 to 0.25 μm thick) to a thicker porous substrate, which provides stability. Membranes can be made from a number of different organic and inorganic materials. The membranes used for wastewater treatment are typically organic. The principal types of membranes used include polypropylene, cellulose acetate, aromatic polyamides, and thin-film composite (TFC). The choice of membrane and system configuration is based on minimizing membrane clogging and deterioration, typically based on pilot-plant studies.

Driving Force. The distinguishing characteristic of the first four membrane processes considered in Table 2 (MF, UF, NF, and RO) is the application of hydraulic pressure to bring about the desired separation. Dialysis involves the transport of constituents through a semipermeable membrane on the basis of concentration differences. Electrodialysis involves the use of an electromotive force and ion-selective membranes to accomplish the separation of charged ionic species.

Removal Mechanisms. The separation of particles in MF and UF is accomplished primarily by straining (sieving), as shown on Figure 2a. In NF and RO, small particles are rejected by the water layer adsorbed on the surface of the membrane which is known as a *dense* membrane (see Figure 2b). Ionic species are transported across the membrane by diffusion through the pores of the macromolecule comprising the membrane. Typically NF can be used to reject constituents as small as 0.001 μm whereas RO can reject particles as small as 0.0001 μm. Straining is also important in NF membranes, especially at the larger pore size openings.

Size of Separation. The pore sizes in membranes are identified as macropores

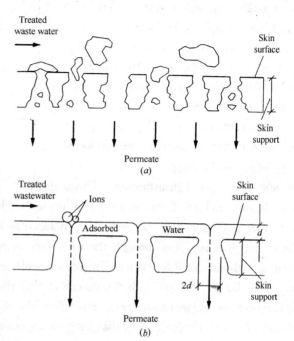

Figure 2 Definition sketch for the removal of wastewater constituents
(a) removal of large molecules and particles by sieving (size exclusion) mechanism and (b) rejection of ions by adsorbed water layer

($>$50 nm), mesopores (2 to 50 nm), and micropores ($<$2 nm). Because the pore sizes in RO membranes are so small, the membranes are defined as dense. The classification of membrane processes on the basis of the size of separation is shown in Table 2. There is considerable overlap in the sizes of particles removed, especially between NF and RO. Nanofiltration is used most commonly in water-softening operations in place of chemical precipitation.

Membrane Configurations and Membrane Operation

In the membrane field, the term *module* is used to describe a complete unit comprised of the membranes, the pressure support structure for the membranes, the feed inlet and outlet permeate and retentate ports, and an overall support structure. The principal types of membrane modules used for water treatment are (1) tubular, (2) hollow fiber, and (3) spiral wound. Plate and frame and pleated cartridge filters are also available but are used more commonly in industrial applications.

The operation of membrane processes is quite simple. A pump is used to pressurize the feed solution and to circulate it through the module. A valve is used to maintain the pressure of retentate. The permeate is withdrawn, typically at atmospheric pressure. As constituents in the feedwater accumulate on the membranes (often termed membrane fouling), the pressure builds up on the feed side, the membrane flux (i.e., flow through membrane) starts to decrease, and the percent rejection also starts to decrease (see Figure 3). When the performance has deteriorated to a given level, the membrane modules are taken out of service and backwased and/or cleaned chemically. The operational configurations and parameters for the various membrane processes are considered in the following discussion.

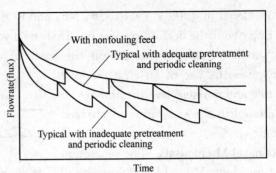

Figure 3 Definition sketch for the performance of a membrane filtration system

Microfiltration and Ultrafiltration. Three different process configurations are used with microfiltration and ultrafiltration units as illustrated on Figure 4. In the first configuration known as *cross flow* (Figure 4a) the feedwater is pumped with cross flow tangential to the membrane. Water that does not pass through the membrane is recirculated through the membrane after blending with additional feedwater. The second configuration, also known as cross flow (Figure 4b), is similar to the first with the exception that the water that does not pass through the membrane is recirculated to a storage reservoir. The third configuration is known as direct feed (also *dead-end*) (Figure 4c) in that there is no cross flow. All of the water applied to the

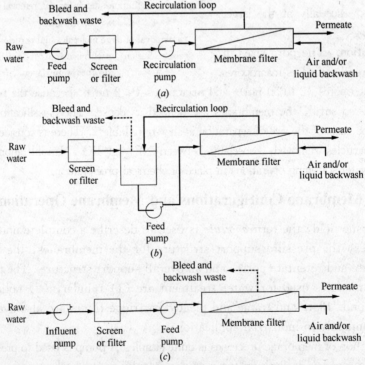

Figure 4 Typical operational modes for MF and UF membrane processes
(a) cross flow, (b) cross flow with reservoir, and (c) direct feed

membrane passes through the membrane. Raw feedwater is used periodically to flush the accumulated material from the membrane surface

For the cross-flow mode of operation (see Figure 4a and b), the transmembrane pressure is given by the following expression:

$$P_{tm} = \left[\frac{P_f + P_c}{2}\right] - P_p \tag{1}$$

where P_{tm} = transmembrane pressure gradient, kPa
P_f = inlet pressure of feed stream, kPa
P_c = pressure of concentrate stream, kPa
P_p = pressure of permeate stream, kPa

The overall pressure drop across the filter module for the cross-flow mode of operation is given by

$$P = P_f - P_p \tag{2}$$

where P = pressure drop across module, kPa
P_f and P_p as defined above

For the direct-feed mode of operation (see Figure 4c) the transmembrane pressure is given by the following expression:

$$P_{tm} = P_f - P_p \tag{3}$$

where P_{tm} = transmembrane pressure gradient, kPa
P_f and P_p as defined above

The total permeate flow from a membrane system is given by

$$Q_p = F_w A \tag{4}$$

where Q_p = permeate stream flowrate, kg/s
F_w = transmembrane water flux rate, kg/(m² · s)
A = membrane area, m²

As would be expected, the transmembrane water flux rate is a function of the quality of the feed stream, the degree of pretreatment, the characteristics of the membrane, and the system operating parameters.

The recovery rate r is defined as

$$r, \% = \frac{Q_p}{Q_f} \times 100 \tag{5}$$

where Q_p = permeate stream flow, kg/s
Q_f = feed stream flow, kg/s

It should be noted that there is a difference between the recovery rate (which refers to the water) and the rate of rejection (which refers to the solute) as given below:

$$R, \% = \frac{C_f - C_p}{C_f} \times 100 = 1 - \frac{C_p}{C_f} \times 100 \tag{6}$$

The corresponding mass balance equations are

$$Q_f = Q_p + Q_c \tag{7}$$
$$Q_f C_f = Q_p C_p + Q_c C_c \tag{8}$$

Three different operating modes can be used to control the operation of a membrane process with respect to flux and the transmembrane pressure (TMP). The three modes are (1) constant flux in which the flux rate is fixed and the TMP is allowed to vary (increase) with time; (2) constant TMP in which the TMP is fixed and the flux rate is allowed to vary (decrease) with time, and (3) both the flux rate and the TMP are allowed to vary with time. Traditionally, the constant-flux mode of operation has been used. However, based on the results of a recent study with various wastewater effluents (Bourgeous et al., 1999), it appears the mode in which both the flux rate and the TMP are allowed to vary with time may be the most effective mode of operation.

Reverse Osmosis. When two solutions having different solute concentrations are separated by a semipermeable membrane, a difference in chemical potential will exist across the membrane (Figure 5). Water will tend to diffuse through the membrane from the lower-concentration (higher-potential) side to the higher-concentration (lower-potential) side. In a system having a finite volume, flow continues until the pressure difference balances the chemical potential difference. This balancing pressure difference is termed the *osmotic pressure* and is a function of the solute characteristics and concentration and temperature. If a pressure gradient opposite in direction and greater than the osmotic pressure is imposed across the membrane, flow from the more concentrated to the less concentrated region will occur and is termed *reverse osmosis* (see Figure 5c).

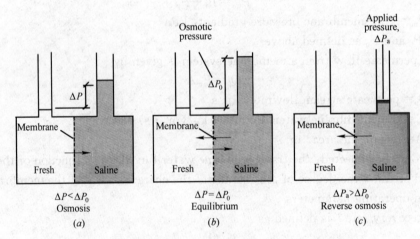

Figrue 5 Definition sketch of osmotic flow
(a)osmotic flow, (b)osmotic equilibrium, and(c)reverse osmosis

A number of different models have been developed to determine the surface area of membrane and the number of arrays required (see Figure 6). The basic equations used to develop the various models are as follows. Referring to Figure 1, the flux of water through the membrane is a function of the pressure gradient:

$$F_w = k_w (\Delta P_a - \Delta \Pi) = \frac{Q_p}{A} \tag{9}$$

where F_w = water flux rate, kg/(m² · s)
  k_w = water mass transfer coefficient involving temperature, membrane characteristics, and solute characteristics, s/m
  ΔP_a = average imposed pressure gradient, kPa

$$=\left[\frac{P_f+P_c}{2}\right]-P_p$$

$\Delta\Pi$ = osmotic pressure gradient, kPa

$$=\left[\frac{\Pi_f+\Pi_c}{2}\right]-\Pi_p$$

Q_p = permeate stream flow, kg/s

A = membrane area, m^2

Some solute passes through the membrane in all cases. Solute flux can be described adequately by an expression of the form

$$F_i=k_i\Delta C_i=\frac{Q_pC_p}{A} \qquad (10)$$

where F_i = flux of solute species i, kg/(m$^2 \cdot$ s)

k_i = solute mass transfer coefficient, m/s

ΔC_i = solute concentration gradient, kg/m^3

$$=\left[\frac{C_f+C_c}{2}\right]-C_p$$

C_f = solute concentration in feed stream, kg/m^3

C_c = solute concentration in concentrate stream, kg/m^3

C_p = solute concentration in permeate stream, kg/m^3

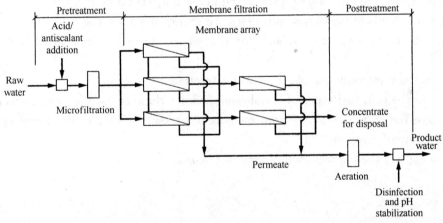

Figure 6 Typical flow diagram for reverse osmosis membrane process with pre- and posttreatment

New Words and Phrases

electrodialysis (ED)　　*n.* 电渗析
module　*n.* 模块，模数，基本单位
semipermeable membrane　半透膜
retentate　*n.* (在渗析过程中未能通过半透膜而被保留下的)截留物，滞留物

flux　*n.* 通量
fouling　*n.* 污垢，沾污
lumen　*n.* 内腔
hollow fiber membrane　中空纤维膜
spiral-wound membrane　卷式膜
molecular weight cutoff　截留分子量

dalton   n. 道尔顿（质量单位）
solute   n. 溶质
exclusion   n. 去除，排除
nanofiltration（NF） n. 纳滤
dialysis   n. 渗析
asymmetric   adj. 不均匀的，不对称的
composite   adj. 合成的，复合的
TFC：thin-film composite（membrane）
cellulose acetate   醋酸纤维素
polyamide   n. 聚酰胺
polypropylene   n. 聚丙烯
aromatic   adj. 芬芳的，芳族的

cyst   n. ［生物］（动、植物的）胞，包囊，膀胱，囊肿
concentration differences   浓度差
ion-selective membrane   离子选择性膜
macromolecule   n. 大分子，高分子
plate and frame   板框式
pleated cartridge filter   折叠滤芯过滤器（主要用于微滤，且专用于出水病毒的浓缩）
deteriorate   v.（使）恶化
transmembrane pressure   砖膜压力
osmotic pressure   渗透压

Questions

1. What is the role of the membrane?
2. Please explain the meanings of *feed stream*, *permeate*, *concentrate and flux*?
3. Try to explain the meaning of fouling and molecular weight cutoff.
4. How many kinds of membrane processes are there? What are they?
5. What are the removal mechanisms for the separation of particles in MF, UF, NF and RO?
6. What is the commonly use of NF in water treatment?
7. What are the principal types of membrane modules that are used for water treatment?
8. What are the meanings of the transmembrane pressure（TMP）, the recovery rate r and the rate of rejection?
9. Try to explain the phenomenon of *reverse osmosis*.

Reading Material

Membrane Fouling

The term *fouling* is used to describe the potential deposition and accumulation of constituents in the feed stream on the membrane. Membrane fouling is an important consideration in the design and operation of membrane systems as it affects pretreatment needs, cleaning requirements, operating conditions, cost, and performance. Fouling of the membrane can occur in three general forms：(1) a buildup of the constituents in the feedwater on the membrane surface，(2) the formation of chemical precipitates due to the chemistry of the feedwater, and (3) damage to the membrane due to the presence of chemical substances that can react with the membrane or biological agents that can colonize the membrane.

Membrane Fouling Caused by Buildup of Solids. Three accepted mechanisms resulting in resistance to flow due to the accumulation of material within a lumen (see Figure 7) are (1) pore narrowing, (2) pore plugging, and (3) gel/cake formation caused by concentration polarization. Gel/cake formation, caused by concentration polarization, occurs when the majority of the solid matter in the feed is larger than the pore sizes or molecular weight cutoff of the membrane. Concentration polarization can be described as the buildup of matter close to or on the membrane surface that causes an increase in resistance to solvent transport across the membrane. Some degree of concentration polarization will always occur in the operation of a membrane system. The formation of a gel or cake layer, however, is an extreme case of concentration polarization where a large amount of matter has actually accumulated on the membrane surface, forming a gel or cake layer. The mechanisms of pore plugging and pore narrowing will occur only when the solid matter in the feedwater is smaller than the pore size or the molecular weight cutoff.

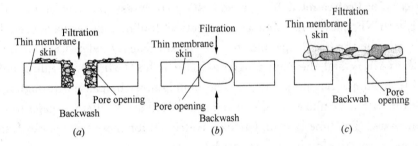

Figure 7 Modes of membrane fouling
(a) pore narrowing, (b) pore plugging, and (c) gel/cake formation polarization

Control of Membrane Fouling. Typically, three approaches are used to control membrane fouling: (1) pretreatment of the feedwater, (2) membrane backflushing, and (3) chemical cleaning of the membranes. Pretreatment is used to reduce the TSS and bacterial content of the feedwater. Often the feedwater will be conditioned chemically to limit chemical precipitation within the units. The most commonly used method of eliminating the accumulated material from the membrane surface is backflushing with water and/or air. Chemical treatment is used to remove constituents that are not removed during conventional backwashing. Chemical precipitates can be removed by altering the chemistry of the feedwater and by chemical treatment. Damage of the membrane due to deleterious constituents typically cannot be reversed.

Pertreatment for Nanofiltralien and Reverse Osmosis. A very high-quality feed is required for efficient operation of a nanofiltration or reverse osmosis unit. Membrane elements in the reverse osmosis unit can be fouled by colloidal matter and constituents in the feed stream. The following pretreatment options have been used singly and/or in combination.
1. Pretreatment of a secondary effluent by chemical clarification and multimedia filtration or by multimedia filtration and ultrafiltration is usually necessary to

remove colloidal material.
2. Cartridge filters with a pore size of 5 to 10 μm have also been used to reduce residual suspended solids.
3. To limit bacterial activity it may be necessary to disinfect the feedwater using either chlorine, ozone, or UV radiation.
4. The exclusion of oxygen may be necessary to prevent oxidation of iron, manganese, and hydrogen sulfide.
5. Depending on the type of membrane, removal of chlorine (with sodium bisulfite) and ozone may be necessary.
6. The removal of iron and manganese may also be necessary to decrease scaling potential.
7. To inhibit scale formation, the pH of the feed should be adjusted (usually with sulfuric acid) within the range from 4.0 to 7.5.

Regular chemical cleaning of the membrane elements (about once a month) is necessary to restore the membrane flux.

Assessing Need for Pretreatment for NF and RO. To assess the treatability of a given wastewater with NF and RO membranes, a variety of fouling indexes have been developed over the years. The three principal indexes are the silt density index (SDI), the modified fouling index (MR), and the mini plugging factor index (MPFI). Fouling indexes are determined from simple membrane tests. The sample must be passed through a 0.45 μm Millipore filter with a 47 mm internal diameter at 210kPa (30 lb/in^2) gage to determine any of the indexes. The time to complete data collection for these tests varies from 15 min to 2 h, depending on the fouling nature of the water.

The most widely used index is the SDI. The SDI is defined as follows:

$$\text{SDI} = \frac{100(1 - t_i/t_f)}{t} \tag{11}$$

Where t_i = time to collect initial sample of 500mL
t_f = time to collect final sample of 500mL
t = total time for running the test

The silt density index is a static measurement of resistance that is determined by samples taken at the beginning and end of the test. The SDI does not measure the rate of change of resistance during the test. Recommended SDI values are reported in Table 3.

Approximate values for fouling indexes   Table 3

Membrane process	Fouling index	
	SDI	MFI, s/L^2
Nanofiltration	0~2	0~10
Reverse osmosis hollow fiber	0~2	0~2
Reverse osmosis spiral wound	0~3	0~2

The modified fouling index (MFI) is determined using the same equipment and procedure used for the SDI, but the volume is recorded every 30 s over a 15-min filtration period. Derived from a consideration of cake filtration, the MFI is defined as follows:

$$\frac{1}{Q} = a + \mathrm{MFI} \times V \tag{12}$$

where Q = average flow, L/s
  a = constant
  MFI = modified fouling index, s/L^2
  V = volume, L

The value of the MFI is obtained as the slope of the straight-line portion of the curve obtained by plotting the inverse flow versus the cumulative volume (see Figure 8). Recommended MFT values are reported in Table 3.

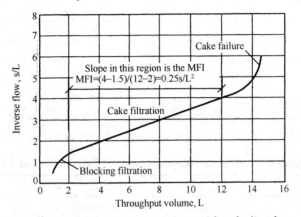

Figure 8 Typical plot to determine the modifieg fouling factor

New Words and Phrases

colonize *vt.* 殖民，定居
gel *n.* 凝胶体
concentration polarization 浓差极化

polarization *n.* 偏振(现象)，极化(作用)
deleterious *adj.* 有害的，有毒的
bisulfite *n.* 亚硫酸氢盐，酸式亚硫酸盐

Application of Membranes

With evolving health concerns and the development of new and lower-cost membranes, the application of membrane technologies in the field of environmental engineering has increased dramatically within the past 5 years. The increased use of membranes is expected to continue well in the future. In fact, the use of conventional filtration technology may be a thing of the past within 10 to 15 years, especially in light of the need to remove resistant organic constituents of concern. Typical applications of membrane technologies for wastewater treatment are reported in Table 1. The principal applications of the various membrane technologies for the removal of specific constituents found in wastewater are summarized in Table 2. Typical operating ranges in terms of operating pressures and flux rates, along with the types of membranes used, are reported in Table 3.

Typical applications for membrane technologies in wastewater treatment   Table 1

Applications	Description
Microfiltration and ultrafiltration	
Aerobic biological Treatment	Membrane is used to separate the treated wastewater from the active biomass in an activated-sludge process. The membrane separation unit can be internal immersed in the bioreactor or external to the bioreactor. Such processes are known as membrane bioreactor (MBR) processes
Anaerobic biological Treatment	Membrane is used to separate the treated wastewater from the active biomass in an anaerobic complete-mix reactor
Membrane aeration biological treatment	Plate and frame, tubular, and hollow membranes are used to transfer pure oxygen to the biomass attached to the outside of the membrane (see Figure 2a). Such processes are known as membrane aeration bioreactor (MABR) processes
Membrane extraction biological treatment	Membranes are used to extract degradable organic molecules from inorganic constituents such as acids, bases, and salts from the waste stream for subsequent biological treatment (see Figure 2b). Such processes are known as extractive membrane bioreactor (EMBR) processes
Pretreatment for effective disinfection	Used to remove residual suspended solids from settled secondary effluent or from the effluent from depth or surface filters to achieve effective disinfection with either chlorine or UV radiation for reuse applications
Pretreatment for nanofiltration and reverse osmosis	Microfilters are used to remove residual colloidal and suspended solids as a pretreatment step for additional processing
Nanofiltration	
Effluent reuse	Used to treat prefiltered effluent (typically with microfiltration) for indirect potable reuse applications such as groundwater injection. Credit is also given for disinfection when using nanofiltration

Table 1(Continued)

Applications	Description
	Nanofiltration
Water softening	Used to reduce the concentration of multivalent ion contributing to hardness
	Reverse osmosis
Effluent reuse	Used to treat prefiltered effluent (typically with microfiltration) for indirect potable reuse applications such as groundwater injection. Credit is also given for disinfection when using reverse osmosis
Effluent dispersal	Reverse osmosis processes have proved capable of removing sizable amounts of selected compounds such as NDMA
Two-stage treatment for boiler use	Two stages of reverse osmosis are used to produce water suitable for high-pressure boilers

Application of membrane technologies for the removal of specific constituents found in wastewater[a]   Table 2

Constituent	Membrane technology				Comments
	MF	UF	NF	RO	
Biodegradable organics		√	√	√	
Hardness			√	√	
Heavy metals			√	√	
Nitrate			√	√	
Priority organic pollutants		√	√	√	
Synthetic organic compounds			√	√	
TDS			√	√	
TSS	√	√			TSS removed during pretreatment for NF and RO
Bacteria	√[b]	√	√	√	Used for membrane disinfection. Removed as pretreatment for NF and RO with MF and UF
Protozoan cysts and oocysts and helminth ova	√	√	√	√	
Viruses			√	√	Used for membrane disinfection

[a] Specific removal rates will depend on the composition and constituent concentrations in the treated wastewater.
[b] Variable performance.

Typical characteristics of membrane technologies used in wastewater-treatment applications   Table 3

Membrane technology	Typical operating range, μm	Operating pressure		Rate of flux		Membrane details	
		lb/in^2	kPa	Gal/(ft^2·d)	L/(m^2·d)	Type	Configuration
Microfiltration	0.08~2.0	1~15	7~100	10~40	405~1600	Polypropylene, acrylonitrile, nylon, and polytetrafluoroethylene	Spiral wound, hollow fiber, plate and frame

Table 3(Continued)

Membrane technology	Typical operating range, μm	Operating pressure		Rate of flux		Membrane details	
		lb/in^2	kPa	Gal/(ft^2·d)	L/(m^2·d)	Type	Configuration
Ultrafiltration	0.005~0.2	10~100	70~700	10~20	405—815	Cellulose acetate, aromatic polyamides	Spiral wound, hollow fiber, plate and frame
Nanofiltration	0.001~0.01	75~150	500~1000	5~20	200~815	Cellulose acetate, aromatic polyamides	Spiral wound, hollow fiber
Reverse osmosis	0.0001~0.001	125~1000	850~7000	8~12	320~490	Cellulose acetate, aromatic polyamides	Spiral wound, hollow fiber, thin-film composite

Note: kPa×0.1450=lb/in^2
L/(m^2·d)×0.024542=gal/(ft·d)

Typical energy consumption and product recovery values for various membrane systems are presented in Table 4. In reviewing the information presented in Table 4, it is important to note that the reported operating pressure values for all of the membrane processes excluding electrodialysis, are considerably lower than comparable values of 5 years ago. It is anticipated that operating pressures will continue to go down as new membranes are developed. At the present time where the use of membranes is being considered, special attention must be devoted to the characteristics of the wastewater to be processed. Advantages and disadvantages of MF and UF and RO membrane technology are compared in Table 5.

Typical energy consumption and product recovery values for various membrane systems   Table 4

Membrane process	Operating pressure		Energy consumption, kWh per		Product recovery, %
	lb/in^2	kPa	1000gal	m^3	
Microfiltration	15	100	0.1	0.4	94~98
Ultrafiltration	75	525	0.8	3.0	70~80
Nanofiltration	125	875	1.4	5.3	80~85
Reverse osmosis	225	1575	2.7	10.2	70~85
Reverse osmosis	400	2800	4.8	18.2	70~85
Electrodialysis			2.5	9.5	75~85

Advantages and disadvantages of membrane treatment technologies   Table 5

Advantages	Disadvantages
Microfiltration and ultrafiltration	
• Can reduce the amount of treatment chemicals	• Uses more electricity; high-pressure systems can be energy-intensive

Table 5 (Continued)

Advantages	Disadvantages
Microfiltration and ultrafiltration	
• Smaller space requirements (footpint); membrane equipment require 50 to 80 percent less space than conventional plants • Reduces labor requirements; can be automated easily • New membrane design allows use of lower pressures; system cost may be competitive with conventional wastewater-treatment processes • Removes protozoan cysts, oocysts, and helminth ova; may also remove limited amounts of bacteria and viruses	• May need pretreatment to prevent fouling; pretreatment facilities increase space needs and overall costs • May require residuals handling and disposal of concentrate • Requires replacement of membranes about every 3 to 5 years • Scale formation can be a serious problem. Scale-forming potential difficult to predict without field testing • Flux rate (the rate of feedwater flow through the membrane) gradually declines over time. Recovery rates may be considerably less than 100 percent • Lack of a reliable low-cost method of monitoring performance
Reverse osmosis	
• Can remove dissolved constituents • Can disinfect treated water • Can remove NDMA and other related organic compounds • Can remove natural organic matter (a disinfection by-product precursor) and inorganic matter	• Works best on groundwater or low solids surface water or pretreated wastewater effluent • Lack of a reliable low-cost method of monitoring performance • May require residuals handling and disposal of concentrate • Expensive compared to conventional treatment

Microfiltration. Microfiltration membranes are the most numerous on the market, are the least expensive, and as reported in Table 3, are commonly made of polypropylene, acrylonitrile, nylon, and polytetrafluoroethylene. Typical operating information for microfiltration and ultrafiltration membrane technologies used for wastewater including operating pressures and flux rates are also presented in Table 3. Microfiltration technologies, as discussed below, can be used in a variety of ways in wastewater-treatment and water reuse systems.

In advanced treatment applications, microfiltration has been used, most commonly as a replacement for depth filtration to reduce turbidity, remove residual suspended solids, and reduce bacteria to condition the water for effective disinfection and as a pretreatment step for reverse osmosis. Corresponding performance data are presented in Table 6. Typical performance data reported in the literature are also included in Table 6 for the purpose of comparison.

Table 6 Performance summary for the Dublin San Ramon Sanitary District MF for the period from 4/00 through 12/00[a]

Constituent	MF influent, mg/L	MF effluent, mg/L	Average reduction, %	Reduction reported in literature, %
TOC	10~31	9~16	57	45~65
BOD	11~32	<2~9.9	86	75~90

Table 6(Continued)

Constituent	MF influent, mg/L	MF effluent, mg/L	Average reduction, %	Reduction reported in literature, %
COD	24~150	16~53	76	70~85
TSS	8~46	<0.5	97	95~98
TDS	498~622	498~622	0	0~2
NH_3-N	21~42	20~35	7	5~15
NO_3-N	<1~5	<1~5	0	0~2
PO_4^-	6~8	6~8	0	0~2
SO_4^{2-}	90~120	90~120	0	0~1
Cl^-	93~115	93~115	0	0~1
Turbidity	2~50NTU	0.03~0.08NTU	>99	

a Typical flux rate during test period was 1600 L/(m² · d)

A relatively recent development, the use of membranes for biological treatment, promises to be one of the most important uses of membranes in wastewater treatment. As reported in Table 1, membranes have been used for both aerobic and anaerobic treatment of wastewaters. Typical membrane bioreactors (MBRs) are illustrated on Figure 1. On Figure 1a, the membrane separation unit is internal, immersed in the bioreactor. Treated effluent is withdrawn from the bioreactor with the application of a vacuum (on the order of 50kPa). On Figure 1b, the membrane separation unit is external to the bioreactor. The aeration system installed below the membrane separation unit is used to clean the hollow fibers continuously by the shearing action of the air bubbles as they rise through the liquid.

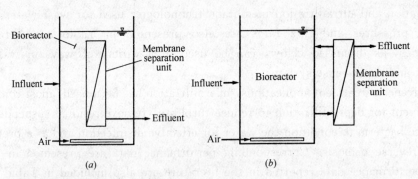

Figure 1 Schematic flow diagrams for the membrane bioreactor activated-sludge process
(a)with internal membrane biosolids separation unit and(b)with external biosolids separation unit

Typical performance data for the MBR activated-sludge process are presented in Table 7. As reported in Table 7, the quality of the effluent is ideal for a number of reuse application or for further processing by nanofiltration or reverse osmosis. In addition to offering excellent performance, MBRs require a considerably smaller aerial footprint. It is also interesting to note that MBRs have also been used for the anaerobic treatment of wastewater. The current literature abounds with articles delineating the use of membranes in a variety of wastewater-treatment applications.

Typical performance data for membrane bioreactor used to treat domestic wastewater Table 7

Parameter	Unit	Typical	Parameter	Unit	Typical
Effluent BOD	mg/L	<5	Effluent TN	mg/L	<10
Effluent COD	mg/L	<30	Effluent turbidity	NTU	<1
Effluent NH_3	mg/L	<1			

Performance summary for the Dublin San Ramon Sanitary District RO for the period from 4/1999 through 12/1999[a] Table 8

Constituent	RO influent, mg/L	RO effluent, mg/L	Average reduction, %	Reduction reported in literature, %
TOC	9~16	<0.5	>94	85~95
BOD	<2~9.9	<2	>40	30~60
COD	16~53	<2	>91	85~95
TSS	<0.5	~0	>99	95~100
TDS	498~622	9~19	0	90~98
NH_3-N	20~35	1~3	96	90~98
NO_3-N	<1~5	0.08~3.2	96	65~85
PO_4^-	6~8	0.1~1	~99	95~99
SO_4^{2-}	90~120	<0.5~0.7	99	95~99
Cl^-	93~115	0.9~5.0	97	90~98
Turbidity	0.03~0.08NTU	0.03NTU	50	40~80

[a] Typical flux rate during test period was $348L/(m^2 \cdot d)$.

In addition to the MBR process, plate and frame, tubular, and hollow membranes have been used to transfer pure oxygen to the biomass attached to the outside of the membrane (see Figure 2a). Such processes are known as membrane aeration bioreactor (MABR) processes. In another application, membranes are used to extract degradable soluble organic molecules from inorganic constituents in a waste stream (see Figure 2b).

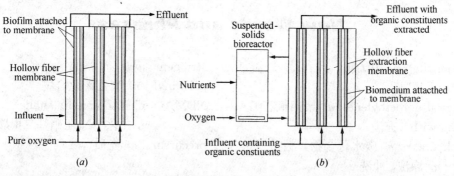

Figure 2 Schematic flow diagrams for alternative biological treatment processes employing membranes
(a) membrane aeration bioreactor and (b) extractive membrane bioreactor with external treatment unit

The extracted organic constituents are treated in an external bioreactor. Such processes are known as extractive membrane bioreactor (EMBR) processes.

Ultrafiltration. Ultrafiltration (UF) membranes are used for many of the same applications as described above for microfiltration. Some UF membranes with small pore sizes have also been used to remove dissolved compounds with high molecular weight, such as colloids, proteins, and carbohydrates. The membranes do not remove sugar or salt. Ultrafiltration is used typically in industrial applications for the production of high-purity process, rinse water. Typical operating data are presented in Table 3.

Nanofiltration. Nanofiltration, also known as "loose" RO, can reject particles as small as 0.001 μm. Nanofiltration is used for the removal of selected dissolved constituents from wastewater such as the multivalent metallic ions responsible for hardness. The advantages of nanofiltration over lime softening include the production of a product water that meets the most stringent reuse water quality requirements. Because both inorganic and organic constituents and bacteria and viruses are removed, disinfection requirements are minimized. Although most NF facilities use polyamide TFC membranes in a spiral-wound configuration, more than ten different types of membranes are available. Other membranes include polyamide hollow fiber, polyvinyl acetate spiral wound, and asymmetric cellulose acetate in a tubular configuration.

Reverse Osmosis. Worldwide, reverse osmosis (RO) is used primarily for desalination. In wastewater treatment, RO is used for the removal of dissolved constituents from wastewater remaining after advanced treatment with depth filtration or microfiltration. The membranes exclude ions, but require high pressures to produce the deionized water. Typical operating information for reverse osmosis used for wastewater including operating pressures and flux rate rates are reported in Table 3. Corresponding performance data are presented in Table 8. Typical performance data reported in the literature are also included in Table 8. As noted above, care should be used in applying the performance data reported in Table 8 as it has been found that the performance of RO is also site-specific, especially with respect to fouling. Disinfection of the RO feedwater is usually practiced to minimize or limit the bacterial growth on the membrane. Care must be taken with polyamide and TFC membranes because they are sensitive to chemical oxidants. The need for cleaning depends on how long the flux rate is maintained.

New Words and Phrases

acrylonitrile *n.* 丙烯腈
nylon *n.* 尼龙
polytetrafluoroethylene *n.* 聚四氟乙烯
abound with 充满
carbohydrate *n.* 碳水化合物，糖类
rinse *n.* 漂洗，冲洗
stringent *adj.* 严格的
polyvinyl *n.* 聚乙烯化合物
NDMA(n-nitrosodimethylamine)
　　n. ［化］N-亚硝基二甲胺
precursor *n.* 先质

Questions

1. In advanced treatment applications, what is the most common use of MF?
2. Try to explain the process of membrane bioreactors (MBRs).
3. Do you think UF membranes can be used to remove sugar or salt?
4. What is the purpose of disinfection of the RO feedwater?
5. What are the characteristics of NF purification?

Reading Material

Electrodialysis

In the electrodialysis process, ionic components of a solution are separated through the use of semipermeable ion-selective membranes. Because the electrodialysis process is being evaluated for a variety of reuse applications, the purpose of the following discussion is (1) to introduce the theory of electrodialysis and (2) to consider some applications.

Theory of Electrodialysis. Application of an electrical potential between the two electrodes causes an electric current to pass through the solution, which in turn causes a migration of cations toward the negative electrode and a migration of anions toward the positive electrode (see Figure 3). Because of the alternate spacing of cation-and anion-permeable membranes, cells of concentrated and dilute salts are formed. Wastewater is pumped through the membranes, which are separated by spacers and assembled into stacks. The wastewater is usually retained for about 10 to 20 days in a single stack or stage. Dissolved solids removals vary with the (1) wastewater temperature, (2) amounts of electrical current passed,

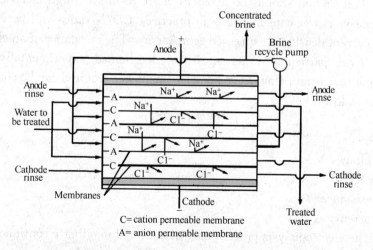

Figure 3 Schematic of electrodialysis unit

(3) type and amount of ions, (4) permselectivity of the membrane, (5) fouling and scaling potential of the wastewater, (6) wastewater flowrates, and (7) number and configuration of stages.

The current required for electrodialysis can be estimated using Faraday's laws of electrolysis. Because one Faraday of electricity will cause one-gram equivalent of a substance to migrate from one electrode to another, the number of gram equivalents removed per unit time is given by

$$\text{Gram eq/unit time} = QN\eta \tag{1}$$

where Q = flowrate, L/s
N = normality of solution, eq/L
η = electrolyte removal as a fraction

The corresponding expression for the current for a stack of membranes is given by

$$I = \frac{FQN\eta}{nE_c} \tag{2}$$

where I = current, amp
F = Faraday's constant
     = 96485 amp·s/gram equivalent = 96485 A·s/eq
n = number of cells in the stack
E_c = current efficiency expressed as a fraction

In the analysis of the electrodialysis process, it has been found that the capacity of the membrane to pass an electrical current is related to the current density (*CD*) and the normality (*N*) of the feed solution. Current density is defined as the current in milliamperes that flows through a square centimeter of membrane perpendicular to the current direction. The relationship between current density and the solution normality is known as the *current density to normality* (*CD/N*) ratio. High values of the ratio are indicative that there is insufficient charge to carry the current. When high ratios exist, a localized deficiency of ions may occur on the surface of the membrane, causing a condition called *polarization*. Polarization should be avoided, as it results in high electrical resistance leading to excessive power consumption. In practice, *CD/N* ratios will vary from 500 to 800 when the current density is expressed as mA/cm². The resistance of an electrodialysis unit used to treat particular water must be determined experimentally. Once the resistance R and the current flow I are known, the power required can be computed using Ohm's law as follows:

$$P = E \times I = R(I)^2 \tag{3}$$

where P = power, W
E = voltage, V
   = $R \times I$
R = resistance, Ω
I = current, A

Application. The electrodialysis process may be operated in either a continuous or a batch mode. The units can be arranged either in parallel to provide the necessary hydraulic capacity or in series to effect the desired degree of demineralization. A typical flaw diagram for electrodialysis membrane process with pretreatment is shown on Figure 4. Makeup water, usually about 10 percent of the feed volume, is required to wash the membranes continuously. A portion of the concentrate stream is recycled to maintain nearly equal flowrates and pressures on both sides of each membrane. Sulfuric acid is fed to the concentrate stream to maintain a low pH and thus minimize scaling. Typical operating parameters for the electrodialysis process are reported in Table 9.

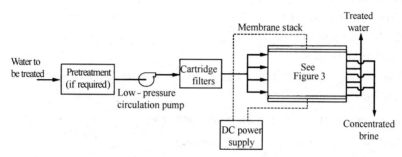

Figure 4 Typical flow diagram for electrodialysis membrane process with pretreatment

Typical operating parameters for electrodialysis units   Table 9

Parameter	Unit	Range	Parameter	Unit	Range
Detention time in stack	d	10~20	Salt-removal efficiency	%	40~60
CD/N ratio	mA/cm²	500~800	Current efficiency	%	85~95
Membrane resistance, Ω	ohms	4~8	Concentrate stream flow	% of feed	10~20

Problems associated with the electrodialysis process for wastewater renovation include chemical precipitation of salts with low solubility on the membrane surface and clogging of the membrane by the residual colloidal organic matter in wastewater-treatment plant effluents. To reduce membrane-fouling, activated carbon pretreatment, possibly preceded by chemical precipitation and some form of multimedia filtration, may be necessary.

Pilot Studies for Membrane Applications

Because every wastewater is unique with respect to its chemistry, it is difficult to predict a priori how a given membrane process will perform. As a result, the selection of the best membrane for a given application is usually based on the results of pilot studies. Membrane fouling indexes can be used to assess the need for pretreatment. In some situations, manufacturers of membranes will provide a testing service to identify the most appropriate membrane for a specific water or wastewater.

The elements that comprise a pilot plant include (1) the pretreatment system, (2) tankage for flow equalization and cleaning, (3) pumps for pressurizing the membrane, recirculation, and backflushing with appropriate controls (e.g., variable-frequency drives), (4) the membrane test module, (5) adequate facilities for monitoring the performance of the test module, and (6) an appropriate system for backflushing the membranes. The information collected should be sufficient to allow for the design of the full-scale system and should include as a minimum the following items:

Membrane operating parameters
    Pretreatment requirements including chemical dosages
    Transmembrane flux rate correlated to operating time
    Transmembrane pressure
    Washwater requirements
    Recirculation ratio
    Cleaning frequency including protocol and chemical requirements
    Posttreatment requirements

Typical water quality measurements may include:

Turbidity	Temperature
Particle counts	Heterotrophic plate count
Total organic carbon	Other bacterial indicators
Nutrients	The specific constituents that can
Heavy metals	limit recovery such as silica, barium,
Organic priority pollutants	calcium, and sulfate
Total dissolved solids	Biotoxicity
pH	

Disposal of Concentrated Waste Streams

Disposal of the concentrated waste streams produced by membrane processes represents the major problem that must be dealt with in their applications. The principal methods now used for the disposal of the concentrated waste streams are reported in Table 10. While small facilities can dispose of small concentrated waste streams by blending with other wastewater flows, this approach is not suitable for large facilities. The concentrate from NF and RO facilities will contain hardness, heavy metals, high-molecular-weight organics, microorganisms, and often hydrogen sulfide gas. The pH is usually high due to the concentration of alkalinity, which increases the likelihood of metal precipitation in disposal wells. As a result, most of the large-scale desalination facilities are located along coastal regions, both in the United States and in other parts of the world. For inland locations, long transmission lines to coastal regions are being considered. While controlled evaporation is technically feasible, because of high operating and maintenance costs this approach is used where no other alternatives are available, and the value of product water is high.

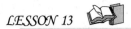

Disposal options for concentrated brine solutions from membrane processes   Table 10

Disposal	Description
Ocean discharge	The disposal option of choice for facilities located in the coastal regions of the United States. Typically, a brine line, with a deepocean discharge, is used by a number of dischargers Combined discharge with power-plant cooling water has been used in Florida. For inland locations truck, rail hauling, or pipeline is needed for transportation
Surface water discharge	Discharge of brines to surface waters is the most common method of disposal for concentrated brine solutions
Land application	Land application has been used for some low-concentration brine solutions
Discharge to wastewater collection system	This option is suitable only for very small discharges such that the increase in TDS is not significant (e.g., less than 20 mg/L)
Deep-well injection	Depends on whether subsurface aquifer is brackish water or is otherwise unsuitable for domestic uses
Evaporation ponds	Large surface area required in most areas with the exception of some southern and western states
Controlled thermal evaporation	Although energy-intensive, thermal evaporation may be the only option available in many areas

New Words and Phrases

alternate spacing　交替间隔
permselectivity　*n.* 选择透过性
normality　*n.* 标准状态，当量浓度
milliampere　*n.* 毫安培
makeup water　补充水
a priori　[拉丁语] 先前
variable-frequency　变频

protocol　*n.* 草案，协议，规程
heterotrophic　*adj.* 异养的
barium　*n.* 钡
biotoxicity　*n.* 生物毒性
subsurface aquifer　地下含水层
brackish　*adj.* 咸味的

LESSON 14

Advanced Oxidation Processes

Advanced oxidation processes (AOPs) are used to oxidize complex organic constituents found in wastewater that are difficult to degrade biologically into simpler end products. When chemical oxidation is used, it may not be necessary to oxidize completely a given compound or group of compounds. In many cases, partial oxidation is sufficient to render specific compounds more amenable to subsequent biological treatment or to reduce their toxicity. The oxidation of specific compounds may be characterized by the extent of degradation of the final oxidation products as follows (Rice, 1996):

1. *Primary degradation*. A structural change in the parent compound.

2. *Acceptable degradation (defusing)*. A structural change in the parent compound to the extent that toxicity is reduced.

3. *Ultimate degradation (mineralization)*. Conversion of organic carbon to inorganic CO_2.

4. *Unacceptable degradation (fusing)*. A structural change in the parent compound resulting in increased toxicity.

Theory of Advanced Oxidation

Advanced oxidation processes typically involve the generation and use of the hydroxyl free radical ($HO·$) as a strong oxidant to destroy compounds that cannot be oxidized by conventional oxidants such as oxygen, ozone, and chlorine. With the exception of fluorine, the hydroxyl radical is one of the most active oxidants known. The hydroxyl radical reacts with the dissolved constituents, initiating a series of oxidation reactions until the constituents are completely mineralized. Nonselective in their mode of attack and able to operate at normal temperature and pressures, hydroxyl radicals are capable of oxidizing almost all reduced materials present without restriction to specific classes or groups of compounds, as compared to other oxidants.

Advanced oxidation processes differ from the other treatment processes discussed (such as ion exchange or stripping) because wastewater compounds are degraded rather than concentrated or transferred into a different phase. Because secondary waste materials are not generated, there is no need to dispose of or regenerate materials.

Technologies Used to Produce Hydroxyl Radicals ($HO·$)

At the present time, a variety of technologies are available to produce $HO·$ in the aqueous phase. Of the technologies, only ozone/UV, ozone/hydrogen peroxide, ozone/UV/

hydrogen peroxide, and hydrogen peroxide/UV are being used on a commercial scale.

Ozone/UV. Production of the free radical HO· with UV light can be illustrated by the following reactions for the photolysis of ozone:

$$O_3 + UV(\text{or } h\nu, \lambda < 310 \text{ nm}) \longrightarrow O_2 + O(^1D) \qquad (1)$$

$$O(^1D) + H_2O \longrightarrow HO\cdot + HO\cdot \text{ (in wet air)} \qquad (2)$$

$$O(^1D) + H_2O \longrightarrow HO\cdot + HO\cdot \rightarrow H_2O_2 \text{ (in water)} \qquad (3)$$

where O_3 = ozone

UV = ultraviolet radiation (or $h\nu$ = energy)

O_2 = oxygen

$O(^1D)$ = excited oxygen atom. The symbol (^1D) is a spectroscopic notation used to specify the atomic and molecular configuration (also known as a singlet oxygen)

HO· = hydroxyl radical. The dot (·) that appears next to the hydroxyl and other radicals is used to denote the fact that these species have an unpaired electron.

As shown in Eq. (2), the photolysis of ozone in wet air results in the formation of hydroxyl radicals. In water, the photolysis of ozone leads to the formation of hydrogen peroxide [see Eq. (3)]. Because the photolysis of ozone in water leads to the formation of hydrogen peroxide, which is subsequently photolyzed to form hydroxyl radicals, the use of ozone in this application is generally not cost-effective. In air, the ozone/UV process can degrade compounds through direct ozonation, photolysis, or reaction with the hydroxyl radical. The ozone/UV process is more effective when the compounds of interest can be degraded through the absorption of the UV irradiation as well as through the reaction with the hydroxyl radicals. A schematic flow diagram of the processes is illustrated on Figure 1.

Ozone/Hydrogen Peroxide. For compounds that do not adsorb UV, AOPs involving ozone/H_2O_2 may be more effective. A schematic flow diagram of the processes is illustrated on Figure 2. Compounds in water such as trichloroethylene (TCE) and

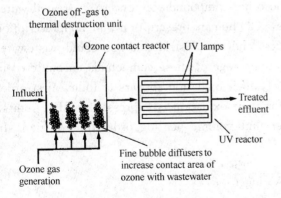

Figure 1 Schematic representation of advanced oxidation process involving the use of ozone and UV radiation

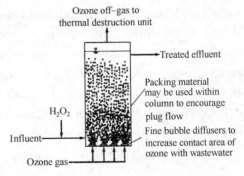

Figure 2 Schematic representation of advanced oxidation process involving the use of ozone and hydrogen peroxide

perchloroethylene (PCE) have been reduced significantly with AOPs using hydrogen peroxide and ozone to generate HO·. The overall reaction for the production of hydroxyl radicals using hydrogen peroxide and ozone is as follows:

$$H_2O + 2O_3 \longrightarrow HO· + HO· + 3O_2 \tag{4}$$

Hydrogen Peroxide/UV. Hydroxyl radicals are also formed when water containing H_2O_2 is exposed to UV light (200 to 280nm). The following reaction can be used to describe the photolysis of H_2O_2:

$$H_2O_2 + UV(\text{or } h\nu, \lambda \approx 200 \sim 280\text{nm}) \longrightarrow HO· + HO· \tag{5}$$

In some cases the use of the hydrogen peroxide/UV process has not been feasible because H_2O_2 has a small molar extinction coefficient, requiring high concentrations of H_2O_2 and not using the UV energy efficiently. A schematic flow diagram and a typical installation of the hydrogen peroxide/UV process are shown on Figure 3.

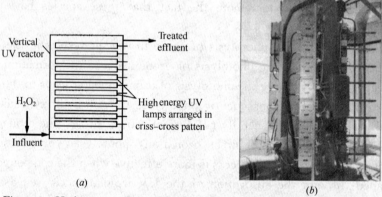

Figure 3 Hydrogen peroxide and UV radiation advanced oxidation process
(a) schematic flow diagram. The hydrogen peroxide feed system and storage container are placed in a contained area and (b) photograph of typical vertical-flow UV reactor

Most recently, the hydrogen peroxide/UV process has been applied to the oxidation of trace constituents found in treated water. The process has been studied for the removal of N-Nitrosodimethylamine (NDMA) and other compounds of concern in treated water including (1) sex and steroidal hormones, (2) human prescription and nonprescription drugs, (3) veterinary and human antibiotics, and (4) industrial and household wastewater products. At the relatively low concentration range of these compounds encountered in treated water (typically in the μg/L range), their oxidation appears to follow first-order kinetics. The electrical energy required for their oxidation is expressed in EE/O units, defined as the electrical energy input per unit volume per log order of reduction. In equation form, the EE/O is given by

$$EE/O = \frac{EE_i}{V[\log(C_i/C_f)]} \tag{6}$$

where EE/O = electrical energy input per log reduction, kWh/(m³ · log order of reduction)
EE_i = electrical energy input, kWh
V = volume of liquid treated, m³

C_i = initial concentration, ng

C_f = final concentration, ng

Based on currently available technology, the required EE/O value for a one-log order of reduction (i.e., 100 to 10) of NDMA is on the order of 21 to 265 kWh/($10^3 m^3$ · log order) [0.08 to 1.0 kWh/(10^3 gal · log order)] with a 5 to 6 mg/L dose of H_2O_2, although in some cases it did not appear that the peroxide was necessary. The required EE/O value will vary significantly with the characteristics of the treated water.

Other Processes. Other reactions that yield HO· include the reactions of H_2O_2 and UV with Fenton's reagent and the adsorption of UV by semiconductor metal oxides such as TiO_2 suspended in water, which acts as a catalyst.

Applications

Based on numerous studies, it has been found that combined AOPs are more effective than any of the individual agents (e.g., ozone, UV, hydrogen peroxide). AOPs are usually applied to low COD wastewaters because of the cost of ozone and/or H_2O_2 required to generate the hydroxyl radicals. Material that was previously resistant to degradation may be transformed into compounds that will require further biological treatment. The application of AOPs for the disinfection of treated wastewater and for the treatment of refractory organic compounds is considered below. Some operational problems are also identified.

Disinfection. Because it was recognized that free radicals generated from ozone were more powerful oxidants than ozone alone, it was reasoned that the hydroxyl free radicals could be used effectively to oxidize microorganisms and refractory organic materials in water. Unfortunately, because the half-life of the hydroxyl free radicals is short, on the order of microseconds, it is not possible to develop high concentrations. With extremely low concentrations, the required detention times for microorganism disinfection are prohibitive.

Oxidation of Refractory Organic Compounds. For the reasons cited above hydroxyl radicals are not used for conventional disinfection; instead they are used more commonly for the oxidation of trace amounts of refractory organic compounds found in highly treated effluents. The hydroxyl radicals, once generated, can attack organic molecules by radical addition, hydrogen abstraction, electron transfer, and radical combination.

1. *By radical addition.* The addition of the hydroxyl radical to an unsaturated aliphatic or aromatic organic compound (e.g., C_6H_6) results in the production of a radical organic compound that can be oxidized further by compounds such as oxygen or ferrous iron to produce stable oxidized end products. In the following reactions the abbreviation R is used to denote the reacting organic compound.

$$R + HO· \longrightarrow ROH \tag{7}$$

2. *By hydrogen abstraction.* The hydroxyl radical can be used to remove a hydrogen atom from organic compounds. The removal of a hydrogen atom results in the formation of a radical organic compound, initiating a chain reaction where the radical organic compound reacts with oxygen, producing a peroxyl radical, which can react with

another organic compound, and so on.

$$RH + HO \cdot \longrightarrow R \cdot + H_2O \tag{8}$$

3. *By electron transfer.* Electron transfer results in the formation of ions of a higher valence. Oxidation of a monovalent negative ion will result in the formation of an atom or a free radical.

$$R^n + HO \cdot \longrightarrow R^{n-1} + OH^- \tag{9}$$

4. *By radical combination.* Two radicals can combine to form a stable product.

$$HO \cdot + HO \cdot \longrightarrow H_2O_2 \tag{10}$$

In general, the reaction of hydroxyl radicals with organic compounds, at completion, will produce water, carbon dioxide, and salts.

Operational Problems

High concentrations of carbonate and bicarbonate in some wastewater can react with $HO \cdot$ and reduce the efficiency of advanced oxidation treatment processes. Other factors can also affect the treatment process, such as suspended material, pH, type and nature of the residual TOC, and other water constituents. Because the chemistry of the wastewater matrix is different for each wastewater, pilot testing is almost always required to test the technical feasibility, to obtain usable design data and information, and to obtain operating experience with a specific AOP.

New Words and Phrases

amenable *adj.* 应服从的
parent compound 母体化合物
reduced material 还原性物质
photolysis *n.* 光分解，光解作用
spectroscopic *adj.* 分光镜的
notation *n.* 符号
singlet oxygen 纯态氧，一单氧
unpaired electron 未配对电子
trichloroethylene (TCE) *n.* 三氯乙烯
perchloroethylene (PCE) *n.* 全氯乙烯
molar extinction coefficient 摩尔消光系数
steroidal *adj.* 甾族的
hormone *n.* 荷尔蒙，激素
prescription drug 处方药

nonprescription drug 非处方药
veterinary *n.* 兽医
  adj. 医牲畜的，兽医的
antibiotics *n.* 抗生素，抗生学
reagent *n.* 试剂
hydrogen abstraction reaction 夺氢反应
unsaturated aliphatic organic compound
  不饱和脂肪族有机化合物
aromatic organic compound 芳香族有机化合物
ferrous *adj.* 铁的，含铁的，亚铁的
peroxyl (hydrogen peroxide) *n.* 过氧化氢

Questions

1. What are the advantages of advanced oxidation processes?
2. What technologies are available to produce $HO \cdot$ in the aqueous phase?

3. What is the meaning of EE/O unit?
4. What is *hydrogen abstraction*?
5. What factors can affect the advanced oxidation processes?

Reading Material

Distillation

Distillation is a unit operation in which the components of a liquid solution are separated by vaporization and condensation. Along with reverse osmosis, distillation can be used to control the buildup of salts in critical reuse applications. Because distillation is expensive, its application is generally limited to applications such as (1) a high degree of treatment is required, (2) contaminants cannot be removed by other methods, and (3) inexpensive heat is available. The purpose of this section is to introduce the basic concepts involved in distillation. As the use of distillation for wastewater reclamation is a recent development, the current literature must be consulted for the results of ongoing studies and more recent applications.

Distillation Processes

Over the past 20 years, a variety of distillation processes, employing a variety of evaporator types and methods of using and transferring heat energy, have been evaluated or used. The principal distillation processes are (1) boiling with submerged-tube heating surface, (2) boiling with long-tube vertical evaporator, (3) flash evaporation, (4) forced circulation with vapor compression, (5) solar evaporation, (6) rotating-surface evaporation, (7) wiped-surface evaporation, (8) vapor reheating process, (9) direct heat transfer using an immiscible liquid, and (10) condensing-vapor-heat transfer by vapor other than steam. Of these types of distillation processes, multistage flash evaporation, multiple-effect evaporation, and the vapor-compression distillation appear most feasible for the reclamation of municipal wastewater.

Multiple-Effect Evaporation. In multiple-effect evaporation several evaporators (boilers) are arranged in series, each operating at a lower pressure than the preceding one. In a three-stage, vertical-tube evaporator (see Figure 4), after the influent water is pretreated, it enters

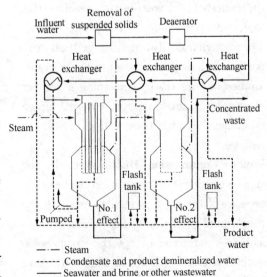

Figure 4 Schematic of multiple-effect evaporation distillation process

the heat exchanger in the last stage (No. 2) and progressively warms as it goes through the heat exchangers in the other effects (i. e. , stages). As the water moves through the heat exchangers, it condenses the water vapor emanating from the various effects. When the progressively warmed influent water reaches the first stage, it flows down the internal periphery of vertical tubes in a thin film, which is heated by steam. The wastewater feed to the second effect comes from the bottom of the first effect. If entrainment is kept low, almost all of the nonvolatile contaminants can be removed in a single evaporation step. Volatile contaminants, such as ammonia gas and low-molecular-weight organic acids, may be removed in a preliminary evaporation step, but if their concentration is so small that their presence in the final product is not objectionable, this step with its added cost can be eliminated.

Multistage Flash Evaporation. Multistage flash evaporation systems have been used commercially in desalination for many years. In the multistage flash process (see Figure 5), the influent wastewater is first treated to remove TSS and deaerated before being pumped through heat transfer units in the several stages of the distillation system, each of which is maintained at a lower pressure. Vapor generation or boiling caused by reduction in pressure is known as flashing. As the water enters each stage through a pressure-reducing nozzle, a portion of the water is flashed to form a vapor. In turn, the flashed water vapor condenses on the outside of the condenser tubes and is collected in trays (see Figure 5). As the vapor condenses, its latent heat is used to preheat the wastewater that is being returned to the main heater, where it will receive additional heat before being introduced to the first flashing stage. When the concentrated wastewater reaches the lowest-pressure stage, it is pumped out. Thermodynamically, multistage flash evaporation is less efficient than ordinary evaporation. However, by combining a number of stages in a single reactor, external piping is eliminated and construction costs are reduced.

Vapor - Compression Distillation. In the vapor - compression process an increase in pressure of the vapor is used to establish the temperature difference for the transfer of heat. The basic schematic of a vapor - compression distillation unit is shown on Figure 6. After initial heating of the wastewater, the vapor pump is operated so that the vapor under

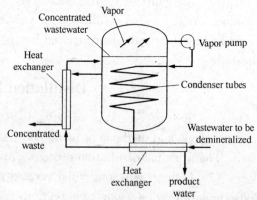

Figure 5　Schematic of multistage flash evaporation distillation process

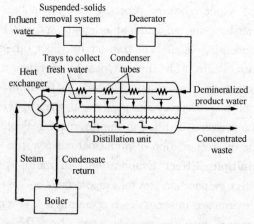

Figure 6　Schematic of vapor-compression distillation process

higher pressure can condense in the condenser tubes, at the same time causing the release of an equivalent amount of vapor from the concentrated solution. Heat exchangers can conserve heat from both the condensate and the waste brine. The only energy input required during operation is the mechanical energy for the vapor pump. Hot concentrated wastewater must be discharged at intervals to prevent the buildup of excessive concentrations of salt in the boiler.

Performance Expectations in Reclamation Applications

The theoretical thermodynamic minimum energy required to raise the temperature of wastewater and to provide the latent heat of vaporization is about 2280 kJ/kg. Unfortunately, because of the many irreversibilities in an actual distillation process, the thermodynamic minimum energy requirements are of little practical relevance in the practical evaluation of distillation processes. Typically, about 1.25 to 1.35 times the latent heat of vaporization will be required.

The principal issues with the application of the distillation processes for wastewater reclamation are the carry-over of volatile constituents found in treated wastewater and the degree of subsequent cooling and treatment that may be required to renovate the distilled water.

Operating Problems

The most common operating problems encountered include scaling and corrosion. Due to temperature increases, inorganic salts come out of solution and precipitate on the inside walls of pipes and equipment. The control of scaling due to calcium carbonate, calcium sulfate, and magnesium hydroxide is one of the most important design and operational considerations in distillation desalination processes. Controlling the pH minimizes carbonate and hydroxide scales. Most inorganic solutions are corrosive. Cupronickel alloys are used most commonly in seawater desalination. Other metals that are used include aluminum, titanium, and monel.

New Words and Phrases

vaporization n. 汽化，蒸发［作用］
condensation n. 冷凝作用，凝结作用
immiscible adj. 不能混合的，不溶混的
multistage flash evaporation 多级闪蒸
entrainment n. 夹带，夹杂
nonvolatile adj. 非挥发性的
deaerate vt. 脱气

condenser n. 冷凝器
latent heat 潜热
irreversibility n. 不可逆性
renovate vt. 修复，更新
magnesium hydroxide 氢氧化镁
cupronickel n. 白铜，铜镍合金
monel n. 蒙乃尔铜-镍合金

LESSON 15

Introduction to the Activated-sludge Process

To provide a basis for the process designs presented in the subsequent sections, it will be useful to consider (1) a brief summary of the historical development of the activated-sludge process, (2) a description of the basic process, (3) a brief review of the evolution of the activated-sludge process, and (4) an overview of recent process developments.

Historical Development

The activated-sludge process is now used routinely for biological treatment of municipal and industrial wastewaters. The antecedents of the activated-sludge process date back to the early 1880s to the work of Dr. Angus Smith, who investigated the aeration of wastewater in tanks and the hastening of the oxidation of the organic matter. The aeration of wastewater was studied subsequently by a number of investigators, and in 1910 Black and Phelps reported that a considerable reduction in putrescibility could be secured by forcing air into wastewater in basins. In experiments conducted at the Lawrence Experiment Station during 1912 and 1913 by Clark and Gage with aerated wastewater, growths of organisms could be cultivated in bottles and in tanks and would greatly increase the degree of purification obtained (Clark and Adams, 1914). The results of the work at the Lawrence Experiment Station were so striking that knowledge of them led Dr. G. J. Fowler of the University of Manchester, England to suggest experiments along similar lines be conducted at the Manchester Sewage Works where Ardern and Lockett carried out valuable research on the subject. During the course of their experiments, Ardern and Lockett found that the sludge played an important part in the results obtained by aeration, as announced in their paper of May 3, 1914 (Ardern and Lockett, 1914). The process was named *activated sludge* by Ardern and Lockett because it involved the production of an activated mass of microorganisms capable of aerobic stabilization of organic material in wastewater (Metcalf & Eddy, 1930).

Description of Basic Process

By definition, the basic activated-sludge treatment process, as illustrated on Figure 1*a* and *b*, consists of the following three basic components: (1) a reactor in which the microorganisms responsible for treatment are kept in suspension and aerated; (2) liquid-solids separation, usually in a sedimentation tank; and (3) a recycle system for returning solids removed from the liquid-solids separation unit back to the reactor. Numerous process configurations have evolved employing these components. An important feature of the activated-sludge process is the formation of flocculent settleable solids that can be removed by gravity settling in sedimentation tanks. In most cases, the activated-sludge process is employed in conjunction with physical and chemical processes that are used for the preliminary and primary treatment of wastewater, and posttreatment, including disinfection and possibly filtration.

Historically, most activated-sludge plants have received wastewaters that were pretreated by primary sedimentation, as shown on Figure 1a and b. Primary sedimentation is most efficient at removing settleable solids, whereas the biological processes are essential for removing soluble, colloidal, and particulate (suspended) organic substances; for biological nitrification and denitrification; and for biological phosphorus removal. For applications such as treating wastewater from smaller-sized communities, primary treatment is often not used as more emphasis is placed on simpler and less operator-intensive treatment methods. Primary treatment is omitted frequently in areas of the world that have hot climates where odor problems from primary tanks and primary sludge

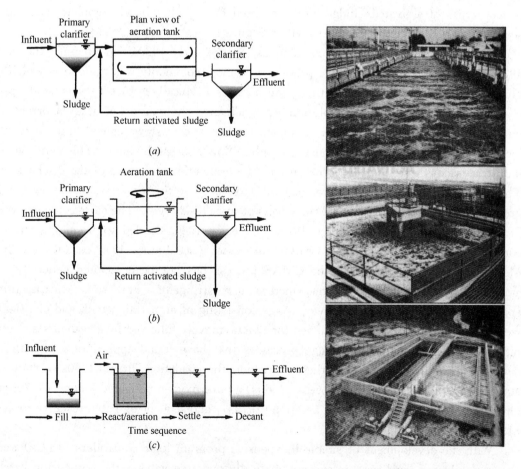

Figure 1 Typical activated-sludge processes with different types of reactors
(a) schematic flow diagram of plug-flow process and view of plug-flow reactor, (b) schematic flow diagram of complete-mix process and view of complete-mix activated-sludge reactor, and(c)schematic diagram of sequencing batch reactor process and view of sequencing batch reactor

can be significant. For these applications, various modifications of conventional activated-sludge processes are used; including sequencing batch reactors, oxidation ditch systems, aerated lagoons, or stabilization ponds.

Evolution of the Activated-Sludge Process

A number of activated-sludge processes and design configurations have evolved since its early conception as a result of (1) engineering innovation in response to the need for higher-quality effluents from wastewater treatment plants; (2) technological advances in equipment, electronics, and process control; (3) increased understanding of microbial processes and fundamentals; and (4) the continual need to reduce capital and operating costs for municipalities and industries. With greater frequency, activated-sludge processes used today may incorporate nitrification, biological nitrogen removal, and/or biological phosphorus removal. These designs employ reactors in series, operated under aerobic, anoxic, and anaerobic conditions, and may use internal recycle pumps and piping. The general types of activated-sludge processes used (i.e., plug flow, complete mix, and sequencing batch reactor) are illustrated on Figure 1.

Since the process came into common use in the early 1920s and up until the late 1970s, the type of activated-sludge process used most commonly was the one in which a plug-flow reactor with large length to width ratios (typically $>10:1$) was used (see Figure 1a). In considering the evolution of the activated-sludge process, it is important to note that the discharge of industrial wastes to domestic wastewater collection systems increased in the late 1960s. The use of a plug-flow process became problematic when industrial wastes were introduced because of the toxic effects of some of the discharges. The complete-mix reactor was developed, in part, because the larger volume allowed for greater dilution and thus mitigated the effects of toxic discharges. The more common type of activated-sludge process in the 1970s and early 1980s tended to be single stage, complete-mix activated-sludge (CMAS) processes (see Figure 1b), as advanced by McKinney (1962). In Europe, the CMAS process has not been adopted generally as ammonia standards have become increasingly stringent. For some nitrification applications, two-stage systems (each stage consisting of an aeration tank and clarifier) were used with the first stage designed for BOD removal, followed by a second stage for nitrification. Other activated-sludge processes that have found application, with their dates of major interest in parentheses, include the oxidation ditch (1950s), contact stabilization (1950s), Krause process (1960s), pure oxygen activated sludge (1970s), Orbal process (1970s), deep shaft aeration (1970s), and sequencing batch reactor process (1980).

With the development of simple inexpensive program logic controllers (PLCs) and the availability of level sensors and automatically operated valves, the sequencing batch reactor (SBR) process (see Figure 1c) became more widely used by the late 1970s, especially for smaller communities and industrial installations with intermittent flows. In recent years, however, SBRs are being used for large cities in some parts of the world.

The SBR is a fill-and-draw type of reactor system involving a single complete-mix reactor in which all steps of the activated-sludge process occur. Mixed liquor remains in the reactor during all cycles, thereby eliminating the need for separate sedimentation tanks.

In comparing the plug-flow (Figure 1a) and complete-mix activated-sludge (CMAS) (Figure 1b) processes, the mixing regimes and tank geometry are quite different. In the CMAS process, the mixing of the tank contents is sufficient so that ideally the concentrations of the mixed-liquor constituents, soluble substances (i.e., COD, BOD, NH_4-N), and colloidal and suspended solids do not vary with location in the aeration basin. The plug-flow process involves relatively long, narrow aeration basins, so that the concentration of soluble substances and colloidal and suspended solids varies along the reactor length. Although process configurations employing long, narrow tanks are commonly referred to as plug-flow processes, in reality, true plug flow does not exist. Depending on the type of aeration system, back mixing of the mixed liquor can occur and, depending on the layout of the reactor and the system reaction kinetics, nominal plug flow may be described more appropriately by the series of complete-mix reactors.

Activated-sludge process designs before and until the late 1970s generally involved the configurations shown on Figure 1a and b. However, with interest in biological nutrient removal, staged reactor designs consisting of complete-mix reactors in series been developed (see Figure 2). Some of the stages are not aerated (anaerobic or anoxic stages) and internal recycle flows may be used. For nitrification, a staged aerobic reactor design may also be used to provide more efficient use of the total reactor volume than a single-stage CMAS process. Pilot-plant studies are sometimes used to evaluate and optimize biological nutrient-removal processes.

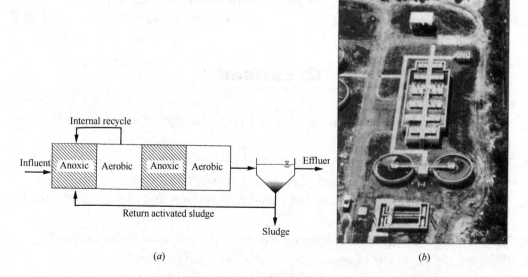

Figure 2 Bardenpho process with staged reactors for biological nitrogen removal
(a) schematic diagram of staged process and (b) view of a staged Bardenpho treatment plant in Palmetto, FL, the first of its type in the United States

Recent Process Developments

As noted above, numerous modifications of the activated-sludge process have evolved in the last 10 to 20 years, aimed principally at effective and efficient removal of nitrogen and phosphorus. Nearly all of the various modifications are based on the same fundamental principles of biological treatment.

Because of the development of improved membrane design, principally for water treatment applications, membrane technology has been found increasing application for enhanced solids separation for water reuse, and more recently for use in suspended growth reactors for wastewater treatment. Membrane biological reactors (MBRs), which may change the look of wastewater- treatment facilities in the future.

Because the design and operation of the activated-sludge process is becoming more complex, computer modeling is an increasingly important tool to incorporate the large number of components and reactions necessary to evaluate activated - sludge performance.

New Words and Phrases

biological treatment   生物处理
antecedent   *n.* 先辈
hasten   *v.* 催促，促进，加速
putrescibility   *n.* 易腐烂
cultivate   *vt.* 培养
sequencing batch reactor (SBR)   序批式反应器
oxidation ditch system   氧化沟系统
aerated lagoon   曝气塘
stabilization pond   稳定塘
plug-flow   *n.* 柱塞流
complete-mix   完全混合式
anoxic   *adj.* 缺氧的
mitigate   *v.* 减轻
parentheses   *n.* 圆括号，插入语，插曲
nitrification   *n.* [化]硝化作用
PLC: Program Logic Control   程序逻辑控制

Questions

1. What are the basic components that activated - sludge treatment process must consist of?
2. What is the important feature of the activated-sludge process?
3. What constituents can the biological processes remove?
4. What are the reasons of activated - sludge processes and design configurations evolvement?
5. What is the advantage of complete-mix reactor in the activated-sludge process?
6. What are the conditions of sequencing batch reactor development?
7. What type of reactor can be used to describe the nominal plug flow?

LESSON 15

Reading Material

Operational Problems Of the Activated-sludge Process

The most common problems encountered in the operation of an activated-sludge plant are bulking sludge, rising sludge, and *Nocardia* foam. Because few plants have escaped these problems, it is appropriate to discuss their nature and methods for their control.

Bulking Sludge

In many cases MLSS with poor settling characteristics has developed into what is known as a *bulking sludge* condition, which defines a condition in the activated-sludge clarifier that can cause high effluent suspended solids and poor treatment performance. In a bulking sludge condition, the MLSS floc does not compact or settle well, and floc particles are discharged in the clarifier effluent. With good settling sludge, sludge levels may be as low as 10 to 30 cm at the bottom of the clarifier. In extreme bulking sludge conditions, the sludge blanket cannot be contained and large quantities of MLSS are carried into the system effluent, potentially resulting in violation of permit requirements, inadequate disinfection, and clogging of effluent filters.

Two principal types of sludge bulking problems have been identified. One type, *filamentous bulking*, is caused by the growth of filamentous organisms or organisms that can grow in a filamentous form under adverse conditions, and is the predominant form of bulking that occurs. The other type of bulking, *viscous bulking*, is caused by an excessive amount of extracellular biopolymer, which produces a sludge with a slimy, jellylike consistency (Wanner, 1994). As the biopolymers are hydrophilic, the activated sludge is highly water-retentive, and this condition is referred to as *hydrous bulking*. The resultant sludge has a low density with low settling velocities and poor compaction. Viscous bulking is usually found with nutrient-limited systems or in a very high loading condition with wastewater having a high mount of rbCOD.

Bulking sludge problems due to the growth of filamentous bacteria are more common. In filamentous growth, bacteria form filaments of single-cell organisms that attach end-to-end, and the filaments normally protrude out of the sludge floc. This structure, in contrast to the preferred dense floc with good settling properties, has an increased surface area to mass ratio, which results in poor settling. On Figure 3, a good settling, dense nonfilamentous floc is contrasted to floc containing filamentous growth. Many types of filamentous bacteria exist, and means have been developed for the identification and classification of filamentous bacteria found commonly in activated-sludge systems. The classification system is based on morphology (size and shape of cells, length and shape of filaments), staining responses, and cell inclusions. Sludge bulking can be caused by a variety of factors, including wastewater characteristics, design limitations, and operational issues. Individual items associated with each of these categories are identified in Table 1.

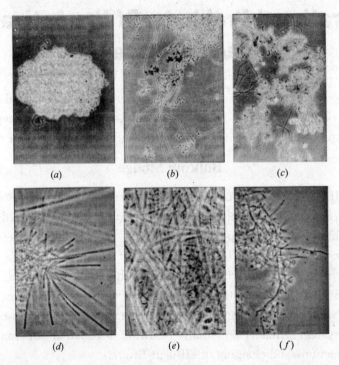

Figure 3 Examples of good and poor settling floc particles
(a) nonfilamentous good settling floc, (b) floc particles bridged by filamentous microorganisms, (c) floc particles with limited filamentous microorganisms and secondary form, (d) filaments extending from floc causing poor settling, (e) *Thiothrix* filaments with sulfur granules, and (f) type 1701 filamentous microorganism observed under low dissolved oxygen conditions

Factors that affect sludge bulking   Table 1

Factor	Description
Wastewater characteristics	Variations in flowrate
	Variations in composition
	pH
	Temperature
	Septicity
	Nutrient content
	Nature of waste components
Design limitations	Limited air supply
	Poor mixing
	Short circuiting (aeration tanks and clarifiers)
	Clarifier design (sludge collection and removal)
	Limited return sledge pumping capacity
Operational issues	Low dissolved oxygen
	Insufficient nutrients
	Low F/M
	Insufficient soluble BOD

Activated-sludge reactor operating conditions (low DO, low F/M, and complete-mix operation) clearly have an effect on the development of filamentous populations. One of the kinetic features of filamentous organisms that relates to these conditions is that they are very competitive at low substrate concentrations whether it be organic substrates, DO, or nutrients. Thus, lightly loaded complete-mix activated-sludge systems or low DO (<0.5 mg/L) operating conditions provide an environment more favorable to filamentous bacteria than to the desired floc-forming bacteria.

Filamentous bacteria such as *Beggiatoa* and *Thiothrix* grow well on hydrogen sulfide and reduced substrates, respectively, that would be found in septic wastewaters. When the influent wastewater contains fermentation products such as volatile fatty acids and reduced sulfur compounds (sulfides and thiosulfate), *Thiothrix* can proliferate. Prechlorination of the wastewaters has been done in some cases to prevent their growth. Besides causing bulking problems in activated-sludge systems, *Beggiatoa* and *Thiothrix* can create problems in fixed-film systems, including trickling filters and rotating biological contactors.

In the control of bulking, where a number of variables are possible causes, a checklist of items to investigate is valuable. The following items are recommended: (1) wastewater characteristics, (2) dissolved oxygen content, (3) process loading, (4) return and waste sludge pumping rates, (5) internal plant overloading, and (6) clarifier operation. One of the first steps to be taken when sludge setting characteristics changes is to view the mixed liquor under the microscope to determine what type of microbial growth changes or floc structure changes can be related to the development of bulking sludge.

Wastewater Characteristics

The nature of the components found in wastewater or the absence of certain components, such as trace elements, can lead to the development of a bulked sludge. If it is known that industrial wastes are being introduced into the system either intermittently or continuously, the quantity of nitrogen and phosphorus in the wastewater should be checked first, because limitations of both or either are known to favor bulking. Nutrient deficiency is a classic problem in the treatment of industrial wastewaters containing high levels of carbonaceous BOD. Wide fluctuations in pH are also known to be detrimental in plants of conventional design. Variations in organic waste loads due to batch-type operations can also lead to bulking and should be checked.

Dissolved Oxygen Concentration

Limited dissolved oxygen has been noted more frequently than any other cause of bulking. If the problem is due to limited oxygen, it can usually be confirmed by operating the aeration equipment at full capacity or by decreasing the system SRT, if possible, to reduce the oxygen demand. The aeration equipment should have adequate capacity to maintain at least 2 mg/L of dissolved oxygen in the aeration tank under normal loading conditions. If 2 mg/L of oxygen cannot be maintained, installation of improvements to the existing aeration system may be required.

Process Loading/Reactor Configuration

The aeration SRT should be checked to make sure that it is within the range of generally accepted values. In many cases, complete-mix systems with long SRTs and subsequent low F/M ratios experience filamentous growths. In such systems, the filamentous organisms are more competitive for substrate. Laboratory research and full-scale investigations have led to activated-sludge design configurations that provide conditions favoring the dominance of *floc-forming* bacteria over filamentous organisms. Reactors in series with various types of environmental conditions, i.e., aerobic, anoxic, and anaerobic, are generally used to augment or replace a complete-mix reactor. The series configurations are called selector processes because they provide conditions that cause selection of floc-forming bacteria in lieu of filamentous organisms as the dominant population.

Internal Plant Overloading

To avoid internal plant overloading, recycle loads should be controlled so they are not returned to the plant flow during times of peak hydraulic and organic loading. Examples of recycle loads are filtrate from sludge dewatering operations and supernatant from sludge digesters.

Clarifier Operation

The operating characteristics of the clarifier may also affect sludge settling characteristics. Poor settling is often a problem in center-feed circular tanks where sludge is removed from the tank directly under the point where the mixed liquor enters. Sludge may actually be retained in the tank for many hours rather than the desired 30min and cause localized septic conditions. If this is the case, then the design is at fault, and changes must be made in the inlet feed well and sludge withdrawal equipment.

Temporary Control Measures

In an emergency situation or while the aforementioned factors are being investigated, chlorine and hydrogen peroxide may be used to provide temporary help. Chlorination of return sludge has been practiced quite extensively as a means of controlling bulking. A typical design for a low (5 to 10 h) τ system uses 0.002 to 0.008 kg of chlorine per kg MLSS·d. Although chlorination is effective in controlling bulking caused by filamentous growths, it is ineffective when bulking is due to light floc containing bound water. Chlorination normally results in the production of a turbid effluent until such time as the sludge is free of the filamentous forms. Chlorination of a nitrifying sludge will also produce a turbid effluent because of the death of the nitrifying organisms. The use of chlorine also raises issues about the formation of trihalomethanes and other compounds with potential health and environmental effects. Hydrogen peroxide has also been used in the control of filamentous organisms in bulking sludge. Dosage of hydrogen peroxide and treatment time depend on the extent of the filamentous development.

Rising Sludge

Occasionally, sludge that has good settling characteristics will be observed to rise or float to the surface after a relatively short settling period. The most common cause of this phenomenon is denitrification, in which nitrites and nitrates in the wastewater are converted to nitrogen gas. As nitrogen gas is formed in the sludge layer, much of it is trapped in the sludge mass. If enough gas is formed, the sludge mass becomes buoyant and rises or floats to the surface. Rising sludge can be differentiated from bulking sludge by noting the presence of small gas bubbles attached to the floating solids and the presence of more floating sludge on the secondary clarifier surface. Rising sludge is common in short SRT systems, where the temperature encourages the initiation of nitrification, and the mixed liquor is very active due to the low sludge age.

Rising sludge problems may be overcome by (1) increasing the return activated-sludge withdrawal rate from the clarifier to reduce the detention time of the sludge in the clarifier, (2) decreasing the rate of flow of aeration liquor into the offending clarifier if the sludge depth cannot be reduced by increasing the return activated-sludge withdrawal rate, (3) where possible, increasing the speed of the sludge-collecting mechanism in the settling tanks, and (4) decreasing the SRT to bring the activated sludge out of nitrification. For warm climates where it is very difficult to operate at a low enough SRT to limit nitrification, an anoxic/aerobic process is preferred to denitrification to prevent rising sludge and to improve sludge settling characteristics.

Nocardia Foam

Two bacteria genera, *Nocardia and Microthrix parvicella*, are associated with extensive foaming in activated-sludge processes. These organisms have hydrophobic cell surfaces and attach to air bubbles, where they stabilize the bubbles to cause foam. The organisms can be found at high concentrations in the foam above the mixed liquor. Both types of bacteria can be identified under microscopic examination. *Nocardia* has a filamentous structure, and the filaments are very short and are contained within the floc particles. *Microthrix parvicella* has thin filaments extending from the floc particles. Foaming on an activated-sludge basin and a microscopic view of Nocardia are shown on Figure 4. The foam is thick, has a brown color, and can build up in thickness of 0.5 to 1 m.

The foam production can occur with both diffused and mechanical aeration but is more pronounced with diffused aeration and with higher air flowrates. Problems of *Nocardia* foaming in the activated sludge can also lead to foaming in anaerobic and aerobic digesters that receive the waste-activated sludge. *Nocardia* growth is common where surface scum is trapped in either the aeration basin or secondary clarifiers. Aeration basins that are baffled with flow from one cell to the next occurring under the baffles, instead of over the top, encourage *Nocardia* growth and foam collection.

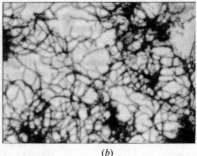

(a) (b)

Figure 4 Nocordia foam
(a) example of foam on an aeration tank and (b) microscopic observation
of gram-stained Nocardia filaments

Methods that can be used to control *Nocardia* include (1) avoiding trapping foam in the secondary treatment process, (2) avoiding the recycle of skimmings into the secondary treatment process, and (3) using chlorine spray on the surface of the *Nocardia* foam. The use of a selector design may help to discourage *Nocardia* foaming, but significant foaming has been observed with anoxic/aerobic processes. The addition of a small concentration of cationic polymer has been used with some success for controlling *Nocardia* foaming. The presence of *Nocardia* has also been associated with the presence of *Nocardia-Microthrix* with fats and edible oils in wastewater. Reducing the oil and grease content from discharges to the collection system from restaurants, truck stops, and meatpacking facilities by effective degreasing processes can help control potential *Nocardia* problems.

New Words and Phrases

MLSS   mixed-liquor suspended solids
bulking Sludge   膨胀污泥
nocardia   *n.* 诺卡氏菌属，土壤丝菌属
filamentous   *adj.* 细丝状的，如丝的
filamentous bacteria   丝状菌
viscous   *adj.* 黏性的，黏滞的
extracellular   *adj.* （位于或发生于）细胞外的
biopolymer   *n.* 生物聚合物
slimy   *adj.* 黏糊糊的，（分泌）黏液的，泥泞的
jellylike   *adj.* 胶体状的
hydrous   *adj.* 含水的
rbCOD   biodegradable chemical oxygen demand

morphology   *n.* 形态学，形态论；词态学
staining   *n.* 着色
cell inclusion   细胞内含物
F/M   food to microorganism ratio
substrate（substratum）   *n.* 培养基，酶作用物，底物，基质
Beggiatoa   *n.* 贝日阿托菌属[属于硫细菌]
thiothrix   *n.* 丝硫细菌属
fermentation   *n.* 发酵
volatile fatty acid   挥发性脂肪酸
thiosulfate   *n.* 硫代硫酸盐（或酯）
proliferate   *v.* 增生扩散
prechlorination   *n.* 预加氯
checklist   *n.* 清单

LESSON 15

granule   *n.* 小粒，颗粒，细粒
SRT（solids reaction time）   represents the average period of time during which the sludge has remained in the system.
septicity   *n.* 腐败性
supernatant（liquor）   *n.* 上层清液
localize   *v.* （使）局部化
bound water   结合水，束缚水
offending   *adj.* 不愉快的，厌恶的
genera   *n.* 类，属

Microthrix parvicella   微丝菌属的一种
pronounced   *adj.* 显著的，明确的
baffle   *n.* 挡板
skimming   *n.* 撇取浮沫，所撇取的浮沫
cationic polymer   阳离子聚合物
edible oil   食用油
meatpacking   *n.* 肉类加工业
degreasing   *n.* 脱脂(法)，除油(法)

LESSON 16

Trickling Filters

Trickling filters have been used to provide biological wastewater treatment of municipal and industrial wastewaters for nearly 100 years. As noted above, the trickling filter is a nonsubmerged fixed-film biological reactor using rock or plastic packing over which wastewater is distributed continuously. Treatment occurs as the liquid flows over the attached biofilm. The depth of the rock packing ranges from 0.9 to 2.5 m (3 to 8 ft) and averages 1.8 m (6 ft). Rock filter beds are usually circular, and the liquid wastewater is distributed over the top of the bed by a rotary distributor. Many conventional trickling filters using rock as the packing material have been converted to plastic packing to increase treatment capacity. Virtually all new trickling filters are now constructed with plastic packing.

Trickling filters that use plastic packing have been built in round, square, and other shapes with depths varying from 4 to 12 m (14 to 40 ft). In addition to the packing, other components of the trickling filter include a wastewater dosing or application system, an underdrain, and a structure to contain the packing. The underdrain system is important both for collecting the trickling filter effluent liquid and as a porous structure through which air can circulate. The collected liquid is passed to a sedimentation tank where the solids are separated from the treated wastewater. In practice, a portion of the liquid collected in the underdrain system or the settled effluent is recycled to the trickling filter feed flow, usually to dilute the strength of the incoming wastewater and to maintain enough wetting to keep the biological slime layer moist.

Influent wastewater is normally applied at the top of the packing through distributor arms that extend across the trickling filter inner diameter and have variable openings to provide a uniform application rate per unit area. The distributor arms are rotated by the force of the water exiting through their opening or by the use of electric drives. The electric drive designs provide more control flexibility and a wider range of distributor rotational speeds than possible by the simple hydraulic designs. In some cases, especially for square or rectangular filters, fixed flat-spray nozzles have been used.

Primary clarification is necessary before rock trickling filters, and generally used also before trickling filters with plastic packing, though fine screens (smaller than 3-mm openings) have been used successfully with plastic packing. With increases in plastic and rubber floatable materials in wastewater, screening of these materials is important to reduce fouling of the packing. In some installations a wire-mesh screen is placed over the top of plastic packing to collect debris that can be vacuumed off periodically.

A slime layer develops on the rock or plastic packing in the trickling filters and contains the microorganisms for biodegradation of the substrates to be removed from the liquid flowing over the packing. The biological community in the filter includes aerobic and facultative bacteria, fungi, algae, and protozoans. Higher animals, such as worms, and snails, are also present.

The slime layer thickness can reach depths as much as 10 mm. Organic material from the liquid is adsorbed onto the biological film or slime layer. In the outer portions of the biological slime layer (0.1 to 0.2 mm), the organic material is degraded by aerobic microorganisms. As the microorganisms grow and the slime layer thickness increases, oxygen is consumed before it can penetrate the full depth, and an anaerobic environment is established near the surface of the packing. As the slime layer increases in thickness, the substrate in the wastewater is used before it can penetrate the inner depths of the biofilm. Bacteria in the slime layer enter an endogenous respiration state and lose their ability to cling to the packing surface. The liquid then washes the slime off the packing, and a new slime layer starts to grow. The phenomenon of losing the slime layer is called *sloughing* and is primarily a function of the organic and hydraulic loading on the filter. The hydraulic loading accounts for shear velocities, and the organic loading accounts for the rate of metabolism in the slime layer. Hydraulic loading and trickling filter sloughing can be controlled by using a wastewater distributor with an electric motor drive to vary rotational speed.

Trickling Filler Classification and Applications

Trickling filter applications and loadings, based on historical terminology developed originally for rock filter designs, are summarized in Table 1. Trickling filter designs are classified by hydraulic or organic loading rates. Rock filter designs have been classified as low- or standard-rate, intermediate-rate, and high-rate. Plastic packing is used typically for high-rate designs; however, plastic packing has also been used at lower organic loadings, near the high end of those used for intermediate-rate rock filters. Much higher organic loadings have been used for rock or plastic packing designs in "roughing" applications where only partial BOD removal occurs.

Low-Rate Filters. A low-rate filter is a relatively simple, highly dependable device that produces an effluent of consistent quality with an influent of varying strength. The filters may be circular or rectangular in shape. Generally, feed flow from a dosing tank is maintained by suction level controlled pumps or a dosing siphon. Dosing tanks are small, usually with only a 2-min detention time based on twice the average design flow, so that intermittent dosing is minimized. Even so, at small plants, low nighttime flows may result in intermittent dosing and recirculation may be necessary to keep the packing moist. If the interval between dosing is longer than 1 or 2 h, the efficiency of the process deteriorates because the character of the biological slime is altered by a lack of moisture.

In most low-rate filters, only the top 0.6 to 1.2 m(2 to 4 ft) of the filter packing will have appreciable biological slime. As a result, the lower portions of the filter may be populated by autotrophic nitrifying bacteria, which oxidize ammonia nitrogen to nitrite and

Design characteristics	Low or standard rate	Intermediate rate	High rate	High rate	Roughing
Type of packing	Rock	Rock	Rock	Plastic	Rock/Plastic
Hydraulic loading, m³/(m²·d)	1~4	4~10	10~40	10~75	40~200
Organic loading, kg BOD/(m³·d)	0.07~0.22	0.24~0.48	0.4~2.4	0.6~3.2	>1.5
Recirculation ratio	0	0~1	1~2	1~2	0~2
Filter flies	Many	Varies	Few	Few	Few
Sloughing	Intermittent	Intermittent	Continuous	Continuous	Continuous
Depth, m	1.8~2.4	1.8~2.4	1.8~2.4	3.0~12.2	0.9~6
BOD removal efficiency, %	80~90	50~80	50~90	60~90	40~70
Effluent quality	Well nitrified	Some nitrification	No nitrification	No nitrification	No nitrification
Power, kW/(10³m³)	2~4	2~8	6~10	6~10	10~20

Historical classification of trickling filters applications   Table 1

Note: m³/(m²·d)×24.5424=gal/(ft²·d)
kg/(m³·d)×62.4280=lb/(10³ft³·d)
kW/(10³ m³)×5.0763=hp/(10³gal)

nitrate forms. If the nitrifying population is sufficiently well established, and if climatic conditions and wastewater characteristics are favorable, a well-operated low-rate filter can provide good BOD removal and a highly nitrified effluent.

With a favorable hydraulic gradient, the ability to use gravity flow is a distinct advantage. If the site is too flat to permit gravity flow, pumping will be required. Odors are a common problem, especially if the wastewater is stale or septic, or if the weather is warm. Filters should not be located where the odors would create a nuisance. Filter flies may breed in the filters unless effective control measures are used.

Intermediate- and High-Rate Filters. High-rate filters use either a rock or plastic packing. The filters are usually circular and flow is usually continuous. Recirculation of the filter effluent or final effluent permits higher organic loadings, provides higher dosing rates on the filter to improve the liquid distribution and better control of the slime layer thickness, provides more oxygen in the influent wastewater flow, and returns viable organisms. Recirculation also helps to prevent ponding in the filter and to reduce the nuisance from odors and flies. Intermediate- and high-rate trickling filters may be designed as single- or two-stage processes. Two filters in series operating at the same hydraulic application rate [m³/(m²·h)] will typically perform as if they were one unit with the same total depth.

Roughing Filters. Roughing filters are high-rate-type filters that treat an organic load of more than 1.6 kg/(m³·d) [100 lb BOD/(10³ft³·d)] and hydraulic loadings up to 190 m³/(m²·d) [3.2 gal/(ft²·min)]. In most cases, roughing filters are used to treat wastewater prior to secondary treatment. Most roughing filters are designed using plastic packing (WPCF, 1988). One of the advantages of roughing filters is the low energy requirement for BOD removal of higher strength wastewaters as compared to activated-sludge aeration. Because the energy required is only for pumping the influent wastewater and recirculation flows, the amount of BOD removal per unit of energy input can increase as the wastewater strength increases until more recirculation is needed to dilute the influent wastewater concentration or to increase wetting efficiency. The energy requirement for a roughing application may range from 2 to 4 kg BOD applied/kWh versus 1.2 to 2.4 kg BOD/kWh for activated-sludge treatment.

Two-Stage Filters. A two-stage filter system, with an intermediate clarifier to remove solids generated by the first filter, is most often used with high-strength wastewater. Two-stage systems are also used where nitrification is required. The first-stage filter and intermediate clarifier reduce carbonaceous BOD, and nitrification takes place in the second stage.

Nitrification. Both BOD removal and nitrification can be accomplished in rock or plastic packing trickling filters operated at low organic loadings. Heterotrophic bacteria, with higher yield coefficients and faster growth rates, are more competitive than nitrifying bacteria for space on the fixed-film packing. Thus, significant nitrification occurs only after the BOD concentration is appreciably reduced. Bruce et al. (1975) demonstrated that the effluent BOD had to be less than 30 mg/L to initiate nitrification and less than 15 mg/L for complete nitrification. Harrem es (1982) considered the soluble BOD, and concluded that a concentration less than 20 mg/L is needed to initiate nitrification. Nitrification can also be accomplished in separate trickling filters following secondary treatment.

New Words and Phrases

dosing *n.* 定量给料
underdrain *n.* 地下排水道
slime *n.* 黏土，黏液
facultative *adj.* 兼性的
fungi *n.* 真菌类，似真菌的
worm *n.* 蠕虫，蚯蚓
snail *n.* 蜗牛
endogenous respiration 内源呼吸

slough *v.* 脱落
siphon *n.* 虹吸管
intermittent *adj.* 间歇，断断续续的
filter fly 滤池蝇
stale *n.* （牲畜等的）尿
ponding *n.* 积水（库），蓄水
autotrophic *adj.* 自养的
heterotroph *n.* 异养生物

Questions

1. What is the trickling filter?
2. Why can a well-operated low-rate filter provide good BOD removal and a highly nitrified effluent?
3. What are the components of the trickling filter?
4. What is the function of the slime layer on the rock or plastic packing in the trickling filters?
5. How to control the slime layer thickness on trickling filter packing?

6. What is the advantage of roughing filters?

Reading Material

Physical Facilities Design of Trickling Filters

Factors that must be considered in the design of trickling filters include (1) type and physical characteristics of filter packing to be used; (2) dosing rate; (3) type and dosing characteristics of the distribution system; (4) configuration of the underdrain system; (5) provision for adequate airflow (i.e., ventilation), either natural or forced air; and (6) settling tank design.

Filter Packing

The ideal filter packing is a material that has a high surface area per unit of volume, is low in cost, has a high durability, and has a high enough porosity so that clogging is minimized and good air circulation can occur. Typical trickling filter packing materials are shown on Figure 1. The physical characteristics of commonly used filter packings, including those shown on Figure 1, are reported in Table 2. Until the mid-1960s, the material used was either high-quality granite or blastfurnace slag. Since the 1960s, plastic packing material, either cross-flow or vertical-flow, has become the packing of choice in the United States.

Where locally available, rock has the advantage of low cost. The most suitable material is rounded river rock or crushed stone, graded to a uniform size so that 95 percent is within the range of 75 to 100 mm (3 to 4 in). The specification of size uniformity is a way of ensuring adequate pore space for wastewater flow and air circulation. Other important characteristics of filter packing materials are strength and durability. Durability may be determined by the sodium sulfate test, which is used to test the soundness of concrete aggregates. Because of the weight of the packing, the depth of rock filters is usually on the order of 2 m (6 ft). The low void volume of rock limits the space available for airflow, and increases the potential for plugging and flow short-circuiting. Because of plugging, the organic loadings to rock filters are more commonly in the range of 0.3 to 1.0 kg BOD/$(m^3 \cdot d)$.

Various forms of plastic packings are shown on Figure 1. Molded plastic packing materials have the appearance of a honeycomb. Flat and corrugated sheets of polyvinyl chloride are bonded together in rectangular modules. The sheets usually have a corrugated surface for enhancing slime growth and retention time. Each layer of modules is turned at right angles to the previous layer to further improve wastewater distribution. The two basic types of corrugated plastic sheet packing are vertical and cross flow (see Figure 1b, c, and d). Both types of packing are reported to be effective in BOD and TSS removal over a wide range of loadings. Biotowers as deep as 12 m (40 ft) have been constructed using plastic

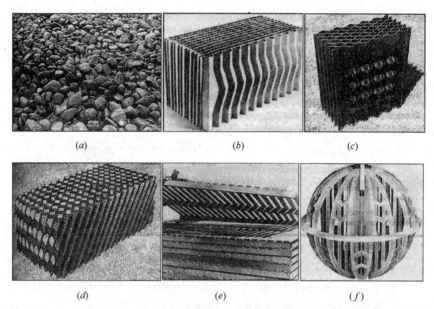

Figure 1 Typical packing material for trickling filters
(a) rock, (b) and (c) plastic vertical-flow, (d) plastic cross-flow,
(e) redwood horizontal, and (f) random pock.
Note: the random pack material is often used in air stripping towers

Physical properties of trickling filter packing materials   Table 2

Packing material	Nominal size, cm	Approx. unit weight, kg/m³	Approx. specific surface area, m²/m³	Void space, %	Application[a]
River rock (small)	2.5~7.5	1250~1450	60	50	N
River rock (large)	10~13	800~1000	45	60	C, CN, N
Plastic—conventional	61×61×122	30~80	90	>95	C, CN, N
Plastic—high specific surface area	61×61×122	65~95	140	>94	N
Plastic random packing—conventional	Varies	30~60	98	80	C, CN, N
Plastic random packing—high specific surface area	Varies	50~80	150	70	N

[a] C=BOD removal; N=tertiary nitrificatin; CN=combined BOD and nitrification.
Note: kg/m³ ×0.0624=lb/ft³.
m²/m³ ×0.0305=ft²/ft³.

packing, with depths in the range of 6 m (20 ft) being more common. In biotowers with vertical plastic packing, cross-flow packing can be used for the uppermost layers to enhance the distribution across the top of the filter. The high hydraulic capacity, high void ratio, and resistance to plugging offered by these types of packing can best be used in a high-rate-type filter. Redwood or other wood packings have been used in the past, but with the limited availability of redwood, wood packing is seldom used currently.

Plastic packing has the advantage of requiring less land area for the filter structure than rock due to the ability to use higher loading rates and taller trickling filter. Grady et al. (1999) noted that when loaded at the similar low organic loadings rates [less than 1.0 kg BOD/$(m^3 \cdot d)$], the performance of rock filters compared to filters with plastic packing is similar. At higher organic loading rates, however, the performance of filters with plastic packing is superior. The higher porosity, which provides for better air circulation and biofilm sloughing, is a likely explanation for the improved performance.

Dosing Rate

The dosing rate on a trickling filter is the depth of liquid discharged on top of the packing for each pass of the distributor. For higher distributor rotational speeds, the dosing rate is lower. In the past, typical rotational speeds for distributors were about 0.5 to 2 min per revolution (WEF, 2000). With two to four arms, the trickling filter is dosed every 10 to 60 s. Results from various investigators have indicated that reducing the distributor speed results in better filter performance. Hawkes (1963) showed that rock trickling filters dosed every 30 to 55 min/rev outperformed a more conventional operation of 1 to 5 min/rev. Besides improved BOD removal, there were dramatic reductions in the *Psychoda* and *Anisopus* fly population, biofilm thickness, and odors. Albertson and Davies (1984) showed similar advantages from an investigation of reduced distributor speed. At a higher dosing rate, the larger water volume applied per revolution (1) provides greater wetting efficiency, (2) results in greater agitation, which causes more solids to flush out of the packing, (3) results in a thinner biofilm, and (4) helps to wash away fly eggs. The thinner biofilm creates more surface area and results in a more aerobic biofilm.

A guideline for trickling filter dosing rate as a function of BOD loading[a]　　Table 3

BOD loading kg/$(m^3 \cdot d)$	Operating dose, mm/pass[b]	Flushing dose, mm/pass[b]
0.25	10~30	≥200
0.50	15~45	≥200
1.00	30~90	≥300
2.00	40~120	≥400
3.00	60~180	≥600
4.00	80~240	≥800

[a] From WEF (2000).

[b] mm/pass represents the amount of liquid applied for each pass of each distributor arm.

Note: kg/$(m^3 \cdot d) \times 62.4280 = $ lb/$(10^3 ft^3 \cdot d)$.

If the high dosing rate is sustained to control the biofilm thickness, the treatment efficiency may be decreased because the liquid contact time in the filter is less. A daily intermittent high dose, referred to as a *flushing dose*, is used to control the biofilm thickness and solids inventory. A combination of a once-per-day high flushing rate and a lower daily sustained dosing rate is recommended as a function of the BOD loading as shown in Table 3. The data in Table 3 are guidelines to establish a dosing range. Optimization of the dosing rate and flushing rate and frequency is best determined from field operation. Flexibility in the distributor design is needed to provide a range of dosing rates to optimize the trickling filter performance.

The rotational speed for a rotary distributor can be determined using the following relationship (Albertson, 1989):

$$n = \frac{(1+R)(q)(10^3 \text{mm/m})}{(A)(DR)(60\text{min/h})} \tag{1}$$

where n = rotational speed, rev/min
$\quad q$ = influent applied hydraulic loading rate, m³/(m² · h)
$\quad R$ = recycle ratio
$\quad A$ = number of arms in rotary distributor assembly
$\quad DR$ = dosing rate, mm/pass of distributor arm

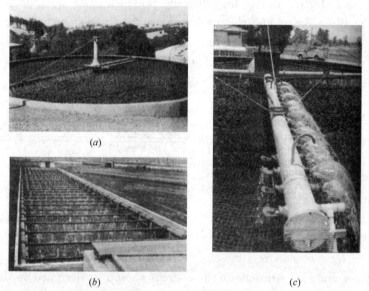

Figure 2 Tyqical distributors used to apply wastewater to trickling filter packing
(a) view of conventional rock filter with two-arm rotary distributor,
(b) view of early (circa 1920) rock filter with a fixed distribution system, and
(c) view of top of tower trickling filter with four-arm rotary distributor

Distribution Systems

A distributor consists of two or more arms that are mounted on a pivot in the center of the filter and revolve in a horizontal plane (see Figure 2). The arms are hollow and contain nozzles through which the wastewater is discharged over the filter bed. The distributor assembly may be driven either by the dynamic reaction of the wastewater discharging from the nozzle or by an electric motor. The flow-driven rotary distributor for trickling filtration has been used traditionally for the process because it is reliable and easy to maintain. Motor drives are used in more recent designs. The speed of rotation, which varies with the flowrate and the organic loading rate, can be determined using Eq. (1). Clearance of 150 to 225mm (6 to 9in) should be allowed between the bottom of the distributor arm and the top of the bed. The clearance permits the wastewater streams from the nozzles to spread out and cover the bed uniformly, and it prevents ice accumulations from interfering with the distributor motion during freezing weather.

Underdrains. The wastewater collection system in a trickling filter consists of underdrains that catch the filtered wastewater and solids discharged from the filter packing for conveyance to the final sedimentation tank. The underdrain system for a rock filter usually has precast blocks of vitrified clay or fiberglass grating laid on a reinforced-concrete subfloor (see Figure 3). The floor and underdrains must have sufficient strength to support the packing, slime growth, and the wastewater. The floor and underdrain block slope to a central or peripheral drainage channel at a 1 to 5 percent grade. The effluent channels are sized to produce a minimum velocity of 0.6 m/s (2 ft/s) at the average daily flowrate. Underdrains may be open at both ends, so that they may be inspected easily and flushed out if they become plugged. The underdrains also allow ventilation of the filter, providing the air for the microorganisms that live in the filter slime. The underdrains should be open to a circumferential channel for ventilation at the wall as well as to the central collection channel.

The underdrain and support system for plastic packing consists of either a beam and column or a grating. A typical underdrain system for a tower filter is shown on Figure 4. The beam and column system typically has precast-concrete beams supported by columns or posts. The plastic packing is placed over the beams, which have channels in their tops to ensure free flow of wastewater and air. All underdrain systems should be designed so that forced-air ventilation can be added at a later date if filter operating conditions should change.

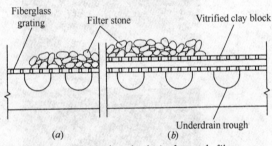

Figure 3 Typical underdrain for rock filter
(a) fiberglass grating and
(b) vitrified clay block

Airflow. An adequate flow of air is of fundamental importance to the successful operation of a trickling filter to provide efficient treatment and to prevent odors. Natural draft has historically been the primary means of providing airflow, but it is not always adequate and forced ventilation using low-pressure fans provides more reliable and controlled airflow.

In the case of natural draft, the driving force for airflow is the temperature difference between the ambient air and the air inside the pores. If the wastewater is colder than the ambient air, the pore air will be cold and the direction of flow will be downward. If the ambient air is colder than the wastewater, the flow will be upward. The latter is less desirable from a mass transfer point of view because the partial pressure of oxygen (and thus the oxygen transfer rate) is lowest in the region of highest oxygen demand. In many

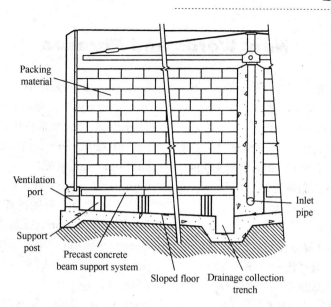

Figure 4 Typical underdrain system for tower filter

areas of the country, there are periods, especially during the summer, when essentially no airflow occurs through the trickling filter because temperature differentials are negligible.

Settling Tanks. The function of settling tanks that follow trickling filters is to produce a clarified effluent. They differ from activated-sludge settling tanks in that the clarifier has a much lower suspended solids content and sludge recirculation is not necessary. All the sludge from trickling filter settling tanks is sent to sludge-processing facilities or returned to the primary clarifiers to be settled with primary solids. Trickling filter performance has historically suffered from poor

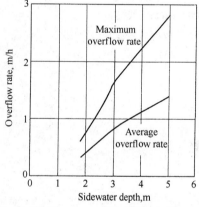

Figure 5 Recommended trickling filterer clarifier overflow rates as a function of the clarifier sidewater depth

clarifier designs. The use of shallow clarifiers for trickling filter applications, with relatively high overflow rates, was recommended in previous versions of the "Ten States Standards". Unfortunately, the use of shallow clarifiers typically resulted in poor clarification efficiency. Clarifier overflow rates recommended currently in the Ten States Standards are more in line with those used for the activated-sludge process. Clarifier designs for trickling filters should be similar to designs used for activated-sludge process clarifiers, with appropriate feed-well size and depth, increased sidewater depth, and similar hydraulic overflow rates. Recommended overflow rates as a function of the clarifier sidewater depth are given on Figure 5. With proper clarification designs, single-stage trickling filters can achieve a less than 20 mg/L concentration of BOD and TSS.

New Words and Phrases

granite　*n.* 花岗岩
blastfurnace slag　高炉灰渣
soundness　*n.* 坚固(性、度)
honeycomb　*n.* 蜂房，蜂巢，蜂脾
corrugated　*adj.* 缩成皱纹的，使起波状的
polyvinyl chloride　聚氯乙烯
biotowers　*n.* 塔式生物滤池
void ratio　孔隙率
rev　*n.* 一次回转，(每分钟的)转速
outperform　*vt.* 做得比……好
Psychoda fly　毛蠓属苍蝇
Anisopus　*n.* ［拉］伪大蚊科
inventory　*n.* 总量，财产目录，清册
pivot　*n.* 枢轴，支点
circa　*adv.* 大约
　　　　prep. 大约

precast　*adj.* 预制的
vitrified clay　釉面陶土
fiberglass　*n.* 玻璃纤维，玻璃丝
reinforced-concrete　钢筋混凝土
subfloor　*n.* 底板
peripheral　*adj.* 外围的
　　　　n. 外围设备
forced ventilation　强制通风
circumferential　*adj.* 圆周的
port　*n.* 端口，入口
post　*n.* 柱
trench　*n.* 沟渠，排水沟
sidewater depth　边墙[处]水深

Anaerobic Treatment

Anaerobic treatment processes include anaerobic suspended growth, upflow and downflow anaerobic attached growth, fluidized-bed attached growth, upflow anaerobic sludge blanket (UASB), anaerobic lagoons, and membrane separation anaerobic processes. The purpose of this section is to present process designs for other anaerobic treatment processes used to remove organic material from liquid streams. The various types of processes are described along with their typical design loadings and treatment process capabilities. Before considering the individual anaerobic treatment processes, it will be helpful to consider the rationale for the use of anaerobic treatment processes.

The Rationale for Anaerobic Treatment

The rationale for and interest in the use of anaerobic treatment processes can be explained by considering the advantages and disadvantages of these processes. The principal advantages and disadvantages of anaerobic treatment are listed in Table 1 and discussed below.

Advantages of Anaerobic Treatment Processes

Of the advantages cited in Table 1, energy considerations, lower biomass yield, fewer nutrients required, and higher volumetric loadings are examined further in the following discussion.

Energy Considerations. Anaerobic processes may be net energy producers instead of energy users, as is the case for aerobic processes. An energy balance comparison for a high-strength wastewater at 20℃ is presented in Table 2. For the conditions given in Table 2, the aerobic process requires 1.9×10^6 kJ/d. On the other hand, the anaerobic process produces a total of 12.5×10^6 kJ/d. Of the total energy produced anaerobically, about 2.1×10^6 kJ/d is required

Advantages and disadvantages of anaerobic processes compared to aerobic processes   Table 1

Advantages	• Less energy required • Less biological sludge production • Fewer nutrients required • Methane production, a potential energy source • Smaller reactor volume required • Elimination of off-gas air pollution • Rapid response to substrate addition after long periods without feeding

Table 1 (Continued)

Disadvantages	• Longer start-up time to develop necessary biomass inventory • May require alkalinity addition • May require further treatment with an aerobic treatment process to meet discharge requirements • Biological nitrogen and phosphorus removal is not possible • Much more sensitive to the adverse effect of lower temperature on reaction rates • May be more susceptible to upsets due to toxic substances • Potential for production of odors and corrosive gases

Comparison of energy balance for aerobic and anaerobic processes for the treatment of a wastewater with the following characteristics: wastewater flowrate=100m^3/d; wastewater strength=10kg/m^3; and temperature=20℃   Table 2

Energy	Value, kJ/d	
	Anaerobic	Aerobic
Aeration$^{a, b}$		-1.9×10^6
Methane produced$^{c, d}$	12.5×10^6	
Increase wastewater	-2.1×10^6	
Temperature to 30℃		
Net energy, kJ/d	10.4×10^6	-1.9×10^6

^{a}Oxygen required=0.8kg/kg COD removed.
^{b}Aeration efficiency=1.52kg O$_2$/kWh and 3600kJ=1kWh
^{c}Methane production=0.35m^3/kg COD removed.
^{d}Energy content of methane=35846kJ/m^3(at 0℃ and 1atm)

to raise the temperature of the wastewater from 20 to 30℃, the low end of the mesophilic temperature range, a more desirable temperature for anaerobic treatment. Thus, the potential net energy production that can be achieved with anaerobic treatment is on the order of 10.4×10^6 kJ/d, or about 5 times the energy required for aerobic treatment.

The wastewater strength is important for comparing energy balances for aerobic and anaerobic processes, where the wastewater temperature must be increased. With the same assumptions used to generate the energy balance presented in Table 2, both the aerobic and anaerobic processes would require the same amount of energy input if the wastewater biodegradable COD concentration is 1270mg/L. At lower COD concentrations, the aerobic process requires less energy. However, heat recovery from the anaerobic effluent stream can modify these values. Further, the lower biomass yield discussed below is still a major advantage offered by anaerobic treatment.

Lower Biomass Yield. Because the energetics of anaerobic processes result in lower biomass production by a factor of about 6 to 8 times, sludge processing and disposal costs are reduced greatly. The fact that less sludge is produced in anaerobic treatment is a significant advantage over aerobic treatment.

Fewer Nutrients Required. Many industrial wastewaters lack sufficient nutrients to support aerobic growth. The cost for nutrient addition is much less for anaerobic processes because less biomass is produced.

Higher Volumetric Loadings. Anaerobic processes generally have higher volumetric organic loads than aerobic processes, so smaller reactor volumes and less space may be required for treatment. Organic loading rates of 3.2 to 32 kg COD/($m^3 \cdot$ d) may be used for anaerobic processes, compared to 0.5 to 3.2 kg COD/($m^3 \cdot$ d) for aerobic processes.

Disadvantages of Anaerobic Treatment Processes

Potential disadvantages also exist for anaerobic processes as reported in Table 1. Operational considerations, the need for alkalinity addition, and the need for further treatment are highlighted further in the following discussion.

Operational Considerations. The major concerns with anaerobic processes are their longer start-up time (months for anaerobic versus days for aerobic process), their sensitivity to possible toxic compounds, operational stability, the potential for odor production, and corrosiveness of the digester gas. However, with proper wastewater characterization and process design these problems can be avoided and/or managed.

Need for Alkalinity Addition. The most significant negative factor that affect the economics of anaerobic versus aerobic treatment is the possible need to add alkalinity. Alkalinity concentrations of 2000 to 3000 mg/L as $CaCO_3$ may be needed anaerobic processes to maintain an acceptable pH with the high gas phase CO_2 concentration. If this amount of alkalinity is not available in the influent wastewater or can not be produced by the degradation of proteins and amino acid, a significant cost may be incurred to purchase alkalinity, which can affect the overall economics of the process.

Need for Further Treatment. Anaerobic processes can also be followed by aerobic processes for effluent polishing to utilize the benefits of both processes. Series reactors of anaerobic-aerobic processes have been shown feasible for treating municipal wastewaters in warmer climates resulting in lower energy requirements and less sludge production.

Summary Assessment

In general, for municipal wastewaters with lower concentrations of biodegradable COD, lower temperatures, higher effluent quality needs, and nutrient removal requirements, aerobic processes are favored at present. For industrial wastewaters with much higher biodegradable COD concentrations and elevated temperatures, anaerobic processes may be more economical. In the future, as more is learned about anaerobic treatment processes, it is anticipated that their use will become more widespread in a variety of applications.

General Design Considerations for Anaerobic Treatment Processes

The type of wastewater and its characteristics are important in the evaluation and design of anaerobic processes. The characteristics presented here apply to the suspended growth, sludge blanket, attached growth, and membrane separation anaerobic processes presented in subsequent sections. Important factors and wastewater characteristics that need to be considered in the evaluation of anaerobic processes for wastewater treatment are discussed below.

Characteristics of the Wastewater

A wide variety of wastewaters have been treated by anaerobic processes including those reported in Table 3. Anaerobic processes are attractive, especially for high strength and warm temperature wastewaters because: (1) aeration is not required, thus saving energy cost, and (2) the low amount of solids generated. Food processing and distillery wastewaters, for example, can have COD concentrations ranging from 3000 to 30000 mg/L. Other considerations that may apply to different wastewater sources are the presence of potential toxic streams, flow variations, inorganic concentrations, and seasonal load variations. Anaerobic processes are capable of responding quickly to wastewater feed after long periods without substrate addition. In some cases with warmer climates, anaerobic treatment has also been considered for municipal wastewater treatment.

Examples of types of wastewater treated by anaerobic processes　　　Table 3

Alcohol distillation	Landfill leachate
Breweries	Pharmaceuticals
Chemical manufacturing	Pulp and paper
Dairy and cheese processing	Slaughterhouse and meatpacking
Domestic wastewater	Soft drink beverages
Fish and seafood processing	Sugar processing

Flow and Loading Variations. Wide variations in influent flow and organic loads can upset the balance between acid fermentation and methanogenesis in anaerobic processes. For soluble, easily degradable substrates, such as sugars and soluble starches, the acidogenic reactions can be much faster at high loadings and may increase the reactor volatile fatty acids (VFA) and hydrogen concentrations and depress the pH. Higher hydrogen concentrations can inhibit propionic and butyric acid conversion. The lower pH can inhibit methanogenesis. Flow equalization or additional capacity must be provided to meet peak flow and loading conditions.

Organic Concentration and Temperature. The wastewater strength and temperature greatly affect the economics and feasibility of anaerobic treatment. Reactor temperatures of 25 to 35℃ are generally preferred to support more optimal biological reaction rates and to provide more stable treatment. Generally, COD concentrations greater than 1500 to 2000 mg/L are needed to produce sufficient quantities of methane to heat the wastewater without an external fuel source. At 1300 mg/L COD or less, aerobic treatment may be the preferred selection.

Anaerobic treatment can be applied at lower temperatures and has been sustained at 10 to 20℃ in suspended and attached growth reactors. At the lower temperatures, slower reaction rates occur and longer SRTs, larger reactor volumes, and lower organic COD loadings are needed. Further, at temperatures in the range from 10 to 20℃, the degradation of long chain fatty acids is often rate limiting. If long chain fatty acids accumulate, foaming may occur in the reactor. When higher SRTs are needed, the solids loss in an anaerobic reactor can become a critical limiting factor. Anaerobic reactors generally produce more dispersed, less flocculent solids than aerobic systems, with effluent TSS concentrations for suspended growth processes in the 100 to 200 mg/L range. For dilute wastewaters, the effluent TSS concentration will limit the possible SRT of the process and treatment potential. Either a lower treatment performance occurs or it is necessary to operate the reactor at a higher temperature. Thus, the method used to retain solids in the anaerobic reactor is important in the overall process design and performance.

Fraction of Nondissolved Organic Material. The composition of wastewater in terms of its particulate and soluble fractions affects the type of anaerobic reactor selected and its design. Wastewaters with high solids concentrations are treated more appropriately in suspended growth reactors than by upflow or downflow attached growth processes. Where greater conversion of particulate organic matter is required, longer SRT values may be needed if solids hydrolysis is the rate-limiting step as compared to acid fermentation or methanogenesis in anaerobic treatment.

Wastewater Alkalinity. With the high CO_2 content (typically in the range from 30 to 50 percent) in the gas produced in anaerobic treatment, alkalinity concentrations in the range from 2000 to 4000 mg/L as $CaCO_3$ are typically required to maintain the pH at or near neutral. The level of alkalinity needed is seldom available in the influent wastewater, but may be generated in some cases by the degradation of protein and amino acids (e.g. meatpacking wastewaters). The requirement to purchase chemicals for pH control can have a significant impact on the economics of anaerobic treatment.

Nutrients. Though anaerobic processes produce less sludge and thus require nitrogen and phosphorus for biomass growth, many industrial wastewaters may sufficient nutrients. Thus, the addition of nitrogen and/or phosphorus may be needed. Depending on the characteristics of the substrate and the SRT value, typical nutrient requirements for nitrogen, phosphorus, and sulfur are in the range from 10 to 13, 2 to 2.6, and 1 to 2 mg per 100 mg of biomass, respectively. The values for nitrogen and phosphorus are consistent with the values for these constituents estimated on the basis of the composition of the cell biomass. Further, to maintain maximum methanogenic activity, liquid phase concentrations of nitrogen, phosphorus, and sulfur on the order of 50, 10, and 5 mg/L, respectively are desirable.

Macronutrients. The importance of trace metals to stimulate methanogenic activity has been noted and discussed by Speece (1996). The recommended requirements for iron, cobalt, nickel, and zinc are 0.02, 0.004, 0.003, and 0.02 mg/g acetate produced, respectively. Examples of increased anaerobic activity were noted after trace additions of iron, nickel, or cobalt. The exact amounts of trace nutrients needed can vary for different wastewaters, and thus trial approaches are used to assess their benefit for anaerobic processes with high VFA concentrations. A recommended dose of trace metals per liter of reactor volume is 1.0 mg $FeCl_2$, 0.1 mg $CoCl_2$, 0.1 mg $NiCl_2$, and 0.1 mg $ZnCl_2$.

Inorganic and Organic Toxic Compounds. Proper analysis and treatability studies are needed to assure that a chronic toxicity does not exist for wastewater treated by anaerobic processes. At the same time, the presence of a toxic substance does not mean the process cannot function. Some toxic compounds inhibit anaerobic methanogenic reaction rates, but with a high biomass inventory and low enough loading, the process can be sustained.

Acclimatization to toxic concentrations has also been shown. Pretreatment steps may be used to remove the toxic constituents, and, in some cases, phase separation can prevent toxicity problems by providing for degradation of the toxic constituents in the acid phase, before exposure of the more sensitive methanogenic bacteria to the toxic constituents.

Solids Retention Time

The solids retention time is a fundamental design and operating parameter for all anaerobic processes. In general, SRT values greater than 20 d are needed for anaerobic processes at 30℃ for effective treatment performance, with much higher SRT values at lower temperatures.

Expected Methane Gas Production

Higher-strength wastewaters will produce a greater amount of methane per volume of liquid treated to provide a relatively higher amount of energy to raise the liquid temperature, if needed. The amount of methane (CH_4) produced per unit of COD converted under anaerobic conditions is equal to 0.35 LNH_4^+/g COD at standard conditions (0℃ and 1atm). The quantity of methane at other than standard conditions is determined by using the universal gas law to determine the volume of gas occupied by one mole of CH_4 at the temperature in question.

Treatment Efficiency Needed

Anaerobic treatment processes are capable of high COD conversion efficiency to methane with minimal biomass production. At SRT values greater than 20 to 50 d, maximum conversion of solids may occur at temperatures above 25℃. However, high-effluent suspended solids (50 to 200 mg/L) are common for anaerobic processes. Without pilot-plant studies and extreme measures to control effluent suspended solids concentrations, such as chemical flocculation or membrane separation, anaerobic processes alone can not be depended on to achieve secondary treatment levels. Some form of aerobic treatment would be necessary to provide effluent polishing, either attached growth or suspended growth processes. For high-strength wastewaters the combination of anaerobic and aerobic treatment can be economical.

Sulfide Production

Oxidized sulfur compounds, such as sulfate, sulfite, and thiosulfate, may be present in significant concentrations in various industrial wastewaters and to some degree in municipal wastewaters. These compounds can serve as electron acceptors for sulfate-reducing bacteria, which consume organic compounds in the anaerobic reactor and produce hydrogen sulfide (H_2S).

Ammonia Toxicity

Ammonia toxicity may be of concern for anaerobic treatment of wastewaters containing high concentrations of ammonium or proteins and/or amino acids, which can be degraded to produce ammonium. Free ammonia (NH_3), at high enough concentrations, is considered toxic to methanogenic bacteria. Ammonia is a weak acid and dissociates in water to form ammonium (NH_4^+) and hydroxyl ions. The amount of free ammonia is a function of temperature and pH. At a pH of 7.5 and at 30 to 35℃, 2 to 4 percent of the ammonium present will be as free ammonia. The toxicity threshold for ammonia has been reported to be 100 mg/L as NH_3-N, but with acclimatization time, higher concentrations may be tolerated. In batch tests, Lay et al. (1998) found a steady inhibition of methanogenic activity as the NH_3-N concentration was increased from 50 to 500 mg/L, with 500 mg/L being the apparent toxicity threshold level.

In stating the toxicity as total ammonium concentration, McCarty (1964) reported toxicity concentration range of 1500 to 3000 mg/L as NH_4-N at pH above 7.4, with 3000 mg/L being toxic at any pH. However, after long-term acclimatization, much higher NH_4-N concentrations without toxicity have been observed. Moen (2000) found no inhibition effects for both thermophilic and mesophilic digestion of municipal sludge with NH_4-N concentrations ranging from 1900 to 2400 mg/L. Others (van Velsen, 1977; Parkin and Miller, 1982) have reported no effect of ammonia toxicity with long-term acclimatized cultures at NH_4-N concentrations in the range of 5000 to 8000 mg/L.

Liquid-Solids Separation

Efficient liquid-solids separation can enhance the performance of anaerobic treatment processes. Because of the low solids synthesis yield coefficient associated with anaerobic treatment, most of the solids wasting is via the treated effluent flow, and thus the degree of solids capture affects the SRT value that can be maintained. Good solids capture improves the effluent quality in terms of TSS concentration, and can also result in a langer SRT in the anaerobic reactor to increase the level of COD conversion.

New Words and Phrases

mesophilic   *adj.* （细菌）嗜温的（亦作 mesophilous），中温的
energetics   *n.* 热力学，动能学，力能学
highlighted   *adj.* 突出的
alcohol distillation   酒精蒸馏
landfill leachate   填埋沥滤液
brewery   *n.* 酿酒厂，啤酒厂
distillery   *n.* 蒸馏间，酿酒厂
pulp and paper   纸浆与造纸
methanogenesis   *n.* 甲烷生成

methanogenic bacteria　产甲烷菌
acidogenic　*adj.*　引起酸化的
butyric acid　*n.*　丁酸
propionic acid　*n.*　丙酸

chronic toxicity　慢性毒性
acclimatization　*n.*　环境适应性，驯化
thermophilic　*adj.*　喜温的，嗜热的，适温的，高温的

Questions

1. Please describe briefly the advantages and disadvantages of anaerobic treatment processes.
2. Which process may be chosen when the COD concentrations are greater than 1500 to 2000 mg/L?
3. What is the reason of the effluent TSS concentrations for anaerobic suspended growth processes can still reach the range of 100 to 200 mg/L?
4. Depending on the characteristics of the substrate and the SRT value, how much nitrogen, phosphorus, and sulfur should be required in anaerobic treatment?
5. Why is the combination of anaerobic and aerobic treatment needed for high-strength wastewaters?
6. What are the recently research fruits on ammonia toxicity?

Reading Material

Anaerobic Treatment Processes

Anaerobic Suspended Growth Processes

Early applications of anaerobic treatment of industrial wastewaters were suspended growth processes, which were initially designed in a similar manner as anaerobic sludge digesters. Three types of anaerobic suspended growth treatment processes are illustrated on Figure 1: (1) the complete-mix suspended growth anaerobic digester, (2) the anaerobic contact process, and (3) the anaerobic sequencing batch reactor, a more recent suspended growth reactor design development. Each of these processes is described below along with general design considerations for suspended growth processes.

Anaerobic Sludge Blanket Processes

One of the most notable developments in anaerobic treatment process technology was the upflow anaerobic sludge blanket (UASB) reactor in the late 1970s in the Netherlands by Lettinga and his coworkers. The principal types of anaerobic sludge blanket processes include (1) the original UASB process and modification of the original design, (2) the anaerobic baffled reactor (ABR), and (3) the anaerobic migrating blanket reactor (AMBR). The ABR process was developed by McCarty and coworkers at Stanford

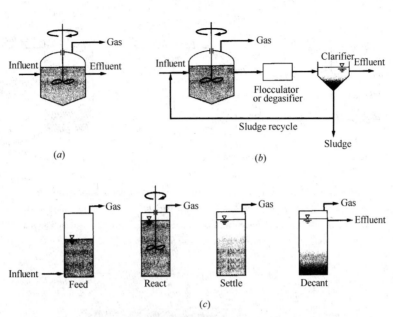

Figure 1 Anaerobic suspended growth treatment processes
(a) complete mix suspended growth anaerobic digester,
(b) anaerobic contact process, and
(c) anaerobic sequencing batch reactor (ASBR)

University in the early 1980s. Work in the late 1990s at Iowa State University has led to the development of the AMBR process. Of these sludge blanket processes, the UASB process is used most commonly, with over 500 installations treating a wide range of industrial wastewaters. A number of pilot studies have been done with the ABR, with a limited number of full-scale installations. In this section all three types of anaerobic sludge blanket processes are described along with their performance, demonstrated process loadings, and key design considerations. The major emphasis is, however, on the UASB process.

Upflow Sludge Blanket Reactor Process

The basic UASB reactor is illustrated on Figure 2a. As shown on Figure 2a, influent wastewater is distributed at the bottom of the UASB reactor and travels in an upflow mode through the sludge blanket. Critical elements of the UASB reactor design are the influent distribution system, the gas-solids separator, and the effluent withdrawal design. Modifications to the basic UASB design include adding a settling tank (see Figure 2b) or the use of packing material at the top of the reactor (see Figure 2c). Both modifications are intended to provide better solids capture in the system and to prevent the loss of large amounts of the UASB reactor solids due to process upsets or changes in the UASB sludge blanket characteristics and density. The use of an external solids capture system to prevent major losses of the system biomass is recommended strongly by Speece (1996). A view of a sludge blanket fixed-film reactor installation is shown on Figure 3.

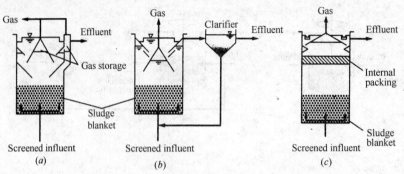

Figure 2 Schematic of the UASB process and some modifications
(a) original UASB process, (b) UASB reactor with sedimentation tank and sludge recycle, and (c) UASB reactor with internal packing for fixed-film attached growth, placed above the sludge blanket

Figure 3 View of UASB reactor equipped with internal packing above the sludge blanket. The exterior physical appearance of a UASB reactor without and with internal packing is the same (see Figure 2c for location of internal packing)

Attached Growth Anaerobic Processes

Upflow attached growth anaerobic treatment reactors differ by the type of packing used and the degree of bed expansion. Three types of upflow attached growth processes are illustrated on Figure 4. In the upflow packed-bed reactor (see Figure 4a) the packing is fixed and the wastewater flows up through the interstitial spaces between the packing and biogrowth. Effluent recycle is generally not used for the packed-bed reactor except for high-strength wastewaters. While the first upflow anaerobic packed-bed processes contained rock, a variety of designs employing synthetic plastic packing are used currently. The anaerobic expanded-bed reactor (see Figure 4b) uses a fine-grain sand to support biofilm growth. Recycle is used to provide upflow velocities, resulting in 20 percent bed expansion. Higher upflow velocities are used for fluidized-bed anaerobic reactors (see Figure 4c), which also contain a fine-grain packing. In fluidized-bed systems, both fluidization and mixing of the packing material occurs. The expanded and fluidized-bed reactors have more surface area per reactor volume for biomass growth and better mass transfer than the upflow packed-bed reactor, but have lower solids capture.

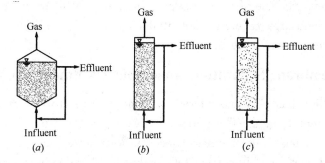

Figure 4 Upflow anaerobic attached growth treatment reactors
(a) anaerobic upflow packed-bed reactor, (b) anaerobic expanded-bed reactor, and (c) anaerobic fluidized-bed reactor

Other Anaerobic Treatment Processes

Numerous other anaerobic processes have been developed and new processes are being developed continuously. Two such processes, the covered anaerobic earthen lagoon process and the membrane separation anaerobic treatment process, are considered briefly in the following discussion.

Covered Anaerobic Lagoon Process

Anaerobic lagoons have been used for high-strength industrial wastewaters, such as meat-processing wastewaters. Detention times ranged from 20 to 50 d with lagoon depths of 5 to 10 m. A schematic of a simple non-proprietary covered anaerobic lagoon process is shown on Figure 5a. A schematic of a proprietary covered anaerobic lagoon process known as the ADI-BVF® reactor is shown on Figure 5b (McMullin et al., 1994). One of

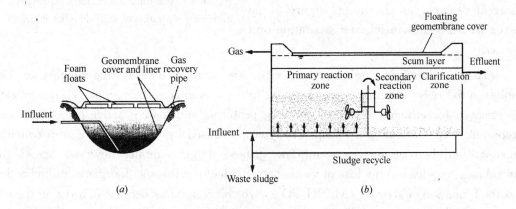

Figure 5 Schematic of covered anaerobic lagoon process
(a) simple nonproprietary design and (b) proprietary ADI-BVF® lagoon process

the main advantages for the covered lagoon processes is their ability to handle a wide range of waste characteristics including solids and oils and greases. Other advantages include simple and relatively economical construction, the large volume that can provide equalization of loads, the use of a low loading, and a high effluent quality. Disadvantages include the large land area required, potential feed flow distribution inefficiencies, and maintenance of the geomembrane cover.

Membrane Separation Anaerobic Treatment Process

Membrane separation has been considered for anaerobic reactors, but the technology is still in a developmental stage. The potential advantages for using membrane separation technology are (1) using higher biomass concentrations in the anaerobic reactor to further reduce its size and increase volumetric COD loadings, (2) allowing much higher SRTs in the anaerobic reactor by almost complete capture of solids that could result in maximum removal of VFAs and degradable soluble COD substances to provide a higher-quality effluent, and (3) maximizing capture of effluent suspended solids to greatly improve the effluent quality from anaerobic treatment. The latter two potential advantages of a longer SRT and low effluent suspended solids concentration should allow anaerobic reactors to produce an effluent quality equal to aerobic secondary treatment processes.

The major design considerations for the application of membrane separation in biological reactors are (1) the membrane flux rate and (2) the ability to prevent fouling of the membrane to sustain acceptable flux rates. In the submerged membrane reactors used for aerobic suspended growth treatment the membranes are placed in the activated sludge reactor and coarse bubble aeration is used to minimize fouling. For anaerobic processes a similar type of gas agitation system might be possible. In current designs, as shown on Figure 6, an external cross-flow membrane separation unit is used.

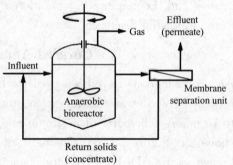

Figure 6 Anaerobic bioreactor with external membrane separation of solids in effluent stream

To control fouling, high liquid velocities are maintained across the membrane. The solids in the reject stream are recycled back to the anaerobic reactor, while clear permeate is removed for effluent discharge. Fouling problems and loss of active cells have been reported. Organic fouling problems are typically caused by the accumulation of colloidal material and bacteria on the membrane surface. High pumping flowrates across the membrane may lead to the loss of viable bacteria due to cell lysis. Inorganic fouling is due to the formation of struvite ($MgNH_4PO_4$), which precipitates because of a rise in the pH as the flow passes through the membranes and CO_2 escapes from the liquid. Observed performance data derived from a limited number of membrane reactor studies are summarized in Table 4. In general, the process organic loading rates are in the range of those used with the sludge blanket and attached growth processes. Further developments in membrane design and fouling control measures could make membrane separation anaerobic reactors a viable technology in the future.

Summary of operating conditions from a limited number of membrane separation anaerobic reactor studies   Table 4

Parameter	Unite	Value Range	Value Typical
COD loading	kg COD/(m^3·d)	2~22	8
τ	d	0.5~15.0	8
SRT	d	30~160	50
MLSS	g/L	8~50	20~25
Solids yield	g VSS/g COD	0.04~0.12	0.08
Final flux	L/(m^2·h)	5~26	18
Specific flux	L/(m^2·h·bar)	2.5~21	14

Note: kg/(m^3·d)×62.4280=lb/(10^{3}ft^3·d)

L/(m^2·h)×0.0245=gal/ft^2·d

New Words and Phrases

decant　　*v.* 滗水，滗析　　　　lysis　　*n.* 溶胞，溶菌
interstitial　　*adj.* 空隙的，形成空隙的　　struvite　　*n.* 鸟粪石
geomembrane　　*n.* 土工膜；隔泥网膜　　liner　　*n.* 衬垫、衬里

LESSON 18

Rotating Biological Contactors

Rotating biological contactors (RBCs) were first installed in West Germany in 1960 and later introduced in the United States. Hundreds of RBC installations were installed in the 1970s and the process has been reviewed in a number of reports. An RBC consists of a series of closely spaced circular disks of polystyrene or polyvinyl chloride that are submerged in wastewater and rotated through it. The cylindrical plastic disks are attached to a horizontal shaft and are provided at standard unit sizes of approximately 3.5 m (12 ft) in diameter and 7.5 m (25 ft) in length. The surface area of the disks for a standard unit is about 9300 m^2 (100000 ft^2), and a unit with a higher density of disks is also available with approximately 13900 m^2 (150000 ft^2) of surface area. The RBC unit is partially submerged (typically 40 percent) in a tank containing the wastewater, and the disks rotate slowly at about 1.0 to 1.6 revolutions per minute. Mechanical drives are normally used to rotate the units, but air-driven units have also been installed. In the air-driven units, an array of cups is fixed to the periphery of the disks and diffused aeration is used to direct air to the cups to cause rotation. As the RBC disks rotate out of the wastewater, aeration is accomplished by exposure to the atmosphere. Wastewater flows down through the disks, and solids sloughing occurs. Similar to a trickling filter, RBC systems require pretreatment of primary clarification or fine screens and secondary clarification for liquid/solids separation.

A submerged RBC design was also introduced in the early 1980s but has seen limited applications. The submergence is 70 to 90 percent and air-drive units are used to provide oxygen and rotation. The advantages claimed for the submerged unit are reduced loadings on the shaft and bearings, improved biomass control by air agitation, the ability to use larger bundles of disks, and ease of retrofit into existing aeration tanks. However, because of the comparatively low levels of dissolved oxygen in the liquid, biological degradation activity by the submerged units may be oxygen-limited. To prevent algae growth, protect the plastic disks from the effects of ultraviolet exposure, and to prevent excessive heat loss in cold weather, RBC units are covered.

The history of RBC installations has been troublesome due to inadequate mechanical design and lack of full understanding of the biological process. Structural failure of shafts, disks, and disk support systems has occurred. Development of excessive biofilm growth and sloughing problems has also led to mechanical shaft, bearing, and disk failures. Many of these problems were related to a lack of conservatism in design and scale-up issue, from pilot-plant to full-scale units. Many of the problems associated with

LESSON 18

earlier installation have been solved and numerous RBC installations are operating successfully.

Process Design Considerations

There are many similarities between RBC design considerations and those described for trickling filters. Both systems develop a large biofilm surface area and rely on mass transfer of oxygen and substrates from the bulk liquid to the biofilm. The complexity in the physical and hydrodynamic characteristics requires that the design of the RBC process be based on fundamental information from pilot-plant and field installations. As for trickling filters, the organic loading affects BOD removal efficiency and the nitrogen loading after a minimal BOD concentration is reached affects the nitrification efficiency. In contrast to the trickling filter where the wastewater flow approaches a plug flow hydraulic regime, the RBC units are rotated in a basin containing the wastewater, so that separate baffled basins are needed to develop the benefits of a staged biological reactor design. The design of an RBC system must include the following considerations: (1) staging of the RBC units, (2) loading criteria, (3) effluent characteristics, and (4) secondary clarifier design. Typical design information for RBCs is presented in Table 1.

Typical design information for rotating biological contactors   Table 1

Parameter	Unit	Treatment level[a]		
		BOD removal	BOD removal and nitrification	Separate nitrification
Hydraulic loading	$m^3/(m^2 \cdot d)$	0.08~0.16	0.03~0.08	0.04~0.10
Organic loading	$g\ sBOD/(m^2 \cdot d)$	4~10	2.5~8	0.5~1.0
	$g\ BOD/(m^2 \cdot d)$	8~20	5~16	1~2
Maximum 1st~ stage organic loading	$g\ sBOD/(m^2 \cdot d)$	12~15	12~15	
	$g\ BOD/(m^2 \cdot d)$	24~30	24~30	
NH_3 loading	$g\ N/(m^2 \cdot d)$		0.75~1.5	
Hydraulic retention time	h	0.7~1.5	1.5~4	1.2~3
Effluent BOD	mg/L	15~30	7~15	7~15
Effluent NH_4-N	mg/L		<2	1~2

[a] Water temperature above 13℃ (55℉).
Note: $g/(m^2 \cdot d) \times 0.204 = lb/(10^3 ft^2 \cdot d)$
$m^3/(m^2 \cdot d) \times 24.5424 = gal/(ft^2 \cdot d)$

Staging of RBC Units. Staging is the compartmentalization of the RBC disks to form a series of independent cells. Based on mass transfer and biological kinetic fundamentals, higher specific substrate removal rates will occur in RBC biofilm at higher bulk liquid substrate concentrations. Because a low effluent substrate concentration and high specific substrate removal rates are generally the ultimate treatment goal, reduced disk area requirements can be realized only by using staged-RBC units.

The RBC process application typically consists of a number of units operated in series. The number of stages depends on the treatment goals, with two to four stages for BOD removal and six or more stages for nitrification. Stages can be accomplished by using baffles in a single tank or by use of separate tanks in series. Staging promotes a variety of conditions where different organisms can flourish in varying degrees from stage to stage. The degree of development in any stage depends primarily on the soluble organic concentration in the stage bulk liquid. As the wastewater flows through the system, each subsequent stage receives an influent with a lower organic concentration than the previous stage. Typical RBC staging arrangements are illustrated on Figure 1.

For small plants, RBC drive shafts are oriented parallel to the direction of flow with disk clusters separated by baffles (see Figure 1*a*). In larger installations, shafts are mounted perpendicular to flow with several stages in series to form a process train (see Figure 1*b*). To handle the loading on the initial units, step feed (see Figure 1*d*) or a tapered system (see Figure 1*e*) may be used. Two or more parallel flow trains should be installed so the units can be isolated for turndown or repairs. Tank construction may be reinforced concrete or steel, with steel preferred at smaller plants. Treatment systems employing RBCs have been used for BOD removal, pretreatment of industrial wastewater, combined BOD removal and nitrification, tertiary nitrification, and denitrification. The principal advantages of the RBC process are simplicity of operation and relatively low energy costs.

The History of RBC Loading Criteria. Based on experience, the performance of an RBC system is related to the specific surface loading rate of total and soluble BOD (sBOD) for BOD removal and NH_4-N for nitrification. For successful treatment, the loading rates must be within the oxygen transfer capability of the system. Poor performance, odors, and biofilm sloughing problems have occurred when the oxygen demand due to the BOD loading has exceeded the oxygen transfer capability. A characteristic of this problem is the development of *Beggiatoa*, a reduced-sulfur oxidizing bacteria, on the outer portion of the biofilm, which prevents sloughing (U.S. EPA, 1984). A thick biofilm can develop to create enough weight to stress the structural strength of the plastic disks and shaft.

Under overloaded conditions, anaerobic conditions develop deep in the attached film. Sulfate is reduced to H_2S, which diffuses to the outer layer of the biofilm, where oxygen is available. *Beggiatoa*, a filamentous bacteria, which is able to oxidize the H_2S and other reduced sulfur compounds, forms a tenacious whitish biofilm that does not slough under the normal RBC rotational sheer conditions. In designing RBC units, it is important to select a low enough BOD loading for the initial units in the staged design to prevent overloading. Odor problems are most frequently caused by excessive organic loadings, particularly in the first stage.

Because the soluble BOD is used more rapidly in the first stage of an RBC system, most manufacturers of RBC equipment specify a specific soluble BOD loading in the range of 12 to 20 g sBOD/($m^2 \cdot d$) [2.5 to 4.1 lb sBOD/($10^3 ft^2 \cdot d$)] for the first stage.

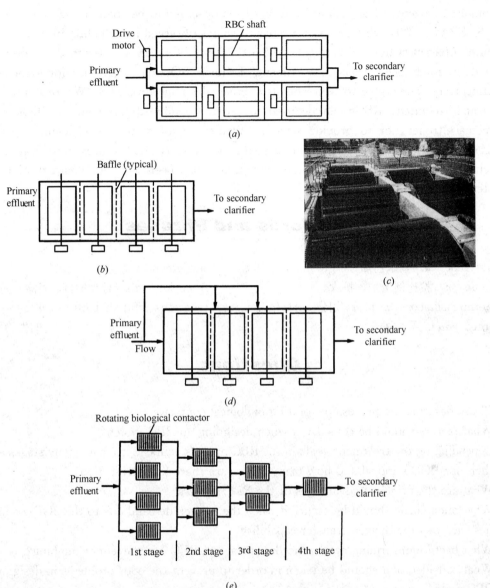

Figure 1 Typical RBC staging arrangements
(a) flow parallel to shaft, (b) flow perpendicular to shaft,
(c) view of RBCs with flow perpendicular to shaft,
(d) step feed flow, and (e) tapered feed flow parallel to shaft

Assuming a 50 percent soluble BOD fraction, the total BOD loading ranges from 24 to 30 g BOD/(m² · d). For some designs that involve higher-strength wastewaters, the loading criteria are met by splitting the flow to multiple RBC units in the first stage or using a step feeding approach as shown on Figure 1d.

For nitrification, the design approach for RBC systems can be very similar to that shown for tertiary nitrification trickling filters after the sBOD concentration is depleted in RBC units preceding nitrification. An sBOD concentration of less than 15 mg/L must be met before a significant nitrifying population can be developed on the RBC disks. The maximum nitrogen surface removal rate has been observed to be about 1.5 g N/(m² · d) (U.S. EPA, 1985), which is quite similar to values observed for trickling filters.

Effluent Characteristics. Treatment systems with RBCs can be designed to provide secondary or advanced levels of treatment. Effluent BOD characteristics for secondary treatment are comparable to well-operated activated-sludge processes. Where a nitrified effluent is required, RBCs can be used to provide combined treatment for BOD and ammonia nitrogen, or to provide separate nitrification of secondary effluent. Typical ranges of effluent characteristics are indicated in Table 1. An RBC process modification in which the disk support shaft is totally submerged has been used for denitrification of wastewater.

New Words and Phrases

polystyrene *n.* 聚苯乙烯
scale-up *n.* 按比例增加，扩大
compartmentalization *n.* 区分，划分，分格化
oriented *adj.* 导向的

turndown *n.* 关闭
retention time 停留时间；阻滞时间
tenacious whitish biofilm 白色坚韧的生物膜

Questions

1. Please describe the process of rotating biological contactors.
2. What factors should be considered when designing an RBC system?
3. Depending on the treatment goals in the RBC process application, how many stages are there for BOD removal and how many stages are there for nitrification?
4. What are the principal advantages of the RBC process?
5. What phenomena should be occurred when the oxygen demand due to the BOD loading has exceeded the oxygen transfer capability?
6. What bacterium forming on the biofilm surface of RBC can prevents sloughing?
7. What consideration should be taken in order to prevent the odor problems in designing RBC units?

Reading Material

Physical Facilities and Process Design for RBC

Physical Facilities for RBC Process

The principal elements of an RBC unit and their importance in the process are described in this section. The suppliers of RBC equipment differ in their disk designs, shafts, and packing support, and configuration designs. The principal elements of an RBC system design are the shaft, disk materials and configuration, drive system, enclosures, and settling tanks.

Shafts. The RBC shafts are used to support and rotate the plastic disks. Maximum shaft length is presently limited to 8.23 m (27 ft) with 7.62 m (25 ft) occupied by disks. Shorter shaft lengths ranging from 1.52 to 7.62 m (5 to 25 ft) are also available. Shaft shapes include square, round, and octagonal, depending on the manufactured. Steel shafts are coated to protect against corrosion and thickness ranges from 13 to 30 mm (0.5 to 1.25 in). Structural details and the life expectancy of the disk shaft are important design considerations.

Disk Materials. High-density polyethylene is the material used most commonly for the manufacture of RBC disks, which are available in different configurations or corrugation patterns. Corrugations increase the available surface area and enhance structural stability. The types of RBC disks, classified based on the total area of disks on the shaft, are commonly termed low- (or standard) density, medium-density, and high-density. Standard-density disks, defined as disks with a surface area of 9300 m^2 (100000 ft^2) per 8.23 m (27 ft) shaft, have larger spaces between disks and are normally used in the lead stages of an RBC process flow diagram. Medium- and high-density disk assemblies have surface areas of 11000 to 16700 m^2 (120000 to 180000 ft^2) per 8.23 m (27 ft) shaft, and are used typically in the middle and final stages of an RBC system where thinner biological growths occur.

Drive Systems. Most RBC units are rotated by direct mechanical drive units attached directly to the central shaft. Motors are typically rated at 3.7 or 5.6 kW (5 or 7.5 hp) per shaft. Air-drive units are also available. The air-drive assembly consists of deep plastic cups attached to the perimeter of the disks, an air header located beneath the disks, and an air compressor. Airflows necessary to achieve design rotational speeds are about 5.3 m^3/min (190 scfm) for a standard-density shaft and 7.6 m^3/min (270 scfm) for a high-density shaft. The release of air into the cups creates a buoyant force that causes the shaft to turn. Both systems have proved to be mechanically reliable. Variablespeed features can be provided to regulate the speed of rotation of the shaft.

Tankage. Tankage for RBC systems has been optimized at 0.0049 m^3/m^2 (0.12 gal/ft^2) of disk area, resulting in a stage volume of 45 m^3 (12000 gal) for a shaft with a disk area of 9300 m^2. Based on this volume, a detention time of 1.44 h is provide for a hydraulic loading of 0.08 m^3/(m^2 · d) [2gal/(ft^2 · d)]. A typical sidewater depth is 1.5 m (5 ft) to accommodate a 40 percent submergence of the disks.

Enclosures. Segmented fiberglass reinforced plastic covers are usually provides over each shaft. In some cases, units have been housed in a building for protection against cold weather, to improve access, or for aesthetic reasons. RBCs are enclosed to (1) protect the plastic disks from deterioration due to ultraviolet light, (2) protect the process from low temperatures, (3) protect the disks and equipment from damage, and (4) control the buildup of algae in the process.

Settling Tanks. Settling tanks for RBCs are similar to trickling filter settling tanks in that all of the sludge from the settling tanks is removed to the sludge processing facilities. Typical design overflow rates for settling tanks used with RBCs are similar to that described for trickling filters with plastic packing.

RBC Process Design

Empirical design approaches have been developed for RBC systems based on pilot-plant and full-scale plant data and that consider such fundamental factors as the disk surface area and specific loadings in terms of g/m^2 disk area $\cdot$ d. Approaches for designing staged RBC systems for BOD removal and nitrification are presented in this section.

BOD Removal. Design models for BOD removal in RBC systems are reviewed in WEF (2000). In a design comparison, the models generally resulted in lower recommended BOD loadings than that determined from manufacturer's literature and were, in some cases, similar for BOD removals below 90 percent. Of these, a second-order model by Opatken (U. S. EPA 1985) is selected to estimate RBC surface area requirements, as the model was developed with data from nine full-scale plants and includes staged reactor designs.

The second-order model was converted to SI units by Grady et al. (1999), and terms were converted to account for disk surface area. The model can be used to estimate the soluble BOD concentration in each stage.

$$S_n = \frac{-1+\sqrt{1+(4)(0.00974)(A_s/Q)\cdot S_{n-1}}}{(2)(0.00974)(A_s/Q)} \tag{1}$$

where S_n = sBOD concentration in stage n, mg/L
  A_s = disk surface area on stage n, m^2
  Q = flowrate, m^3/d

Because Eq. (1) applies only to sBOD concentrations, a secondary clarifier effluent sBOD/BOD ratio of 0.50 is assumed to design for an effluent BOD concentration. Similarly, without sBOD concentration data for the primary effluent fed to the RBC system, an sBOD/BOD ratio of 0.50 to 0.75 can be assumed. Because the design is based on sBOD, the first-stage RBC soluble unit organic loading rate should be equal to or less than 12 to 15 g sBOD/(m^2 $\cdot$ d) to determine the first-stage disk area and effluent sBOD concentration from Eq. (1). The computational procedure used to size an RBC system for BOD removal is summarized in Table 2.

Computation procedure for the design of a rotating biological contactor (RBC) process

Table 2

Item	Description
1	Determine influent and effluent sBOD concentrations and wastewater flowrate
2	Determine the RBC disk area for the first stage based on a maximum sBOD of 12 to 15g sBOD/(m^3 $\cdot$ d)
3	Determine the number of RBC shafts using a standard disk density of 9300m^2/shaft

Table 2(Continued)

Item	Description
4	Select the number of trains for the design, flow per train, number of stages, and disk area/shaft in each stage. For the lower loaded stages a higher disk density may be used
5	Based on the design assumptions made in Step 4, calculate the sBOD concentration in each stage. Determine if the effluent sBOD concentration will be achieved. If not, modify the number of stages, number of per stage, and/or disk area per stage. If the effluent sBOD concentration is met, evaluate alternatives to further optimize the design.
6	Develop the secondary clarifier design

Note: $g/(m^3 \cdot d) \times 0.0624 = lb/(10^3 \text{ ft}^3 \cdot d)$

Nitrification. Treatment systems employing RBC units can be used to develop nitrifying biofilms for nitrification of secondary effluents or at low sBOD loadings where nitrification can occur in BOD removal systems. For tertiary nitrification the same procedure used for the design of trickling filters can be followed. A $r_{n,max}$ value of 1.5 g $N/(m^2 \cdot d)$ is recommended based on field test results(U. S. EPA, 1984). For combined BOD removal and nitrification, nitrification will be prevented or inhibited by the addition of sBOD to the RBC unit. The nitrifying bacteria can compete for space on the RBC disk once the sBOD concentration is reduced to 10 to 15 mg/L.

The sBOD concentration remaining in an RBC tank will be related to the sBOD loading. Pano and Middlebrooks (1983) provide a relationship to show the effect of sBOD loading on the nitrification rates:

$$F_{r_n} = 1.00 - 0.1 \text{sBOD} \tag{2}$$

where F_{r_n} = fraction of nitrification rate possible without sBOD effect

sBOD = soluble BOD loading, $g/(m^2 \cdot d)$

At an sBOD loading rate of 10 g $sBOD/(m^2 \cdot d)$, the nitrification rate is predicted to be zero.

New Words and Phrases

octagonal   *adj.* 八边形的，八角形的
coated   *adj.* 涂上一层的
polyethylene   *n.* 聚乙烯
corrugation   *n.* 成皱，起皱，皱状，波纹

segment   *n.* 段，节，片断
        v. 分割
fiberglass reinforced plastic
    玻璃纤维强化塑料

LESSON 19

Sludge Treatment, Utilization, and Disposal

When the wastewater is treated and discharged to a watercourse, the job is not over. Left behind are the solids, suspended in water, commonly called sludge. Currently sludge treatment and disposal accounts for over 50% of the treatment costs in a typical secondary plant, making this none-too-glamorous operation an essential aspect of wastewater treatment.

Sources of Sludge

The first source of sludge is the suspended solids (SS) that enter the treatment plant and are partially removed in the primary settling tank or clarifier. Ordinarily about 60 percent of the SS becomes *raw primary sludge*, which is highly putrescent, contains pathogenic organs and is very wet (about 96% water).

The removal of BOD is basically a method of wasting energy, and secondary wastewater treatment plants are designed to reduce this high-energy material to low-energy chemicals, typically accomplished by biological means, using microorganisms (the "decomposers" in ecological terms) that use the energy for their own life and procreation. Secondary treatment processes such as the popular activated sludge system are almost perfect systems except that the microorganisms convert too little of the high-energy organics to CO_2 and H_2O and too much of it to new organisms. Thus the system operates with excess of these microorganisms, or *waste activated sludge*. The mass of waste activated sludge per mass of BOD removed in secondary treatment is known as the *yield*, expressed as mass of SS produced per mass of BOD removed. Typically, the yield of waste activated sludge is 0.5 pound of dry solids per pound of BOD reduced.

Phosphorus removal processes also invariably end up with excess solids. If lime is used, the calcium carbonates and calcium hydroxyapatites are formed and must be disposed of. Aluminum sulfate similarly produces solids, in the form of aluminum hydroxides and aluminum phosphates. Even the biological processes for phosphorus removal end up with solids. The use of an oxidation pond or marsh for phosphorus removal is possible only if some organics (algae, water hyacinths, fish, etc.) are periodically harvested.

Sludge Treatment

A great deal of money could be saved, and troubles averted, if sludge could be disposed of as it is drawn off the main process train. Unfortunately, the sludges have three characteristics that make such a simple solution unlikely: They are aesthetically displeasing, they are potentially harmful, and they have too much water.

The first two problems are often solved by *stabilization*, such as *anaerobic* or *aerobic digestion*. The third problem requires the removal of water by either thickening or dewatering. The next three sections cover the topics of stabilization, thickening, and dewatering, and then ultimate disposal of the sludge.

Sludge Stabilization. The objective of sludge stabilization is to reduce the problems associated with two detrimental characteristics—sludge odor and putrescence and the presence of pathogenic organisms. Sludge may be stabilized by use of lime, by aerobic digestion, or by anaerobic digestion.

Lime stabilization is achieved by adding lime [as hydrated lime, $Ca(OH)_2$, or as quicklime, CaO] to the sludge and thus raising the pH to 11 or above. This significantly reduces odor and helps in the destruction of pathogens. The major disadvantage of lime stabilization is that it is temporary. With time (days) the pH drops and the sludge once again becomes putrescent.

Aerobic digestion is a logical extension of the activated sludge system. Waste activated sludge is placed in dedicated tanks, and the concentrated solids are allowed to continue their decomposition. The food for the microorganisms is available only by the destruction of other viable organisms and both total and volatile solids are thereby reduced. However, aerobically digested sludges are more difficult to dewater than are anaerobic sludges and are not as effective in the reduction of pathogens as *anaerobic digestion*, a process illustrated in Figure 1. The biochemistry of anaerobic digestion is a staged process: Solution of organic compounds by extracellular enzymes is followed by the production of organic acids by a large and hearty group of anaerobic microorganisms known, appropriately enough, as the *acid formers*. The organic acids are in turn degraded further by a group of strict anaerobes called *methane formers*. These microorganisms become upset at the least change in their environment, and the success of anaerobic treatment depends on maintenance of suitable conditions for the methane formers. Since they are strict anaerobes, they are unable to function in the presence of oxygen and are very sensitive to environmental conditions like pH, temperature, and the presence of toxins. A digester goes "sour" when the methane formers have been inhibited in some way and the acid formers keep chugging away, making more organic acids, further lowering the pH and making conditions even worse for the methane formers. Curing a sick digester requires suspension of feeding and, often, massive doses of lime or other antacids.

Sludge Thickening. Sludge thickening is a process in which the solids concentration is increased and

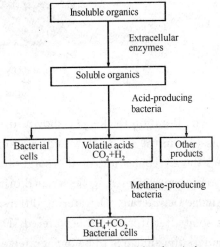

Figure 1 Generalized biochemical reactions in anaerobic sludge digestion

total sludge volume is correspondingly decreased, but the sludge still behaves like a liquid instead of a solid. Thickening commonly produces sludge solids concentrations in the 3% to 5% range, whereas the point at which sludge begins to have the properties of a solid is between 15% and 20% solids. Thickening also implies that the process is gravitational, using the difference between particle and fluid densities to achieve the compaction of solids.

The advantages of sludge thickening in reducing the volume of sludge to be handled are substantial. With reference to Figure 2, a sludge with 1% solids thickened to 5% results in an 80% volume reduction (since 5%=1/20). A concentration of 20% solids, which might be achieved by mechanical dewatering, results in a 95% reduction in volume, with resulting savings in treatment, handling, and disposal costs.

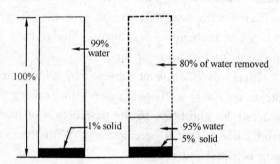

Figure 2 Volume reduction owing to sludge thickening

Two types of nonmechanical thickening operations are presently in use: the *gravity thickener* and the *flotation thickener*. The latter also uses gravity to separate the solids from the liquid, but for simplicity we continue to use both descriptive terms.

A typical gravity thickener is shown in Figure 3. The influent, or feed, enters in the middle, and the water moves to the outside, eventually leaving as the clear effluent over the weirs. The sludge solids settle as a blanket and are removed out of the bottom.

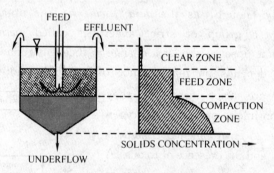

Figure 3 Gravity thickener

A flotation thickener, shown in Figure 4, operates by forcing air under pressure to dissolve in the return flow and releasing the pressure as the return is mixed with the feed. As the air comes out of the solution, tiny bubbles attach themselves to the solids and carry them upward, to be scraped off.

Sludge Dewatering. Dewatering differs from thickening in that the sludge should behave as a solid after it has been dewatered. Dewatering is seldom used as an intermediate process unless the sludge is to be incinerated and most wastewater plants use dewatering as a final method of volume reduction before ultimate disposal.

LESSON 19

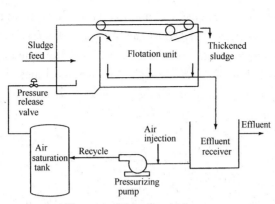

Figure 4   Flotation thickener

In the United States, the usual dewatering techniques are sand beds, pressure filters, belt filters, and centrifuges. Each of these is discussed in the following paragraphs.

Sand beds have been used for a great many years and are still the most cost-effective means of dewatering when land is available. The beds consist of tile drains in sand and gravel, covered by about 26 cm (10 in) of sand. The sludge to be dewatered is poured on the sand. The water initially seeps into the sand and tile drains. Seepage into the sand and through the tile drains, although important in the total volume of water extracted, lasts only for a few days. The sand pores are quickly clogged, and all drainage into the sand ceases. The mechanism of evaporation takes over, and this process is actually responsible for the conversion of liquid sludge to solid. In some northern areas, sand beds are enclosed in greenhouses to promote evaporation as well as to prevent rain from falling into the beds.

If dewatering by sand beds is considered impractical due to lack of land and high labor costs, mechanical dewatering techniques must be used. Three common mechanical dewatering processes are pressure and belt filtration and centrifugation.

The *pressure filter*, shown in Figure 5, uses positive pressure to force the water through a filter cloth. Typically, the pressure filters are built as plate-and-frame filters, in which the sludge solids are captured between the plates and frames, which are then pulled apart to allow for sludge cleanout.

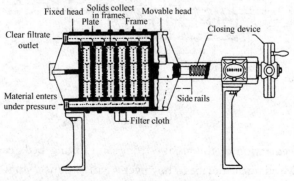

Figure 5   Pressure filters

The *belt filter*, shown in Figure 6, operates as both a pressure filter and a gravity drainage. As the sludge is introduced onto the moving belt, the free water drips through the belt but the solids are retained. The belt then moves into the dewatering zone, where the sludge is squeezed between two belts. These machines are quite effective in dewatering many different types of sludges and are being installed in many small wastewater treatment plants.

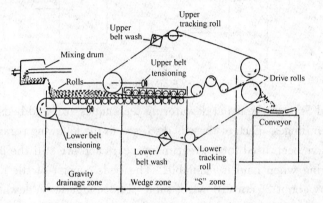

Figure 6 Belt filters

Centrifugation became popular in wastewater treatment only after organic polymers were available for sludge conditioning. Although the centrifuge will work on any sludge, most unconditioned sludges cannot be centrifuged with greater than 60% or 70% solids recovery. The centrifuge most widely used is the *solid bowl decanter*, which consists of a bullet-shaped body rotating on its axis. The sludge is placed in the bowl, and the solids settle out under about 500 to 1000 gravities (centrifugally applied) and are scraped out of the bowl by a screw conveyor (Figure 7). Although laboratory tests are of some value in estimating centrifuge applicability, tests with continuous models are considerably better and highly recommended whenever possible.

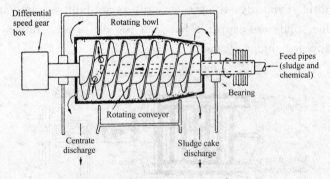

Figure 7 Solid bowl centrifuges

The solids concentration of the sludge from sand drying beds can be as high as 90% after evaporation. Mechanical devices, however, will produce sludge ranging from 15% to 35% solids.

Utilization and Ultimate Disposal

The options for ultimate disposal of sludge are limited to air, water, and land. Strict controls on air pollution complicate incineration, although this certainly is an option. Disposal of sludges in deep water (such as oceans) is decreasing owing to adverse or unknown detrimental effects on aquatic ecology. Land disposal may be either dumping in a landfill or spreading out over land and allowing natural biodegradation to assimilate the sludge into the soil. Because of environmental and cost considerations, incineration and land disposal are presently most widely used.

Incineration is actually not a method of disposal at all but rather a sludge treatment step in which the organics are converted to H_2O and CO_2 and the inorganics are oxidized to nonputrescent ash residue. Two types of incinerators have found use in sludge treatment: multiple hearth and fluid bed. The *multiple hearth incinerator*, as the name implies, has several hearths stacked vertically, with rabble arms pushing the sludge progressively downward through the hottest layers and finally into the ash pit. The *fluidized bed incinerator* is full of hot sand and is suspended by air injection; the sludge incinerated within the moving sand. Owing to the violent motion within the fluid bed, scraper arms are unnecessary. The sand acts as a "thermal flywheel," allowing intermittent operation.

When sludge is destined for disposal on land and the beneficial aspects of such disposal are emphasized, sludge is often euphemistically referred to as *biosolids*. The sludge has nutrients (nitrogen and phosphorus), is high in organic content, and, as discussed, is full of water. Thus, its potential as a soil additive is often highlighted. However, both high levels of heavy metals, such as cadmium, lead, and zinc, as well as contamination by pathogens that may survive the stabilization process, can be troublesome.

Heavy metals entering the wastewater treatment plant tend to concentrate on the sludge solids, and thus far, we have found no effective means of removing these metals from the sludge prior to sludge disposal. Control must therefore focus on maintaining strict rules (industrial pretreatment rules) that prevent the discharge of the metals into wastewater collection systems.

Reduction in the levels of pathogens is often achieved in the sludge digestion process, but the process is not 100% effective. Sludges that receive the equivalent of 30 days anaerobic digestion are classified by EPA as Class B sludges which can be disposed of only on nonagricultural land (golf courses, highway median strips), but a 30-day delay in any use of the land is required. Class A sludges are disinfected by other processes, such as composting and quicklime addition, in which high temperatures act to kill the pathogens, or by nonionizing radiation.

New Words and Phrases

putrescent *adj.* 将腐烂的，腐败的   ecological *adj.* 生态学的，社会生态学的

procreation　*n.* 生产，生殖
invariably　*adv.* 不变地，总是
end up with　以……告终
hydroxyapatite　*n.* 羟磷灰石
marsh　*n.* 湿地，沼泽，沼泽地
hyacinth　*n.* [植] 风信子，洋水仙，水葫芦
avert　*v.* 转移
putrescence　*n.* 腐败，腐烂，坏死
hydrated lime　熟石灰，氢氧化钙
quicklime　*n.* 生石灰
extracellular enzyme　胞外酶
antacid　*adj.* 中和酸性的，抗酸性的　*n.* 抗酸剂
gravity thickener　重力浓缩池
flotation thickener　气浮浓缩
weir　*n.* 堰
scrape　*n.* 刮，擦，擦痕，刮擦声，困境　*vi.* 刮掉，擦掉　*vt.* 刮，擦，擦伤，挖成
incinerate　*vi.* 把…烧成灰，烧弃，焚烧
belt filter　带式滤机
centrifugation　*n.* 离心法，离心分离
solid bowl　无孔转鼓（离心机的）
decanter　*n.* 滗析器，倾析器
assimilate　*v.* 吸收，同化
multiple hearth　多炉膛
fluid bed　流化床
multiple hearth incinerator　多段焚烧炉
rabble blade　耙齿（多段焚烧炉）
ash pit　灰坑
destined　*adj.* 去往……的
euphemistical　*adj.* 婉转的，委婉说法的
soil additive　土壤添加剂
nonionizing　*adj.* 不电离的
tension　*n.* & *vt.* 拉紧

Questions

1. Try to describe the source of sludge.
2. Try to describe the methods of sludge stabilization.
3. Please explain the meaning of sludge thickening.
4. Please explain the principle of a flotation thickener.
5. What is the difference between dewatering and thickening process?
6. What are the usual dewatering techniques in the United States?
7. What is the precondition for the *centrifugation* used in dewater?
8. Try to describe the methods for ultimate disposal of sludge.

Reading Material

Sludge Characteristics

The composition and characteristics of sewage sludge vary widely. Since no two wastewaters are alike, the sludge produced will differ. Furthermore, sludge characteristics change considerably with time. Wastewater sludge typically contains organics (proteins, carbohydrates, fats, oils), microbes (bacteria, viruses, protozoa), nutrients (phosphates and nitrates), and a variety of household and industrial chemicals. The higher the level of heavy metals and toxic compounds, the greater is the risk to humans and the environment. A key physical characteristic is the *solids concentration*, because this defines the volume of sludge that must be handled. It also determines whether the sludge behaves as a liquid or a solid. Sludge tends to act like plastic fluids as the solids concentration increases until a relatively solid state is reached.

The amount of sludge solids generated in a wastewater (or drinking water) treatment system depends largely on the degree of treatment provided and on the amount of chemicals added. Sludge initially forms at the bottom of a clarifier or settling tank in the form of concentrated slurry of solids suspended in water. Its volume depends on the relative amounts of solid material and water. The concentration of the sludge is expressed as a percentage by weight or mass. For example, a mass of 100 kg of liquid sludge that contains 3 kg of solids and 97 kg of water will have a concentration of 3/100 or 3 percent solids. This is equivalent to a solids concentration of 30000 mg/L.

The concentration of solids has a very significant effect on the total volume occupied by the liquid sludge. *The total sludge volume is inversely proportional to the solids concentration*. For example, if the percentage of solids is doubled, say from 3 to 6 percent, then the total sludge volume will be decreased to half its original volume. This is a very important relationship. Increasing the solids concentration in the slurry by a few percentage points can significantly reduce the total sludge volume. This reduces the cost of handling, treating, and disposing of the sludge.

For practical purposes, it can be assumed that the weight or mass per unit volume of liquid sludge is the same as that of pure water. For example, the mass of 1 m³ of water is 1000 kg; the mass of the same volume of a relatively thick sludge (such as 10 percent solids) is only about 1020 kg. The difference of 2 percent can be neglected for design or operational purposes. Based on this, the relationship between sludge concentration and sludge volumes can be expressed as follows:

$$S=\frac{M}{V}\times 100 \tag{1a}$$

or

$$S=\frac{W}{8.34\times V}\times 100 \tag{1b}$$

where S = sludge solids concentation, in percent
 M = dry sludge solids, kg (Equation 1a)
 W = dry sludge solids, lb (Equation 1b)
 V = total sludge volume, L (Equation 1a) or gal (Equation 1b)
 8.34 = number of pounds per gallon (Equation 1b)

Primary sludge typically has a solids concentration of about 7 percent. Secondary sludge has a much lower solids concentration because the suspended solids are mostly biological flocs that settle slowly and do not compact to as high a density as primary sludge. Waste-activated sludge contains only about 2 percent solids or less.

Primary and secondary sludge solids are mostly organic materials, with a volatile fraction of up to 0.8. Primary sludge gives off a strong and offensive odor; it can quickly become septic and difficult to handle. In addition to volume reduction, a basic objective of sewage sludge treatment is to stabilize the biodegradable organic solids and to render the sludge unoffensive and easy to handle.

Water treatment plant sludges are mostly inert chemical precipitates that are relatively stable and unoffensive. Quantities of this type of sludge can vary widely depending on the amount and type of chemicals used and on the composition of the raw water.

The *quantity of primary sludge* produced in a sewage treatment plant depends on the concentration of suspended solids in the raw wastewater and on the TSS removal efficiency. It can be estimated from the following expressions:

$$\text{mass} = E \times \text{TSS} \times Q \tag{2a}$$

$$\text{weight} = E \times \text{TSS} \times Q \times 8.34 \tag{2b}$$

where mass = dry sludge solids, kg (Equation 2a)

weight = dry sludge solids, lb (Equation 2b)

E = TSS removal efficiency, decimal form

Q = sewage flow rate, ML/d (Equation 2a) or mg/d (Equation 2b)

The *quantity of secondary sludge* produced in a sewage treatment plant depends on the BOD concentration and on the fraction of BOD that is converted to biological solids (microbe cells). It can be estimated by the following expressions:

$$\text{mass} = K \times \text{BOD} \times Q \tag{3a}$$

$$\text{weight} = K \times \text{BOD} \times Q \times 8.34 \tag{3b}$$

where K = a coefficient that represents the proportion of BOD converted to biological solids, in decimal form

BOD = applied 5-d BOD, mg/L

The value of K depends on the organic loading or F/M ratio; a typical value for extended aeration or fixed growth systems is $K = 0.25$, and for conventional or step aeration processes, a typical value is $K = 0.35$.

New Words and Phrases

plastic fluid　塑性流体

decimal　*adj*. 十进的，小数的

extended aeration　延时曝气

fixed growth system　固定式生长系统
　　　　　　　（如滴滤池等）

conventional aeration　传统曝气
　　　　　　　（指传统活性污泥法）

step aeration　阶段曝气

Cold Water Supply: I

Drinking Water

Under the Public Health Acts, every dwelling is required to have a potable (drinkable) water supply, and the most important place to provide drinking water in dwellings is at the kitchen sink (see Figure 1). However, because there is a likelihood that all taps in dwellings will be used for drinking, they should all be connected in such a way that the water remains in potable condition. This means that all draw-off taps in dwellings should either be connected direct from the mains supply, or from a storage cistern that is 'protected'.

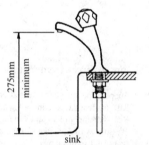

Positioned so that outlet is at least 275mm above bottom of bowl, to allow buckets and other utensils to be filled.
Outlets designed to make hosepipe connections difficult.

Figure 1 Tap at kitchen sink

Drinking water supplies should also be provided in suitable and convenient locations in offices and other buildings, particularly where food and drink is prepared or eaten. If no such locations exist, drinking water should be provided near but preferably not in toilets. However, drinking water fountains may be installed in toilet areas, provided they are sited well away from WCs and urinals and comply with the requirements of BS 6465: Part 1.

To avoid stagnation drinking water points should not be installed at the ends of long pipes where only small volumes of water are likely to be drawn off.

As far as possible pipe runs to drinking water taps should not follow the routes of space heating or hot water pipes or shouldnot pass through heated areas. Where this is unavoidable, both hot and cold pipes should be insulated.

Types of System

Systems in Dwellings. Water may be supplied to cold taps either directly from the mains via the supply pipe or indirectly from a protected cold water storage cistern. In some cases a combination of both methods of supply may be the best arrangement.

Factors to consider when designing a cold water supply system are shown in Figures 2 and 3.

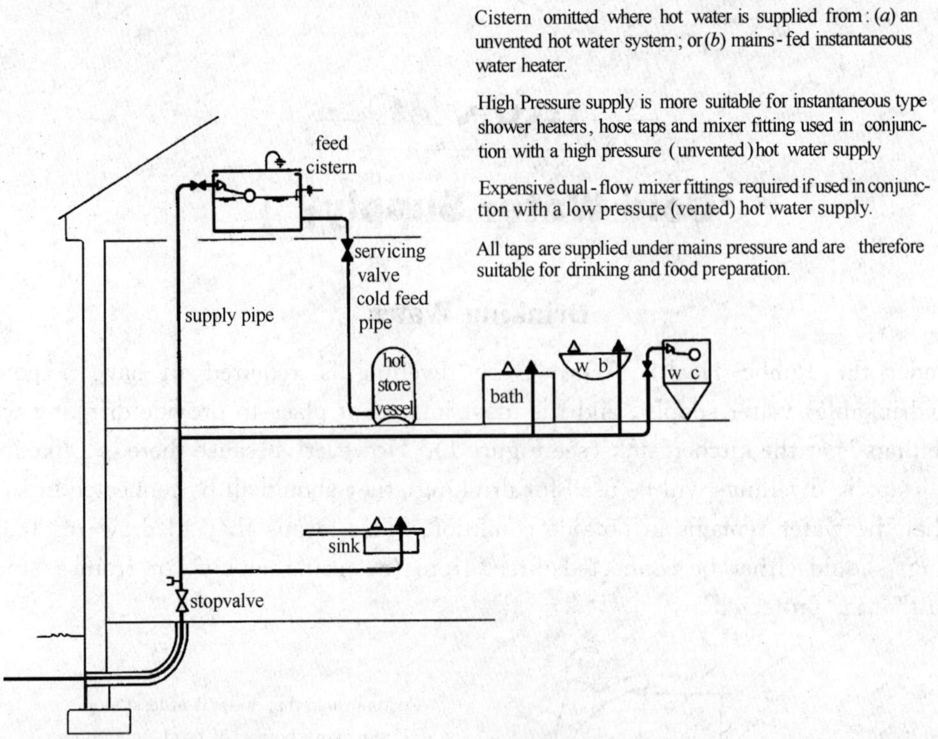
Cistern omitted where hot water is supplied from: (a) an unvented hot water system; or (b) mains-fed instantaneous water heater.
High Pressure supply is more suitable for instantaneous type shower heaters, hose taps and mixer fitting used in conjunction with a high pressure (unvented) hot water supply
Expensive dual-flow mixer fittings required if used in conjunction with a low pressure (vented) hot water supply.
All taps are supplied under mains pressure and are therefore suitable for drinking and food preparation.
feed cistern
servicing valve
cold feed pipe
supply pipe
hot store vessel
bath
w b
w c
sink
stopvalve

Figure 2 Characteristics of supply direct from mains

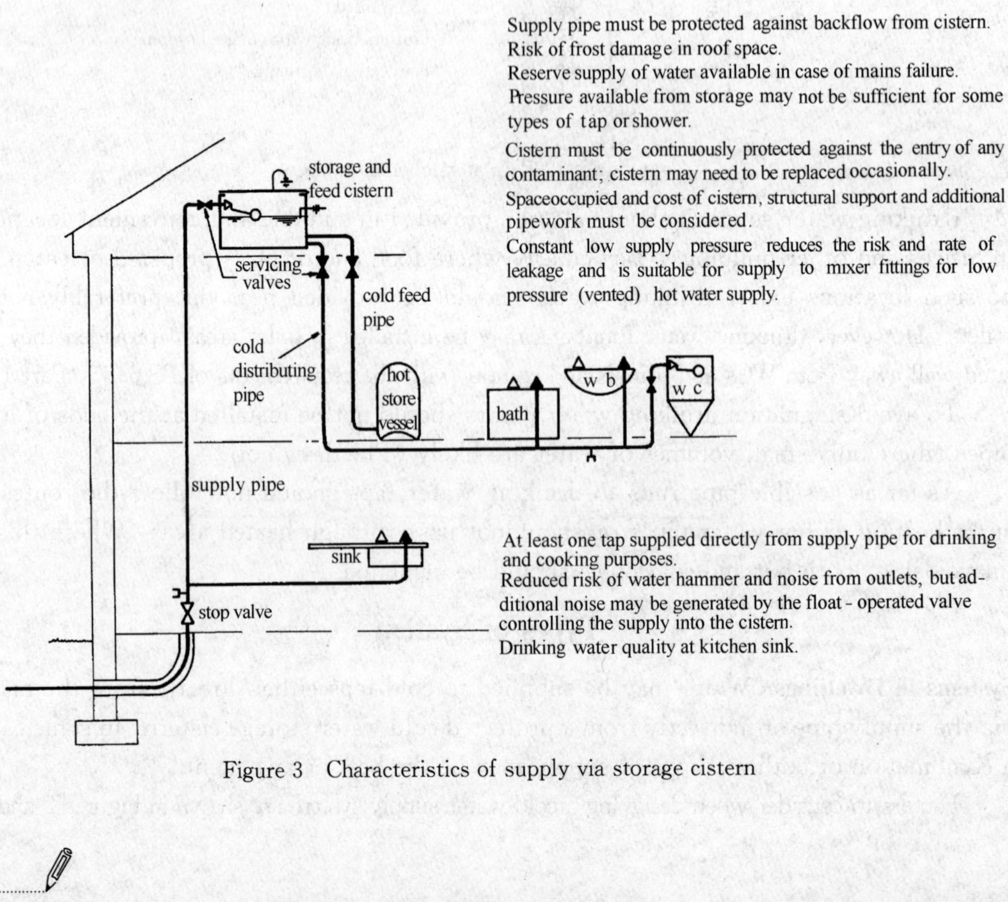
Supply pipe must be protected against backflow from cistern.
Risk of frost damage in roof space.
Reserve supply of water available in case of mains failure.
Pressure available from storage may not be sufficient for some types of tap or shower.
Cistern must be continuously protected against the entry of any contaminant; cistern may need to be replaced occasionally.
Spaceoccupied and cost of cistern, structural support and additional pipework must be considered.
Constant low supply pressure reduces the risk and rate of leakage and is suitable for supply to mixer fittings for low pressure (vented) hot water supply.
storage and feed cistern
servicing valves
cold feed pipe
cold distributing pipe
hot store vessel
bath
w b
w c
supply pipe
sink
stop valve
At least one tap supplied directly from supply pipe for drinking and cooking purposes.
Reduced risk of water hammer and noise from outlets, but additional noise may be generated by the float-operated valve controlling the supply into the cistern.
Drinking water quality at kitchen sink.

Figure 3 Characteristics of supply via storage cistern

LESSON 20

Systems in Buildings other than Dwellings. In the case of small buildings where the water consumption is likely to be similar to that of a dwelling, the characteristics in Figures 2 and 3 should be considered.

For larger buildings such as office blocks, hostels and factories, it will usually be preferable for all water, except drinking water, to be supplied indirectly from a cold water storage cistern or cisterns. Drinking water should be taken directly from the water supplier's main wherever practicable (see Figure 4).

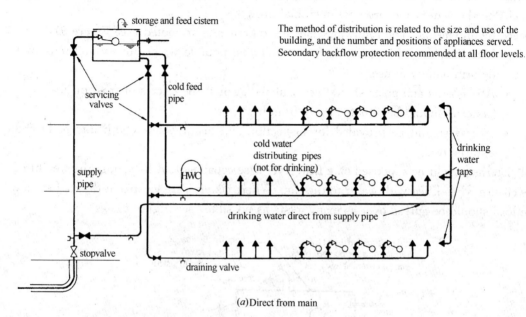

(a) Direct from main

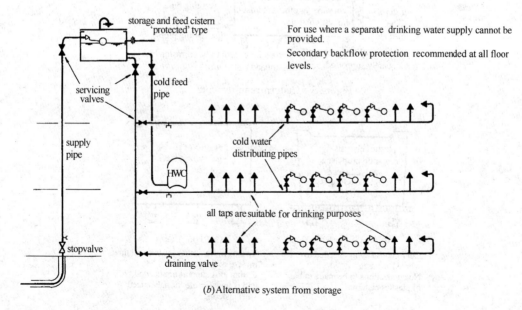

(b) Alternative system from storage

Figure 4　Drinking water supply

Pumped Systems. Where the height of the building lies above statutory levels or when the available pressure is insufficient to supply the whole of a building and the water supplier is unable to increase the supply pressure in the supplier's mains, consideration should be given to the provision of a pumped cold water supply cistern.

Storage Cisterns

Storage cisterns and lids for domestic purposes should not impart taste, colour, odour or toxicity to the water, nor promote microbial growth.

Cistern Requirements. The following cistern requirements are noted (see Figure 5):
- Materials should be suitable for maintaining potable water quality and must not deform unduly in use.
- All cisterns and pipes should be insulated against the effects of frost or heat.
- Cisterns should be situated away from heat.
- Access should be provided for inspection and maintenance (both internally and externally).

All cisterns should be supposed on a firm level base capable of withstanding the weight of the cistern when filled with water to the rim. Where cisterns are located in the roof space, the load should be spread over as many joists as possible (see Figure 6).

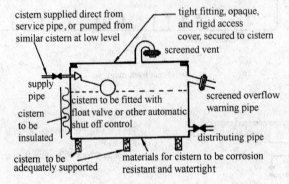

Figure 5 Cistern requirements

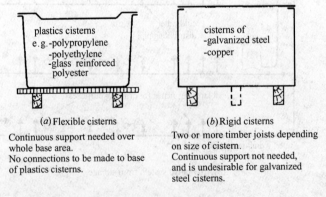

Figure 6 Support for cisterns

Occasionally large cisterns are buried or sunk in the ground. In these cases measures need to be taken to detect leakage and to protect the cistern from contamination (see Figure 7).

Connections to Cisterns. These should be made as shown in Figures 8 and 9.

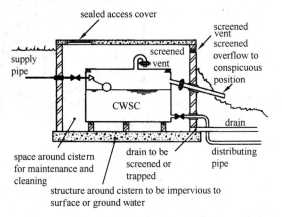

Figure 7 Sunken cisterns

Warning/overflow pipe must be large enough to carry away leakage under worst conditions.
Dimensions are in millimetres.
Cistern must comply with Byelaw 30 if it is used for domestic purposes.

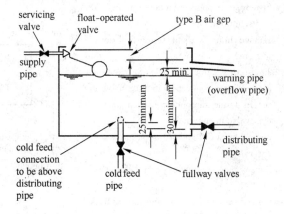

(a) Small cisterns

Washout pipe to be plugged when not in use and must discharge to open air at least 150 mm above any drain.
Overflow pipe must be large enough to carry away leakage under worst conditions.
Cold feed and cold distributing pipes to be fitted with corrosion resistant strainers.
Cold feed pipe to be above distributing pipe.
Dimensions are in millimetres.
Cistern must comply with Byelaw 30 if it is used for domestic purposes.

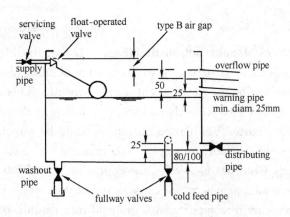

(b) Large cisterns strainers

Figure 8 Connections to cisterns

To avoid *Legionella* cisterns should:
- be small enough to ensure a rapid turnover and thus prevent stagnation.
- have float valves arranged to open and close together.
- have inlet and outlet connections at opposite ends.
- be regularly inspected and maintained in clean condition.
- conform to the requirements of Byelaw 30.

The diagram shows separate overflow pipes. A common overflow pipe or warning pipe may be fitted provided cisterns are linked to form one storage unit

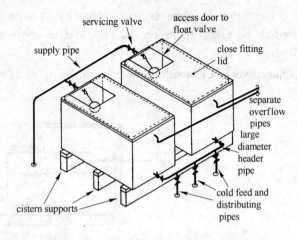

(a) Cisterns connected in parallel

This method is preferred for prevention of *Legionella*.
To take cistern 1 out of commission for cleansing:
- fit temporary connection between link (b) to distributing pipe;
- remove link (a) and cap off close to cisterns.

To take cistern 2 out of commission for cleansing:
- fit temporary connection to float valve in cistern 1 and disconnect branch pipe to float valve in cistern 2;
- remove links (a) and (b) and cap off near cisterns.

Sterilise any pipes and fittings used before they are fitted.
Sterilise cistern and pipes before putting back into service.

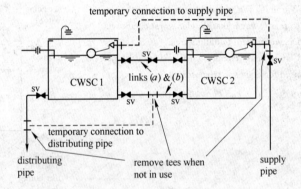

(b) Cisterns connected in series

Figure 9 Linked cisterns

Cisterns Mounted outside Buildings. Whether fixed to the building itself or supported on an independent structure, cisterns outside buildings, see Figure 10, should be enclosed in a well-ventilated, yet draught-proof housing. This should be constructed to prevent the entry of birds, animals and insects, but provide access to the interior of the cistern for maintenance. Ventilation openings should be screened by a corrosion-resistant mesh with a maximum aperture size of 0.65 mm.

Large Cisterns. Generally these provide over 5000 L storage and are often made up of preformed panels or are constructed of concrete. They should preferably be divided into two or more compartments to avoid interruption of the water supply when carrying out repairs or maintenance to the cistern.

Cistern Capacities. Clause 5.3.3 of BS 6700 makes the following recommendations for

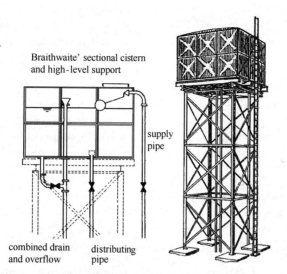

Cistern and pipes to be enclosed and insulated against frost.
Enclosure to be ventilated, but draughtproof, and arranged to prevent the entry of birds, animals and insects.
Overflow/drain pipe must terminate in a conspicuous position above ground level.

Figure 10 Typical exterior storage cistern

houses:

smaller houses	cold water only	—100 L to 150 L
	hot and cold outlets	—200 L to 300 L
larger houses	per bedroom	—100 L

Pipework to and from Cisterns. Supply and distributing pipes to and from cisterns should comply with the following recommendations.
(1) All pipework should be insulated to reduce heat losses and gains, to minimize frost damage, and to prevent condensation.
(2) Pipes should preferably be laid to a fall to reduce the risk of air locks and to facilitate filling and draining.
(3) Pipes should be closely grouped for neatness, but not so close as to gain heat from one another.
(4) Pipes should be securely fixed and adequately supposed.
(5) Only flush pipes fed from a flushing cistern or trough shall deliver water to WCs and urinals.
(6) A cold feed pipe should not be used other than to supply the hot water apparatus for which it is intended.

Warning and Overflow Pipes. Warning and overflow pipes (see Figure 11) serve two purposes:
(1) to give warning that inlet valve to cistern has failed to close.
(2) to remove safely from the buildings any water which does leak from the inflow pipe.

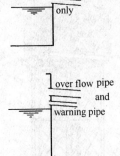

(a) Small cisterns
Small cisterns of up to 1000L nominal capacity must be fitted with a warning pipe and no other overflow pipe.

(b) Medium cisterns
Cisterns of between 1000L and 5000L nominal capacity must be fitted with an overflow pipe and a warning pipe.

Cisterns of more than 5000L nominal capacity may have other warning devices fitted in place of the warning pipe.

Figure 11　Warning and overflow pipes for cisterns

On cisterns of less than 1000L one pipe only will serve both as an overflow pipe and a warning pipe, but on larger cisterns it may be necessary to have a separate pipe for each function.

Note

a potable water: a drinkable water
WC: water closet (WC)
Wb: wash basin
HWC: hot water storage cylinder or hot store vessel
CWSC: cold water storage cistern (storage and feed cistern) (feed cistern)
SV: supply stop valve or servicing valve

New Words and Phrases

draw-off tap　放水龙头
cistern　*n.* 水塔，蓄水池
utensil　*n.* 器具
urinal　*n.* 尿壶，小便池
stagnation　*n.* 停滞
space heating　环流供暖，空间加热
lid　*n.* 盖子，罩，顶
　　vt. 给…盖盖子
microbial growth　微生物增长
insulated　*adj.* 绝缘的，隔热的
rim　*n.* 边，轮缘
unvented　*adj.* 未放气的
deform　*v.* （使）变形

timber　*n.* 木材，木料
joist　*n.* ［建］托梁，小梁
galvanized　*adj.* 镀锌的，电镀的
conspicuous　*adj.* 明显的
mesh　*n.* 网孔，网丝，网眼，筛［目］
impervious　*adj.* 不透水的，不渗透的，密封的
aperture　*n.* 孔，穴，缝隙，（照相机，望远镜等的）光圈，孔径
clause　*n.* 子句，条款
compression fitting　压紧组件
bucket　*n.* 桶，一桶的量，［桶状物］铲斗
Legionella　*n.* 军团菌

tee *n.* 三通，字母T，T形物，球座   fullway valve 全开阀
sterilise *v.* 消毒   draughtproof 不透风的
glass reinforced polyester 玻璃纤维增强聚酯   preformed *adj.* 预成型的，预制成的

Questions

1. In what situation should consideration be given to the provision of a pumped cold water supply cistern?
2. What are the basic requirements for storage cistern?
3. Generally, why should large cisterns be divided into two or more compartments?
4. What are the purposes for warning and overflow pipes?
5. What are the recommendations of supply and distributing pipes to and from cisterns?

Reading Material

Cold Water Supply：Ⅱ

Water Revenue Meters

This section should be regarded as for information only. It is probable that regulations will be made as to water metering matters in due course.

Meters may be fitted by the consumer's contractor or by the water undertaker. Where fitting is done by a private contractor the water supplier will need to be consulted and agreement reached on siting and installation details.

The revenue meter will be supplied by and will remain the property of the water supplier.

The preferred position for the meter is at the boundary of the premises at the end of the communication pipe so that it will register the whole supply (see Figure 12).

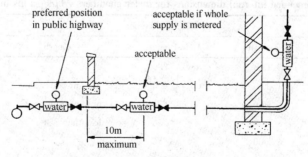

Figure 12 Meter positions

In the case of premises with multiple occupations, e.g. flats, and where underground installations are not practicable, an internal installation may be acceptable provided the whole supply is registered.

Notes on Fitting. The following points on fitting should be noted
- The meter installation should comply with BS5728.
- The meter must be protected from risk of damage by shock or vibration.
- The method of connection should permit meter changes without the use of heat or major disturbance of pipework.
- Connector unions should have flat seats and be complete with 1.5mm thick washers to allow for tolerance on meter lengths.
- Meter lengths — G3/4B meters, 134 mm.
  —G1B meters, see BS 5728.

Flow Rates. Nominal flow rate for the G3/4B meter is 1.5 m^3/h, and for the G1B meter is 2.5 m^3/h.

Continuity Bonding. 'The Institution of Electrical Engineers' Regulations for Electrical Installations do not allow the use of water pipes as an electrode for earthing purposes. However, any metal water supply pipe must be bonded to the electrical installation main earth terminal as near as possible to its point of entry into the building.

A suitable conductor should be installed between pipes on either side of the meter and stopvalves, to protect the installer against electrical fault, and for the maintenance of the earth connection during use, and particularly when the meter is being replaced.

External Meter Installations.

- The chamber should be well constructed of brick, concrete, GRP or PVC, with a cover marked 'Water meter' and fitted with slots or lifting eyes. Covers should not be of concrete.
- Pipes, cables and drains other than meter pipework must not pass through the meter chamber.
- A meter below ground should be installed in the horizontal position to facilitate meter reading.

See Table 1 and Figure 13.

Recommended internal dimensions for meter chambers (dimensions in mm)　　Table 1

Size of meter	Size of chamber			Remarks
	Length	Breadth	Depth	
15 to 20	430	280		
25	600	600	To suit pattern of meter but not less than 750	Or 380 circular
40 to 50	900	600		
80*	1900	750		
100*	2000	750		
150*	2150	750		

* Dimensions for these sizes take account of compound assemblies but do not provide for isolating valves.

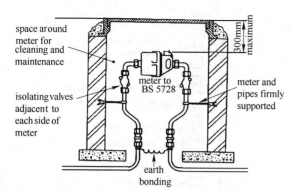

Figure 13 Below ground meter installation

Note Whilst BS 6700 and many Water Authorities favour raising the meter as shown in Figure 13 to make meter reading and changing easier. I would prefer the meter to remain at the same level as the service pipe, as in Figure 14, in order to comply with the water byelaw requirement of 750 mm depth to avoid frost damage.

Internal meters. Internal meters may be fixed horizontally or vertically provided the dial is not more than 1.5 m above floor level and readily visible for reading (see Figure 15).

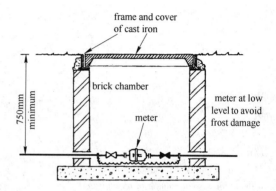

Figure 14 Meter installation to avoid frost damage

Boosted Systems

Water supplies to buildings vary greatly in pressure and quantity available. In some cases this may give rise to intermittent supplies and in others, especially high-rise developments, parts of the building may be above the pressure limit of the mains supply. In these situations there is a case for the use of pumps.

There are two ways that pumps can be used to deal with the above problems. These are by direct boosting and indirect boosting. Indirect systems are more common than direct systems; the latter are rarely permitted by water suppliers because they reduce the mains pressure available to other consumers and can increase the risks of backsiphonage. Under no circumstances should any pump be connected directly to a pipe without first obtaining the written consent of the water undertaker.

Booster pumps can cause excessive aeration. Although this does not cause deterioration of water quality, the 'milky' appearance can cause concern amongst consumers.

Basic systems. The basic systems are as follows:
- simple direct boosting, see Figure 16,
- direct boosting to header and duplicate storage cisterns,
- indirect boosting to storage cistern, see Figure 17,

(a) General requirements

Pipework to be adequately supported.

Meter to be protected from frost, especially in exposed positions, e.g. garage.

Meter in cupboard to be brought forward to within 300 mm of the front of cupboard.

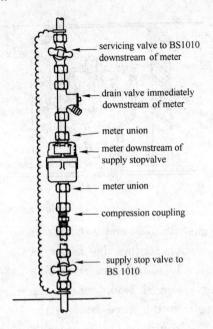

(b) Positioning

Meter in a cupboard may be brought forward for ease of reading provided it is properly supported.

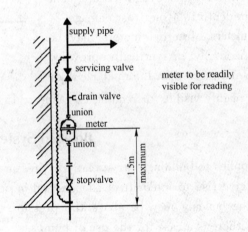

Figure 15 Above ground meter installation

- indirect boosting with pressure vessel.

Pumps and Equipment. Pumps and other associated equipment are usually located within the building being served, preferably as near as possible to the point of entry of the incoming pipe.

Electrically driven centrifugal pumping plant is normally used; pumps and other equipment should be duplicated.

Pumps may be either horizontal or vertical types, directly coupled to their electric motors. A solid foundation is essential for all motors and pumps and anti-vibration mountings should normally be specified.

Automatic control of pumping plant is essential and pressure switches, level switches, or high-level and low-level electrodes should give reliable control. Other methods of control,

LESSON 20

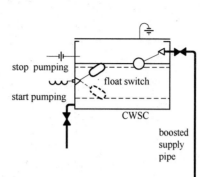

When used for drinking water, the storage vessel should be of the 'protected' type.

Pump control provided by level switch or similar device in the high-level storage cistern.

Pumps switch on when the level of water drops to a predetermined depth (normally about half the depth of the cistern) and they should switch off when the water level rises to about 50mm below the shut-off level of the float-operated valve.

The frequency with which the pumps switch on and off should be limited to reduce wear on them, but the frequency of operation depends on the quantity of water used and stored and on the pump rating.

Where the water supplier permits, pumps are connected to the incoming supply pipe to enable the pressure head to be increased.

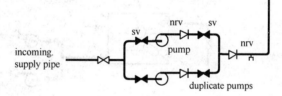

Figure 16 Simple direct boosting

both mechanical and electrical, could be considered. Pumping should be controlled using a pump selector switch and an ON/OFF/AUTO control. Motor starters should incorporate overload protection.

Pumps should be installed in duplicate and sized so that each pump is capable of overcoming the static lift plus the friction losses in both pipework and valves. Where pumps are connected directly to the service pipe, allowance should be made for the minimum operating pressure in the service pipe, since the pump head is added to this and does not cancel out any existing pressure.

Care should be taken in pump and pipe sizing to minimize the risk of water hammer due to surge when pumps are started and stopped.

Transmission of pump and motor noise via pipework can be reduced by the use of flexible connections. Small-power motors of the squirrel cage induction type are suitable for most installations. Low-speed pumps are preferable to promote a long efficient life and reasonably quiet operation. The fitting of motors with sleeve type super-silent bearings

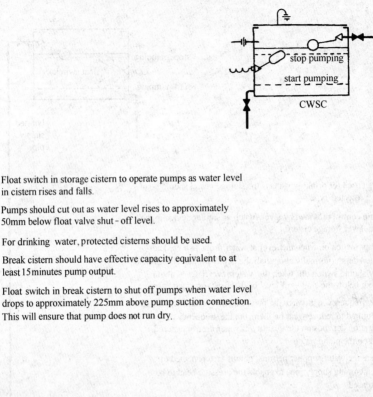

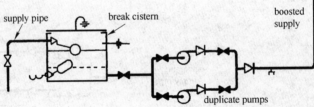

Figure 17　Indirect boosting to storage cistern

should be considered for quiet running.

All pipework connections to and from pumps should be adequately supported and anchored against thrust to avoid stress on pump casings and to ensure proper alignment.

Most small air compressors used for charging pneumatic pressure vessels are of the reciprocating type, either air-cooled or water-cooled. A water-cooled after-cooler for the condensation and extraction of oil and moisture from the compressed air should be installed. The air to be compressed should be drawn from a clean cool source and should be protected from contamination. Check or non-return valves should offer a minimum of frictional loss and should be non-concussive.

The pump room should be of adequate size to accommodate all the plant and also provide adequate space for maintenance and replacement of parts; it should be dry, ventilated and protected from frost and flooding. Entry of birds and small animals must be prevented. Access should be restricted to authorised persons.

Provision should be made for the pumps to be supplied by an alternative electricity supply in the event of mains failure.

Water Softeners

The purpose of water softeners is to reduce scale formation in hot water systems and components (see Figure 18).

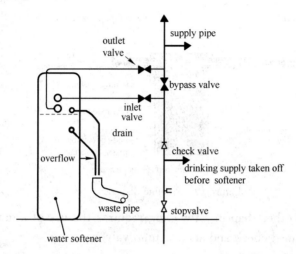

Figure 18　Installation of base exchange water softener

Advantages. Some of the advantages of water softeners are as follows:
(1) Savings in soap and reduction of scum, resulting in:
- reduced expenditure on soap purchase (small savings);
- easier cleaning of appliances;
- cleaner crockery from dishwashers.

(2) Smooth, gentle feel of bath and shower water.
(3) Scale reduction in appliances and components, resulting in:
- longer life for cylinders, immersion heaters and other components;
- less maintenance, e.g. shower outlets less likely to become clogged with fur.

Disadvantages.
(1) Additional installation costs (manufacturers claim a six-year pay back).
(2) Cost of running the unit, e.g. electricity supply and salt.
(3) Drain needed for brine rinse.
(4) User must add salt periodically.

Other Forms of Treatment. BS 6700 deals briefly with water softeners, but does not refer to other forms of treatment, which are shown in Figure 19. It is not the intention here to recommend their use, rather to point out that there are such treatments readily available, and that they can in certain circumstances have a limited application.

Before any of the chemical devices are used, advice should be sought from local water undertakers, particularly regarding toxicity.

Installation. Water softeners should be sited near the incoming supply pipe and where drain access is available.

Electricity supply is required for automatic control and operation.

Water softeners of the salt regenerated type installed in dwellings are considered to be a minor backflow risk and as such a check valve should be installed on the supply pipe before the softener connection.

Drinking water supply should be taken off before the softener, and upstream of check valves.

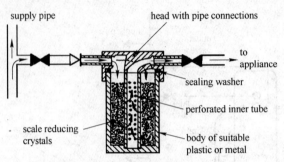

Useful for supplies to instantaneous water heaters.

Figure 19 Pipeline dispenser

A softener located other than in a dwelling requires the use of a double check valve arrangement or a combined check and anti-vacuum valve.

New Words and Phrases

in due course　及时地，在适当时
contractor　n. 订约人，承包人
siting　n. 建筑工地选择，(道路等)定线
premises　n. 前提，前言；(pl.)房屋，房产
union　n. 接头，联轴器，活接；
complete with　包括，连同
washer　n. 垫圈，洗衣人，洗衣机，洗碗机
tolerance　n. 公差，容忍，(食物中残存杀虫剂的)(法定)容许量
bonding　n. 连［搭，焊，胶，粘］接，压焊，粘合，接合
terminal　n. 终点站，接线端，端子，终端
　　adj. 末期，每期的，每学期的
slot　n. 缝，狭槽，细长的孔，硬币投币口，闸门槽
lifting eye　吊眼，吊环
dial　n. 刻度盘，钟面，转盘
byelaw　n. 条例，规则，内部规则
boosting　n. 增［升］压
backsiphonage　n. 倒虹吸
under no circumstances　决不

compression coupling　压紧联轴节
duplicate　vi. 加倍，重写；
　　adj. 两重的，备用的；
　　n. 两倍，复本，备件
reliable　adj. 可靠的，可信赖的
alignment　n. 成直线，(直线)对准；定线
authorise　vt. (authorize) 批准
scale　n. 盐垢
crockery　n. 陶器，瓦器
PVC：聚氯乙烯
GRP：Glass Reinforced Plastic 玻璃纤维增强塑料，玻璃钢
property　n. 性质，特性，器材，物品，财产
highway　n. 公路，大路
cast iron　n. 铸铁，生铁
cupboard　n. 橱，碗碟橱
NRV：non-return valve　单向阀，止回阀
check valve　止回阀，单向阀，逆止阀
break cistern　中间水箱

LESSON 20

coupled   *adj.* 连结的，联系的，偶联的
coupling   *n.* 联结，接合，耦合，联轴器
foundation   *n.* 基础
starter   *n.* 启动器，启动钮
static lift   静扬程
water hammer   水锤
squirrel cage   *n.* 鼠笼(式)
sleeve bearing   套筒轴承，滑动轴承
after-cooler   二次冷却器，后冷却器
plant   *n.* 植物，工厂，车间，设备
      vt. & *vi.* 种植，栽培，培养

LESSON 21

Hot Water Supply: I

The following factors should be considered in the selection and the design of hot water supply systems:
(1) quantity of hot water required;
(2) temperature in storage and at outlets;
(3) cost of installation and maintenance;
(4) fuel energy requirements and running costs;
(5) waste of water and energy.

Hot water supply cannot be considered in isolation from central heating because systems commonly combine both functions. This book, like BS6700, is primarily concerned with hot water supply and refers only to central heating in combined hot water and heating systems up to 44 kW output.

Instantaneous Water Heaters

Instantaneous water heaters (see Figures 1 to 2) should be chosen with the following considerations in mind.

(1) Some of these heaters have relatively high power ratings (up to 28 kW if gas fired) so it is important that adequate gas or electricity supplies are available.

(2) The water in instantaneous water heaters is usually heated by about 55°C at its lowest flow rate, and its temperature will rise and fall inversely to its flow rate.

(3) Where constant flow temperature is important, the heater should be fitted with a water governor at its inflow. Close control of temperature is of particular importance for showers.

(4) To attain constant temperatures on delivery, water flow and pressure must also be constant. Variations in pressure can cause flow and temperature problems when the heater is in use, and when setting up or adjusting flow controls.

(5) The use of multi-point heaters for showers should be avoided, except where the heater only feeds a bath with a shower over it.

(6) Gas-fired heaters fitted in bathrooms must be of the room-sealed type. Room-sealed types are preferred in other locations.

(7) Electrically powered heaters in bathrooms must be protected against the effects of steam and comply with the Regulations for Electrical Installations of the Institution of Electrical Engineers.

(a) Directly supplied heater

Constant flow rate needed to maintain 55℃ temperature difference between feed water and heated water.

Pressure and flow variations will affect temperatures at outlets.

Showers are not recommended because of possible loss of constant temperature control and pressure.

Use only thermostatically controlled shower mixer.

The usual arrangement is direct from the supply pipe as shown here because installation cost is lower. However, supply from storage will give constant flow.

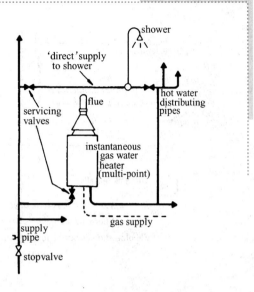

(b) Indirectly supplied heater

High installation cost compared with mains-fed system.

Constant pressure from storage for shower and other fittings gives more stable temperature control.

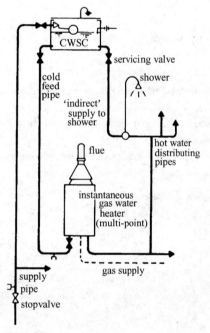

Figure 1 Centralised gas-fired instantaneous water heater installations

Water-jacketed Tube Heaters

The water drawn off for use passes through a heat exchanger in a reservoir of primary hot water (see Figure 3). The size of this reservoir and its heat input determines the volume and rate of flow of hot water that can be provided without an unacceptable temperature drop. The cold water fed to the heater may be from the mains or from a storage cistern.

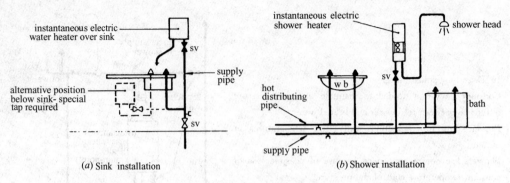

(a) Sink installation (b) Shower installation

Figure 2   Typical uses for instantaneous electric water heaters
Where shower unit is fitted, it will need a minimum head of 10.5m.
Flexible shower outlet may be a contamination risk if nozzle can become submerged

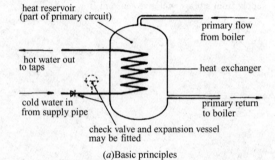

(a) Basic principles

Water-jacketed tube heater is a form of instantaneous heater.

Primary circuit may be vented system or sealed system.

Heat exchanger warms secondary supply water as it passes through.

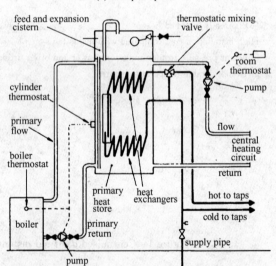

(b) Use of water-jacketed tube heater

Figure 3   Water-jacketed tube heater

Note 1 Primary water from the boiler flows to the heat store as programmed by the cylinder thermostat. Hot water is pumped to the radiator heating circuits and returns to the heat store. Cooler water from the heat store then returns to be reheated in the boiler.

Note 2 Cold water under mains pressure from the supply pipe enters the lower heat exchanger to be partially heated. It then passes through the upper heat exchanger where it is fully heated before being distributed to the taps.
Drawing shows the 'Boilermate' system using a combination unit.

LESSON 21

Storage Type Water Heaters and Boiler Heated Systems

Domestic hot water supply installations of the storage type are either vented or unvented. Figures 4 and 5 illustrate the main features of each.

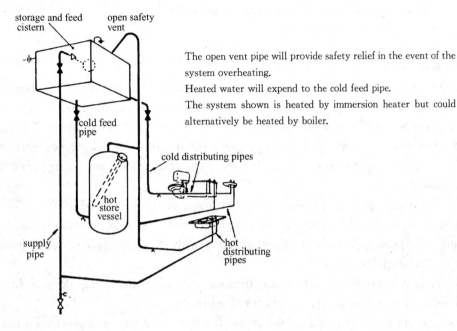

The open vent pipe will provide safety relief in the event of the system overheating.

Heated water will expend to the cold feed pipe.

The system shown is heated by immersion heater but could alternatively be heated by boiler.

Figure 4 Vent hot water system

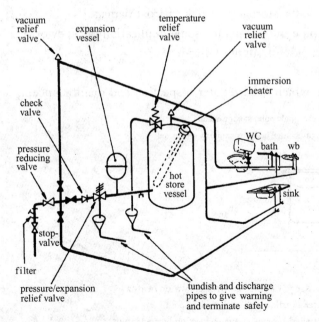

Pressure reducing valve reduces mains pressure to pressure suitable for operating system.

Pressure relief valve guards against excess pressure.

Expansion vessel accommodates expansion of water when heated.

Thermostat (not shown) controls temperature at normal level.

High temperature cut-out (not shown) protects against over-heating of water.

Temperature relief valve allows boiling water and steam to escape if thermostat and thermal cut-out should fail.

Tundish and discharge pipes take relief water to safe place.

Figure 5 Unvented hot water storage system (basic outline of system and components)

Vented Hot Water Storage System. This is fed from a high-level cistern, which provides the necessary pressure at outlets, accommodates expansion due to heated water, and is fitted with an open safety vent pipe to permit the escape of air or steam, and to prevent explosion without the need for any mechanical device.

The vented hot water storage system provides:
- constant low pressure;
- reserve water supply;

but needs:
- protection against the entry of contaminants to cistern (the 'protected' drinking water cistern to the requirements of Byelaw 30 will guard against this).

Unvented hot water storage system. This is usually fed direct from the supply pipe under mains pressure. It does not require the use of a feed cistern or open vent pipe, but relies on mechanical devices for the safe control of heat energy and hot water expansion.

Building regulations require that hot water shall not exceed 100℃. The Approved Document recommends that all unvented hot water storage systems should be of the 'unit' or 'package' type, supplied complete with all safety devices, and should be fired by an 'approved installer'.

A unit system has all safety devices and other operating devices fitted by the manufacturer at the factory, ready for site installation.

A packaged system has all safety devices factory fitted. However, all other operating devices are supplied by the manufacturer in 'kit' form for site assembly.

Features of the unvented hot water storage system are as follows:
- eliminates the need for cold water storage and risk of frost damage;
- may require a larger supply pipe but eliminates some duplication of pipework;
- contains no reserve supply in case of supply failure;
- eliminates cistern refill noise;
- relies on mechanical controls which need regular inspection and maintenance;

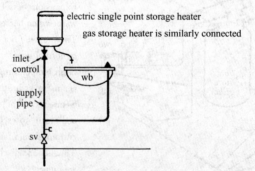

Figure 6 Non-pressure or inlet-controlled water heater
Expansion of heated water overflows through outlet spout.
Outlet must not be obstructed, nor must any connection be made to it.
Can be connected to wash basin or sink if special taps are used to control the inlet and leave the outlet unobstructed.

LESSON 21

For dwellings, cistern must be 'protected'.
Heater capacity (minimum):
○ for small dwellings, 100L to 150L,
○ for off-peak electricity systems, 200L.
Electricity systems are usually in the form of factory lagged and cased hot water cylinder with connections similar to those shown here for a gas installation.

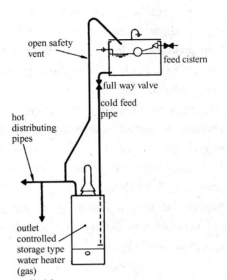

Figure 7 System using outlet-controlled heater

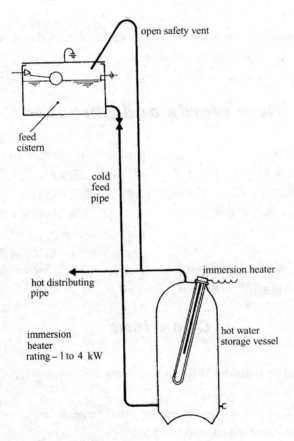

Figure 8 Storage system using immersion heater
The hot store vessel may be a hot water cylinder or a combination unit,
or a specially made, encased and lagged cylinder

- gives better pressure at outlets, particularly at showers;
- allows quicker installation than vented system but involves more costly components.

Non-pressure or inlet-controlled water heaters. These are generally seen as single point heaters fitted either above the appliance with a swivel outlet spout, or under the appliance using special taps to control the flow before the heater inlet. They may be heated by either gas or electricity. See Figure 6.

Pressure or outlet-controlled water heaters. These may be heated by either gas or electricity. Although these are called pressure type heaters, they are generally designed for supply from a feed cistern and are not usually suitable for operation under direct mains pressure. See Figures 7.

Electric immersion heater type storage heaters. Immersion heaters can be used as an independent heat source, or to provide supplementary heat to other centralised boiler systems, see Figures 8.

Note

instantaneous water heater: an appliance in which water is immediately heated as it passes through the appliance.

close control: close-cycle control.

New Words and Phrases

central heating 集中供暖	radiator n. 辐射体，散热器
thermostatic adj. 温度调节装置的，恒温的	off peak 正常的，额定的，非峰值的
	lag n. 滞后，落后
thermostat n. 恒温器，温度调节装置	vt. 用隔热（绝缘，保温）材料保护
water jacket 水套	encase vt. 嵌入、封闭
tundish n. 漏斗	appliance n. 用具，器具
spout n. 喷管，喷口，水柱，喷流，管口	swivel v. & n. 旋转
v. 喷出，滔滔不绝地讲，喷涌	

Questions

1. What factors should be considered in the selection and the design of hot water supply systems?
2. What factors should be considered when the instantaneous water heaters are chosen?
3. Try to explain what a water-jacketed tube heater is.
4. What are the characteristics of the vented hot water storage system?
5. Try to explain what an unvented hot water storage system is.

LESSON 21

Reading Material

Hot Water Supply: II

Primary Circuits

Primary circuits are used for circulation of hot water between the boiler and the hot store vessel and include any radiator circuits (see Figure 9 and 10). They may be vented or unvented. Circulation may be gravity or pumped.

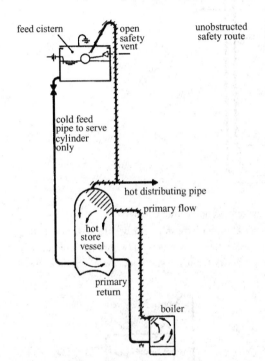

All pipes to be laid to falls to avoid air locks and facilitate draining.

Vent route from top of boiler through cylinder to open vent not to be valved or otherwise closed off.

Minimum sizes for primary circuits to hot store vessels

- 25 mm for solid fuel gravity systems;
- 19 mm for small bore systems;
- 13 mm for pump assisted systems.

Figure 9   Direct system of hot water (vented)

Supplementary Water Heating and Independent Summer Water Heating. It is common practice for supplementary water heating and independent summer water heating to be provided by use of electric immersion heaters in the storage vessel or by gas circulators. Supplementary water heating provided from solar energy or heat pumps is growing in popularity.

Where supplementary electric immersion heating is to be used in conjunction with a boiler, the height of the storage vessel above the boiler should be sufficient to prevent circulation of hot water from the storage vessel to the boiler, when only the immersion heater is in use.

Solar Heating. Solar energy heating can be useful to augment a conventional domestic hot water system (see Figure 11) but, except on hot sunny days, cannot in Britain be considered sufficient to heat hot water to draw-off temperatures.

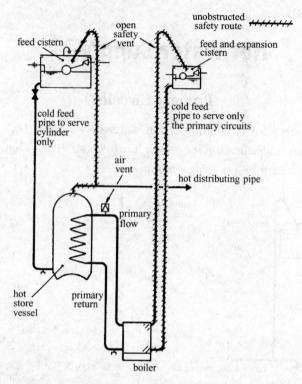

Figure 10 Indirect system of hot water (vented)

Open vent and cold feed pipes to primary circuit must not have valve, or be otherwise closed off.
The open vent and cold feed pipes may be connected to the primary flow and return pipes respectively.
Where vent pipe is not connected to highest point in primary circuit, an air release valve should be installed.

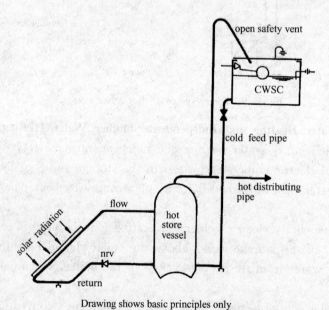

Drawing shows basic principles only

Figure 11 Solar heating system for hot water

Many different designs of solar systems for heating water are possible, from simple direct feed gravity systems to more complex pumped circuits using two indirect storage cylinders or one cylinder with two indirect heating coils.

Heat Pumps. Heat pumps extracting energy from the ground, water, or air at ambient temperatures, can be used to preheat conventional hot water systems, to augment existing systems, or to supply full hot water and central heating requirements, see Figure 12.

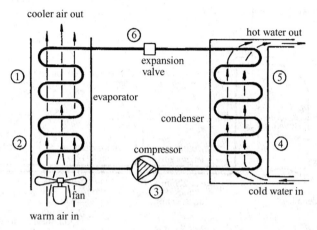

Figure 12 The heat pump - principle

The heat pump works on the 'refrigeration cycle' principle(air to water)
(1) Refrigerant liquid forced under pressure into evaporator.
(2) Heat energy from air absorbed by refrigerant as it is vaporized from liquid to gas.
(3) Compressor 'squeezes' gas which becomes hotter and more compact.
(4) The hotter compacted gas is pumped under pressure into the condenser.
(5) In the condenser the gas becomes liquid and throws off heat which is absorbed into the hot water.
(6) Condensed refrigerant liquid passes through expansion valve, to lower its pressure.

Until such time as a British Standard is available giving recommendations for their use, guidance should be sought from heat pump manufacturers, or the Heat Pump Association.

Secondary Distribution Systems

A secondary hot water distribution system may be one of the following types:
  (1) gravity fed (vented) from a cold water storage cistern;
  (2) gravity fed from a water storage cistern;
  (3) directly supplied under pressure from mains, through an instantaneous water heater or a water jacketed tube heater;
  (4) unvented storage type, directly supplied under pressure from mains.

Connections to hot water storage vessels should be arranged so that the cold water feed pipe is connected near the bottom and hot water supply drawn off from the top of the cylinder, above any primary flow connection or heating element.

Dead legs and Secondary Circulation. To promote maximum economy of energy and water, the hot water distribution system should be designed so that hot water appears quickly at draw-off taps when they are opened. The length of pipe measured from the tap to the water heater or hot water storage vessel should be as short as possible and should not exceed the lengths shown in Figure 13. Where these lengths exceed the values given in Table 1, the pipe should be insulated. Insulation provided should ensure that heat losses from pipes do not exceed the values given in Table 2.

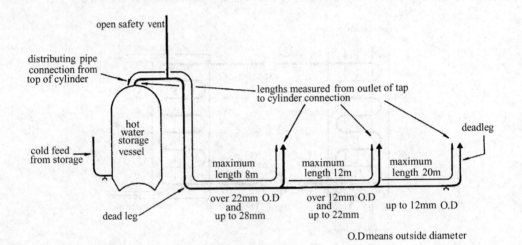

Figure 13 Maximum length of dead legs without insulation
Where lengths of dead legs exceed those shown, pipes should be insulated
Note. '*Dead leg*' means the length of distributing pipe without secondary circulation.

Maximum lengths of uninsulated distributing pipes Table 1

Outside diameter of distributing pipe, mm	Maximum length, m	Outside diameter of distributing pipe, mm	Maximum length, m
Not exceeding 12	20	Exceeding 22 but not exceeding 28	8
Exceeding 12 but not exceeding 22	12	Over 28	3

Maximum permitted rates of heat loss from pipes Table 2

Outside diameter of pipe*, mm	Maximum heat loss, W/m²	Outside diameter of pipe*, mm	Maximum heat loss, W/m²
10	675	40	220
20	400	50 and above	175
30	280		

* For intermediate values of pipe diameter, the corresponding maximum heat loss is found by linear interpolation

Secondary circulation minimises delays in obtaining hot water from taps and reduces waste of water during any delay. Secondary circulation should be considered when short dead legs are impractical and the circuit should be well insulated to reduce the inevitable heat losses from pipe runs. A diagrammatic arrangement of secondary circulation is shown in Figure 14.

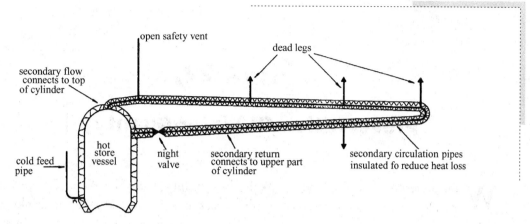

Figure 14 Distribution system with secondary circulation
Lengths of dead legs should not exceed those shown in figure 13
Dead legs feeding spray taps should not be more than 1m long

In systems where it is not possible to attain gravity circulation, a non-corroding circulating pump should be installed to ensure that water within the secondary circuit remains hot. The pump should be located on the return pipe close to the cylinder.

Note

primary circuit: an assembly of pipes and fittings in which water circulates between a boiler or other water heater and the primary heater inside a hot water storage vessel.
primary heater: a heater mounted inside a hot water storage vessel for the transfer of heat to the stored water from circulating hot water.
vented primary circuit: a primary circuit which is provided with a vent pipe.
unvented primary circuit: a primary circuit which is not provided with a vent pipe.
secondary circuit: an assembly of pipes and fittings in which water circulates in distributing pipes to and from a water storage vessel.
secondary system: that part of a hot water system comprising the cold feed pipe, any storage cistern, water heater and flow and return pipework from which hot water for use is conveyed to all points of draw-off.

New Words and Phrases

heating coil   加热盘管，加热旋管
linear interpolation   线性内插法，线性内插
diagrammatic   *adj.* 图表的，概略的
bore   *n.* 汽缸筒，钻孔，孔
refrigerant   *adj.* 制冷的
              n. 制冷剂

LESSON 22

Preservation Of Water Quality: I

Water undertakers in England and Wales have a duty under the Water Act 1989 to provide a supply of wholesome water, which is suitable and safe for drinking and culinary purposes. At the same time, public demand requires that water supplied is of good appearance with minimal colour, taste or odour.

To enable water undertakers to maintain their supplies in wholesome condition and to preserve the quality of water supplied, the act provides water undertakers with powers to enforce their water byelaws, which came into effect on 1 January 1989. Installers and users must ensure that systems and components, which are installed, comply with water byelaws.

BS6700 looks at the preservation of water quality in four main areas.

(1) *Materials in contact with water*. There is not much point in having a good quality water supply if it becomes contaminated by unsuitable pipes, fittings and jointing materials.

(2) *Stagnation of water* and the prevention of bacterial growth particularly at temperatures between 20℃ and 50℃.

(3) *Cross connections* must be prevented between pipes supplied directly under mains pressure and pipes supplied from other sources, such as:

(i) water from a private source
(ii) non-potable water
(iii) stored water
(iv) water drawn off for use.

(4) *Prevention of backflow* from fittings or appliances into services or mains, particularly at point of use, i. e. draw-off taps, flushing cisterns, washing machines, dishwashers, storage cisterns and hose connections. For example, pumps should not be connected so as to cause backflow into the supply pipe, (see Figure 1).

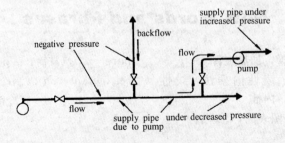

Figure 1 Example of backflow caused by pump installation
Pump may cause pressure drop sufficient to reverse flow in adjacent pipes.

LESSON 22

Backflow prevention forms the largest portion of clause 9 of BS6700 and is prominent in water byelaws, which aim to implement the recommendations of the *Backsiphonage Report* of 1974.

Materinals in Contact with Water

Contamination of water by contacting with unsuitable materials will be avoided if careful attention during design and installation is given to:
- the specification and selection of acceptable materials used in the manufacture of pipes, fittings and appliances;
- the method of installation, and in particular to the method of and materials used when jointing and connecting pipes, fittings and appliances;
- the environment into which pipes, fittings and appliances are to be installed;
- the design of the various elements of installation, especially where differing materials are to be used.

Materials selected for use in contact with water intended for domestic purposes should comply with water byelaws and in particular Part II *Prevention of contamination of water from contact with unsuitable materials or substances*. In general this means compliance is assured where any materials used are manufactured to a relevant British Standard specification, or are listed in the *Water Fittings and Materials Directory* produced under the United Kingdom Water Fittings Byelaws Scheme.

Examples of problems caused by unsuitable materials, and situations which should be avoided are shown in Figures 2 and 3.

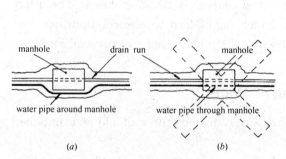

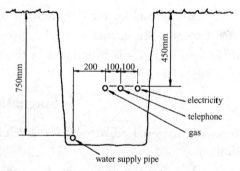

Figure 2 Pipes not to pass through manholes, etc.
  (a)Correct siting (b)Incorrect siting

Figure 3 Positioning of pipelines in trenches
  Dimensions in millimetres

Pipes not to pass through any foul soil, refuse or refuse chute, ash pit, sewer or drain, cess pool or manhole (Byelaw 5).

Pipes made of any material that is susceptible to permeation by gas or to deterioration by contacting with substances likely to cause contamination of water should not be laid or installed in a place where permeation or deterioration is likely to occur. Because plastic pipes in particular are liable to a degree of permeation and deterioration by gas and oil, care should be taken when positioning pipelines to avoid contact in the event of leakages occurring from oil or gas lines, for example, at petrol filling stations. Figure 3 shows the positioning of pipelines in trenches as suggested by the National Joint Utilities Group Report No. 6.

Byelaw 7 refers to pipe materials or other materials that must not cause contamination of water used for domestic purposes.

Substances leached from some materials may adversely affect the quality of water. Although British Standard schemes for the testing of pipes, fittings and materials aim to prevent this, much depends on the installer and the material chosen for a particular application, after taking due account of the nature of the water (see Figure 4).

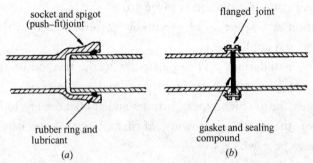

Figure 4 Examples of materials that could cause contamination if not chosen with care
(a)Socket and spigot joint (b)Flanged joint

The use of lead for pipes, cisterns or in solders is prohibited because of the obvious danger of plumbo solvency (Byelaw 9). However, BS 6700 does give details of jointing for lead pipes within its list of jointing methods for potable water pipework because there will be cases when connections have to be made to existing lead pipes.

For soldered joints to copper pipes, lead-free solders should be specified, e.g. tin/silver alloys.

The use of coal tar for the lining of pipes and cisterns is also prohibited. The direct connection between copper and lead pipes, which might lead to electrolytic action and further lead solvency is prohibited in the absence of suitable means to prevent corrosion though galvanic action.

Stagnation of Water

To restrict bacterial growth in stored drinking water, temperatures should be maintained as follows:
- cold water should be stored and distributed at as low a temperature as is practical and preferably below 20℃.
- hot water should preferably be stored at 60℃ to 65℃ and distributed at not less than 50℃. (*Legionella* will not flourish at temperatures above 50℃)

Research into *Legionnaires' Disease* is ongoing. Evidence of this disease occurring has generally been found where pipes and components are not regularly maintained and cleaned, or in parts of systems that cannot easily be cleaned during routine maintenance programmes, e.g. where flushing valves or drain valves are wrongly positioned, or where accumulation of rust and other debris can settle and build-up. Infection by *Legionella* can be prevented through good design, and regular, thorough maintenance. Advice should be sought from the Department of Health for up-to-date information.

LESSON 22

(a) Connections between supply pipe and distributing pipe
No connection shall be made between a supply pipe and a distributing pipe(Byelaw 13).

(b) Supplies from different sources
Installation not permitted. Correct installation is type A air gap on supply pipe.

(c) Temporary connection to sealed system
No closed circuit to be connected to a supply pipe. Important because primary circuits to heating systems are often heavily contaminated with additives.

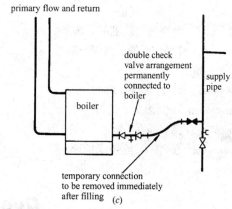

(d) Shower mixer installation
No connection to be made between a supply pipe and a hot or cold distributing pipe(Byelaw 13).
Water could flow from hot store vessel to the drinking tap if the supply pipe should fail.
May be permitted if feed cistern is protected to Byelaw 30 standards and a check valve is fitted to both the hot and cold supplies to the shower.

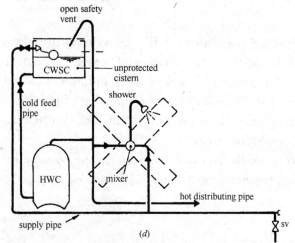

Figure 5 Cross connection hazards

Prevention of Contamination by Cross Connection

No supply pipe, distributing pipe or cistern used for conveying or receiving water supplied by a public water supplier shall be connected so that it can receive or convey water which is not supplied by a public water supplier, except where the water supplied by a public water supplier is discharged through a type A air gap (see Figure 5).

Additives to primary hot water or heating circuits. If a liquid (other than water) is used in any type of heating primary circuit, or if an additive, e. g. a corrosion inhibitor, is used in water in such a circuit, the liquid or additive should be non-toxic and non-corrosive.

New Words and Phrases

wholesome　*adj.*　卫生的,有益的,健康的
culinary　*adj.*　烹调用的,厨房用的
recommendation　*n.*　推荐,介绍(信),建议
specification　*n.*　详述,规格,说明书,规范
foul　*adj.*　污秽的,肮脏的,淤塞的
chute　*n.*　陡槽,滑槽,斜管,斜道
pit　*n.*　坑
cess pool　*n.*　污水坑,粪坑
permeation　*n.*　渗入,透过
socket　*n.*　窝,插孔,插座,(管)套
　　　　v.　套(接),给⋯配插座
spigot　*n.*　栓,龙头,套管,插口
socket and spigot joint　承插接头
flanged joint　法兰连接
gasket　*n.*　垫圈,衬垫
sealing　*n.*　(密,焊)封,封(焊)接;压实填料
solder　*n.*　焊料
　　　　v.　焊接
plumbo solvency　溶铅[能]力
tin　*n.*　[化]锡,马口铁
lining　*n.*　衬里,内层,衬套
galvanic　*adj.*　电流的,以流电所产的
additive　*adj.*　附加的,加成的,添加的
　　　　n.　添加剂

Questions

1. What are the main areas for the water quality preservation?
2. To avoid the contamination of water by contact with unsuitable materials, what careful attention should be taken during design and installation?
3. Please describe the correct positioning of pipelines in trenches.
4. To restrict bacterial growth in stored drinking water, what is the appropriate temperatures range?
5. What are the research fruits about the possible breeding place in drinking water and the preventive methods of *Legionnaires' Disease*?

LESSON 22

Reading Material

Preservation Of Water Quality: II

Backflow Protection

Backflow can include both 'backsiphonage' and 'back pressure'. Appropriate preventative measures should be related to the level of risk, should backflow occur, and will vary according to the nature and use of the supply.

The *Backsiphonage Report* of 1974 divides the levels of risk into three categories.

Class 1 Risk of serious contamination occurring continuously or frequently, and likely to be harmful to health.

Class 2 Risk of contamination by substances, which may be harmful to health, but not continuously or frequently present.

Class 3 Risk of contamination by substances not likely to be harmful to health.

The Department of the Environment *Byelaws Guidance Notes* list appliances that fall into each category, and also gives relevant prevention devices. BS 6700 has similar lists. Examples of backflow risk are shown in Table 1.

Examples of backflow risk Table 1

Source of risk	Examples of recommended protection
Class 1 risk	
WC pan	Approved flushing cistern correctly installed
Bidet	Type A air gap
Class 2 risk	Type A air gap recommended
Sink taps	Double check valve assembly
Hose union taps	Type B air gap
Washing machine	
Class 3 risk	Any of the above devices, or a check valve
Mixer tap	
Water softener (domestic)	

Backflow prevention devices

Type A air gap. See Figures 6 and 7. This is a pipe arrangement where the supply to a cistern or vessel is arranged as follows:

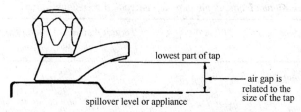

Figure 6 Example of use of type A air gap at draw-off tap
Type A air gap to be visible, measurable and unobstructed.

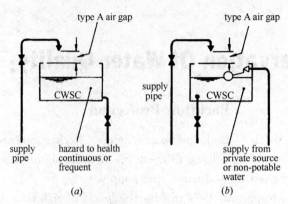

Figure 7 Examples of type A air gap at cisterns
(a)Cistern with hazardous contents (b)Cistern with mixed supplies

Air gap related to size of inlet

Flow from inlet to be into air at atmospheric pressure and not more than 15° from the vertical.

- the cistern or vessel has an unrestricted overflow to atmosphere;
- the supply discharge and its outlet is not obstructed;
- the water is discharged vertically or not more than 15° from the vertical;
- the vertical distance between the discharge pipe outlet and the spill-over level of the cistern or vessel is not less than that shown in Table 2.

Air gaps at taps Table 2

Nominal size of tap or fitting	Vertical distance between tap outlet and spill-over level of receiving appliance mm
Up to and including $\frac{1}{2}$	20
Over $\frac{1}{2}$ and up to and including $\frac{3}{4}$	(See table 3)
Over $\frac{3}{4}$	70

Its principal merit is that is has no moving parts and cannot readily be destroyed by vandals. It is accepted throughout the world.

Type B Air Gap. See Figure 8. In a cistern or other similar vessel, which is open at all times to the atmosphere, the vertical distance between the lowest point of discharge and the critical water level should be one of the following.

(1) sufficient to prevent backsiphonage of water into the supply pipe;
(2) not less than the distances shown in Table 3.

Dimensions of type A air gaps to cisterns (dimensions in mm) Table 3

Bore diameter of feed pipe or outlet	Vertical distance of point of outlet above spill-over level
Up to 14	20
Over 14 up to 21	25
Over 21 and up to 41	70
Over 41	Twice the bore of the feed pipe or outlet

In storage cisterns the type B air gap, as shown in Figure 8(a), is impractical. Its critical water level, which determines the difference in fixing heights between the float operating valve and the warning pipe, cannot be readily calculated. The critical water level will vary from one installation to another depending on the inlet pressure and the length and gradient of the warning pipe.

In most cases it is expected that water undertakers will accept the simpler arrangement seen in Figure 8(b).

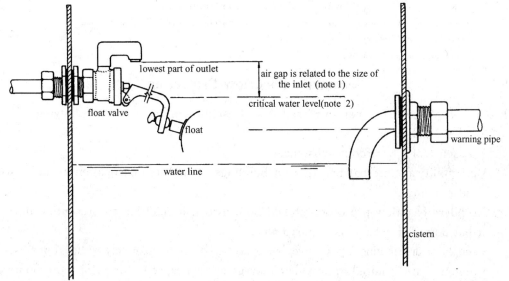

(a) At storage cistern

Note 1 The air gap is related to the size of the inlet and is the minimum permitted vertical distance between the 'critical' water level and the lowest part of the float valve outlet.

Note 2 The critical water level is the highest level the water will reach at the maximum rate of inflow, i.e. float removed.

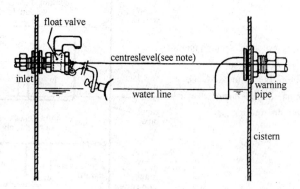

(b) Acceptable alternative to the type B air gap

Figure 8   Type B air gap

This arrangement is acceptable if;
   ○ the cistern complies with Byelaw 30;
   ○ the float operated valve is of the reducing flow type.

A reducing flow type float valve is one which gradually closes as the water level in the cistern rises, e.g. diaphragm float valve to BS 1212: Parts 2 or 3.

In this cistern the critical water level is assumed to be level with the centre line of the float valve body.

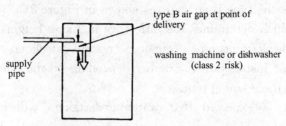

(c) Example of type B air gap to domestic appliance

Figure 8 Type B air gap (continued)

Water Research Centre approved appliance will have protection device built in during manufacture.
Type B air gap to comply with BS 6281:Part 2.
Discharge to be unobstructed.

Secondary Backflow Protection

This is used where there is an increased risk of backflow because of the following:
- exceptionally heavy use;
- presence of a hazardous substance;
- possibility of internal backflow in buildings of multiple occupation, e. g. flats or tall buildings.

Secondary backflow protection should be provided in addition to prevention devices installed at points of use and is required when:
- supply or distributing pipes convey water to two or more separately occupied premises;
- premises are required to provide a storage cistern capacity for 24 or more hours of normal use.

Acceptable arrangements for secondary backflow protection are shown in Figure 9.

(a) Secondary backflow protection on supply pipes
Double check valve preferred.
No need for secondary protection at lowest level.
No part of the branch pipe to be higher than its connection to the common distributing pipe.

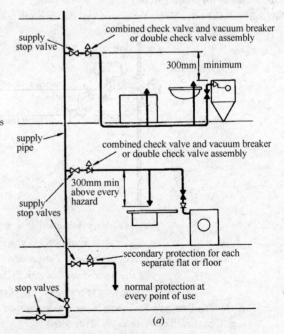

Figure 9 Acceptable arrangement for secondary backflow protection

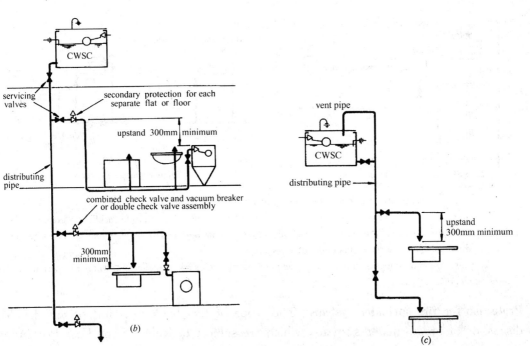

(b) Secondary backflow protection on distributing pipes
No part of the branch pipe to be higher than the distributing pipe.
Double check valve assembly preferred.
No need for secondary protection at lowest level.
(c) Secondary backflow protection on distributing pipes using a vent pipe.
Vent will admit air to prevent backflow.
No need for secondary protection at lowest level

Figure 9   Acceptable arrangement for secondary backflow protection (continued)

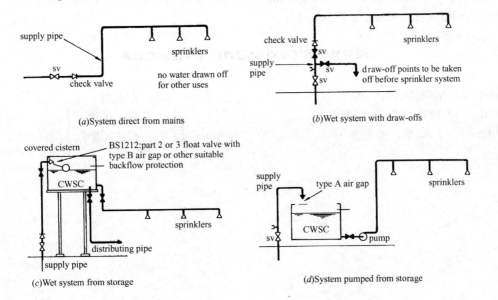

Figure 10   Backflow protection in fire sprinkler systems
Cistern supplied from mains only.
Water for other purposes to be drawn separately from storage cistern.
An uncovered cistern must supply the sprinklers only.

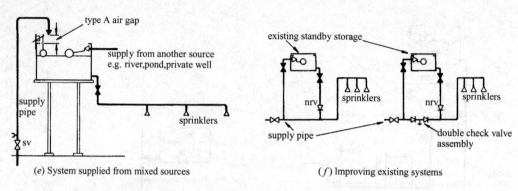

(e) System supplied from mixed sources   (f) Improving existing systems

Figure 10 Backflow protection in fire sprinkler systems (continued)

An alternative to the double check valve arrangement would be a pressure principle backflow preventor. The best solution, provided the effectiveness of the sprinkler system is not reduced, would be to remove the connection between the supply pipe and the sprinkler-distributing pipe.

This installation only applies to the improvement of protection to existing buildings. It will not be permitted in new installations.

Protection for fire sprinkler systems. The scope of this book does not permit detailed discussion of fire sprinkler systems, which are subject to Rules of the Loss Prevention Council and the requirements of the local water undertakers who should be consulted before commencing any installation.

Sprinkler systems are commonly installed, particularly in high-risk situations. They are fired for emergency fire protection only and should be used for no other purpose. Water in them may become stagnant and create contamination risks particularly where substantial volumes are stored in ground level or elevated cisterns. Backflow protection arrangements are shown in Figure 10.

New Words and Phrases

bidet   n. 坐浴盆，净身盆
vandal   n. 故意破坏者；野蛮人
spillover   n. 溢出，溢出管

gradient   adj. 倾斜的
    n. 梯度，坡度
commence   v. 开始，着手

LESSON 23

Pump Stations for Municipal Wastewater: I

General

Depending on their intended purpose and site of installation, pump stations for municipal wastewater are divided into regional stations, pumping wastewater collected from a territory into a higher level main, and central stations, pumping the entire volume of wastewater to treatment facilities.

Pump stations are situated in separate buildings at a distance of not less than 20 m from residential buildings or food enterprises when the station receives up to 50 thousand m^3 per day and not less than 30 m distant when the flow is greater. A protective green belt of not less than 10 m in width is required around the perimeter of pump stations.

With appropriate substantiation, emergency discharges into a water body or storm sewer are located before pump stations. The possibility of installation and the selection of the sites of installation of emergency discharges are approved by the regulatory agencies. Mains before pump stations should be equipped with gates with a drive controlled from the surface, permitting temporary flooding of the main or discharge wastewater through the emergency discharge when there is a failure at the pump station.

The specialized design institutes have developed typical projects for pump stations to pump sanitary and other similar wastewaters, and neutral wastewaters containing no explosive substances.

The pump stations were designed assuming winter ambient temperatures of -20, -30 and $-40°C$, presence or absence of groundwater, for various depths of laying of the incoming main. Small and medium stations are designed for a wastewater flow of up to 80 thousand m^3/day. These stations are equipped with horizontal sewerage pumps—usually not more than three. There are also designs for small stations with non-clogging pumps and submersible electric pumps. Large station designs are developed for flows of $100 \sim 320$ thousand m^3/day. Five pumps are installed at these stations. In all cases the pumps and screens are automatically controlled.

The method of construction of the underground section of the pump stations varies depending on the construction conditions.

Pump Station Appurtenances

Machine Room (Dry Pit). The following major equipment is located in the machine room: the pumps, pumps to supply water for the technical needs of the station, vacuum pumps (if the main pumps are not under water level), drainage pumps, lifting and transport devices and monitoring and measurement instruments.

In order to pump sanitary wastewater and industrial wastewater of similar composition, with a neutral or weakly alkaline pH, sanitary pumps are used: horizontal and vertical. In order to deliver small quantities of water ($5 \sim 20$ m^3/hr) at low head, monoblock submersible sewage pumps are used. In cases of low head lift (up to 5 m) and highly variable flow, auger pumps are used.

When selecting pumps, the catalogs and other materials available from the design organizations and manufacturers should be used.

The horizontal centrifugal pumps of all types, as well as the type FV 144/46 vertical pumps, have two additional modifications each. These modifications differ by the rotor diameter.

In the machine room, in addition to the operable pumps, reserve pumps are required: for two operable pumps there is one reserve pump; for three or more operable pumps there are two reserve pumps. At stations with three operable pumps with capacity up to 360 m^3/hr each, it is permissible to provide a single reserve unit when there is a second in stock.

Two vacuum pumps with a circulating water tank are installed (one of them is reserve). Their capacity is chosen to provide filling of the intake pipes and pump casing in $3 \sim 5$ minutes.

In order to pump water from the drain pit in the machine room to the wet pit, the GNOM type pumps are used. These are centrifugal self-priming or vertical sanitary pumps (at large stations). The quantity of wastewater pumped is measured by flow meters, Venturi nozzles or tubes.

Screen Rooms and Wet Pits. Large floating matter is removed by mechanically cleaned screens with shredders or by comminutors. Sluice gates are provided in the canals leading to the screens. The volume of screenings retained, the width of gaps in the screens, the velocity of wastewater in them and the number of reserve units are determined in accord with SNiP standard 11-32-74.

In order to suspend the sediment in wet pits, a device connected to a pressurized pipe, which is also used to empty the system must be provided. Means for washing screens and other equipment, usually hoses with nozzles, are used in screen room.

Lifting and Transport Devices. For installation and operation of equipment at the stations, the following should be provided: for loads up to 1 tonne, fixed beams with grapple forks or manual suspended beam cranes; up to 5 tonnes, manual suspended beam cranes; and over 5 tonnes, manual bridge cranes. When loads are lifted over 6 m or when the machine room is over 18 m long, electrical lifting and transport equipment should be used.

The load capacity of the lifting and transport equipment is chosen in accord with the maximum weight of the equipment and fittings in the assembled form. At pump stations equipped with beam cranes and bridge cranes, areas should be designated for service of the crane mechanisms and electrical equipment.

Hydraulic Computation of Pump Stations

Selecting Pumps and Pressurized Pipe Systems. When selecting pumps, the following should be considered:

(1) The total capacity of operable pumps should equal the maximum design flow of wastewater or slightly exceed it;

(2) The number and capacity of the pumps should permit a stable station operating regime during periodic variations of the water flow;

(3) Pumps of the same type should be used.

The required pump head, m, is determined by the equation:

$$H=H_g+h_{lh}+h_{lp}+h_r \tag{1}$$

where H_g = the geometric head, m;
h_{lh} = the headloss in the suction pipe, m;
h_{lp} = the headloss in the pressure pipe (outside and inside the pump station), m;
h_r = the reserve for discharge of the liquid from the pipe (usually 1m).

For stations with storage capacity in the wet pit, the design level of wastewater is taken to be the height of the mean water level in the wet pit; for stations without storage capacity, the design elevation is taken to be the water level in the main at the minimum inflow.

When the pressure pipe is connected to a receiving sump or a gravity-flow canal above the water level in them, the wastewater discharge level is considered to be the top of the discharge pipe; when water is discharged below the water surface in a receiving sump, the design level is taken to be the level of water in this sump; when the pressure pipe passes over a high section of the terrain with a ground level above the water level at the destination point, the level is taken as the top of the pipe in the raised area.

The head losses in pipes consist of the loss on friction and local resistance. The losses on friction along the pipes are determined from the computation tables for pressure pipes. The local resistances, m, are computed by the equation:

$$h_l=\Sigma \zeta \frac{v^2}{2g} \tag{2}$$

where v is the design velocity of the water through the pipe, m/sec; g is the gravity constant, m/sec^2; and ζ is the coefficient of local resistance (taken from the hydraulic handbooks).

The order of the hydraulic computation of a pump station is as follows:

(1) Approximate determination of the diameter and number of the pressure pipes in accord with the maximum inflow of wastewater;

(2) Determination of the required pump head for these pressure pipes;

(3) From the wastewater flow and the pump head according to the catalogs the pumps are preliminarily chosen;

(4) On the curves representing the pump head, efficiency and power as a function of capacity (at a constant rotation speed) plot the pipeline characteristics Q-H, plotted on the same scale; for this purpose determine the head loss in the pipes at various values of the water flow and add to these losses the geometric head; the point of intersection of the Q-H curve of the pump and the Q-H curve of the pipe represents the operable point for a pump.

The final selection of pipes and pumps should be made with consideration of all the possible variants and based on technical economic computations.

Figure 1 presents the simplest case of computation, which is the operation of a single pump with a single discharge pipe. The point A of intersection of the curves Q-H and Q-H_p is the computation point for pump operation. The flow Q_f corresponds to the pump capacity at the head H_f; the efficiency of the pump is determined by point B, and the power demand by point C.

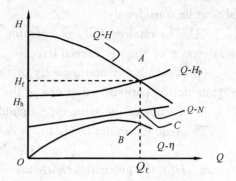

Figure 1 Characteristic curves for the operation of one pump into one discharge

The Change in the Characteristics of Centrifugal Pumps. The characteristics of a pump may be changed depending on the rotation speed of the pump rotor. The new characteristic curve is plotted on the basis of the following functions:

$$Q/Q_1 = n/n_1;\quad H/H_1 = (n/n_1)^2;\quad N/N_1 = (n/n_1)^3$$

where Q, H and N = the pump capacity, head and power at a given rotation speed n;

Q_1, H_1 and N_1 = the same, at a new rotation speed n_1.

The range of utilization of pumps is significantly expanded by cutting the rotors, which changes the efficiency slightly. Cutting is allowed within 20% of the nominal rotor diameter (depending on the speed of the pump). The change in the pump characteristics when the rotors are cut is determined by the following formulas:

$$Q_1/Q = D_{cut}/D_n;\quad H_1/H = (D_{cut}/D_n)^2;\quad N_1/N = (D_{cut}/D_n)^3$$

where Q, H and N = the pump parameters at the nominal rotor diameter D_n;

Q_1, H_1 and N_1 = the same, at the cut rotor diameter D_{cut}.

The Pump Brake Power. The pump brake (power consumed), kW, is determined by the equation:

$$N = QH/102\eta \tag{3}$$

where Q = the pump capacity, m³/sec;

H = the pump head, m;

η = the efficiency of the pump, corresponding to the operable point of the pump.

The pump power is chosen with a safety factor depending on the brake power.

Pump Suction Head. The allowable geometric suction head of the pump H_{gh}, m (the height of installation of the pump axis above the minimum water level in the reservoir) is determined by the formula

$$H_{gh} = H_{vac} - [H_p + v^2/(2g)] \tag{4}$$

where H_{vac} = the allowable vacuumetric head, m;

H_p = the loss on friction and local resistances in the intake pipe, m;

v = the velocity in the intake section of the suction pipe, m/sec.

The manufacturer usually indicates H_{vac} for normal atmospheric pressure (given in the catalogs) at a water temperature of 20℃. When pumps are installed in regions where the atmospheric pressure differs from normal, and also for different water temperatures, appropriate correction factors are used for the vacuumetric suction head.

Parallel Operation of Pumps. For parallel operation pumps with the same or with slightly different heads can be used. The characteristic curves of pumps, Q-H, operating in parallel, are plotted graphically by adding their capacities at various heads (Figure 2).

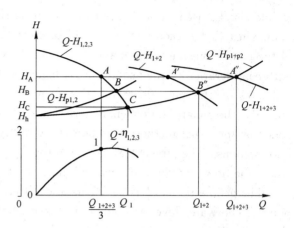

Figure 2 Characteristics of parallel operation of three identical pumps on two pressurized pipes.

In order to obtain the total characteristic curve for three pumps, Q-H_{1+2+3}, triple the capacity for one pump at different heads (ordinates). The characteristic curve for parallel operation of two pipes, Q-H_{p1+p2}, is plotted similarly (here the values of H reflect the geometric head and the headlosses both in the external pipe and in the internal systems). The total capacity of three pumps is determined by the pump operation computation point A''. The delivery and head of each pump are determined by the point A. In order to determine the efficiency of a pump, a vertical line from point A to the intersection with the Q-η curve (point 1) should be drawn.

In order to simplify the computation of complex pumping systems (pumps with different capacity, different lengths or diameters of the internal pipes from the individual pumps, etc.), it is recommended that the method of plotting the adjusted pump characteristics should be used. For this purpose the operating characteristics of the intake and pressure pipes within the pump station and the ordinates of the resulting characteristic curves from the ordinates of the characteristics of the corresponding pumps should be graphically determined. Adjusted in this manner to the point where the pressure pipe exits from the pump station, the pump characteristic curves may be added in the usual manner.

When computing the parallel operation of two or several pump stations into a common pressurized pipe (Figure 3), the method of adjusted characteristic curves

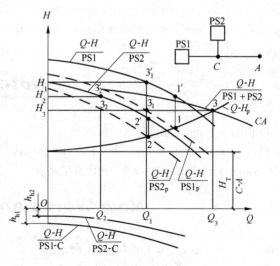

Figure 3 Characteristic curves of parallel operation of two pump stations

should also be used. For this purpose the total characteristics of parallel operation of the pumps installed at each station should be plotted. On the same graph the characteristics of the pipes from the pump stations to point C where the flows merge should be plotted with consideration of the geometric lift height h_{h1} and h_{h2} between them. Subtracting the ordinates of the pipe characteristics from the ordinates of the corresponding pump stations, the pump station characteristics are obtained adjusted to point C, which are added by the usual method to obtain the total operating characteristics of the pumps of both stations. The pipe characteristic in this case is plotted for the segment from point C where the flows merge to the water intake point A.

The geometric head is taken as the difference between the water levels at these points. The water level at point C is taken as the height of the axis of the pipe. The characteristic intersection point 3 is the operable point of the system. This point determines the capacity Q_3 of the two pump stations. Points 3_1 and 3_2 characterize the capacity of stations 1 and 2, respectively; points $3'_1$ and $3'_2$ characterize the heads on these stations. Points 1 and $1'$, 2 and $2'$ show the capacity and head of the pump stations during independent operation of each of them.

Sequential Operation of Pumps and Pump Stations. The use of pumps for sequential operation to increase the head should be approved by the manufacturer (if this is not considered in the pump certificate). In order to obtain the total operating characteristic of sequentially connected pumps, the heads created by them in the separate operation are added. On the resulting graph of the operating characteristic of the pipe and characteristic of the pumps the operable point of the pump is found at the intersection. In the computations the head losses in the pump connection lines must be considered since these losses may be significant.

In the sequential pumping the lower and upper pumps stations are analyzed in the same way as sequentially installed pumps at a single station. For greater operating reliability, it is recommended that a slight additional head should be provided before the upper station.

Note

operating regime   工作（操作）体制
allowable geometric suction head of the pump   安装高度
allowable vacuumetric head   允许真空高度

New Words and Phrases

main   *n.* 总干管，干渠，电力线，电网，电源
substantiation   *n.* 实体化，证明，证实
vacuum pump   *n.* 真空泵
drainage pump   *n.* 排水泵
monoblock   *adj.* 整体的
auger pump   *n.* 螺旋泵
rotor   *n.* ［机］转子，回转轴，转动体，叶轮

operable pump	*n.* 工作泵	beam	*n.* 梁，桁条，柱，电波，横梁
reserve pump	*n.* 备用泵	grapple	*n.* 抓斗、抓钩
intake pipe	*n.* 吸水管，取水管	forks	*n.* 抓斗，分歧点，（音、论、分、树）叉
pump casing	*n.* 泵壳	crane	*n.* 起重机
drain pit	*n.* 积水坑，排水坑	fitting	*n.* 配件，装备，装置
wet pit	*n.* 集水井，湿井，排水井	pressure pipe	*n.* 压水管
self-priming	*adj.* 启动时不用注水的，自吸	the design level	设计水位
shredder	*n.* 撕碎机，粉碎机	local resistance	局部阻力
comminutor	*n.* 粉碎机（污水预处理）	merge	*v.* 合并，并入，结合，吞没，融合
tonne	*n.* 公吨（=1,000公斤或称 metric ton）	appurtenances	*n.* 附属物，附属设备

Questions

1. What major equipment is located in the machine room?
2. What should be considered for the amount of reserve pumps and the capacity of vacuum pumps?
3. What should be considered when choosing the lifting and transport devices?
4. What should be considered when selecting pumps?
5. Please write out the equations describing the pump characteristic rule for a new rotation speed of the pump rotor.
6. Please write out the equations describing the pump characteristic rule when the rotors are cut.
7. What is meaning of the allowable geometric suction head of the pump H_{gh}?

Reading Material

Pump Stations for Municipal Wastewater: II

Computing the Storage Capacity of a Wet Pit

The storage capacity of a wet pit is determined depending on the wastewater inflow, the pump capacity and their operating regime. The minimum storage volume should be not less than a 5 minute maximum capacity of a single pump.

    The storage capacity is checked for the frequency with which the pumps are shut off and turned on. The number of shut off-turn on operations per hour should not be greater than five for automatic operation of pumps and three for manual control; at a motor power of automatically controlled pumps over 50kW, it is recommended that the pumps be shut off no oftener than three times an hour. If the initially determined storage capacity does not meet these conditions, it should be increased correspondingly. The respective check is performed graphically by plotting an integral graph of the inflow and pumping wastewater for one hour for the mean (50% of the maximum) and minimum inflows during operation of a single pump.

Figure 4 presents an example of a check of the storage capacity for pump switching with manual control. The water is pumped by a type FG-450/22.5 pump, the capacity of which is 450 m³/hr, which corresponds to the maximum inflow. The required reservoir capacity in accord with the 5 minute storage condition is: $W_r = 37.5 m^3$. A capacity of 40 m³ is chosen. The graph shows that the number of times the pump is shut off-turned on in one hour at the mean and minimum inflows does not exceed three. Consequently, no increase in the reservoir capacity is required.

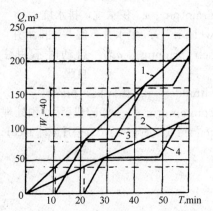

Figure 4 Graph of the inflow and pumping of wastewater:
1) mean wastewater inflow;
2) minimum inflow;
3) and 4) operating regimes of type FG-450/22.5 pump.

On large pump stations the wet pit is usually transformed into a distribution canal with sufficient length and depth to accomodate the intake pipes from all pump units.

Pump Station Layout

When designing pump stations for sanitary sewage, the wet pit, screen room, machine room, and the utility and service rooms are usually located in a single building.

The underground section of small and medium-size stations is usually circular. When the main is at a shallow depth, the rectangular shape is more practical, since the equipment is more easily contained in a rectangular room. The shape of the underground section of large stations is chosen depending on the hydrogeological conditions, the depth to which the main is laid and the method of performing the work on the basis of a technical-economic comparison of the variants.

The underground section of the buildings is usually rectangular in shape, since in this case standardized structural elements may be used in the construction.

The wet pit and the screen building should be separated from the machine room by a continuous water-impermeable partition. Connection between them (a door) is permitted only in the unflooded section of the building with measures to prevent the entry of wastewater into the machine room during flooding of the station. The pumps are usually installed under water (below the upper water level in the wet pit).

The pump units and other appurtenances should be arranged so as to permit convenient access to them for service and maintenance. It is recommended that the pump units be installed on a single level, perpendicularly to the wall separating the machine hall from the wet pit.

When determining the dimensions of the stations, the clearances between the equipment, the size of the installation area, and the composition of the utility and service rooms are chosen in accord with SNiP 11-32-74.

The receiving reservoirs of stations with capacity over 100 thousand m^3/day are divided into two sections without an increase in the total volume.

The machine room floor is given a slope of 0.03~0.05 toward the collecting channel; the slop of the bottom of the wet pit towards suction sumps is taken at not less than 0.1m. The depth of the operable section of the wet pit should be taken at not less than 1.5~2.0m for small and medium stations and 2.5m for large stations. The roof of the reservoir is situated 0.5m above the highest computed water level in it. The dimensions of the installation openings in the walls of the stations are chosen so that the equipment may be transported through them. Automobile access to the installation openings is provided.

Examples of the layouts of municipal pump stations are presented in Figure 5.

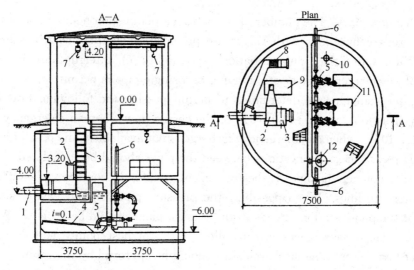

Figure 5 Pump station with three horizontal pumps:
1) main, 2) charging channel, 3) mechanically cleaned screen, 4) pipe for suspending sediment, 5) intake pipe, 6) pressure pipe, 7) manual block and tackle, 8) screen with manual cleaning and perforated trough, 9) shredder, 10) pump to supply water for gland sealing, 11) horizontal sewerage pumps, 12) drain pump.

Pipe Designs

Pipes within Pump Stations. The station pipe layout is chosen with consideration of the possibility of disconnection of any pump for maintenance without disrupting the operation of the station.

The intake pipes (separate for each pump) are installed with a slope of not less than 0.005 to the pump. Installation of check valves and screens on the intake lines is not permitted.

Steel pipes in the form of large elements, as well as plastic pipes, are used; flanges are welded to the pipes only to connect to fittings and pumps.

The design velocities of the water in the pipes are given in Table 1.

Velocity of water in pipes Table 1

Pipe diameter, mm	Velocity in pipe, m/sec	
	Intake	Pressure
To 250	0.7~1.0	1.0~1.5
From 300 to 800	1.0~1.5	1.2~2.0
Over 800	1.2~1.5	1.8~2.5

The pipes are laid on the floor surface or in channels to permit convenient construction. Mechanized control should be provided for shut-off valves over 400 mm in diameter, and for any diameter when remote or automatic control is used. A check valve and a gate valve are installed on the pressure pipe, and a gate valve is provided on submerged intake pipes.

External Pressure Pipes. The number of pipes from a pump station should be not less than two, and cross-connections with valves are provided when their length is great (over 2 km). With appropriate substantiation (possibility of interruptions in operation, presence of an emergency tank, etc.) laying of a single pipe is permitted.

The pipe diameters are determined to permit passing the following flow during an emergency situation: not less than 70% of the design flow when an emergency discharge is available; 100% when an emergency discharge is not available. The possibility of using reserve pumps and cross-connections between the pipes should be considered.

Primarily nonmetallic pipes (asbestos cement, reinforced concrete, plastic) should be used for pressure lines. When possible, the pressure pipes should have a slope in the direction of the pump station. Bends in the vertical plane should be avoided. Where such bends occur, air release valves are installed at the highest point, and discharges are provided at low points. The discharge sites should be approved by the sanitary inspection agencies.

Pump Station Sanitary Engineering Facilities

Water Supply and Sewerage. Pump stations are provided with potable and process water supply service. The stations are supplied with water from the water system of a populated area or an industrial plant. With appropriate substantiation, artesian wells may be used.

The process water is used for hydraulic sealing of the packing glands of the main pumps, to wash screenings from the screens, to lubricate the screen bearings, and wash the wet pit. The pressure in the process water system is usually dictated by the required pressure for hydraulic sealing of the packing glands of the sewage pumps, which is usually taken at 2~3 m above the head developed by the pumps. When the station has large vertical pumps, the required head to wash the seal rings of the impeller, which exceeds the pump head by 10 m, should be considered.

The water from the inlet of the potable system to the process water system should be through a tank ("siphon breaking tank"), which is installed in a room of the pump station at a high level. From the tank the water is pumped into the process system by a pump designed for the maximum possible water flow. There is a second such pump in reserve. For small and medium stations hot water for the showers and lavatories is prepared at local heating facilities; for large stations the water is heated in a heating system in the pump station building.

The wastewater from the sanitary facilities of small and medium size stations is discharged into the wet pit before screens, and for large stations it is recommended that the sanitary facilities be connected to external sewerage networks.

Heating and Ventilation. Design of heating and ventilation for pump stations should be based on SNiP 11-32-74 and 11-33-75. In all cases the possibility of connecting the station to the heating mains of a populated area or plant should be determined. When this is not possible, a central heating system of medium capacity with small heat transfer area cast iron boilers should be used.

New Words and Phrases

integral   *adj.* 完整的，整体的，[数学] 积分的，构成整体所需要的
   n. 积分，完整，部分
hydrogeological   *adj.* 水文地质的
partition   *n.* 分割，划分，分开，隔离物
   vt. 区分，隔开，分割
gland   *n.* [解剖] 腺，[机械] 填料盖，压盖，密封装置
flange   *n.* 边缘，轮缘，凸缘，法兰
   vt. 给…装凸缘

asbestos cement   *n.* 石棉水泥
artesian   *adj.* 喷水井的，自流井的
artesian well   *n.* 自流井
impeller   *n.* 叶轮
lavatory   *n.* 厕所，〈英〉抽水马桶，〈美〉洗脸盆，浴室
block and tackle   *n.* [机] 滑轮，滑轮组

LESSON 24

Pump Stations for Industrial Wastewater, Stormwater, Sediments and Sludges

Pump Stations for Industrial Wastewater

Specificities of the Design of Pump Stations. Industrial wastewaters are quite variable in composition, which has a decisive effect on the selection of the pumps and other equipment and is reflected to a certain degree on the design solutions with regard to size of pump stations.

For example, when the water to be pumped is high in viscosity or when it contains a high concentration of solids (sludge), there is an increase in the headloss, with a consequent increase in the required head of the pumps and the power of the electric motors. The presence of abrasive impurities in the wastewater leads to the necessity of using abrasive-resistant metals for pumps and fittings. At a high wastewater temperature there is a decrease in the suction height of the pumps. When pumping corrosive acid-containing wastewater, use acid-resistant pumps, pipes and equipment, with anticorrosion protection of the wet pit. The presence of substances in the water that give off explosive or combustible gases and vapors requires the installation of explosion-proof pumps and electrical equipment. Explosion hazard conditions should also be taken into consideration when designing building structures.

When pumping sludge there should be taps on the pressure pipes for washing of the intake lines, which may increase the area of the machine rooms in stations. There are also other specific features that should be considered when designing these pump stations.

Pump stations may be located either in individual buildings or in rooms connected to industrial buildings, and also directly in plant divisions. In the latter case the wastewater should not give off gases and vapors, which are toxic or explosive when mixed with air (with the exception of those cases where the contamination of the air by gases or vapors is related primarily to the industrial process). The receiving reservoirs for wastewaters containing flammable or explosive (with air) substances are situated outside the pump station building.

The combined installation of pumps in the same machine room for pumping wastewater of different types, excluding water containing explosive and flammable substances is permitted. When explosive and flammable substances are present, a separate room should be provided in the machine room.

When pumping corrosive wastewater, separate pump stations are usually provided with two wet pits, which should be accessible for external inspection and maintenance.

LESSON 24

Wet pits, floors and pump foundations in the machine room should have anticorrosion protection. Wet pits may be located in the same room with the pumps. When necessary, the pump station is located in an industrial building where, in accord with the conditions of the industrial process, the necessary measures are taken for anticorrosion protection of the structures and equipment.

The electrical power supply for continuously operated pump stations for industrial wastewater should be uninterrupted. The number of pressure pipes is taken at not less than two, each with capacity of 100% of the design quantity of wastewater. Usually, all pumps have separate intake pipes.

Pumps to pump sludges should be located only below the liquid level, with mandatory provision for washing the intake and delivery lines of the sludge pipes.

Selection of Pumps for Industrial Wastewaters. Examples of Pump Station Layouts

The nomenclature of the pumps produced by the machine plants in the country is rather well known, and the selection of pumps for industrial wastewaters presents no significant problem. Of primary interest are centrifugal pumps of various types. For noncorrosive wastewaters with a low concentration of mechanical impurities, general purpose pumps can be used. In a number of cases sanitary pumps may be used to pump industrial wastewater and sewerage sludge.

When water contains various specific contaminants, pumps for suspended solids, sludge, sand, acid-resistant pumps, petroleum product pumps, etc. can be used.

The number of operable pumps is chosen in accord with the design inflow of wastewater, and the number of reserve pumps depending on the number of operable pumps (Table 1).

Number of operable and reserve pumps for industrial wastewaters — Table 1

Wastewaters	No. of pumps	
	Operable	Reserve
Acidic	1	1+1
	2	2
	3	2
	4	3
	≥5	50%
Alkaline and salt-containing	1	1
	2	1
	≥3	2
Containing abrasive solids	1	2
	≥2	2
Sludge-containing	1	1
	≥2	2

For other types of industrial wastewaters, the number of reserve pumps is chosen the same as for pumping sanitary wastewaters.

Pump stations are usually deep structures. Their layout depends on the nature of wastewater, the purpose of pump stations and local conditions. Two pump stations for pumping various wastewaters may be presented as examples.

Figure 1 shows a pump station for water-containing petroleum products and petroleum-containing sediments (a typical design), located at facilities for treating petroleum-containing wastewater. The machine room is situated at a depth of 6.6 m in a 10 m diameter shaft. The wet pits are located outside the station. In the machine room there are three petroleum pumps and two sanitary pumps (for sediment) with explosion-safe electric motors. In the surface section of the station there are the electrical distribution box and ventilation rooms. A monorail hoist with manual control and a block and tackle are provided to lift the equipment. The intake pipes of the sediment pumps are provided with back washing.

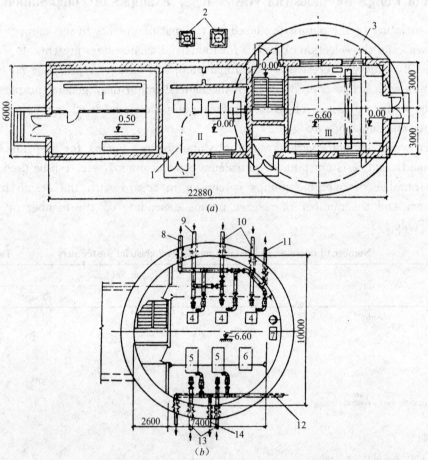

Figure 1   Pump station for water-containing petroleum products and petroleum-containing sediments
(a) plan of underground section, (b) plan of shaft, Ⅰ) electrical distribution box, Ⅱ) ventilation chamber, Ⅲ) machine room,
1) monorail hoist, 2) ventilation pipes, 3) rail hoist, 4) pumps for petroleum products, 5) sludge pumps, 6) pump to supply water to packing glands of main pumps, 7) drain pump, pipes to supply water and sediments, 8) to oil-water separation reservoirs, 9) from petroleum collection reservoir, 10) from oil-water separation reservoirs, 11) to plant feedstock tanks, 12) to sludge pond, 13) from sludge reservoir, 14) pipe to evacuate sludge system.

LESSON 24

The Headlosses for Viscous Liquids. The headlosses in pipes are determined by the equation:

$$h = \frac{\lambda L v^2}{2gd} \quad (1)$$

where L = the design length of the pipe, m, equal to the actual length plus the length equivalent to the losses on the local resistances;

v = the velocity of the liquid, m/sec;

g = the gravity constant, m/sec^2;

d = the internal diameter of the pipe, m.

The coefficient of hydraulic resistance λ depends on the numerical value of the Reynolds number Re:

$$\text{Re} = vd/\nu \quad (2)$$

Where ν = the kinematic viscosity of the liquid, cm^2/sec.

At Re<2320 the regime of liquid flow is laminar. In this case the valve of λ is determined by the equation:

$$\lambda = 64/\text{Re} \quad (3)$$

At Re>2320 the regime of the liquid flow is turbulent. When pumping industrial wastewater or water-containing products, usually 2320<Re≤100000, and the value of λ is determined by the equation

$$\lambda = 0.3164/\sqrt[4]{\text{Re}} \quad (4)$$

When pumping wastewater in a mixture with viscous liquids (petroleum products, tars), the hydraulic resistance coefficients should be determined by computation for the mean viscosity of the mixture, using the Eq. (1) through (4). The presence of viscous liquids in industrial wastewaters has a certain effect on the characteristics of centrifugal pumps (a slight decrease in the capacity and an increase in the power consumption).

Suction Head for Industrial Wastewaters. The greatest geometric suction head, m, of the pumps, corresponding to the difference in elevations of the pump axis and the free surface of the mixture being pumped, is determined by the equation

$$h = \frac{H_{vac} - h_{vap}}{\gamma_m} + \frac{H_{bar} - 10}{\gamma_m} - h_l - \frac{v_{in}^2}{2g} \quad (5)$$

where H_{vac} = the vacuumetric head, determined by the reading of a vacuum-meter during operation of the pump on cold water (factory data);

h_{vap} = the pressure of the vapor of the water or other liquid in the pumped water (taken as the greatest pressure at the corresponding temperature);

H_{bar} = the barometric pressure at the elevation of pump installation: 101.32 kPa (10.33 m of water column) at sea level; 100.13 kPa (10.21 m of water column) at an altitude of 100 m and 97.68 kPa (9.96 m of water column) at an altitude of 300 m;

h_l = the total head in the suction pipe;

v_{in} = the velocity of the liquid in the intake connector of the pump;

γ_m = the specific gravity of the mixture being pumped.

Pump Stations for Stormwater and Combined Systems

Pump stations for stormwater are designed for the capacity corresponding to the design duration and intensity of rain as established for the design of the stormwater collection lines. It is recommended that the number of operable pumps should be not less than two, reserve pumps are not provided. At pump stations for partially separated and combined systems, pumping both industrial-sanitary wastewater and stormwater, two groups of pumps are provided. The second group is activated only during a rain. At pump stations for storm water, high capacity-low head pumps are usually required. Propeller pumps are most practical.

Wet pits at pump stations for partially separated and combined sewerage systems are provided with a spillway device and a wall separating them into two sections, one for the effluent in dry weather and the other during a rain; two separate reservoirs may also be installed.

The volumes of wet pits or their sections for the influent in dry weather are determined in the same manner as the capacity of wet pits for sanitary sewerage. When there is additional inflow during a rain, the capacity is computed as for a storage tank, but the capacity should be not less than the volume of water entering in the time required to turn on the pump of the greatest capacity.

Mechanically cleaned screens or comminutors are installed before wet pits. The gaps in the screens must correspond to the type of pump. The number of pressure pipes from the pump station should be not less than two. Their diameter is determined to provide passage of the effluent in dry weather when there is a failure on one pipe in the presence of an emergency outfall, and to pass the entire design flow during a rain when there is no emergency outfall.

Pump Stations for Sludges

Design features and examples. Stations for sludge differ from sanitary sewerage stations by the absence of screens and shredders. Standard sanitary pumps are usually used to pump sludge. The sludge reservoir (wet pit) may be combined with the pump station or be separate. Its capacity is determined by the quantity of sludge from a one-time discharge from primary settling tanks or digestors. The volume of the sludge reservoir for the recirculated, activated sludge in activated sludge processes are determined by the 15-minute capacity of the largest operable pump. Water should be supplied from pressure lines to wash the pump intake lines.

When pumping certain types of industrial sludges, for example heavy iron-and-steel works sludges such as generated at gas purification facilities at blast furnace divisions or scale-containing sludges, pumps and equipment made of abrasive resistant materials should be used. In these cases wet pits should have a significant slope of the bottom in the direction of the pump sump. It must be possible to wash the sludge lines, and in certain cases reserve lines are required.

Figure 2 shows a pump station for sludge from industrial wastewater settling tanks, equipped with three plunger pumps (one reserve). The station also has pumps for washing pipes, emptying the settling tanks, and pumping out floating scum. A ventilation chamber and a room for electrical equipment are located in the annex to the surface section of the station. A monorail hoist with manual control is used in the machine room. All equipment is explosion-proof.

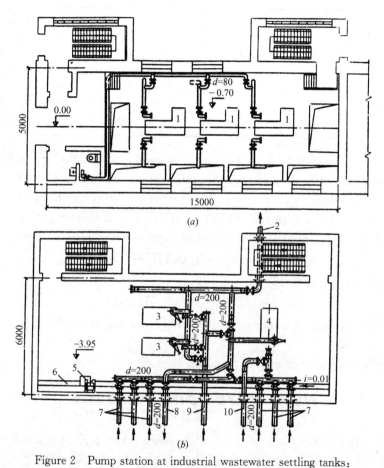

Figure 2 Pump station at industrial wastewater settling tanks:
(a) plan of surface section, (b) plan of underground section, 1) plunger pumps for raw sludge to treatment, 2) pipeline to deliver sludge to treatment or to storage, 3) centrifugal pumps to pump scum from a scum tank to a storage tank, 4) pump for emptying settling tanks and supplying wash water, 5) sump, 6) channel, 7) raw sludge intake pipes, 8) pipe for emptying settling tanks, 9) pipe from scum tank, 10) wash water tank.

Headloss in the Pumping of Sludges. Sanitary wastewater sludges may be considered as a colloidal system with a slightly higher viscosity than pure water. In addition, the viscosity depends on the flow velocity. At a sludge velocity greater than 1 m/sec, the headloss in pipes decreases as compared with the losses when pumping pure water, and on the contrary, at a low sludge velocity the headloss increases. An increase in the moisture content of the sludge to 99.0%~99.5% gives it practically the properties of pure water.

Design of sludge pressure pipes for sanitary sewerage systems should be based on the lowest permissible design velocities of flow of raw and digested sludges, as well as thickened activated sludge. According to SNiP 11-32-74, the lowest permissible velocities are taken from Table 2.

Lowest permissible sludge velocities in sludge pipes   Table 2

Sludge Moisture,%	Sludge velocity, m/sec, at sludge pipe diameter, mm	
	150~200	250~400
92	1.4	1.5
93	1.3	1.4
94	1.2	1.3
95	1.1	1.2
96	1.0	1.2
97	0.9	1.0
98	0.8	0.9

When pumping industrial wastewaters with a significant quantity of solids, as well as sludges separated from these wastewaters, the design velocity of the liquid in pipes should be not less than the critical velocity V_{cr}, mm/sec. This prevents formation of bottom sediments in pipes. According to the data of the VNIIG (The All-Union Research-Scientific Institute of Hydrology) Institute, at a particle size in the wastewater up to 0.07 mm

$$v_{cr}=0.2(1+3.43\sqrt[4]{P_w d^{0.75}}) \tag{6}$$

and at a particle size up to 0.15 mm

$$v_{cr}=0.255(1+2.48\sqrt[3]{P_w}\sqrt[4]{d}) \tag{7}$$

where P_w = the content of particles in wastewater, %, For sludges P_w = 5 to 7% by volume;

d = the internal diameter of pipe, m.

New Words and Phrases

monorail hoist 单轨吊车
rail hoist 桥式吊车
stormwater collection line 暴雨收集管线
blast furnace （鼓风）炉
kinematic viscosity 动力黏性
abrasive n. 研磨剂
    adj. 研磨的
corrosive adj. 腐蚀的，蚀坏的，腐蚀性的
    n. 腐蚀物，腐蚀剂
combustible adj. 易燃的
tackle n. 工具，复滑车，滑车，用具，装备
mandatory adj. 命令的，强制的

nomenclature n. 术语，命名法
evacuate v. 疏散，排泄
tar n. 焦油，柏油
barometric adj. 大气压力的
propeller pump n. 螺旋泵，轴流泵
spillway n. 溢洪道，泄洪道
digestor (=digester) n. 消化池
plunger pump n. 活塞泵
annex n. 附件，附属构筑物，边（群）房
   vt. 并吞，附加
hydrology n. 水文学，水文地理学

LESSON 24

Questions

1. What will affect on the characteristics of centrifugal pumps if viscous liquids are present in industrial wastewaters?
2. What are the specific features that should be considered when designing corrosive wastewater pump stations?
3. What are the specific features that should be considered when designing sludges pump stations?
4. When pumping industrial wastewater or water-containing products, what equation can be used to determined the value of the coefficient of hydraulic resistance λ ?
5. How to confirm the capacity of sludge reservoir?
6. Please talk about the relationship between the headloss in pipes and the sludge velocity.

Reading Material

Other Lifting Devices

Ejectors and Air Lifts for Wastewater and Sludges

Ejectors. Ejectors (jet pumps) are used for wastewaters, heavily loaded with suspensions, sludges, semisolid residues, and grit and sand. Due to the absence of moving parts and the simplicity and reliability of the device, these installations are much more efficient than sanitary or sand pumps.

An ejector installation is equipped with a pump delivering the ejecting water to the ejector, the ejector itself and the slurry pipe (Figure 3). The ejecting liquid under pressure (Figure 4) is supplied through a pipe to the nozzle and flows from it at a high velocity, which creates a vacuum in the receiving chamber, which draws in the pumped liquid. In the mixing chamber, into which the resulting mixture flows, the kinetic energy of the flow is transformed to pressure energy. In the diffuser, due to the decrease in the velocity of the flow, there is a further increase in pressure, which permits the mixture to be transported through the slurry pipe to the site of its discharge.

When designing ejecting installations, compute the ejecting water delivery system (the intake and pressure pipes and the pump) and the slurry delivery system (the ejector and the slurry pipes). K. A. Shcheglov proposed that ejectors be designed (with sufficient accuracy for practical purposes) by superimposing the characteristic curve of the ejecting water pump on the characteristic curve of the ejector and superimposing the characteristic curve of the ejector on the characteristic curve of the slurry pipe.

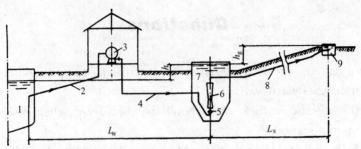

Figure 3 Ejector installation

1) water reservoir, 2) suction pipe, 3) pump for ejecting water, 4) pressure pipe, 5) ejector nozzle, 6) ejector housing, 7) tank with sludge sump, 8) slurry pipe, 9) tank to receive slurry, h_g) geometric height of slurry lift, L_w) length of ejecting water pipeline, L_s) length of slurry pipe.

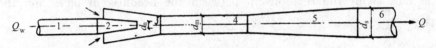

Figure 4 Diagram of ejector

1) ejecting water pipe, 2) nozzle, 3) receiving chamber, 4) mixing chamber, 5) diffuser, 6) slurry pipe; d_n, d_m and d_s) diameter of nozzle, mixing chamber and slurry pipe, respectively.

The ejector characteristic is plotted on the basis of the equation for the rate of outflow of the ejecting water from the nozzle, m/sec:

$$v = \zeta_n \sqrt{2gH_n} \tag{8}$$

where ζ_n = the velocity coefficient for the nozzle, equal to 0.95;

g = the gravity constant, m/sec^2;

H_n = the water pressure at the nozzle exit, m.

According to B. E. Fridman, an ejector can be designed using the equation:

$$\alpha = 0.516m - (m^2 + 2m)\beta/4.53 + 0.34 \tag{9}$$

where α is the suction coefficient:

$$\alpha = \frac{\gamma_{in}Q_{in}}{\gamma_w Q_w} \tag{10}$$

where γ_{in} and γ_w = the densities of the pumped and ejecting liquids, g/m;

Q_{in}, Q_w = the flow rates of the pumped and ejecting liquids, m/sec.

The total flow of liquid (slurry), m^3/sec, pumped by the ejector, is

$$Q = Q_{in} + Q_w \tag{11}$$

Substituting the value of Q_w from Eq. (10) into the resulting equation yields:

$$Q = Q_{in}\left(1 + \frac{\gamma_{in}}{\alpha \gamma_w}\right) \tag{12}$$

The ratio of heads is

$$\beta = \frac{H}{\zeta_n^2 H_n} \tag{13}$$

where H = the total dynamic ejector head, m.

The ratio of areas of the cross sections is:

$$m = F_m/F_n \qquad (14)$$

where F_m and F_n = the cross-sectional areas of the mixing chamber and the nozzle outlet, respectively, m².

The efficiency of the ejector for each point of the curve is determined by the equation:

$$\eta = \alpha \cdot \beta \qquad (15)$$

The characteristic curve of an ejector and diameters d_n of nozzle and d_m of mixing chamber are determined as follows:

1. Using Eq. (12), and the design flow of the pumped liquid Q_{in}, the total flow rate Q of the ejector is determined assuming the coefficient α equals 1.

2. The diameter of the slurry pipe is chosen on the basis of critical velocity, and then the headlosses, the geometric lift height and, consequently, the total ejector head H are found.

3. The ratio β is chosen:

at $H = 3 \sim 6$m................ $\beta = 0.1 \sim 0.2$
at $H = 6 \sim 15$m................ $\beta = 0.2 \sim 0.3$

4. The ratio m is found from the condition $\beta m = 1$, at which the ejector has the maximum efficiency. This efficiency value is in effect only under certain conditions: the distance from the nozzle outlet to the mixing chamber is equal to or slightly less than $2d_n$, the length of the mixing chamber (of cylindrical shape) is $(6 \sim 7)d_m$, the angle of the diffuser is 8 to 10°, and the vacuummetric lift is not greater than 1 m.

5. According to Eq. (13), the required head at the nozzle H_n is determined.

6. Using Eq. (10) the preliminary value of the ejecting water flow Q_w is found.

7. Eq. (8) is used to compute the nozzle cross-sectional area and diameter.

$$F_n = \frac{Q_w}{v} = \frac{Q_w}{\zeta_n \sqrt{2gH_n}}; \quad d_n = \sqrt{\frac{4F_n}{\pi}}$$

8. Eq. (14) is used to determine the value of F_m and the corresponding value of d_m. For ejectors pumping slurry from grit chambers, d_m should be not less than 70 mm, thus when designing an ejector, d_m is designated first, and the dimension d_n is computed by the equation $d_n = d_m/\sqrt{m}$.

9. Substituting $v = Q_w/F_n$ into Eq. (8) yields:

$$H_n = \frac{Q_w^2}{\zeta_n^2 F_n^2 2g} \qquad (16)$$

Using this equation, and assuming the series of values of Q_w, the corresponding values of H_n can be found and the curve Q_w-H_n for the ejector can be constructed.

10. A pump is chosen with a capacity close to the previously determined value Q_w, and the curve of the available pressure at the nozzle is plotted. For this purpose the Q-H curve for pipes conveying the ejecting liquid is subtracted from the Q-H characteristic curve of the pump. Then the resultant curve is superimposed on the nozzle characteristic and the point of intersection is found, which determines the required Q_w and H_n.

11. The ejector characteristic curve is constructed similarly. For this purpose, the principal ejector formulas relating the quantities β, α, η, Q and H are used.

Correspondingly, for various values of β, Q_w and H_n various values of Q and H can be found. For convenience of computation a table can be used.

12. The Q-H characteristic of the slurry pipe is plotted and superimposed on the ejector characteristic. The point of intersection of the characteristics, corresponding to the resulting value of Q_w, determine the total capacity of the ejector, and the efficiency and suction flow values.

Air lift installations. At small and medium-size biological treatment plants, air lift installations can be used for pumping the recycled activated sludge to the distribution canal. Their advantages are simplicity of design, operational reliability and absence of moving parts. The drawbacks are a low efficiency and the necessity of deep submergence of the air lift chambers.

The operating efficiency of the air lift depends on the relative submergence:

$$k = h/(H+h) \qquad (17)$$

where h = the depth of submergence of the air lift (from the level in the chamber to the location of the air input), m;

H = the height of the liquid lift (from its level in the chamber to the discharge opening), m.

It is recommended that the coefficient k be taken at 0.5 to 0.6.

The specific consumption of compressed air per unit volume of pumped liquid depends on the L/H ratio and is determined from the following design equation:

$$\log \frac{Q}{q} = \frac{2}{\sqrt{L/H}} - 1 \qquad (18)$$

where $L = H + h$ = the length of the air lift, m;

Q = the air flow, m³/sec;

q = the liquid flow, m³/sec.

This equation is correct only at $H \leqslant 5$m and when the ratio $L/H > 2$.

With a low height of the liquid lift (to 10 m) the specific air flow may be assumed approximately at 1 to 2.5 m³ per m³ of liquid supplied (the higher value for a higher lift height).

The minimum pressure, Pa, of the compressed air supplied to the air lift may be found using the equation

$$P_{min} \geqslant h\gamma \cdot 10^4 \qquad (19)$$

where h = the depth of submergence of the air lift, m;

γ = the density of the pumped liquid, tonne/m³.

The velocity of the flow of liquid at the intake to the air mixing device is usually 1.2 to 2 m/sec, and the velocity of the water-air mixture at the discharge opening should not be greater than 6~7 m/sec. The velocity of the compressed air in the air supply pipe is assumed in the range from 10 to 20 m/sec depending on the pressure.

The diameter and number of the openings in the air distribution devices are determined in accord with the velocity of the air passage through the openings, equal to 2~3 m/sec. The design number of openings is increased by 20%~30% with consideration of their clogging.

The efficiency of the air lift is determined by the equation

$$\eta_a = \frac{qH}{Q \cdot 23\log(p_1/p_0)} \qquad (20)$$

where p_1 = the air pressure before the air lift, Pa;

p_0 = the atmospheric pressure, Pa.

The capacity of the air lift is affected by the design of its parts. For example, experience shows that it is more practical to use smoothly rounded discharge pipes.

Pumping Installations with Screw, Inclined Archimedean Screw, Submersible, and Nonclogging Pumps and Pneumatic Pumping Devices

Pump installations with type 1V6/10Kh horizontal screw pumps are designed to pump and also to meter solutions of aluminum sulfate and lime.

In order to extend the service life of the pump the abrasive substances (sand, particles of lime) should first be removed from the solution, which is accomplished by sedimentation of the liquid in the service tank (the solution is taken from the upper part of the tank).

A type VTs22-131-03 speed control is installed between the pump and the electric motor, permitting metering of the fed solution depending on the wastewater flow.

The screw pump has the following characteristics: capacity 0.45~4.3 m³/hr; pressure at the discharge 0.6 MPa (6 kg/cm²); head not less than 0.5 m; rotor speed 200~1200 min^{-1}; motor power 4 kW; weight of the unit 385 kg.

Pump stations with inclined Archimedean screw pumps (lifts) are designed to pump wastewaters to low heights (2~7 m). These lifts, operating on the Archimedean screw principle, have a number of advantages over pumps of other types. They have a simple design, and require no preliminary screening or shredding. The size of refuse, which may be pumped, is determined principally by the diameter of the screw and the screw spacing. Instead of valves there are simpler gate cutoffs; there is no need for pressure pipes.

An installation with two screw lifts (one reserve) is presented in Figure 5. The diameter of the screw for this installation is 800 mm; the water feed at speeds 59, 64 and

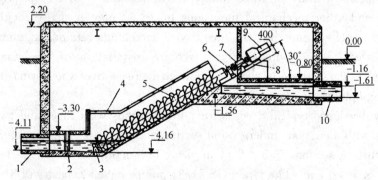

Figure 5 Pump station with two screw lifts

1) intake main, 2) stoplogs, 3) lower screw bearing, 4) handrail, 5) screw lift, 6) upper screw bearing, 7) bearing unit, 8) gear frame, 9) gear-motor, 10) discharge main.

75 min^{-1} is 360, 390 and 460 m^3/hr respectively, at a lift height of 2.5 m.

Pump stations with type TsMK monoblock submersible electric pumps are designed for small sewerage systems to pump sanitary and noncorrosive industrial wastewaters. The use of the type TsMK pumps permits construction of compact stations, which reduces the construction costs by a factor of 2 to 3.

Kharkov developed a typical pump station design (Figure 6) for two TsMK 16-27 pumps (one of them reserve) with capacity of 16 m^3/hr and head of 27 m; the pump power requirement is 3.3 kW, at 40% efficiency. The station consists of an underground circular shaft 2 m in diameter. The depth of laying of the gravity flow feeder main can be 3, 4 and 5 m. A container screen can be raised by a manual hoist to discharge the screenings into a special container, transported by a truck. The pump unit is equipped with a device for automatic connection to the pressure pipe, which permits lowering and, when necessary (for example, for inspection, maintenance) lifting the pump out of the shaft. The type SAUNA electric motor control system included in the pump unit permits automatic start-up and shut-off the pump depending on the water level in the reservoir.

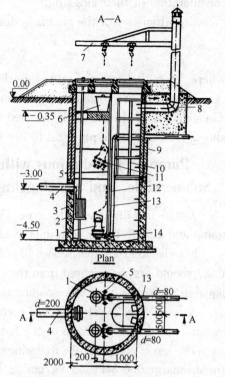

Figure 6 Pump station with two monoblock submersible pumps
1) electric pump, 2) screen container, 3) gate screen, 4) feeder main, 5) guide pipe, 6) container, 7) hoist, 8) ventilation pipe, 9) lugs, 10) railing, 11) electric pump when raised or lowered, 12) chain to raise or lower pump, 13) discharge pipe, 14) joint.

Pump stations with nonclog-type FGS pumps are also designed for small sewerage systems. A specific feature of these pumps is the possibility of free passage of fibrous matter, rags and other mechanical inclusions up to 50 mm in size through the pump, bypassing the impeller, and thus the quantity of screenings retained at pump stations is greatly decreased. These pumps do not require installation of mechanically cleaned screens and shredders; there is also a significant increase over the normal time between pump cleaning operations.

Kharkov developed typical designs for pump stations with three and two type FGS-81/31 pumps with a circular underground section of 5 and 5.5 m in diameter, and with a rectangular surface section, 7.5×6 m in size. The depth at which the feeder main is located is 4, 5.5 and 7 m. The type FGS 81/31 pumps have a capacity of 81 m^3/hr, head of 31 m, and electrical motor power of 22 kW.

At these pump stations the water enters a wet pit through a screen, which is raised on guides by a monorail hoist to the ground level, where the screenings are transferred into a container and hauled by a truck. The quantity of screenings does not exceed 60 kg per day.

Pump stations with a type UPPV-20 pneumatic device are designed to pump sanitary and noncorrosive industrial wastewaters and may be used at industrial sites having a compressed air system. This installation pumps water over a distance of up to 100 m and has a head of 7 m, which provides a lift of the wastewater up to 5 m relative to the feeder pipe (Figure 7).

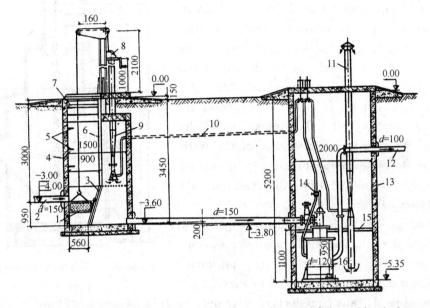

Figure 7 Pneumatic pump stations with capacity of 5~20 m³/hr and head of 7 m
1) perforated container, 2) feeder main, 3) screen with gap of 16mm, 4) receiving sump,
5) lugs, 6) guide for the perforated container, 7) woods cover, 8) manual type PL-90 hoist,
9) ventilation ejector, 10) compressed air pipe, 11) ventilation pipe, 12) pressure pipe,
13) shaft, 14) three-position stopcock, 15) wooden deck, 16) type UPPV-20 pneumatic pump.

The use of pneumatic pumps is more efficient at a wastewater flow up to 5 m³/hr at a pumping distance up to 10 m. Pneumatic installations may be used at plants for local pumping of wastewater when difficulties are encountered in connecting discharges from industrial buildings to an industrial site sewerage system. These installations operate automatically without using electrical power and are simple and reliable in operation.

Kharkov developed a typical design for a pneumatic pump station with capacity of 5~20 m³/hr and head up to 7 m. The station consists of two sections: a wet pit of 1.5 m diameter and a dry pit of 2.5 m diameter. The feeder main is laid at depths of 3 or 4 m. The wet pit contains a screen with manual cleaning preceded by a trash collector, consisting of a perforated metal container, which is raised to the ground surface along steel guides by means of a manual winch. The dry pit contains a type UPPV-20 pneumatic pump. The operable pressure of the air at the intake to the pump is 0.2~0.6 MPa (2~6 kg/cm²), and inside it 0.07~0.12 MPa (0.7~1.2 kg/cm²); its weight is 550 kg.

The pneumatic installation (Figure 8) consists of a welded external reservoir of 720 mm diameter and an internal cylinder, which contains a float with a conical valve. The internal cylinder is connected to a feeder pipe 150 mm in diameter, and in the reservoir is a pipe 100 mm in diameter and the compressed air pipe. The float is connected by a plunger to a three-way stopcock on the compressed air pipe. When the reservoir is filled with wastewater, the position of the valve is automatically changed, providing alternating operating cycles of the installation. The reservoir is filled with water when it is under atmospheric pressure. After that the reservoir is cut off from the atmosphere, the compressed air is fed, the intake valve for wastewater is closed; and discharge of the water due to the increase in the pressure pipe occurs. When liquid is removed from the reservoir, the cycle is repeated.

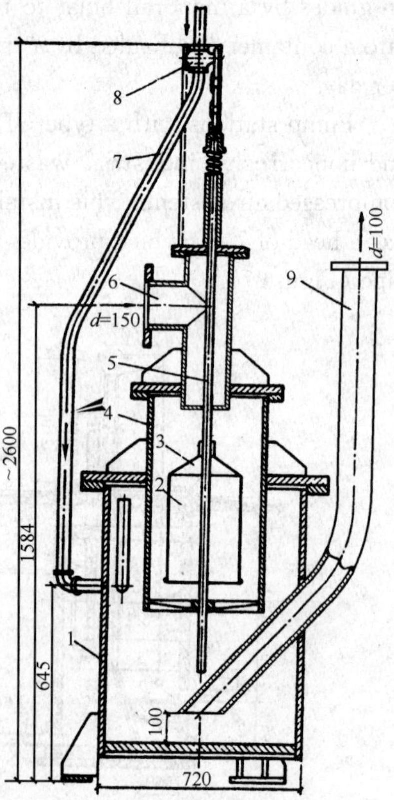

The compressed air is supplied to the pneumatic pump station from the industrial compressor stations. The compressed air pressure in the pneumatic installation is automatically reduced to a level equal to the actual head, thus no reduction valve need be installed.

The capacity of the pneumatic installation changes automatically depending on the wastewater lift height due to the change in the discharge rate. The capacity of the installation may be determined approximately by the Q-H curve plotted on the basis of actual measurements.

In order to ventilate the pits there is periodically operating forced exhaust ventilation, turned on for 5~10 minutes before descending into the sump. The ventilator is an injector, to which compressed air is connected.

Figure 8 Type UPPV-20 pneumatic installation
1) welded reservoir, 2) float, 3) conical valve, 4) internal cylinder, 5) plunger, 6) feeder pipe, 7) compressed air pipe, 8) three-way stopcock, 9) pressure pipe.

New Words and Phrases

submersible electric pump 潜水电泵	stoplog *n.* 闸板、挡板
coefficient *n.* [数] 系数	bearing *n.* 轴承,方向,方位
superimpose *v.* 添加,双重,叠加	handrail *n.* 栏杆,扶手
air lift *n.* 气升泵	gear *n.* 齿轮,传动装置
screw pump *n.* 螺旋(杆)泵	*v.* 调整,(使)适合,换挡
Archimedean *adj.* 阿基米得的	compact *adj.* 紧凑的,紧密的,简洁的

LESSON 24

	n. 契约，合同
hoist	*n.* 起重机，升起
lug	*n.* 突出物，把(手)，悬臂，接线片
joint	*n.* 接头，接合处，接合，关节
	adj. 共同的，联合的，连接的，合办的
	vt. 连接，接合，使有接头
	vi. 贴合，生节
fibrous	*adj.* 含纤维的，纤维性的
inclusion	*n.* 包含，内含物
stopcock	*n.* ［机］管闩，活塞，活栓，旋塞阀

trash	*n.* 无价值之物，垃圾，废物
winch	*n.* 绞盘，绞车
weld	*vt.* 焊接
	n. 焊接，焊缝
conical	*adj.* 圆锥的，圆锥形的
plunger	*n.* 潜水者，活塞
installation	*n.* 安装，装置，就职
ventilation	*n.* 通风，流通空气，换气
laying	*n.* 布置，敷设，瞄准

289

REFERENCES

1. R. H. Garrett (2000), ***Hot and Cold Water Supply***, British Standards Institution, Blackwell Publishing
2. J. Jeffrey Peirce, Ruth F. Weiner, and P. Aarne Vesilind (1997) ***Environmental Pollution and Control***, **4th ed**, Butterworth-Heinemann
3. George Tchobanoglous, Franklin L. Burton, H. David Stensel (2003) ***Wastewater Engineering: Treatment and Reuse***, **4th ed**, McGraw-Hill, New York
4. V. N. Samokhin (1986) ***Design Handbook of Wastewater Systems***, Allerton Press, Inc., New York
5. Jerry A. Nathanson (2003) ***Basic Environmental Technology: Water Supply, Waste Management, and Pollution Control* (Fourth Edition)**, Pearson Education., publishing as Prentice Hall